PURITANS, PLAGUES, AND PROMISES

COLE, CLARKE, AND COLLIER IN ENGLAND TO AMERICA

WILLIAM E. "BILL" COLE

PURITANS, PLAGUES, AND PROMISES
Cole, Clarke, and Collier in England to America
by William E. "Bill" Cole
1. HIS036020 History / United States / Colonial Period (1600-1775)
2. BIO006000 Biography & Autobiography / Historical
3. REF013000 REFERENCE / Genealogy & Heraldry

ISBN: 979-8-88636-019-6 (hardcover)
ISBN: 979-8-88636-020-2 (paperback)
ISBN: 979-8-88636-021-9 (ebook)

Library of Congress Control Number: 2023905728

Cover designer: Lewis Agrell

Printed in the United States of America

Authority Publishing
13389 Folsom Blvd #300-256
Folsom, CA 95630
800-877-1097
www.AuthorityPublishing.com

Puritans, Plagues, and Promises by William E. "Bill" Cole
Early Book Reviews

Historians, scholars, and genealogists are going to love this book. The narrative style of writing is engaging and the level of detail throughout is exceptional. Great job!

Jeff Evans, Professional Indexer for twenty-five years.

Having a family tree is good, but telling an ancestor's story breathes life into the names, dates, and places representing a real person. Bill's book masterfully shows how this is done. He skillfully weaves the fabric of his 16th and 17th century Cole ancestors' lives and makes one feel what it was like to be a Puritan in those perilous times. After numerous close calls with the authorities and plagues, the Coles decide the best course of action was to get the family to the emerging Plymouth Colony. He fixes a clear image of that experience on the reader's mind where once there was a hazy idea. Highly recommended.

Michael J. Cole, retired Brigadier General, U.S.A.F.

Beginning in the small English village of Weedon Bec with an introduction to a previously unknown ancestor, Bill Cole grabs his readers and leads them on a journey through time and English history. As we follow the Cole, Clarke, and Collier families from England to America, it becomes clear that like all of us, we are shaped by events around us. An excellent storyteller, Bill is meticulous in his research, and thorough in his description of the times. He certainly "cracked the code" of the elusive Cole family and more. I highly anticipated this book on many fronts: as a personal family historian, archivist, Mayflower descendant, avid reader and yes, Cole descendant. Puritans, Plagues and Promises did not disappoint!

Patricia M. Donohoe, former Vice President, Eastham Historical Society.

As a descendant of Jane (Yates) (Clarke) Collier, through daughters born to both her Clarke and Collier husbands, I am more than a bit biased in my interest. It was difficult waiting for my chance to read Bill's book. Bill's excellent articles in the Mayflower Descendant (Volumes 69 and 71) had introduced me to details of the Yates, Clarke, Arnold, Collier, and Cole families. But those detailed research articles were just an appetizer to the meal which is this book. Bill does an excellent job in establishing a series of themes and then making history come to life through stories involving a series of interconnected people who lived out that history. Bill's approach includes weaving plenty of details into the story he has crafted. While on my first pass through the book, I found myself drawn to hasten my pace, having made the decision that I would be rereading this book to be able to spend sufficient time on the notes and excerpts from the historical documents which Bill had so painstakingly included in this book. As a descendant and researcher of these people, I also know that my copy of this book is going to become flagged with many post-it notes highlighting all sorts of things.

Ronald E. Benson Jr., Ph.D., genealogical researcher and author
[including "Discovering more about Lieutenant Marcus Cole…" **Nutmegger** (Vol. 45), and "Philip and Chloe (Cole) Goff…" **OGSQ** (Vol. 54)].

DEDICATION

Dedicated first to my grandfather, Perry Ogden Cole (1870-1967). An important role model in my youth, he taught me the importance of God and family in one's life. My relationship with him stimulated my interest in genealogy.

Also dedicated to the great-grandson, Hunter Justin Cole, of my brother, Norman Harold Cole. Born in 2015, the year my English origins research project started, Hunter is the thirteenth great-grandson of Daniel Cole (1614-1694). Daniel Cole emigrated from England to America's Plymouth Colony during the Great Puritan Migration to New England from 1620-40. With findings revealed in *Puritans, Plagues, and Promises*, Hunter is the seventeenth-generation male Cole descendant in our family's branch. Our Cole family history now dates back more than five hundred years—a half millennium.

CONTENTS

ACKNOWLEDGEMENTS

I acknowledge generations of researchers and writers whose dedicated work and findings have guided me throughout my quest. Two years after my English origins research project launched, I contacted several Cole cousins to share some early breakthrough findings.

> "We have stood on the shoulders of many Cole genealogy giants who have invested countless hours and energy of research to get us to this point. Now we need to pick up the genealogical baton!"[1]

Many historians, scholars, and genealogists wrote works that continue to influence our understanding of the past. What follows is a listing of authors whose publications I relied upon to propel me to complete this publication. I apologize in advance for leaving anyone out. Listed in chronological sequence and referencing the year of just one work for each person, my acknowledgement is for their many contributions, scholarship, and dedication to building up the knowledge base in our field. If you see some you do not recognize, make a concerted effort to find their works. As my friend and colleague, Bud Gardner, co-author of a best-selling book, wrote, "When you write, your words echo down the ages."[2]

1609	William Strachey	1945	George F. Willison	2005	James Shapiro
1619	William Brewster	1958	Edmund S. Morgan	2006	Nathaniel Philbrick
1624	Edward Winslow	1966	John G. Hunt	2007	Caleb H. Johnson
1649	John Winthrop	1967	Patrick Collinson	2007	David Charles Cole
1650	William Bradford	1973	Robert S. Wakefield	2008	Joseph L. Black
1669	Nathaniel Morton	1979	W.J. Shiels	2012	Jeremy Dupertuis Bangs
1720	Daniel Neal	1986	Eugene A. Stratton	2014	Rodney Gragg
1813	Benjamin Brook	1986	Martha C. Howell	2014	Susan A. Roser
1861	Samuel Hopkins	1987	Helene Holt	2015	Jaqueline Dinan
1888	John A. Goodwin	1992	David Underdown	2015	Ruth Goodman
1887	Frank T. Cole	2000	Christopher Haigh	2020	Jonathan Mack
1908	Joseph O. Curtis	2003	Robert Brenner	2020	Michael E. McCarthy
1920	Charles Pope	2004	Robert Bucholz	2020	Graham Taylor
1925	Anna C. Kingsbury	2005	Sue Allan	2020	Robert Charles Anderson

---

[1] William E. Cole, personal archive, email 2 February 2017.
[2] Jack Canfield et al, *Chicken Soup for the Writer's Soul* (Deerfield Beach: Health Communications, 2000): 256.

RESEARCH SPONSORS

A few individuals and organizations financially sponsored this research project as it progressed. First and foremost, I acknowledge and give special thanks to Scott L. Semans, my nephew. His interest, encouragement, and financial support contributed heavily to this work's completion and images acquisition. The American Society of Genealogists awarded me a grant in 2022. Alicia Crane Williams, a fellow of ASG, spearheaded my application, which was greatly appreciated. Two client organizations, Kitchen Mart, Inc. of Sacramento, California, and Abacus Plumbing, Heating, Air Conditioning, and Electrical in Houston and Austin, Texas, encouraged me and supported my research. A sincere thank you to the leaders of both organizations: Dave and Tamara Hollars and Alan O' Neill. You are very special people and leaders. I am blessed to have you as close friends.

SPONSORS

This publication includes original source record images not previously published from as early as 1550. In part, these historic genealogical breakthrough images are brought to you by the following organizations and individuals who sponsored at least one image:

American Society of Genealogists.
Abacus Plumbing, Heating, Air Conditioning, & Electrical in Houston, Texas.
Kitchen Mart, Inc. of Sacramento, California.
Ronald E. Benson, my distant cousin.
David Charles Cole, my sixth cousin.
John Anholm Cole, in memory of his father, Jeffrey Anholm Cole, my first cousin.
Michael John Cole, my Y-DNA cousin.
Stephen Dandridge Cole, my eighth cousin.
Anne Cole Linscott and brother, James Stuart Cole, in memory of their father, Charles Henry Cole, Jr.
John and Patricia Donohoe, my distant cousin.
Dave and Tamara Hollars, my clients and friends.
Claire Diane Jaynes, my niece, in memory of her mother, Diane Cole Semans.
Alan O'Neill, my client and friend.
Scott L. Semans, my nephew.
Jerrine A. Stanbury, my distant cousin.

DONORS

Additional thanks are extended for donations from my friend and business colleague, Harold C. Krause; my friend and researcher, Richard Cameron Williams; and cousins Sharon Stevens and Sandra Cole Roe.

ENCOURAGERS

Others have encouraged me as I researched and began sharing my findings. Many volunteer their time and talents for their respective organizations. Thank you all!

Julia Johns	Secretary (former)	Weedon Bec Hist. Society, Northamptonshire, England
Angela Marin	President	Northamptonshire Family Historical Society, England
Helen Baker	Volunteer	Long Buckby Hist. Society, Northamptonshire, England
Else Churchill	President	Society of Genealogists, London, England
Tony Sharp	Historian	London/Southwark, England
Patricia M. Donohoe	Vice President (former)	Eastham Historical Society, Eastham, MA
Eileen A. Seaboldt	President	Eastham Historical Society, Eastham, MA
Dr. Donna D. Curtin	Executive Director	Pilgrim Hall Museum, Plymouth, MA
Timothy A. White	Assistant Registrar	Plymouth Colony Registry of Deeds, Plymouth, MA
Mark Schmidt	Executive Director	General Society of Mayflower Descendants, Plymouth, MA
Christopher C. Child	Editor	*Mayflower Descendant*, New England Hist. Gen. Society
Cécile Engeln	Editorial Director	American Ancestors and New England Hist. Gen. Society
Susan A. Roser	Editor (former)	*Mayflower Quarterly*
Timothy A. Martin	Vice President	Falmouth Genealogical Society, MA
Nancy Moffett	President	Santa Clara County Hist. and Genealogical Society, CA
Linda Sanders	Program Chair	Santa Clara County Hist. and Genealogical Society, CA
David Wolff	President	Stanislaus County Genealogical Society, Modesto, CA
Janet Wolff	Vice President	Stanislaus County Genealogical Society, Modesto, CA
Ingeborg Carpenter	President	Sacramento German Genealogy Society, Sacramento, CA
Richard Hanson	Vice President	Sacramento German Genealogy Society, Sacramento, CA
Bonnie Cosgrove	Volunteer	Sacramento German Genealogy Society, Sacramento, CA
Amy Chidester	Volunteer	Sacramento German Genealogy Society, Sacramento, CA
Robert L. Bone	Photographer	Rancho Mission Viejo, CA
Tony Johns	Photographer	Weedon Bec, Northamptonshire, England

ENGLAND'S ARCHIVES STAFF

In my historic genealogical presentations, whether in person or virtual, I often reference England's underutilized treasure troves containing hidden genealogical gems. Without archives' staff who preserve, care for, and help researchers access their holdings, publications like this one would be impossible. Despite challenging shutdowns for long stretches during the COVID-19 pandemic, staff members in England's archives have been exemplary. Each group held records for genealogical mysteries that were long thought to be unsolvable. Sincere thanks and appreciation are due to all of them.

Eton College Archives	Windsor, England.
Northamptonshire Archives	Northampton, England (cited as NRO).

The National Archives	Kew, Surrey, England.
The British Library	London, England.
Lambeth Palace	London, England.
Society of Genealogists	London, England.
London Metropolitan Archives	London, England.
Grocers' Guild Archives	London, England.
Merchant Taylors' Guild Archives	London, England.

From all of us ancestor searchers to the staff of archives, libraries, and other repositories worldwide, we collectively say thank you. We, and our descendants, are eternally grateful.

RESEARCH TEAM

A hearty thanks and job well done is due to my English research partner, Nicola Waddington, M.A. Waddington is a registered archivist who heads up a UK Archives and Community History Consultancy firm, Archives Alive. Nicola has partnered with me from the very beginning of my English origins research project. We decided to give it a try right after she told me she doubted if she could help me. Our skills proved to be complementary. We each brought different ways of looking at clues and facts obtained. For one who is not a genealogist, her contributions enabled historic genealogical breakthroughs that might never have occurred without her. Eight years after we started our work together, she may know as much about Plymouth Colony, its people and history, and the Great Puritan Migration to New England as do many seasoned American genealogists and researchers.[3]

Also acknowledged for a job well done is Simon Neal, M.A., AGRA. Simon transcribed and translated many primary source records in old English and Latin that Nicola and I uncovered. One record discovered was so difficult to decipher and interpret, we translated it four times with four different experts for comparison purposes. Simon's work proved to be the most accurate. Excellent work, Simon! Thank you.

THANKS TO THREE SPECIAL LADIES

Stephanie Chandler heads up Authority Publishing, located in Folsom, California. *Puritans, Plagues, and Promises* is my third publication with her team. She is also Founder and CEO of the Non-Fiction Author's Association. Thanks, Stephanie, to you and your team. Much appreciated!

Dr. Ellen A. Koehler, Ph.D. in Intellectual and Cultural History, is an independent scholar[4] and Worship Pastor of Epiclesis, an Ancient-Future Faith Community in Sacramento, California.[5] Ellen is a friend and colleague who has stuck with me through thick and thin to help make this book a reality. For more than a year, she has coached me

---

[3] Nicola Waddington, M.A., "Archives Alive," http://www.archivesalive.co.uk.

[4] *Clerestory Notes.* https://www.clerestorynotes.com.

[5] "Our Pastors," *Epiclesis: An Ancient Future Faith Community.* https://epiclesis.org/our-pastors/.

with manuscript reviews, fact-checking, stylistic advice, and grammar corrections. Thank you, Ellen!

To my wife, Kristy L. Cole, love and kisses! She is an angel. Kristy has tolerated my countless hours and sacrificed much to allow me the freedom, flexibility, and focus to accomplish this all-consuming passion. She is the love of my life. This year, we celebrate our Golden Wedding Anniversary. Thank you, dear!

A LEGACY AND LABOR OF LOVE

I have often said this is my legacy project. This labor of love is the culmination of a lifetime quest to find my roots in England. Thank you, Grandpa Cole, for inspiring me to venture on this path and persevere to provide this legacy work. For my fellow researchers and genealogists, my five Cole nephews and nieces, many great nephews and nieces, and several great-great nieces and nephews, plus countless other Cole, Clarke, and Collier descendants—cherish the information. As you will discover, we owe much to those who went before us. Enjoy and Cheers!

PRELUDE

Good King Cole,
And he call'd for his Bowle,
And he call'd for Fidler's three;
And there was Fiddle, Fiddle,
And twice Fiddle, Fiddle,
For 'twas my Lady's Birth-day,
Therefore we keep Holy-day
And come to be merry[6]

Did King Cole really exist? I've often said that my ultimate genealogical goal would be to connect my Cole line to him. In February 2015, I found myself committed to an ambitious project. Already a seasoned genealogical researcher, sitting in my office over a cup of coffee, I was struck by one glaring question: "With all the great genealogists and researchers who came before me, why wasn't anyone able to crack the code regarding the Cole ancestry?" What were they missing, and why? For generations, researchers have searched in vain for the English origins of three brothers: Job, John, and Daniel Cole, plus Daniel's wife Ruth. In 2007, David Charles Cole wrote,

> The English forebears of Daniel Cole may never be known with certainty.[7] Tragically, we may [also] never know the lineage of Ruth, the matriarch . . . [and] faithful wife of Daniel for more than 50 years who nurtured and raised their 11 children under difficult and harsh conditions. Ruth died on December 15, 1694 at age 67, one week before Daniel died at age 80.[8]

Prior genealogists proposed that Ruth Cole's maiden surname, not indicated in any record, was Chase, Chandler, or Collier. Susan E. Roser wrote in 2010, "Ruth Cole's identity is not known with certainty. . . . her existence is known only from her death records."[9] Those statements were my tipping point, when I re-read both books in late 2014. I was determined to break through any-and-all brick walls to solve these age-old mysteries. I was determined to prove what had never been accomplished before—my branch's Cole connection to England. *Puritans, Plagues, and Promises* culminates a four-decade quest to accomplish that and more.

---

[6] Opie and P. Opie, *The Oxford Dictionary of Nursery Rhymes* (Oxford University Press, [1951] 1997): 156–8. The song is first attested in William King's *Useful Transactions in Philosophy* in 1708–9.

[7] David Charles Cole, *A Cole Family in America* (Philadelphia: Xlibris, 2007): 2.

[8] Cole, 35.

[9] Susan E. Roser, *Early Descendants of Daniel Cole of Eastham, Massachusetts* (Markham, Ont.: Stewart Publishing, 2010): 4.

My Journey's Beginning

An inquisitive fire about my Cole family's origins was stoked early and still burns brightly. It's a passion that harkens back to the day of my birth, fostered from my earliest memories, and reflects an innate drive we all share to answer two fundamental questions: Who am I? From whom and from where do I come?

In the late 1940s, my grandfather, Perry Ogden Cole, came to live with my parents in Whittier, California. On his seventy-eighth birthday, a camera captured his image in our front yard on August 18, 1948.

A retired school principal, Perry politely posed in his suit pants, dress shirt, and suspenders. He appeared more relaxed than normal. Most images show him in a three-piece suit. That same day, my mother went into labor. At 2:26 that afternoon, I was born.

When the telephone rang to inform the family, Grandpa answered. He most likely thought, "What a grand birthday gift!" With my father away at work, Grandpa Cole couldn't wait until his son, Harold Myron Cole, returned from work. He wanted to see his newest grandson. There was no debate.

Perry O. Cole, 78th birthday.
Cole personal archive. (0.1)

Grandpa walked out the front door at 505 North Alta Avenue, down the front steps, headed around the curve past Lou Henry Hoover Elementary School, crossed Hadley Street, and hiked up the hill to Murphy Memorial Hospital. After his half mile trek, he inquired about seeing the baby and his mother.

As Mom cradled her newborn son in her arms while still in the hospital bed, two nurses entered the room with quizzical looks on their faces. One said, "Ma'am, there's a . . . a . . . gentleman outside. He's very anxious to see the baby!" Of course, the nurses made a quick assumption—this elderly man was the baby's father. Fortunately, the confusion cleared quickly. Grandpa Cole entered the room to see—what in his eyes—was his very special birthday gift![10]

Another special gift is the accompanying photograph. Grandpa brought this framed photograph of father's family with him when he came to live with us. Taken in 1882 in

William E. Cole, August 1948.
Cole archive. (0.2)

---

[10] Family story told by the author's mother, Beatrice Rosamond "Kay" Cole.

front of John Emery Cole's farmhouse built just outside Mason City, Iowa, this photographic image, in its original frame, hung in my bedroom from my earliest memories. It is still in my bedroom today.[11]

Cole Family Home in Iowa 1882. Cole personal archive. (0.3)

Our shared birthdays created a special bond. Fond memories of Grandpa Cole teaching me to play Chinese Checkers and Parchesi exist from a very young age. He used games as a forum to pass along his values, the importance of family, and his faith in God. After my early years, he moved back to Santa Maria where he previously served in the public school system—both there and in San Luis Obispo. Grandpa Cole lived in a modest one-bedroom apartment at 602 Church Street—the western end unit closet to the street.

A few times each year, Dad and Mom took me on the three-hour drive to visit him. We continued our game-playing chats, and I often sat on his lap when he told me a story. Each summer's highlight was a Cole family "picnic" on the weekend nearest his birthday. The venue alternated yearly between San Luis Obispo's Cuesta Park and Santa Maria's Waller Park. The menu was always the same: barbequed Santa Maria-style steak with sides of beans, garlic bread, and assorted salads. Delicious! Hosted by Grandpa Cole's children, my father and his five siblings, the privileged seat next to Grandpa was mine—each of us with our

---

[11] William E. Cole, Cole archive.

own birthday cake. My cousin, Sharon Stevens, told me she never understood why I <u>always</u> got to sit next to Grandpa . . . until she finally realized it was my birthday too!

At each picnic, a designated sibling faithfully recorded each attendee's name, and where they lived. Often reported were the names of any family members missing, engagements, and anniversaries. A local newspaper article appeared annually featuring our Cole family honoring their father's birthday and usually included his picture. Having taught or served in the area as a school principal for more than twenty years, he was respected and well-known as an educator and a Presbyterian church elder. Genealogist alert: how would you like to have in your files a collection of articles like these with this much information about your family? I treasure them still.

Grandpa and I shared nineteen birthday celebrations. After he passed away at age ninety-seven, our Cole family continued the reunion tradition for many years. In 2020, interrupted by COVID-19, we gathered on Zoom for the first time in a long time to celebrate Perry O. Cole's 150th birthday!

In 1980, my genealogy quest began. Because of my special relationship with Grandpa Cole, I wanted to know the entire story of his life. Fortunately, he had printed some basic genealogical information and written a short autobiography. As the youngest Cole grandchild with an interest in family history, others gladly entrusted me with family papers and photographs. Within two decades, our ancestral connection was proven to Daniel and Ruth Cole. They emigrated to America during the Great Puritan Migration to New England from 1620-1640. They lived in Plymouth Colony and were one of the founding families of Nauset/Eastham on Cape Cod. Even though I was working full time, I completed my General Society of Mayflower Descendants certification as a descendant of Stephen Hopkins and his daughter, Constance. One of her descendants married a Cole.[12] With that accomplished, it was time to take on another genealogical challenge.

TWO STARTING QUESTIONS

I framed my project's initial efforts with two straightforward research questions: 1) Who are the English ancestors of Job, John, and Daniel Cole? 2) Who is the mysterious Ruth, wife of Daniel Cole? With a single undocumented lead, I contacted an English genealogist in Lancashire, England. He did not find any connections and exhausted what was available. One month into the project, I hit a brick wall. I asked him if he knew anyone else who might be able to help me. He said, "If anyone can, Nicola Waddington's the one." I thanked him for his effort and candor. I promptly sent Ms. Waddington an email inquiry.

Nicola replied she was an archivist, not a genealogist. She was skeptical and wasn't sure if she would be able to help me. I thought to myself, "An archivist—that's interesting. I'm a seasoned genealogist with lots of experience. But I don't know English records and archives. Since those who tried before me could not crack the code, maybe it's time to try something different."

---

[12] William E. Cole is General Society of Mayflower Descendants No. 91332 from Gold River, California.

INTRODUCTION

My English origins research project unearthed more discoveries than I ever imagined possible. Blessed with gifts I never expected to receive, the journeys of ancestors great and small emerged from the depths of England's archives. The more my English research partner and I discovered, the more the stories grew.[13] In writing my manuscript's initial draft, a realization hit me like a ton of bricks.

The relevance of *Puritans, Plagues, and Promises* goes far beyond this author's ancestors. While it is about them, it is also about the ancestors of some twenty thousand other English men, women, and children who emigrated to New England from 1620-40 during the Great Puritan Migration. Their stories describe *Puritans* whose faith was tested, and who were persecuted, martyred, and honored; *Plagues* that decimated entire families and passed over others; and *Promises* made, broken, fulfilled, unfulfilled, and sometimes deferred.

Their stories are riveting. They reveal extraordinary journeys of people who were adventurous, brave, and daring. What emerges from these pages is a collection of connected stories that contain challenges and challengers, triumphs and tragedies, trials and tribulations, and the pursuit of *Promises* great and small.

An Epic Story

The overarching journey is one of epic proportions. Powerful people, forces, and motivations clash in England and establish colonies in America. The official religion of the Crown swings back and forth between Catholicism and Protestantism, highlighted during the reigns of Henry VIII, Edward VI, Mary I, and Elizabeth I. The sixteenth century's second half reveals conflicts of conscience between Puritans, powerful leaders in the Church of England, and reigning monarchs. As the Reformation took hold and developed in England, Puritans emerged.

At the dawn of the seventeenth century, these conflicts escalated, propelling some into exile and thereafter compelling many to venture further, emigrating to the New World. Their efforts display tests, triumphs, and tragedies which come clearly into focus. Their skirmishes over the right to their "own private judgment" and the necessity of acting in accordance with their "own conscience" led to diverse battles on many fronts: religious, political, legal, and economic. Powerful forces collide—often with the consequence of life or death. They foretell of future battles in America two hundred years later, to be fought over issues that include the separation of Church and State, the rule of law versus a monarch's absolute rule, and freedoms and rights held dear but sometimes taken for granted. They include freedoms of religion and the press; the rights to a jury of peers and to a just, speedy trial; and the prohibition of self-incrimination. Many late-sixteenth and early-seventeenth century

---

[13] Nicola Waddington, M.A., heads up Archives Alive, a UK-based consultancy headquartered in Canterbury, England.

battles created precedents for England and the American colonies. They foreshadowed, and led to, founding documents of the United States of America including the Declaration of Independence, the Constitution, the Bill of Rights, and other Constitutional Amendments.

While the story of intrepid Pilgrims seeking religious freedom has been told time and time again, their story and the stories of others closely connected to them—which included my ancestors and probably yours—deserved a new exploration of fascinating people and complex events that led to Plymouth Colony's struggles and successes. While religious freedom was an important part of the story, it wasn't the only factor. Also important were political, legal, and economic forces. All are explored in *Puritans, Plagues, and Promises*.

CREATIVE NONFICTION NARRATIVE

As more details surfaced during the research project, several discoveries altered pre-conceived notions about these men, women, and children. To better understand what, why, and how events unfolded the way they did required a greater in-depth historical context than I imagined. It also required adopting a new writing style.

In previous publications, I mainly let facts speak for themselves and wrote stories from my perspective. But this project's magnitude of discoveries required more—much more. The epic nature of this story required me to adapt my style using a new template. It enabled me to do something I teach in genealogical and historical presentations: how to breathe life into our genealogy and history with the power of stories. In this work, I poured everything I've learned into it.

Stories that emerged right from chapter one captured details of people's lives in one of the most turbulent times in Elizabethan England's history. They required adjustments in writing style, approach, and methods which allowed me to reach beyond presenting the facts and figures of our genealogical finds. I found that to be a good thing. As often happens with just facts and figures, non-genealogists' eyes glaze over. But let me be clear: this passionate genealogist adheres to strict and accepted professional genealogical standards. Facts and figures are sacrosanct. But bringing them to life in an approachable and engaging way required a new approach that differs from many works in this genre. It required CNN—but not the news channel. The overarching style employed in *Puritans, Plagues, and Promises* is a Creative Nonfiction Narrative.

While the facts and figures are nonfiction as are the people, a dose of creative license breathes life into the cast of characters—in this case the author's ancestors and those within their circle of associates. Real people, including in-laws, friends, colleagues, peers, partners, and ministers, are placed squarely into their historical context. With creative license, their stories and the facts of their lives are overlayed with thoughts, emotions, spoken words, and prayers—since many were Puritans. In other words, facts and figures meet flesh and blood.

The real-life characters in this historical narrative are real people who face real-life challenges spanning the second half of the sixteenth century through the first third of the seventeenth century. That's four score years of real people, history, and stories. Without the benefit of today's technology such as audiotapes, video recordings, and the like, they often had carefully scribed documents, letters, and, as you will later discover, amazingly detailed court records. From those, plausible and believable stories emerge. Carefully researched, they represent what they most likely would have thought, felt, spoke, and prayed.

Puritans, Plagues, and Promises emerges as an historically accurate and representative story about the bold and courageous English men, women, and children who lived in the latter half of the sixteenth century and the first third of the seventeenth century. This interlaced set of generational stories follows interconnected families who experienced one of the most tumultuous times in England's colorful history. They were real people who faced real challenges. They experienced trials, tribulations, and testing. They lived their lives consistent with their consciences. They overcame obstacles with determination and perseverance, and ultimately triumphed over their challenges. This work is relevant and representative of all of them. *Puritans, Plagues, and Promises* is truly an epic story.

SECTION ONE: PURITANS

Section One delves deeply into the history of the Puritans and their movement in England. Decades before *Mayflower's* voyage to the New World was conceived, what was their movement about? What hardships and ordeals did they experience? In one of the most tumultuous religious periods in English history, the Puritans withstood challenges and challengers with courage while their faith was tested.

The opening chapter springs to life with clandestine meetings held by Puritan clergymen in response to directives emanating from the Archbishop of Canterbury in the 1580s. A thrilling story emerges when a series of inflammatory pamphlets are printed in secret and distributed throughout England. Today, these pamphlets are viewed as literary masterpieces—the first English example of popular political sarcasm known to be printed. Incensed ecclesiastical officials hunt for the culprits. Determined Puritans stay one step ahead of the officials' henchmen by hiding, dismantling, and moving a secret printing press in the dead of night several times. They manage to elude ecclesiastical enforcers, publishing seven pamphlets before they are finally caught, questioned, and hauled off to jail in London. The resulting trials riveted attention on the issue of Church and State in England.

The author's ancestors, their vicar, and their community were all involved. They faced adversity from powerful people in England. In this volume, you will experience how ordinary people from a small village supported the Puritan cause while they experienced these extraordinary events. They met the challenges head-on without flinching and kept their faith during this turbulent period in England's colorful history. More than thirty years before the *Mayflower's* epic voyage, some Puritan leaders were arrested, imprisoned in London, put on trial, and summarily executed. Do you know the names of these martyrs? You will. Why they were executed might surprise you. But when you read the historical record of conversations between the Archbishop of Canterbury and Queen Elizabeth after the executions, you will most likely be saddened, shocked, and possibly enraged.

Section One concludes with the chronicle of nine zealous Puritans on trial, including the Cole family's vicar. Eight Puritan ministers and a much-revered theologian are detained in prison, deprived of their living, their families, and their liberty during the reign of Elizabeth I. They face Her Majesty's handpicked advisors in the Courts of the High Commission and the Star Chamber on charges of treason and sedition. A complex series of trials in the early 1590s provided legal precedents that made their way into the legal systems of both England and what became the United States of America, some two hundred years later.

SECTION TWO: PLAGUES

Section Two begins with an unusual example of how the Plague of 1593 resulted in conditions that brought freedom, liberty, and new opportunities for a few fortunate ones who survived. This surprising outcome is a lesson in how silver linings often appear from dark clouds—a lesson we can learn from even today. Cole, Clarke, and Collier family members and their close circle of colleagues and friends were particularly impacted by the plagues that ravished England in the late-sixteenth and early-seventeenth centuries. Their stories provide specific examples that reveal how entire families were affected. These seemingly indiscriminate episodic events besieged countryside villagers and residents of London equally—with life and death consequences. Without regard to status, whether victims were of nobility or commoners, merchants or farmers, plagues decimated some but spared others. And plagues were not a onetime event. They often came in waves, some in short succession that seemed to hit indiscriminately. These stories are accounts of courage in the face of painful adversity—narratives that show how even tragic circumstances can turn into inspiration with the Promises of new beginnings.

These interconnected families all experience plagues. While mourning those lost, their strong Puritan faith enabled them to celebrate God's protection for those who lived. For those who lost children, spouses, parents, and friends, we are left to contemplate what might have been if those who perished had survived or if some survivors had not. For us now, as for those living then, this close look at Plagues brings into sharp focus how difficult and precious life could be for England's people in the late sixteenth and early seventeenth centuries.

These stories tell us much about people's character in the face of pain and sorrow. Qualities of perseverance and faith shine forth when one considers the alternatives. Coming out of successive waves of plague, some had no choice but to rebuild their lives. Some rebuilt merchant enterprises and some started over. For some, it forced generational change. For others, it provided prospects to start anew. But one thing is certain. Plagues affected all facets of everyday existence in England in dramatic ways. Considering our collective experiences worldwide with the Covid-19 pandemic from 2020-22, the sufferings and triumphs of our predecessors become more relatable and even more inspirational. Their real-life examples are valuable models of perseverance and hope for our lives today.

Section Two ends with a different type of plague. The Cole family is plagued by a vindictive attorney. It's another riveting story, with difficulties encountered yielding another silver lining. Though the court cases were ultimately resolved in their favor, they caused undue hardship on the Coles and their extended family. But on a personal note, researching the court records enabled this Passionate Genealogist to identify with certainty the mother of the Cole brothers who immigrated to America, Frances, plus her entire family. It revealed a new branch of our family tree and provided the answer to a long-sought and perplexing mystery—another historic genealogical breakthrough.

Section Three: Promises

While the story of intrepid Pilgrims seeking religious freedom has been told time and time again, their story and the stories of others closely connected to them, which included my ancestors and perhaps yours, deserved a fresh exploration of fascinating people and complex events that led to Plymouth Colony's struggles and successes. While religious freedom was an important part of the story, it wasn't the only factor. Also important were political, legal, and economic forces. All are explored in *Puritans, Plagues, and Promises*.

Section Three explores the Promises offered on both sides of the Atlantic Ocean. Spanning the late sixteenth century and into the first third of the seventeenth century, England's push to colonize America and compete with the Spanish, French, and Dutch explorers expanded its trade opportunities dramatically outward from the Isle of Britain. It helped further the global aspirations of three English monarchs—Elizabeth I, James I, and Charles I. At times, this golden age of exploration offered Promises of vast natural resources and virgin land, while it also exploited the same. It also exploited indigenous peoples and even its own merchants. All this created an age of Promises—some fulfilled, others unfulfilled, and still others deferred. But what it really did was to offer an alternative path for religious nonconformists, including Puritans, to remain subjects of the Crown while escaping the forces that sought to control their religious beliefs and worship by going into exile far, far away. This section about such Promises offers insights into an era of trade growth and prosperity that dramatically increased opportunities for England's merchants as well as the Puritan faithful.

The author descends from two *Mayflower* passengers and one of the Merchant Adventurers, the investor group that underwrote the voyage and founding of Plymouth Colony in New England. But this section does not start with the *Mayflower*. It first explores previous English colonization efforts in America. One of the author's ancestors was the only *Mayflower* passenger who had been to America before. His previous journey involved one of the first recorded episodes of a ship experiencing and surviving a hurricane. Shipwrecked on Devil's Isle, Stephen Hopkins, the other passengers, and crew all lived on a deserted island. This section chronicles the dynamics between a ship captain and a future governor of the colony, a mutiny involving the author's ancestor, the rebuilding of two ships from the original ship's wreckage, and the continuation of the journey to Virginia's Colony and Jamestown. This exciting adventure tale provided the plot inspiration for one of Shakespeare's last plays.

New research findings about the author's Merchant Adventurer ancestor, an investor "from the very beginning," provide new insights and illuminate understandings of the various forces that created *Mayflower*'s epic voyage and the new colony in New England. The author explores factors that exiled the Leiden Separatists, their decision to emigrate to America, the epic voyage of the *Mayflower* in 1620, and Plymouth Colony's early struggles for survival. What is unique to this narrative is its multi-faceted view of the events from both the colonists' and adventurers' perspectives. Why is this voyage and its subsequent colony so important? It was not the first. Nor was it the most prosperous. What propelled its founding and settlement? What marks this as a watershed moment for both England and America? Why is 1620 burned into our collective consciousness? What has prevented it from fading into the dimness of ancient history? As author Nathaniel Philbrick wrote in 2006, "The Pilgrims had come to America not to conquer a continent but to re-create their modest communities in Scrooby and in Leiden."[14]

This final section delves into the complex relationship between the Leiden Separatists, commonly known as Pilgrims, and their investors. Their relationship was at times loving, and at other times antagonistic or even hostile. It shines new light on vivid details of the voyage, the passengers' arrival in America, and their early struggles to survive and prosper. By spotlighting events on both sides of the ocean, not only what the Leiden Separatists faced, but also what their investors faced, this fresh perspective brings new insights to an old story.

---

[14] Nathaniel Philbrick, *Mayflower: A Story of Courage, Community, and War* (New York: Penguin Books, 2006): 347.

THIS AUTHOR'S HOPE FOR YOU

My sincere desire is for you to be caught up in an approachable and engaging narrative as you follow the journeys of interconnected families living in interesting, tumultuous, and consequential times. *Puritans, Plagues, and Promises* covers one of the most turbulent times in England's colorful history. It chronicles much of the founding of New England in America.

Stories of people facing momentous choices emerge, as facts and figures meet flesh and blood. They thought, felt, spoke, and prayed the way they did because they were *Puritans*. We identify with real challenges they faced including *Plagues* and other trials and tribulations. We see how they lived their lives consistent with their consciences and with courage and perseverance. Their determination and faith led them to ultimately triumph over their challenges. In turn, that allowed them to pursue their hopes and dreams—the *Promises* they sought beyond England and across a great expanse of ocean.

Puritans, Plagues, and Promises is an epic story. And their stories are our story. My hope is that you will love and cherish it as much as I did. Researching, discovering, and writing the narrative of their lives and experiences in this way breathes life into their genealogy with the power of story. Cheers!

A NOTE ON TECHNICAL CONVENTIONS

<u>Dates</u>: Throughout this work, dates are presented such that they conform to the current modern calendar. Most original sources both in England and America during this time period used split years i.e. 1598/9 to record events. In this example, 1 January – 24 March was from the year 1599, while 25 March – December 31 was from 1598. The dates presented here conform to the modern calendar and keep the actual records' dates and do not add ten days to account for the Julian calendar corrections that were implemented in England in 1751.

<u>Spellings, capitalizations, and punctuations</u>. Documents researched in the sixteenth and seventeenth centuries contain unusual or inconsistent spelling, capitalization, and punctuation variations. It was not unusual to find different spellings of the same person throughout the same document. The same is true in early books of this era. While the author has made every attempt to be consistent in the book's text to standardize the names, word spellings, punctuations, etc. there may be some variations based on accessing different source documents. In terms of unusual capitalizations, source documents often contain capitalized nouns to emphasize their importance or power—for example, Church, State, Oath, Schism, Declaration, etc. One final note: the author has chosen to capitalize church and state when the terms refer to the historical relationship between Church and State as institutions.

<u>Original source documents</u>. Primary sources quoted, transcribed, and translated, as much as was feasible, retained the original word spellings, capitalizations, etc. As a result, readers will occasionally see names that are spelled one way in the book's text and another way in the quoted passages.

<u>Prayers</u>: You will note that prayers prayed by the Puritans are placed and set off in quotation marks. They were crafted in the style and language consistent with what they would have been familiar with. These include the *Book of Common Prayer*, 1559, and the Geneva Bible of 1599.

SECTION ONE

PURITANS

CHAPTER 1

CHALLENGES, CHALLENGERS, AND CLASSES

Northamptonshire Vicar Travels to Daventry

In the early morning mist, vicar William Proudlove strode through the quiet village of Weedon Bec and recalled all that had transpired here during the last two eventful years. A seasoned clergyman, Proudlove vividly remembered the chaos he inherited upon arrival. Some parishioners had stopped attending local worship services entirely, and several others traveled to attend elsewhere. While not surprising, given similar events happening throughout England, it was serious. The vicar knew what had always been true: the life of an English village centered on the life of its church. How the parish was in turmoil!

From day one, Proudlove assumed responsibility as shepherd for his flock with great care. A man in his fifties, he approached his tasks with the renewed vigor of a man twenty years younger. He intentionally nurtured his parishioners, and they responded eagerly and with spiritual growth. That delighted him and rejuvenated his spirit. But Proudlove knew it was the Lord's doing, and he was most grateful. He certainly acknowledged what his heart knew to be true, "On my own, I am weak. But in the Lord, that is where my strength is."

When Proudlove recognized the humble abode up ahead, he whispered to himself, "Ahhh . . . here we are." When he quietly tapped his knuckles on the door, Thomas Cole pushed back his chair from the modest table, rose from his seat, and breathed a quiet sigh. He whispered, to no one in particular, "It must be vicar Proudlove." He had been expecting him before dawn.

Cole recalled when Proudlove arrived two years before. The vicar had stepped into a tumultuous situation. In fairness, Cole thought, Proudlove's predecessor—vicar Thomas Deane—had followed the long-serving and well-loved vicar, John Ringrose. Ringrose was instituted 14 May 1562.[1] His previous two-year calling was as the Rector of Pitsford.[2]

As Weedon Bec's spiritual leader, Ringrose had shepherded his flock and ministered to Thomas Cole, his family, and the other villagers for a quarter of a century. Vicar Ringrose faithfully implemented Puritan reforms to develop his parishioners' godly character.[3] In 1576, when eight clergy were examined by diocesan authorities as to their skill level, he received the rating of *bene eruditus*, the highest level of competence. Five of these clerics

---

[1] John Bridges, *The History and Antiquities of Northamptonshire, Vol. 1.* (London: T Payne, 1791): 453-4. Accessed on *The Internet Archive.* Viewed 1 December 2017. https://archive.org/.

[2] "The Clergy of the Church of England Database 1540-1835." https://theclergydatabase.org.uk/. Hereinafter CCEd.

[3] Puritans referred to themselves as godly.

"and John Ringrose of Weedon Bec were known Puritans or associated with vigorous Puritan centres."[4]

With such meritorious service, following Ringrose would be tough for his replacement. But with increasing pressure emanating from the archbishop, the diocese knew change was required. When Ringrose resigned on 6 March 1587, diocesan authorities made it clear to the new vicar, Thomas Deane, that his responsibility was to ensure absolute adherence to the Church of England's *Book of Common Prayer*. Many Puritan-leaning vicars refused to adhere to mandated practices they felt had no Biblical basis and were remnants of Roman Catholicism. But now, even small deviations, previously overlooked, were no longer acceptable.

Parishioners were to be fined for non-attendance. They were required to kneel to take Communion. Vicars were to adhere strictly to the official dress code and wear a surplice and the vestments. Even more troubling for Puritans was the strict edict that allowed only homilies read from Scripture and eliminated the preaching of sermons. By extension, that eliminated small group Bible studies, often held in homes to discuss Sunday sermons, which Puritan vicars had proliferated throughout England and parishioners embraced.

From the moment vicar Thomas Deane arrived in Weedon Bec on 22 March 1587,[5] he set about dismantling the spiritual disciplines fostered by his predecessor. But these diocesan-mandated changes enforced by Deane were too much for the parishioners to handle. As it must have appeared to Thomas Cole, church conformity and uniformity seemed more important to ecclesiastical authorities than the parishioners' deepening faith and spiritual growth.

After a brief volatile period of disruption, Cole was undoubtedly amazed when he saw the Lord work what appeared to be a miracle. After just three months, vicars Deane and Proudlove exchanged positions. William Proudlove, the Rector of Lamport since 1577, became the parish vicar of Cole's village on 30 June 1587.[6] Thomas Deane replaced him as the Rector of Lamport—nineteen miles distant. Upon hearing the news, Cole would have assuredly exclaimed, "Praise be to God!"

When vicar Proudlove accepted the challenge of taking over the troubled parish, he received cautious acceptance from the parishioners. As Proudlove reinstituted many reforms in line with Ringrose's teaching, everything changed for the better. In a little over two years, his spiritual impact on the congregation had been dramatic. What at first had been cautious acceptance from the parishioners turned to unbridled joy. This early morning, Thomas Cole undoubtedly reflected on how much vicar Proudlove's stature had grown in two short years. Vicar Proudlove was now firmly in place as the parish's spiritual leader. He had earned the respect of the entire village.

Likewise, Thomas Cole was well-respected in his village. He often served at the twice-annual Baron of the Manor Court hearings, either as juror or homage, for various

[4] W. J. Shiels, *The Puritans in the Diocese of Peterborough: 1558-1610* (Northampton: Northamptonshire Record Society, v. 30, 1979): 93.
[5] CCEd.
[6] CCEd.

presentments.[7] While most cases were issues of land tenancy rights which concerned payment, fines, or transitions, Cole might adjudicate conflicts or complaints among tenants, as well as perform administrative responsibilities. Vicar Proudlove recognized Cole's talents and selected him to serve as a parish churchwarden. Both positions, one secular and one religious, required clear-thinking men, respected in the community with good writing abilities. Thomas Cole was such a man.

Cole's village, Weedon Bec in the shire of Northampton, is an ancient village. Built on a Roman road as a prime transit route from London across the East Midlands toward Wales, cattle droves trod the road to market. Weedon comes from two Anglo-Saxon words: *Weoh*, meaning a Shrine or Holy Place, and *Dun*, meaning Hill. The earliest known written occurrence of the name is found in an Anglo-Saxon Charter dated 944 AD. Bec is a village in Normandy, where there was an important Abbey.[8] Two small hamlets, Upper Weedon and Lower Weedon, sprang forth surrounding this "holy hill." They were separated by farms and shared land. Upon Cole's arrival, he would have heard about Weedon's *Fable of the Geese*.

In about 1540 John Leland was travelling around England on Royal business and visited Weedon. He reported a little from the south side of the chirch yarde ys a faire chapel dedicate to S. Werburge, that sum tyme was a nunne at Wedon. Saint Werburgh died in about 700 A.D. and the story of her life was recorded by more than one medieval monk. . . . Werburgh was said to be the daughter of Wulfhere, King of Mercia, which was the part of Britain which might today be called the Midlands. She was always very devout and became a nun at Ely. After the death of her father, his brother Ethelred succeeded him, and asked his niece to take charge of the nunneries in Mercia.

In 1095, Goscelin records . . . one miracle performed by Werburgh . . . involving the geese which were feeding from the fields of Weedon, where she was living at the time. When told of the damage which this was causing she ordered that the geese be called to her. She then told them to leave, and not return. In the words of Goscelin, as translated from the Latin by Rev. W.G. Griffin: And there was no further delay. That whole gathering flew off and away, so that not even one small bird of that species has ever been seen on that territory . . . so it has been widely recounted.[9]

Hearing Proudlove's knock, Cole rose from his candle-lit table, unlatched his door, and embraced his vicar and friend. After hushed but pleasant greetings, vicar William Proudlove thanked Cole for the loan of his horse. The vicar reiterated how grateful he was and did not expect to return until nightfall. As Proudlove mounted Cole's horse, he waved goodbye and leaned toward a well-worn path heading north. Proudlove thought to himself, "I am so blessed! I did not want my energy expended with a five-mile hike to Daventry. Today's meeting is too important for me to be late or tired upon arrival!"

---

[7] Homage is a court official similar to a judge. Presentment was the term for a court case locally overseen.

[8] from the Abbey of Bec-Hellouin, in Normandy, France.

[9] "Weedon Tales," *Weedon Bec Parish Council*. Viewed on 15 January 2019. http://www.weedonbec-village. co.uk/weedon-tales.html.

As the vicar rode astride the horse and away from the village, the misty morning dissipated. At daybreak, the idyllic countryside of the shire of Northampton unfolded before his eyes. Proudlove thought, "How beautiful and perfect is God's creation!" After a brief admiring gaze at the horizon, he wondered, "What has led me here?" A flood of recollections from his youth and years in ministry cascaded through his mind.

As a young lad, Proudlove was aware of church matters. Born about 1535, he overheard family discussions of Henry VIII's "Great Matter"—the need to produce a male heir. That ultimately led to the king's break with the Pope and the start of the Church of England.

Raised as a Catholic, Proudlove would have initially felt confused as England converted to Protestantism. But not much changed on the surface. Keeping basic church customs and rituals made his adjustment relatively easy. Of course, the old monasteries became the Crown's property—filling the king's coffers. That reminded Proudlove of a familiar childhood rhyme.

> Little Jack Horner sat in a corner
> Eating a Christmas pie;
> He put in his thumb,
> And pulled out a plum,
> And said, "What a good boy am I!"[10]

As he recited the rhyme, he recalled its meaning. In the 1530s, Jack Horner was a steward to the last Abbot of Glastonbury, Richard Whiting. After the Dissolution of the Monasteries, a legend emerged that Whiting sent little Jack Horner to London in hopes of placating King Henry with a Christmas pie filled with twelve manor deeds. On the journey, Jack supposedly opened the pie and extracted the deed of the Manor of Mells in Somerset, which the plum represents. This fable is understandably denied by the present Lord, Thomas Horner.

In 1538, the birth of King Henry's son, Edward, settled the Great Matter—a male royal heir was finally secured. In his final years, Henry VIII specified a succession plan in his will.

> This document bequeathed the throne to, first, Edward. Should the new king die without heirs, Henry's eldest daughter, Mary, would follow; if she should die childless, she would be succeeded by Elizabeth. It is a measure of Henry's power and prestige that his wishes, even in death, were not seriously questioned despite the facts that they reversed previous legislation delegitimizing the two princesses, and that Edward VI was only 9 years of age . . . when he came to the throne.[11]

Henry VIII, King of England, ex-communicated Catholic who had become Supreme Head of the Church of England, drew his last breath in the early hours of the morning on

[10] Ellen Castelow, "Nursery Rhymes," *Historic UK: The History and Heritage Accommodation Guide.* Viewed on 4 October 2021. https://www.historic-uk.com/CultureUK/Nursery-Rhymes/.
[11] Robert Bucholz and Newton Key, *Early Modern England 1485-1714: A Narrative History* (Oxford: Blackwell Publishing Ltd., 2004): 97-8.

28 January 1547. With him was his Archbishop of Canterbury, Thomas Cranmer. Having been summoned to the king's bedside just after midnight, Cranmer held Henry's hand in his, read a reformed statement of faith, and prayed.

Edward VI was crowned on 20 February 1547. Henry had surrounded Edward with "a regency council made up of prominent Protestant peers and clergymen." Included in this inner circle was Edward's uncle, Edward Seymour, the Earl of Hertford. The brother of Henry VIII's third wife, Jane Seymour, Edward was promptly named Lord Protector of the Realm and Duke of Somerset. In his role, Seymour "was something of a reformer, issuing some 76 proclamations in just two years."[12] Lacking Henry's political skills, his social and economic policies proved unpopular with nobility and the ruling class.

> [Seymour] asked Parliament to repeal the Treason Act, the Act for Burning Heretics, the Six Articles, and all restrictions on printing and reading the Bible. English men and women were now more free to discuss religion and religious alternatives than ever before… Bibles and Protestant tracts flooded into England, where they were read and debated avidly, especially at the two universities and among urban professionals and merchants.[13]

PURITAN REFORMS ACCELERATE

With the accession of Edward, Proudlove no doubt felt relief the Tudor Dynasty was intact. For a lad entering his teenage years, stability in England's monarchy was of prime importance. The likelihood of war, internal rival clashes, and a draft into military service diminished dramatically with a smooth transition of monarchs.

Edward VI's intellectual prowess developed rapidly with scholarly interests in Greek, Latin, French, astronomy, and music. Surrounded with puritan-leaning Protestant advisors committed to reforms within the church, King Edward's commitment to advance Protestant reforms propelled Puritans forward, and the Church of England toward greater alignment with other Reformation initiatives on the Continent. But support for these changes was not universally accepted. Rooted in church tradition for generations, particularly in the northern provinces,

Edward VI. Wikimedia Commons. Public domain. (1.1)

some nobles and members of the ruling elite resisted reforms. When King Edward recognized the severity of his health issues at age fifteen, he sought to ensure the ongoing Puritan

---

[12] Bucholz and Key, 98.
[13] Bucholz and Key, 99.

reform movement. In June 1553, Edward VI wrote his will designating Lady Jane Grey and her male heirs as successors to the Crown. Lady Jane was a committed Protestant supportive of reforms already made in the Church of England. Since Edward's will eliminated his two half-sisters, Mary and Elizabeth, from the line of succession on account of their illegitimacy, he thought any claims they might promote under the Third Succession Act were thwarted.

Edward VI died on 6 July 1553, and the Privy Council proclaimed Lady Jane Grey queen within four days. As she awaited coronation sequestered in the Tower of London, an all too predictable power struggle ensued. Support for Mary grew quickly, and most of Jane's supporters abandoned her. The Privy Council suddenly changed sides. Mary was proclaimed queen on 19 July 1553, thus deposing Jane. After twelve tumultuous days, Edward VI's half-sister and Henry VIII's eldest daughter, Mary Tudor, became Queen Mary I—just as specified in her father's will.

Mary I. Wikimedia Commons. Public domain. (1.2)

Mary never abandoned her Catholic faith during Edward's reign, and celebrated Mass in her private estates. While she initially declared her intention to keep England Protestant, she progressively increased pressure on Protestants. After Mary's marriage to Philip of Spain (later King Philip I of Spain) in 1554, she rapidly worked to revert England to Catholicism. Acts were passed requiring clergy and supporters to renounce their Protestant faith. Although it might have been confusing to him at times, William Proudlove, born Catholic and a convert to Protestantism, most likely adjusted once again given his Catholic upbringing.

As Proudlove nudged his horse forward, he glanced at the beautiful countryside. The beauty of God's Creation brought another flood of memories. He thought about those required shifts of faith early as he began his ministry. He was admitted as Rector of Braceborough under the patronage of two gentlemen, Richard Leytus and William Leitus, on 4 November 1555.[14] Proudlove recalled starting his first clergy assignment with excitement. But even then, at about age twenty, he had heard reports of persecutions that troubled him. He remembered feelings of anguish about clergy and supporters summoned to affirm their allegiance to the queen and renounce their Protestant faith.

In what became known as "Marian persecutions" for those who refused—the consequences were severe. Those refusing to swear the *ex-officio* oath to Queen Mary, were declared heretics. They could be excommunicated from England's reinstated Catholic church, imprisoned, expelled from England, or even worse. The first major event occurred on 4 February 1555. Refusing to renounce his faith, John Rogers, a translator of the Bible into English, was burned at the stake.[15]

---

14 "William Prowdelove [*sic*]," CCeD.

15 Bucholz and Key, 107.

The Burning of Master John Rogers, translator of the
Bible into English, 1555. Public domain. (1.3)

In the span of forty-five months through November 1558, more than three hundred souls refused to publicly renounce their faith and sacrificed their mortality. The choice presented at their trials was labeled "turn or burn." Queen Mary I's subjects bestowed on her a new title: "Bloody Mary." Thirty-four individuals died in prison, while 237 men and 52 women were burned at the stake as heretics.[16] One man experienced the worst possible sentence—he was hanged, drawn, and quartered. Designed to place absolute terror and fear in the hearts and minds of those who might follow his example, this gruesome torture was carried out in a public square—often with many spectators.

The condemned man would usually be sentenced to the short drop method of hanging, so that the neck would not break. The man was usually dragged alive to the quartering table, although in some cases men were brought to the table dead or unconscious. A splash of water was usually employed to wake the man if unconscious, then he was laid down on the table. A large cut was made in the gut after removing the genitalia, and the intestines would be spooled out on a device that resembled a dough roller. Each piece of organ would be burned before the sufferer's eyes, and when he was completely disembowelled, his head would be cut off. The body would then be cut into four pieces, and the king would decide where they were to be displayed. Usually the head was sent to the Tower of London and…

---

[16] Bucholz and Key, 107.

the other four pieces were sent to different parts of the country. The head was generally par-boiled in brine to preserve the appearance of the head in display, while the quarters were more often prepared in pitch, for longer-lasting deterrent displays.[17]

Given these public displays of torture, Proudlove recalled a well-known rhyme that may have been penned to commemorate the policies of Mary I. He quietly recited it.

> Mary, Mary quite contrary
> How does your garden grow,
> With silver bells and cockle shells
> And pretty maids all in a row.[18]

One interpretation is this. As a devout Catholic, Mary ascended the throne on the death of her Protestant half-brother Edward—then restored the Catholic faith to England; hence "Mary, Mary quite contrary." The "garden" refers either to the country itself or represents cemetery markers of those executed. The "silver bells" and "cockle shells" were instruments of torture used on Protestant martyrs to "persuade" them to change faith, and the "pretty maids all in a row" refers to the mass execution of female Protestants.

Vicar Proudlove's recollection of these events, some thirty years later, must have troubled him. He very likely asked himself, "Was history about to repeat itself in these different times under these different circumstances?" He must have pondered, "What would I do if confronted with refusing to recant my Puritan beliefs as a Protestant before my current ecclesiastical authorities? Could that happen in today's England? I am meeting my peers today to discuss whether or not we might be on a similar path. I fear it may be so—not as Catholics, but as Puritans." He kicked his horse's flanks harder to hasten the pace.

During Mary I's reign with its trials and tribulations, her half-sister, Elizabeth Tudor, kept a low profile. Elizabeth had remained privately Protestant. When Queen Mary died unexpectedly in 1558, Elizabeth ascended to the English throne. With another transition underway, her subjects wondered what policies the new queen would favor. What tone would she set for her reign? They anxiously watched and waited. From the beginning of her reign, Elizabeth's subjects scrutinized her every move for any sign—even in her smallest gesture.

Knowingly, Elizabeth carefully choreographed the messages she wanted to convey. On 15 January 1559, the queen's coronation procession entered London amid bells, bonfires, and demonstrations designed to elicit jubilation. She undoubtedly had rehearsed what she was about to do for all to see. "When a girl in an allegorical pageant presented her with a Bible in English translation—banned under Mary's reign—Elizabeth kissed the book, held it up reverently, and then laid it on her breast." Elizabeth had mastered the art of political and courtly theater. One observer noted she had a gift and style that won the hearts of her

---

[17] "Hanged, drawn and quartered," *Wikipedia*. Viewed on 9 September 2020. https://en.wikipedia.org/wiki/Hanged,_drawn_and_quartered.

[18] "Mary, Mary, Quite Contrary," *All Nursery Rhymes*. Viewed 20 July 2021. https://allnurseryrhymes.com/mary-mary-quite-contrary.

people. Upon her procession's arrival at Westminster Abbey in broad daylight, the abbot and monks greeted her with candles in their hands. Elizabeth dispatched them with a sweeping hand gesture saying, "Away with those torches! We can see well enough."[19]

Moving resolutely and rapidly, Queen Elizabeth purged Catholic members from her Privy Council. On the morning of her accession, Elizabeth appointed Sir William Cecil to be her principal secretary of state. Cecil oversaw a tight circle of trustworthy advisors.[20]

Elizabeth quickly formed her government and issued proclamations. She restructured the enormous royal household. With her carefully orchestrated moves, Elizabeth's subjects recognized that England had decisively returned to Protestantism. The Queen's early signals encouraged reformers and rekindled their hopes for reform within the Church of England—Promises of what the Reformation had earlier initiated. Reformers hoped to purify the church from vestiges, symbols, and practices of Catholicism and its liturgy. This Bible verse captures the essence and expectation of these reforms. "Since we have these promises, dear friends, let us purify ourselves from everything that

Sir William Cecil, Lord Burghley.
Wikimedia Commons.
Public domain. (1.4)

contaminates body and spirit, perfecting holiness out of reverence for God."[21]

Proudlove recalled what this meant for him personally. With Elizabeth I on the throne and England once again Protestant, he was free of the priestly restrictions on marriage and children. He soon met Isabella. "Ah, my sweet woman. What a great wife and mother she is. My children adore her. I am so blessed!"

While Elizabeth's goal was to purge the remnants of Catholicism in Protestant England, she anticipated her subjects' need for stability. She did not want them to experience the whiplash that occurred from the transitions started by her father, Henry VIII. In 1533, the same year Elizabeth was born, Henry broke away from Roman Catholicism and founded

---

[19] "Accession of Elizabeth I," *Britannica*. Viewed 20 July. https://www.britannica.com/biography/Elizabeth-I/Accession.

[20] Elizabeth relied heavily upon the advice of Nicholas Bacon, Francis Walsingham, and Nicholas Throckmorton. Nicholas was the uncle of Job Throkmorton associated with the *Martin Marprelate* tracts.

[21] 2 Corinthians 7:1 (New International Version). Puritans in this era would have used an earlier translation, the Geneva Bible. The 1599 edition of 2 Corinthians 7:1 reads, "Lest by overmuch urging them he should dismay their tender minds, he proveth that all that he said, proceeded of the great good will he bare unto them: and therefore they should not be offended, that he made them sorry, and brought them to repentance not to be repented of."

the Church of England. His son Edward furthered Protestant reforms starting in 1547, which yielded to Elizabeth's half-sister, Mary, who reverted England to Catholicism in 1553, and Elizabeth was reinstalling Protestantism in 1558. In the span of one generation, England's parishioners had experienced four major ecclesiastical shifts. Elizabeth realized

Coronation Portrait of Elizabeth I, 1559.
Wikimedia Commons.
Public domain. (1.5)

stability in the church and monarchy should be her priority. As she came to the throne in 1558, Elizabeth worked with her Privy Council to create a religious settlement that would unite the country into one church. They began with the two Supremacy Acts created under Henry VIII and slightly altered them. The Act of Supremacy 1559 made Elizabeth the Supreme Governor of the Church of England. The word choice of Supreme Governor was distinctly important. Her father, Henry VIII, was titled the Supreme Head of the Church, which caused considerable concern for Puritans. They recognized the Supreme Head of the Church to be Jesus Christ, as described in the Bible. But the title of Supreme Governor distanced and blocked the Catholic Church from any oversight over the workings and beliefs of the Church of England. Elizabeth sought to maintain the ultimate authority over the English Church.

The Act of Uniformity 1559 reintroduced the *Book of Common Prayer,* which defined the church's liturgy, specified the order and content of worship services, and began to differentiate how the churches, and their priests (now vicars), should look and behave. Thirteen months after Elizabeth's coronation, she appointed one of the most recognized and respected clergymen as her Archbishop of Canterbury, Matthew Parker. Parker supervised the revision of the forty-two doctrinal articles developed by Archbishop Thomas Cranmer in 1553. This resulted in the Thirty-Nine Articles on which the Church of England doctrinally rests. They were printed in 1563. One year later, the first known use of the term Puritan occurred—derived from the word purify.[22]

Archbishop Parker organized a new translation of the Bible and personally translated Genesis, Matthew, and some Pauline letters. As it was known, this Bishops' Bible became the official English Bible in 1567.[23] Even so, Puritans preferred the Geneva Bible which became available in 1560. During the reign of Mary I, many exiled English clergymen were familiar with its framework used by Calvin and others on the European continent.

---

[22] Thomas Fuller, in his *Church History* (1655), dates the first use of Puritan to 1564. (See "Thomas Fuller (1608-1661)," A Puritan's Mind. Viewed on 1 February 2020. https://apuritansmind.com/puritan-favorites/Thomas-fuller-1608-1661/).

[23] "Matthew Parker," *Britannica*.

While Elizabeth I supported early basic reforms, her desire for conformity and uniformity outweighed further reform efforts. What had been hoped-for reforms under Elizabeth, and perceived by some Puritans as Promises, were seriously hampered. But some prominent men continued their reform efforts, including one early Puritan convert, Sir Richard Knightley.

Sir Richard Knightley, 1567.
Wikimedia Commons.
Public domain. (1.6)

One of three members of Parliament[24] representing the shire of Northampton, Knightley's estate was located at Fawsley, six miles west of Weedon Bec. He directly controlled some 850 acres as heir for a Royal grant received from Henry VIII in 1538. Because Sir Richard's second wife was the daughter of Edward Seymour, the first Duke of Somerset and Lord Protector of his nephew, Edward VI, "he was likely the most influential and prominent Puritan supporter in Parliament." In addition, from 1569, Knightley "was almost continuously concerned with musters and military matters in the area, either as a deputy lieutenant or, when there was no lord lieutenant, as a commissioner for musters."[25]

In 1562, William Proudlove was called to be Fawsley's parish vicar. With Knightley's patronage, Proudlove confidently embraced Puritan reforms and started his ministry the same year as vicar John Ringrose did in nearby Weedon Bec. In 1587, after Ringrose resigned his ministry, Knightley most certainly endorsed Proudlove as an excellent choice to follow him.

During his five-mile ride, Proudlove recalled not only his ministry, but also how he carefully tailored his teachings and studies to prepare his Weedon Bec parishioners for whatever may lie ahead. With access to English language Bibles for nearly fifty years, they were deepening in their spiritual growth. While Proudlove was pleased with his flock's developing faith, he acknowledged it wasn't because of him. God ordained him to be his messenger for this exact moment. God equipped him for his will to be done in the here and now.

In doing God's assigned tasks, Proudlove also recognized that his churchwarden, Thomas Cole, possessed special characteristics. Cole's spiritual growth was evident. The vicar knew, in this thirty-first year of Elizabeth's reign (1589), that diocesan pressure was intensifying. Events were cascading and coming to a head. Conflict seemed inevitable. Proudlove's discernment led him to believe that Thomas Cole might play a significant role in whatever

---

24 Hereinafter referred to as MP (Member of Parliament) or MPs (Members of Parliament).

25 "Knightley, Sir Richard (1533-1615)," *The History of Parliament*. Viewed on 10 September 2020. https://www.historyofparliamentonline.org/.

lay ahead. And he couldn't have been more correct on both accounts. Conflict was ahead, and Thomas Cole would be drawn in. As the scenery changed, the vicar sat up on his horse and spotted a church tower on the horizon. It shone brightly as the morning sun glanced off the sandstone-colored stones. Built after the eleventh century Norman Conquest, it had been a prominent Daventry landmark since medieval times. Proudlove fixed his gaze on the sunlit tower rising above the market town. He sighed out loud, "Ah, there it is. O Lord, what do you have in store for us this day?"

The Daventry meetings began about five years before. Initially, Proudlove traveled nineteen miles from the village of Lamport. He thought, "Today's ride is easy compared to the strenuous travel to attend meetings at their beginning. But it was such a blessing to reconnect with vicar Ringrose in those early meetings!" Proudlove smiled as he recalled how God had orchestrated Ringrose's endorsement for the position exchange that allowed him to start his new ministry in Weedon Bec. He lifted a prayer of gratitude: "I am most thankful, Lord, for the blessings of the shortness of the journey and especially for the ease on my aging bones!" Proudlove realized the additional blessing of meeting privately with other reform-minded vicars. Their discussions of the serious diocesan directives were informative. And reporting on actions emanating from the bishop—at best confusing and at times ominous—were comforting indeed.

But most assuredly, he had felt God's calling to engage fully right from the beginning of these meetings. Away from the eyes and ears of bishops and their hand-picked selectmen, God created a haven for open dialogue among these concerned clergymen to discern a path ahead. Yet these secret discussions could be seen as a violation of their ordination vows. But with many hours devoted to prayer and studying these reforms, his heart was at peace. His spirit was awakened and convicted him this cause was righteous. Proudlove must have smiled at the New Testament verse, "The prayer of a righteous man availeth much, if it be fervent."[26] As he considered today's discussion topics, there was little doubt that these ecclesiastical directives came right from the Archbishop of Canterbury's office.

Throughout England, concerned vicars, some more bent on Puritan reforms than others, were meeting sans permission or authorization. Without ecclesiastical oversight, they risked discipline or censure at best, possible removal from their positions . . . or even worse. Proudlove most surely asked, "Lord, what part am I to play in all this? How am I being called to bring about necessary reforms within the Church of England?" He lifted up an affirmation:

"Lord, we know thy Truth—Jesus Christ is Head of the Church. The Church is the Body of Christ. The Head of the Church is not Queen Elizabeth, the Archbishop of Canterbury, the Catholic Pope, or anyone but thy son, Jesus Christ. That's what Scripture says!"

Above all else, Proudlove wanted to please God and be obedient to his calling.

For important matters, Puritans turned first to the Holy Scriptures. In 1539, the first authorized translation of the Bible into English reached the shores of England. By

---

[26] James 5:16 (Geneva Bible 1599)

the beginning of King Edward's reign in 1547, average parishioners had direct access to the Scriptures. But in Queen Mary's reign, they were again interpreted through a Catholic priest in Latin—incomprehensible to most English parishioners. With Queen Elizabeth's early support and the English translation of the Geneva Bible available since 1560, Bible studies proliferated.

Puritans collectively believed their supreme authority was not human, but divine. Puritans tested new directives by searching Scripture for confirmation. If answers were not forthcoming, they consulted with other "godly" Christians. Together, they would discern whether something was from God or simply a man-made edict. That was the impetus for these meetings.

As Proudlove pondered these factors, it may have brought to mind an Old Testament verse he paraphrased in a matter-of-fact tone: "Here I am, Lord. Speak, for your servant is listening."[27] He also recalled the promising reforms implemented right before he became Lamport's rector in 1577 under the previous Archbishop of Canterbury, Edmund Grindal.

When Elizabeth appointed Grindal to his position on 29 December 1575, Puritans including Proudlove rejoiced. Most clergymen felt the same as what Puritan Alexander Nowell wrote about Grindal: "a man of the greatest wisdom and ability to govern, and unto whom the other bishops with great *contentation* would submit themselves."[28] As soon as he was confirmed, an anonymous letter from a Privy Councillor surfaced and affirmed Grindal's appointment: "It is greatly hoped for the godly and well-affected of this realm that your lordship will prove a profitable instrument in that calling; especially in removing the corruptions in the Court of the Faculties, which is one of the greatest abuses that remain in this Church of England. . . . That there may be . . . consultation had with some of your brethren how some part of those Romish dregs remain in [the Church] offensive to the godly, may be removed.[29]"

Archbishop Edmund Grindal. Wikimedia Commons. Public domain. (1.7)

Despite the Puritans' hoped-for *Promises* of reforms, Queen Elizabeth wanted the Puritan practice of prophesying to cease. "Prophesying," at that time, was considered to include Bible studies and small group discussions in homes to discuss sermons preached in Sunday's worship services. Embraced by Puritan vicars and parishioners, particularly those now

---

[27] 1 Samuel 3:10

[28] Robert Charles Anderson, *Puritan Pedigrees: The Deep Roots of the Great Migration to New England* (Boston: New England Historic Genealogical Society, 2018): 147, footnote 10. "In this context *contentation* means "acquiescence in or acceptance of the situation."

[29] Patrick Collinson, *The Elizabethan Puritan Movement*. (Oxford: Clarendon Press 1967): 161.

in Proudlove's care, these meetings were occasionally held without a clergyman present. Sometimes groups of vicars met and included laymen in the discussion. These practices were not in conformity with the *Book of Common Prayer* and attracted concerns of some diocesan officials. Subsequently, the queen issued an edict through her Privy Council to ban prophesying. In addition, Elizabeth also asked Archbishop Grindal to suppress preaching. She favored a return to the previous practice of adhering only to Scripture readings.[30]

Rather than accepting Queen Elizabeth's edict outright, Archbishop Grindal consulted with his bishops. He found that two-thirds of them felt the church benefitted from the practices of prophesying and preaching. The archbishop detailed his case in a lengthy 6,000-word letter to his queen. Defending his stance, he unflinchingly wrote: "I choose rather to offend your earthly Majesty than to offend the heavenly Majesty of God."[31] He allowed the practices to continue. In June 1577, Queen Elizabeth suspended Grindal's jurisdictional duties but not his spiritual functions. She believed, as did most European royal monarchs, a threat to church hierarchy was a threat to her rule. But Grindal stood firm. Finally in January 1578, the queen reaffirmed her desire to deprive Archbishop Grindal of his position. While the Privy Council dissuaded her from this action, Grindal sequestered at home.

Archbishop John Whitgift. Wikimedia Commons. Public domain. (1.8)

After a 1581 Convocation, a petition for Grindal's reinstatement was sent to Queen Elizabeth—which she denied. Near the end of 1582, Elizabeth asked Grindal to resign. He declined but did apologize. She intended to reinstate him, but his weakened condition led to his death on 6 July 1583. In essence, the Archbishop of Canterbury, the most powerful church official in England, lived out his final six years under house arrest either self-imposed or from the queen. His crime? Disobedience to Her Majesty, Queen Elizabeth.[32]

Within six weeks of Grindal's demise, Queen Elizabeth appointed John Whitgift as Archbishop of Canterbury on 24 August 1583. He was confirmed a month later. As Proudlove recalled these events, he surely exclaimed, "That's when this all started—the day Whitgift became Archbishop

---

[30] Known as homilies.

[31] Collinson, 196.

[32] 150 years later in his *History of the Puritans*, author Daniel Neal called him "the good old archbishop," "of a mild and moderate temper, easy of access and affable even in his highest exaltation," "upon the whole . . . one of the best of Queen Elizabeth's bishops." From "Edmund Grindal," *Wikipedia*. Viewed on 15 September 2020. https://en.wikipedia.org/wiki/Edmund_Grindal.

of Canterbury! Oh, how the church has suffered!" The early Promises of Puritan reforms must have seemed a far distant memory.

Archbishop of Canterbury John Whitgift was an imposing figure of "middle stature, strong and well-shaped, of a grave countenance and brown complexion, black hair and eyes, his beard neither long nor thick."[33] He was also known as the queen's favorite—a very powerful position.

Archbishop Whitgift acted swiftly. At the queen's urging, he intentionally clamped down and enforced oversight where his predecessors had not. His first act was to issue the following articles. They were sent to the bishops on the 19th of October, who were "required to supply the archbishop with information as to conformity in their dioceses."[34] Queen Elizabeth did not question Whitgift's consultation with the bishops—in stark contrast to her objection to Grindal's actions. Within weeks, Whitgift issued his first directives.

Articles Touching Preachers and Other Orders for the Church A.D. 1583

That none be permitted to preach, read, catechise, minister the sacraments, or to execute any other ecclesiastical function unless he consents and subscribes to the Articles following:

1. That Her Majesty, under God, hath, and ought to have, the sovereignty and rule over all manner of persons born within her realms . . . either ecclesiastical or temporal, soever they be.
2. That the Book of Common Prayer, and of ordering bishops, priests and deacons, containeth in it nothing contrary to the word of God . . . and that he himself will use the form of the said book prescribed in public prayer and administration of the sacraments, and none other.
3. That he alloweth the book of Articles, agreed upon by the archbishops and bishops of both provinces, and the whole clergy in Convocation holden at London in the year of our Lord God 1562 . . . and that he believeth all the Articles therein contained to be agreeable to the word of God.[35]

Commonly known as the Three Articles, most clergy had no major issues with article one or three. But article two referenced strict adherence to the *Book of Common Prayer*. Therefore, it forbade preaching and prophesyings ingrained in Puritan practices. From the Puritans' perspective, once again, the Church of England had dramatically changed direction. The hoped-for reforms by vicars and others aligned with Ringrose and Proudlove were being pushed aside.

---

[33] Described by his biographer, Sir George Paule, in his *Life of the Most Reverend and Religious Prelate John Whitgift, Lord Archbishop of Canterbury* (London: Thomas Snodham, 1612).
[34] "Articles Touching Preaching and Other Orders for the Church, A.D. 1583," *Luminarium: Encyclopedia Project*. Viewed 1 September 2021. http://www.luminarium.org/encyclopedia/articles1583.htm.
[35] C N Trueman, "The Three Articles," *The History Learning Site*. Viewed 17 Mar 2018. https://www.historylearningsite.co.uk.

With Archbishop Grindal's death in July and John Whitgift's appointment as Archbishop of Canterbury in September, Proudlove and his Puritan colleagues witnessed "a decisive climacteric in the history of the Reformed Church of England. The new Archbishop quickly justified the fears of the Puritans and their supporters."[36] With Archbishop Whitgift, reforms that had been acceptable or overlooked before, were no longer tolerated. This reversal was likely viewed as Promises not fulfilled, and their ministries became increasingly difficult.

As Daventry's church tower and market loomed ahead, Proudlove probably wondered, "Will Thomas Cartwright be there? It has been so rumored. He is certainly the most respected divine of our generation. And we need inspiration for the matters at hand."

THOMAS CARTWRIGHT

Thomas Cartwright, a Cambridge student at St. John's College, had attended three years when Edward VI died. With Mary I's accession in 1553, Cartwright left his studies to become a clerk to a counsellor at law. He kept up his divinity studies independently. After Elizabeth's accession, Cartwright resumed his studies and was elected a fellow of St. John's in

Thomas Cartwright, born c 1535. Wikimedia Commons. Public domain. (1.9)

1560. About 1563, he removed to Trinity College as one of eight senior fellows. "He allowed himself only five hours' sleep in the night, to which custom he closely adhered to the end of his days."[37] As his career progressed, he was revered as one of the most important Puritan divines in England.

During Elizabeth I's August 1564 state visit to Cambridge, Thomas Cartwright opposed Thomas Preston, a fellow of King's College, in a philosophical and theological debate. Cartwright's performance revealed extraordinary abilities and gave "the greatest satisfaction, both to the queen and the other auditors."[38]

He accepted an opportunity to serve as the Ireland archbishop's chaplain in 1565-7. After his return to England, he was appointed the Lady Margaret professor of divinity at Cambridge in 1570. When he preached at St. Mary's, the sexton found it necessary to take down the church windows because he was so popular. When he

---

36 Shiels, 48.

37 Benjamin Brook, *The Lives of the Puritans: Containing a Biographical Account of Those Divines who Distinguished Themselves in the Cause of Religious Liberty from the Reformation under Queen Elizabeth to the Act of Uniformity in 1562*, Vol. II (London: James Black, 1813): 136. (*Internet Archive*. Viewed 29 October 2021. https://archive.org.)

38 Brook, 137.

lectured on the New Testament's Book of Acts, Cartwright inveighed bitterly against the hierarchy and constitution of the Church of England. He compared it unfavorably to the ancient Christian church structure as captured in the Book of Acts. His preaching brought to a head the Puritan attitude on church ceremony and organization. Dr. John Whitgift, the university vice chancellor, zealously opposed him.

Cartwright's lectures provoked a reprimand letter from Archbishop Grindal, addressed to university chancellor, Sir William Cecil, who was instructed to silence Cartwright. Cartwright defended his conduct and declared his aversion to anything seditious or contentious. He also affirmed he taught nothing that did not naturally flow from God's word. His defense elicited Cecil's support. Cartwright then delivered a set of propositions to the vice-chancellor including: 1) abolishing the titles and functions of archbishops and archdeacons; 2) giving congregations more say into selection of their ministers; and 3) requiring that every minister should have the charge of a particular congregation, which eliminated at-large ministers. In response, the university's vice-chancellor Whitgift deprived him of his fellowship in December 1570. Cartwright then left England to study with Theodore Beza in Geneva.

When Cartwright returned to England in 1572, he was on track to become professor of Hebrew at Cambridge. But he expressed sympathy for the *Admonition to the Parliament for the Reformation of Church Discipline,* which turned some supporters against him. When its authors, John Field and Thomas Wilcox, were imprisoned, Cartwright published petitions on their behalf. He maintained Holy Scripture was the only standard of discipline and government, as well as its doctrine.

> We mean not to take away the authority of the civil magistrate, to whom we wish all blessedness, and for the increase of whose godliness we daily pray; but that Christ, being restored to his kingdom, may rule in the same by the scepter of his word.[39]

Whitgift published replies in opposition to Cartwright's petitions. These public written debates did not further Cartwright's stature, and he lost some supporters.

On 11 December 1573, Cartwright was summoned to appear in London by special order of the High Commission.[40] To escape arrest, he concealed himself and went abroad. He officiated as a clergyman to English residents at Antwerp, Belgium, and at Middelburg, the capital of the Dutch province of Zeeland. In 1576, Thomas Cartwright, assisted by Edmund Snape of Northampton, established a necessary structure for Huguenot ministers in the Channel Islands churches in Jersey and Guernsey. Scottish King James VI, the future King of England who would later succeed Queen Elizabeth, offered Cartwright a chair at the prestigious St. Andrews University in Scotland.[41] Cartwright declined and again settled as pastor at Antwerp.

In 1583, Queen Elizabeth asked Theodore Beza of Geneva to publish a refutation of the Rhenish translation of the New Testament. Beza declined, saying the queen had a person far

---

[39] Brook, 144.
[40] One of England's highest courts of law, its judges included Elizabeth I's Privy Council members.
[41] "James VI and I," *Wikipedia*. Viewed 20 May 2020. https://en.wikipedia.org/wiki/James_VI_and_I.

better qualified in her own kingdom. He declared him to be Thomas Cartwright. Solicited for the project by some of the most learned and celebrated divines at Cambridge, Cartwright undertook the work and perfected it through the seventeenth chapter of the Bible's *Book of Revelation*. But Dr. John Whitgift forbade him to proceed, and the work was laid aside.[42]

In 1585, Cartwright left Antwerp and returned to England without permission. Apprehended and imprisoned in London, he began drafting a revised *Book of Discipline*. The First Earl of Leicester, Robert Dudley, admired Cartwright and supported excellent preaching for which Cartwright was well known. Since Dudley wielded great influence in circles that mattered—including his title as the Queen's Favorite—he secured Cartwright's release. Dudley then employed him as master of his Lord of Leicester's Hospital in Warwick.

Lord of Leicester Hospital.
Wikimedia Commons. Public domain. (1.10)

Since the hospital was not subject to diocesan oversight, Cartwright received substantial public opportunities to articulate his views. While he opposed Independents of the Church of England, such as Brownists, his views were clearly Presbyterian. However even within a national Presbyterian church, it is unlikely he would have tolerated nonconformity or the separation of church and state. As he developed his *Book of Discipline* draft, he most certainly wondered, "What will the reaction be?"

With Dudley's support, Cartwright's influence widened. The Warwick hospital was located twenty-two miles west of Daventry—a market town in Northampton. Daventry was an ideal meeting site for Puritan ministers comprised of Sir Richard Knightley protégés including vicar William Proudlove. In the shires of Warwick and Northampton, Puritan activity like this was now well established. In fact, meetings like these now comprised a widespread movement of reform that reached throughout England. "The influx of new recruits brought in by patrons predisposed to Puritanism, were building up to some sort of crisis."[43]

While Proudlove and his colleagues were in awe of Cartwright's intellect and convictions, his views were still controversial. The thought of creating an *ecclesia in ecclesia* was outside everyone's frame of reference. Other thoughts most surely raced through the vicar's mind as he rode toward his meeting. "This gathering is perhaps <u>the</u> most important ever. I need to give these matters my undivided and utmost attention. Together, we must prayerfully discern a fundamental question: what is God calling us to do?"

On this late August morning, Proudlove kicked his horse's flanks smartly to hurry on—anxious to see his peers again. He anticipated they felt the same. Why? The past year's

---

[42] Published in 1618 for which he received 100 pounds.
[43] Shiels, 44.

discussions and debates intensified dramatically. Increased pressure weighed heavily upon everyone involved. That pressure came from the most famous mystery man in England—a man whom no one knew.

MARTIN MARPRELATE WRITES AND STRIKES

In October 1588, a thousand copies of a pamphlet, *The Epistle,* written by a mysterious Martin Marprelate, were distributed throughout England. *The Epistle* unveiled an underground Puritan movement previously cloaked in shadows and brought it into full public view. The first in a series of seven pamphlets created a firestorm within the Church of England.

> The Martin Marprelate tracts are the most famous pamphlets of the English Renaissance; to their contemporaries, they were the most notorious. Printed in 1588 and 1589 on a secret press carted across the English countryside from one sympathetic household to another, the seven tracts attack the Church of England, particularly its bishops (hence the pseudonym 'Mar-prelate') and advocate a Presbyterian system of church government. Scandalously witty, racy, and irreverent, the Marprelate tracts are the finest prose satires of their era. Their colloquial style and playfully self-dramatizing manner influenced the fiction and theater of the Elizabethan Golden Age.[44]

These works are now considered literary masterpieces. They owe their existence to a courageous and well-known London Puritan printer. Robert Waldegrave published works for reformers within the Church of England and also published works by Continental and Scottish religious reformers including Martin Luther, John Calvin, and John Knox. Waldegrave was twice imprisoned in 1586–7 for publishing works critical of the Church of England.

In February 1588, the Star Chamber decreed a publishing restriction on him. Undeterred, Waldegrave anonymously published John Udall's *The State of the Churche of England Laid Open*, or *Diotrephes*. On 16 April, officials confiscated Waldegrave's press and almost all his type, together with copies of Udall's book. With his books burned, the press seized, and his type destroyed, Waldegrave was rendered incapable of supporting his wife and six children. However, he escaped with a box of type hidden beneath his cloak.

Waldegrave set up a secret new press in the manor of Elizabeth Crane. Located in East Mosley, Surrey, about thirteen miles southwest of London—directly across the River Thames and within sight of the queen's favored residence Hampton Court Palace. One might ask: was the location of this secret press intentionally defiant?

The Epistle's mysterious author skewered church authorities by name! Martin Marprelate's prose, steeped in parody and sarcasm, pointed out what many Puritans felt but dared not say.

---

[44] Joseph L. Black, editor, *The Martin Marprelate Tracts: A Modernized and Annotated Edition* (Cambridge: 2008): frontispiece.

Now judge you, good readers, whether Martin saith not true, that there is too much cozenage nowadays among the clergy men. This sentence following of Master Dean's hath as good sense as the former, page 655. The D. citeth these words out of the *Learned Discourse*: *God grant that instead of ordinary forms of prayers, we have preaching in all places.* And instead of Amen, God forbid say I, quoth of the Doctor, with another prayer to the contrary (now mark my masters, whether you can find any sense in this contrary prayer, for I assure you reverend Martin can find none), if it be his good will not so much (good Lord) to punish us, that this our brethren's prayer should be granted. If this be a senseless kind of writing, I would there were never a lord bishop in England.[45]

Martin did not stop at merely skewering Bishop Dean. Without hesitation, he directly attacked the highest ecclesiastical authority in England, Archbishop of Canterbury John Whitgift.

May it please your honorable worships, to let worthy Martin understand why your Canterburiness and the rest of the lord bishops favor papists and recusants, rather than puritans? For if a puritan preacher, having a recusant in his parish, and shall go about to deal with the recusant for not coming to church: sir, will the recusant say, you and I will answer the matter before his grace (or other the high commissioners, as lord bishops, seevillians[46] (I mean) popish doctors of the bawdy courts).[47]

Martin issued harsh words for the archbishop's treatment of his colleague, printer Robert Waldegrave. Martin aimed his attention squarely at the archbishop.

And now that Waldegrave hath neither press nor letters, his grace may dine and sup the quieter. But look to it brother Canterbury, certainly without your repentance, I fear me, you shall be Hildebrand indeed. Waldegrave hath left house and home, by reason of your unnatural tyranny: having left behind him a poor wife and six orphans, without anything to relieve them. (For the husband you have bereaved both of his trade and goods.) Be you assured that the cry of these will one day prevail against you, unless you desist from persecuting.[48]

In addition, Martin referenced Thomas Cartwright's eminence.

Briefly, may it please you to let the gospel have a free course, and restore unto their former liberty in preaching all the preachers that you have put to silence: and this far is my first suit. My second suit is a most earnest request unto you, that are the hinderers of the publishing of [it, that] the confutation of the Rhemish Testament by Master Cartwright may be published.[49]

---

[45] Black, 15.
[46] Black, 222, footnote 109: *seevillians* punning on the high commission civilians (authorities on civil law) as "see-villians" (with "see" referring to episcopal *see* or seat).
[47] Black, 22-3.
[48] Black, 24.
[49] Black, 27.

With his distinctly dramatic flair, Martin Marprelate again directly addressed John Whitgift with this simple phrase. "I hope you have not long to reign. Amen."[50]

After specific examples of persecuted clergymen, Martin Marprelate put forth five "Conditions of Peace to be inviolably kept forever, between the reverend and worthy Master Martin Marprelate gentleman on the one party, and the reverend fathers his brethren, the lord bishops of this land."[51] After detailing them and providing pages of scathing text filled with names and examples, Martin Marprelate closes *The Epistle* with this directive:

> Favor learning more than you do, and especially godly learning. Stretch your credit, if you have any, to the furtherance of the gospel. You have joined the profanation of the magistracy, to the corruption of the ministry; leave this sin. All in a word, become good Christians, and so you shall become good subjects, and leave your tyranny. And I would advise you, let me hear no more of your evil dealing.[52]

One can almost hear the mysterious author add, "Take that, Archbishop Whitgift!" As Whitgift and other authorities fumed, Martin Marprelate's readers gasped. They also laughed out loud and loved the tracts. With irrepressible irreverence, Martin brought hilarious commentary to serious matters. He opened up what obviously were pent-up feelings about volatile issues. As one would expect, church officials' reactions were unforgiving. Furiously, they lashed out demanding to know who wrote it. Without success, they searched for those involved in publishing what they considered to be heresy.

Feeling the heat, the press was dismantled in early November 1588 and stored briefly in a hidden cart. Then it was moved stealthily at night nearly one hundred miles in two weeks' time. Its new secret location: Sir Richard Knightley's estate in Fawsley, in the shire of Northampton. Elected to Parliament this same year, Knightley was a conspicuous member of the Puritan faction in Parliament. Vicar Proudlove had earlier served in Knightley's Fawsley parish beginning in 1562.

Even before Knightley became an MP, a revolutionary bill was introduced in Parliament sponsored by MPs from the Midlands and East Anglia. It asked for the Genevan liturgy to be authorized in the Church of England. It called for the *Book of Common Prayer* to be replaced. The *Book of Common Prayer* contained instructions particularly disturbing to Puritans. A few examples, not biblically specified and perceived to be remnants of Catholicism, included:

1. The use of texts from the Apocrypha, believed by Puritans among others to be a collection of corrupt human texts—not divinely-inspired. [53]
2. The required reading of homilies at the exclusion of genuine preaching.
3. That clergy must wear distinctive Anglican vestments.
4. That clerics must be addressed as priest versus minister.

---

[50] Black, 29.
[51] Black, 34.
[52] Black, 45.
[53] These texts were eliminated from the Bible's Kings James Version in 1610.

5. That parishioners must kneel at communion.
6. That parishioners were to be fined for non-attendance at worship.
7. Signing of the cross and an interrogation of infants must occur at baptism.

The response to the submitted bill was swift and direct. "Parliamentary activity ended abruptly with a royal assertion of prerogative in matters ecclesiastical and the imprisonment in the Tower of five members, including Peter Wentworth, MP for Northampton."[54]

Martin Marprelate addressed all these issues and more in his pamphlets. By late November 1588, a second Martin Marprelate pamphlet, *The Epitome*, appeared—again with a thousand copies printed for distribution. "At forty-six pages, *The Epitome* was shorter than *The Epistle*."[55] But it was totally recognizable coming from the same press and with the same type as *The Epistle*.

The Epitome offered "a sustained response to John Bridges' *Defence of the Government Established in the Church of Englande* (1587).[56] Besides Bridges, Martin took aim at John Aylmer, Bishop of London, another of the most powerful clergymen in England. Martin also commented on various harsh reactions to *The Epistle*.

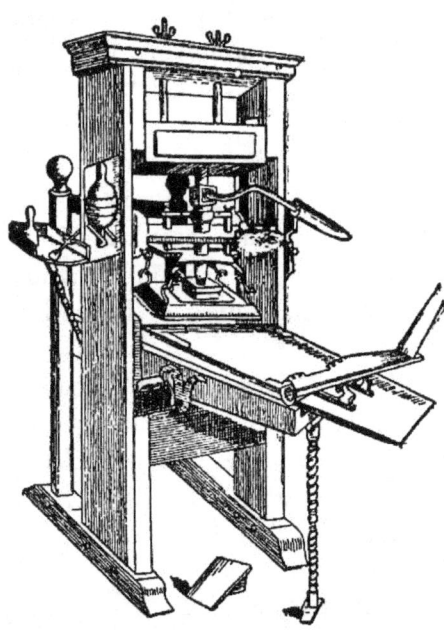

Early Printing Press. Engraving attributed to Willem Janszon Blaeu (1571-1638). Public domain. (1.11)

Why my clergy masters, is it even so with your terribleness? May not a poor gentleman signify his good will unto you by letter . . . Every archbishop is a petty pope, so is every lord bishop. You are all the pack of you, either hirelings or wolves. . . . If you dare answer my reasons, let me see it done. Otherwise, I trow, my friends and sons will see you one day deposed. The puritans are angry with me, I mean the puritan preachers. And why? Because I am too open. Because I jest . . . I am plain, I must needs call a spade a spade, a pope a pope.[57]

The *Martin Marprelate* tracts "marked the beginning of the end of the most famous pamphlet war in Elizabethan England."[58] In January 1589, rumors forced the press to be dismantled and hidden temporarily in a Norton farmhouse near Daventry.

Traveling primarily in the dead of night, in secret along one hundred miles of the old Roman road, Watling Street, it took two weeks to arrive

---

54 Shiels, 51.
55 Black, 49.
56 Black, 49.
57 Black, 53.
58 Black, lv.

at Whitefriars, Coventry. The secret press was then sequestered at the home of Sir Richard Knightley's nephew, John Hales.

A thousand copies of the third tract, *Certain Mineral and Metaphysical Schoolpoints,* were printed at the Hales estate in late January/early February 1589. Another thousand copies of tract four followed, *Hay Any Work for Cooper.* It took three weeks to print its lengthy text of fifty-eight pages. With its distribution in March 1589, the stinging public criticism published by Martin Marprelate caused a rising crescendo of concerns. Citing some Puritan ministers' disapproval, Robert Waldegrave refused to print any further tracts. He left England for the Continent.

Retorts and rebuttals published by church officials amplified the issues. However, they did not match Martin's style. It had captured the public's attention and imagination. They eagerly awaited the next tract to read about who would be criticized and what he would say. This escalating public war of dueling pamphlets increased the urgency and fervent pursuit to find Martin Marprelate and destroy his ability to publish such inflammatory criticism. In anticipation, the secret press was again moved. Its next destination: Wolston Priory in Warwickshire near Coventry—at the estate of Sir Roger Wigston. Two more tracts of thirty-two pages were produced in about a week each. John Hodgkins agreed to take over the publishing effort, and enlisted two printers, Valentine Simms and Arthur Thomlin, to support his efforts. They distributed fifteen hundred copies of tract five, *Theses Martinianae,* in early July and the same amount for tract six, *The Just Censure and Reproof of Martin Junior* in late July. *Just Censure* issued this scathing criticism.

> I protest and affirm that the foresaid John Whitgift, alias Canterbury, which nameth himself archbishop of Canterbury, is no minister at all in the church of God, but hath and doeth wrongfully usurp and invade the name and seat of the ministry, unto the great detriment of the church of God, the utter spoil of the souls of men, and the likely ruin of this commonwealth, together with the great dishonour of her Majesty and the state. And in this case do I affirm all the lord bishops in England to be.[59]

> I do protest and affirm that the true church of God ought to have no more to do with Jo. Canterbury his brothers and their synagogue, namely, with their antichristian courts of faculties, etc., with their officers of commissaries, archdeacons, chancellors, officials, dumb ministers, etc., than with the synagogue of Satan. And that he their head and pope, together with his foresaid rabble, are not to be accounted for that church, whose censures we are to reverence and obey, and in the unity whereof we are to remain.[60]

Word was received that the next tract was ready. Hodgkins had a press waiting for him at home in Lancashire and made the decision to print there. He told his two assistants, Simms and Thomlin, to pack up their supplies "for feare of being taken at Wolston." Leaving the press, the three printers left at night for a six-day, hundred-mile journey to Warrington, Lancashire—midway between Liverpool and Manchester. They arrived on

---

[59] Black, 178.
[60] Black, 179.

4 August 1589. At a rented house in Newton Lane near Manchester, the three printers unpacked their supplies and set up Hodgkins' press. On 14 August, agents of Henry Stanley, the Fourth Earl of Derby, caught up with them. After Stanley's interrogation, the three printers were dispatched and arrived in London by 23 August. With information divulged in interrogations, the final curtain call was about to fall on the *Martin Marprelate* tracts.

Even with this setback, the press did not stay dormant. Through the efforts of John Penry, Job Throkmorton, and their Northampton supporters, an initial run of a seventh tract was completed without qualified printers. However, Robert Waldegrave, who had accepted an offer from James VI of Scotland to become the king's printer, stopped in Wolston to help get a second run completed. With the quality substantially improved, Waldegrave continued his journey north to Scotland. He printed more than one hundred books there.

When published and distributed in late September 1589, *The Protestation of Martin Marprelate* struck another blow. The tract opened with the capture of printer Hodgkins, his assistants, and the press. "With three men now in custody and in danger of torture, was the work of publicizing reform ultimately worth the risks they had undertaken? Martin's answer is yes."[61]

Martin stated for the record that bishops were "our vile servile dunghill ministers of damnation, that viperous generation, those scorpions."[62] How's that for fire and brimstone preaching? One can almost hear Martin saying: "Take that, bishops!"

But what of Martin Marprelate himself? The tracts' writing styles were immediately analyzed and compared with known works. But more than four centuries after they were published, the authors were never definitively proved. However, one scholar offers his observations.

> The Marprelate project was a communal operation, Job Throkmorton and John Penry wrote the tracts and Penry managed the press, but many others contributed. Throkmorton and Penry drew heavily on material gathered over the years by John Field from reform-minded contributors from across the country. John Udall was present in the early stages. Producing and circulating the books required several printers and two presses, suppliers of ink and paper, the sympathetic members of four large households, and several wholesale and probably scores of local distributers. The community that produced and distributed the Marprelate tracts was a broadly constituted one: it included women as well as men, and its members ranged from prominent local gentry with aristocratic support, to local magistrates, merchants, and clergy, to respectable widows, journeyman workers, and servants. All risked being charged with treason.[63]

Besides upsetting the Church of England's leadership, the tracts created friction among Puritans. Some felt Martin Marprelate had gone too far. A line had been crossed. They did not want to be embroiled in an intensified battle with ecclesiastical authorities.

---

[61] Black, 193.
[62] "History of the Puritans under Elizabeth I," *Wikipedia*. Viewed 10 September 2019. https://en.wikipedia.org/wiki/History_of_the_Puritans_under_Elizabeth_I.
[63] Black, lvi.

As the morning sun illuminated the townscape, vicar William Proudlove recognized the Daventry meeting place ahead. Unaware the seventh *Martin Marprelate* tract was about to be published, he noted how summer was already starting its annual transition to autumn. He dismounted, took a deep breath, unlatched the front door, and entered a room filled with his Puritan peers.

CLASSIS, CLASSES, AND CONFERENCES

Archbishop Whitgift's *Articles Touching Preachers and Other Orders for the Church, A.D. 1583,* stimulated Puritans to meet consistently in independent groups without ecclesiastical oversight or permission. While many different reform approaches emerged for the Church of England, none dominated. There were Barrowists, Brownists, Congregationalists, Separatists, non-separating Congregationalists, Independents, and Presbyterians to name the most common. With so many different strains and no common vision, ecclesiastical authorities, Royalists, and the general populace lumped them into one overarching label: Puritans—which was not a compliment.[64] This was the Puritans' environment in England.

Referred to as a *classis* for a singular meeting, or *classes* for a group of meetings, the prototype for these *classes* might have occurred before Archbishop Whitgift was appointed. On 22 October 1582, in what later became known as the Dedham *Conference,* thirteen Puritans subscribed and met monthly. Its genesis might have been even earlier, in the 1581 Convocation that petitioned Queen Elizabeth to reinstate Archbishop Grindal. After that petition was rejected, the Dedham *Classis* subscribers included Edmund Chapman, Richard Crick, and Richard Dow. Subscribers rotated principal roles and directly controlled admission to their fellowship, choices of moderator, and preachers. Choices were made by consent of the whole. A meeting's first half focused on preaching, and the second half focused on broader *conference* topics.

Publication of Whitgift's *Articles* intensified the formation of other *classes* on a much broader scale starting about 1584. In a relatively short period of time, *classes* spread rapidly in many county shires throughout England including Coventry, Essex, Kent, Northampton, Oxford, Sussex, Suffolk, and Warwick. By the late 1580s in scores of market towns, *classes*

> were held in private houses in the towns where they were located . . . and began with election of a moderator by secret ballot after a prayer for guidance. Thus elected, the moderator took charge of the meeting and a roll was called, latecomers sitting in order as they came. The work of the moderator was to set out the questions to be discussed and, following the discussion, to make a summary of the debate. Matters requiring censure were also taken up by the moderator, whose authority lasted until the next meeting, which was usually to be held within three weeks; the date of that meeting was always fixed before the classis disbanded. The moderator was empowered to call the classis together sooner if urgent business required dispatch.[65]

---

[64] At this time in England, Puritan was an all-encompassing derogatory term applied broadly to any who sought deviation from the Church of England's *Book of Common Prayer.*

[65] Shiels, 55.

In addition, Puritan *conferences* were held periodically on a regional basis—again without oversight or permission. One *conference*, held annually at Cambridge during a popular fall festival in this university town, gave Puritans and their supporters opportunities to share ideas, learn from each other, and create forums for discussion of relevant topics. There was certainly much to discuss.

They felt reform efforts had not properly progressed. In their view, the Church of England still retained too many "papist" remnants leftover from Queen Mary's reign. Whitgift's Three Articles—which effectively banished Puritan liturgical practices—set back the reform-minded Puritans even further. But they did not abandon their efforts. As a result, official diocesan visitations increased. Puritan supporters responded by proposing an ecumenical reform bill to Parliament. It addressed their concerns regarding the liturgical practices prescribed by the Church of England in the *Book of Common Prayer*. The bill was rejected outright by Queen Elizabeth.

The focus of *classes* then shifted to Cartwright's revised *Book of Discipline* draft. Discussions centered on three major elements: "First, the nature and extent of subscription to the *Book of Discipline*; second, the establishment of an eldership in the parishes; and finally, the use of discipline and censure among the membership."[66] Cartwright's draft promoted the concept of Presbyterianism within episcopacy, which was popular in Protestant churches on the Continent as well as in Scotland. Presbyterianism is not church doctrine. Rather, and significantly, Presbyterianism is a form of governance regarding church structure and discipline. Cartwright's embrace of this church governing structure is reflected in his *Book of Discipline*. But he never advocated separation from the Church of England.

Cartwright promoted a Presbyterian church structure featuring elder-led congregations operating with increased input or control over local matters within a group of churches—a presbytery. He advocated local oversight and input for discipline matters and the calling of "ministers."[67] His proposal opposed strictly hierarchical clerical appointments directed solely by a regional bishop.

As could be predicted with any reform of this magnitude, "The *Book of Discipline* received a very mixed reception among puritans in different parts of the country. . . . Many puritans sympathized with its programme but were uncertain about setting up such an obvious *ecclesia in ecclesia*."[68] This concept of a "church within a church" was not only contrary to Whitgift's policies; it was also foreign to England's society. For centuries, every facet of English life—families, towns, land rights, church, state, and the monarchy itself—functioned in, and was accustomed to, hierarchical structures. Above all, Archbishop John Whitgift knew Queen Elizabeth's desire for conformity was to protect her supreme authority as monarch.

---

[66] Shiels, 55.
[67] Puritans referred to themselves as ministers instead of Church of England vicars.
[68] Shiels, 52.

STRUCTURE AND SUBSTANCE OF *CLASSIS* AND *CLASSES*

In Northamptonshire, three *classes* were held in Daventry, Northampton, and Kettering. In addition, Puritans

> established a meeting not provided for in the *Book of Discipline* but one reminiscent of the order establishing the exercises in 1571, that is an assembly of the whole shire attended by two delegates from each *classis*. . . . The assembly met, usually every six to eight weeks, to discuss matters beyond the scope of the individual classes, and to keep in touch with events elsewhere. They elected their own moderator, who was said to have authority over all the other classes until the next meeting of the assembly and conducted correspondence with puritan leaders . . . for the county and the assembly issued advice to the *classes* so that they might "the better direct themselves and their churches accordingly."[69]

Because Martin Marprelate highlighted Puritanism's strength in Northamptonshire, "attention was drawn to the activities of the Midland classes . . . and challenged the mayor and constables of Northampton to apprehend those involved in their publication, [which] helped to tighten a net already closing on the puritans."[70] In essence, diocesan officials knew where to concentrate their visitation efforts. As a result, this county's *classes* are well-documented. Its extensive network of clandestine *classes* was well-organized. In the accompanying map image, each "x" represents known Puritan clergymen in this East Midlands County, with more than eighty identified.

---

[69] Shiels, 54.
[70] Shiels, 59.

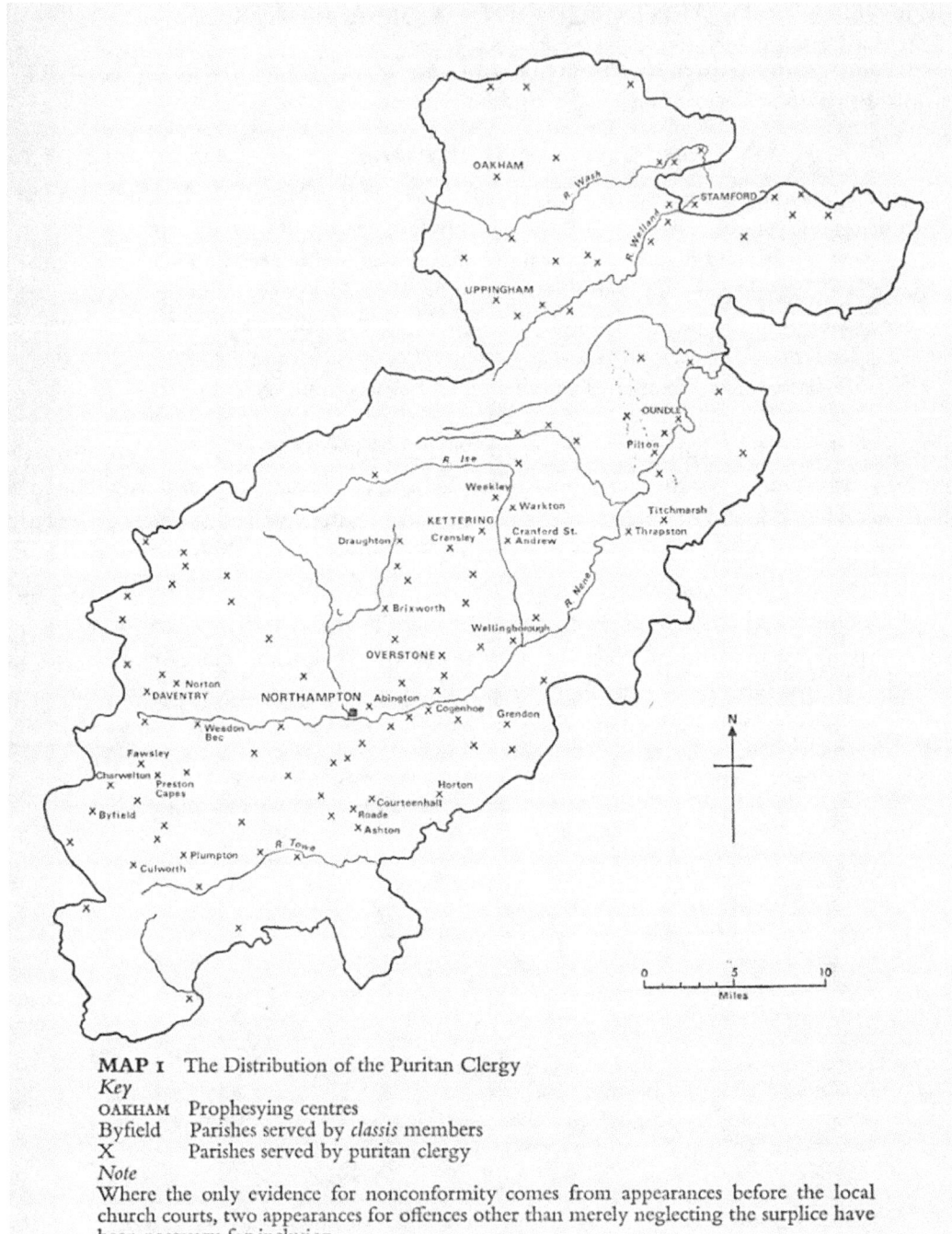

MAP I The Distribution of the Puritan Clergy
Key
OAKHAM   Prophesying centres
Byfield   Parishes served by *classis* members
X   Parishes served by puritan clergy
Note
Where the only evidence for nonconformity comes from appearances before the local church courts, two appearances for offences other than merely neglecting the surplice have been necessary for inclusion.

The Distribution of Puritan Clergy in Northamptonshire.
With kind permission granted by author, W. J. Shiels.[71] (1.12)

---

[71] Shiels, 53.

The "*classes* of the diocese involved twenty-eight of the parochial clergy as members, and a few others as sympathizers. The Daventry *Classis* was smallest in number but represented a cohesive group of Knightley protégés."[72] Located in a tight corridor within a few miles of Daventry and circling Sir Richard Knightley's estate, the group consisted of:

1. Simon Rogers, Rector of Byfield, located just eight miles south of Daventry. Rogers started his service there on 18 August 1579.
2. Edward Sharpe, Fawsley's vicar. He served there in the 1580s.
3. John Barbone, Charwelton's vicar. He was presented on 20 April 1581.
4. John Elliston, Preston Capes' vicar, began his service there on 18 February 1583. In 1584, Elliston came into conflict with his parishioners over tithes. With complaints about him, "the vicar was presented for departing from the *Book of Common Prayer*."[73] In addition, when he "refused to wear the surplice, to sign with the cross in baptism or to church new mothers after childbirth: angry parishioners got him deprived."[74]
5. Robert Smarte replaced Elliston at Preston Capes on 30 June 1585. John Elliston then became Plumpton's rector in East Sussex. He started there on 20 April 1586.
6. Andrew King, Culworth's vicar, started on 23 May 1583. King was a divine of considerable eminence who had first been cast into prison for nonconformity in 1573.
7. William Proudlove, Weedon Bec's vicar, started there on 30 June 1587. He was "one representative of an older generation of nonconformists."[75]

Thomas Cartwright, a regular participant in Warwick, might occasionally have participated in the Daventry *Classis*. It is twenty-two miles distant from his Warwick hospital. Sir Richard Knightley likewise may have stopped by when in residence at his Fawsley Hall estate, only six miles from Daventry. Another noteworthy Puritan was also located nearby. "Well-known separatist, John Penry, married into a Northampton family" and was a visitor to the Northampton *Classis*.[76]

WHAT WAS THE CONTENT OF *CLASSES*?

Moderators of *classes* set agendas and led the meetings. An assigned scribe took minutes to provide a record. From the Warwickshire *Classis*:

> The brethren assembled together in the name of God, having heard and examined by the word of God, and according to their best abilities and judgment, a draught of discipline essential and necessary for all times, have thought good to testify concerning it as follows:—We

---

[72] Shiels, 60, 52.
[73] Shiels, 43.
[74] Christopher Haigh, "The Taming of Reformation: Preachers, Pastors and Parishioners in Elizabethan and Early Stuart England," (*History*, Volume 85, no. 280 (October 2000)): 572-588. *JSTOR*. Viewed 18 June 2020. https://jstor.org/stable/24425938.
[75] Shiels, 52.
[76] Shiels, 54.

acknowledge and confess the same to be agreeable to God's most holy word, so far as we are able to judge or discern of it, excepting some few points, which we have sent to our reverend brethren of this assembly, for their further resolution.

We affirm it to be the same which we desire to be established in this church, by daily prayer to God, which we promise (as God shall offer opportunity, and give us to discern it so expedient) by humble suit unto her majesty, her honourable council and the parliament, and by all other lawful and convenient means, to further and advance, so far as the laws and peace of the present estate of our church will suffer it, and not enforce the contrary. We promise to guide ourselves and to be guided by it, and according to it.

For a more special declaration of some points more important and necessary, we promise uniformly to follow such order, when we preach the word of God, as in the book is by us set down, in the chapters of the office of ministers of the word, of preaching, of sermons, of sacraments, of baptisms, and of the Lord's supper. Further, also, we follow the order set down in the chapters of the meetings, as far as it concerneth the ministers of the word. For which purpose, we promise to meet together every six weeks in classical conferences, with such of the brethren here assembled, as for their neighbourhood may fit us best, and such others as by their advice, we shall desire to be joined with us.

The like we promise for provincial meetings every half year from our conferences to send unto them, being divided according to the order following. Also, that we will attend the general assembly every year, and at all parliaments, and as often as by order it shall be thought good to be assembled.

John Oxenbridge	Thomas Cartwright
Humphrey Fenn [*sic*]	Matthew Hulme
Edward Gellibrand	Anthony Nutter
Hercules Cleveley	Daniel Wight [*sic*]
Leonard Fetherston	Edward Lord
John Ashbye	Edmund Littleton.[77]

Unfortunately for the Puritans, these meeting minutes fell into the hands of diocesan authorities. This document disclosed *classes* discussions, the intent of the *Book of Discipline* draft, and identified its participants. With it, a dozen Puritans were targeted for interrogations.

As one of the Daventry *Classis'* eldest members, William Proudlove was greeted warmly by his peers. But as he entered, he sensed a high level of tension that permeated the room. Serious discussions lay ahead. After dispatching the meeting's procedural aspects, all could see that the past year's events were building to a climax of epic proportions.

As the meeting began, the moderator summarized a few key items. He reviewed how the *Martin Marprelate* tracts boasted of the strength of Northampton's Puritans. In fact, Martin

---

[77] "Edmund Littleton," *Bible Study Tools*. Viewed on 15 February 2021. https://www.biblestudytools.com/history/brook-lives-puritans-volume-1/edmund-littleton.html. (From Benjamin Brook, *The Lives of the Puritans*, Volume 1.)

challenged the mayor and constables to apprehend those involved in their publication. In essence, he dared authorities to tighten the net on the network of committed Puritans.

The moderator recounted how, during the pursuit of Martin Marprelate, Edmund Snape, the "chief-man" curate at St. Peter's Northampton and leader of its *classis*, had already become a prime target of diocesan officials. Snape had a knack for, and history of, attracting attention and controversy. When he received his first diocese assignment in 1575, Snape refused it unless the Northampton congregation at St. Peter's directly called him, which they immediately did. After he left to join Cartwright in the Channel Islands and returned a year later, "Snape preached and spoke of the church as a 'chosen generation' which comprised 'here one and there one picked out of the prophane and common multitude and put apart to serve the Lord.'"[78] This Puritan-leaning belief was not accepted by the Church of England.

The moderator added that Edmund Snape was identified as one who convinced Sir Richard Knightley to allow Robert Waldegrave's secret printing press to set up at his Fawsley estate. *The Epitome* was printed there. During the search for the perpetrators, Snape was warned of an impending visitation. "Snape was so apprehensive that he hid his books in the house of one of his congregation [*sic*] but some of his personal papers were seized, as was much incriminating evidence about the Warwickshire classes when the house of Edmund Littleton was searched."[79]

The *classis* moderator paused, sighed, and looked into the eyes of his peers. Then he reported an even more troubling event. Two weeks previously, diocesan agents seized three Puritan colleagues near Manchester. They were setting up the secret Martin Marprelate printing press in a rented house. Examined and detained for a week, they then were dispatched to London. Rumors indicated they might be imprisoned. More details were sketchy. But it was believed, that somehow, some way, another *Martin Marprelate* tract was about to be published.

The moderator's report created an uproar and much consternation among the *classis* members. Questions immediately flew around the room. "What will happen next? Are you expecting a diocesan visit? Will we get visited as well? How prepared are your parishioners? Is your church united or splintered in our cause?"

As the most senior member, Proudlove stood up, and a silence fell upon the room. He interjected his thoughts and voiced his wisdom. "These are all good questions, but will the answers lead us to the path most pleasing to God? Let us present our supplications in prayer right now! We need to operate in his strength—not from our own."

After lengthy prayers and shared discernment, the *classis* moderator stressed that everyone needed to prepare and anticipate a visitation. As the final agenda item, an upcoming regional *conference* was announced in Cambridge for the following week. Designated Northamptonshire representatives were Edmund Snape, William Fludd, and Thomas Stone. Cartwright would attend representing Warwickshire. Proudlove thought, "Ah, that explains why he was unable to be with us today as had been rumored."

---

[78] Shiels, 57.
[79] Shiels, 59.

The Cambridge provincial *conference* in September 1589 is well-documented.

In early September, puritan delegates from London, the Midlands and East Anglia met in Cambridge for a provincial conference. It was Stourbridge Fair time, by now a regular occasion for a general meeting at the university. . . . The conference took place in St. John's College, a community still, as ever, deeply divided in religion, and it was perhaps inevitable that rumours of this 'presbytery' should spread beyond Cambridge.

The meeting-place was the Master's Lodge, at that time occupied by a senior fellow and the leading puritan at St. John's, Henry Alvey . . . The list of delegates to the conference consists for the most part of hardened, professional presbyterian leaders: Cartwright himself for Warwick, Snape, Fludd and Stone from Northamptonshire, Gifford for Essex, Walter Allen for Suffolk, Thomas Barber for London and Chaderton of Cambridge. A more surprising name was that of William Perkins of Christ's College, then on the threshold of his great theological reputation, for Perkins, so far as we know, played little other part in the presbyterian movement.

The moderator was a local Cambridgeshire minister, John Harrison, vicar of Histon. Stone, Perkins and Barber all admitted . . . that their conference had to do with the *Book of Discipline*. According to Barber "they did correct, alter and amend divers imperfections" in the Book . . . having "perfected" it, they "did then and there . . . voluntarily agree amongst themselves that so many as would should subscribe to the said *Book of Discipline* after that time." . . . The Discipline had been under consideration for at least four years.[80]

After the weight of the reports and their discussions settled on the Daventry *Classis* members, they had no other agenda items left. They ended their meeting by reciting the Lord's Prayer in unison.

"Our Father which art in heaven, hallowed be thy Name. Thy kingdom come; Let thy will be done, even in earth, as *it is* in heaven; Our daily bread give us for the day; And forgive us our sins, for even we forgive every man that is indebted to us; And lead us not into temptation, but deliver us from evil: for thine is the kingdom, and the power, and the glory for ever. Amen."[81]

These committed Puritans embraced one last time before departing. Proudlove most surely reflected, "Yes indeed. The stage is set for an epic conflict."

---

[80] Collinson, 400-2.
[81] Matthew 6:9-13 (Geneva Bible 1599)

CHAPTER 2

TRIALS AND TRIBULATIONS

VICAR PROUDLOVE RETURNS FROM THE DAVENTRY *CLASSIS*

As William Proudlove mounted his borrowed horse for the ride home, dusk enveloped the landscape. With discussions fresh in mind, Proudlove could not help thinking of what was ahead. A weightiness, not present before, gave him pause. As he was prone to do, the vicar offered up another prayer. "Lord, give me strength to persevere. Thou hast placed me here at this time for this purpose. May I be found faithful, and thy presence with me every step of the way." The vicar hurried the pace home. He hoped to arrive before darkness fully descended.

When he arrived at Cole's home, Proudlove was greeted by Thomas Cole's son. In his twenties, John was a young man in his prime. Vicar Proudlove surmised, "I'm sure he would be a prime catch for a fortunate young woman. God, please allow me to bless their union when the time arrives." John Cole informed the vicar that his father was out and unavailable for the evening. Proudlove stressed to John, "Make sure your father knows it is urgent for us to meet tomorrow." John promised he would.

Proudlove grasped John's hand, thanked him, and set off quickly as darkness fell. With purposeful strides, he was anxious to be home. His wife, Isabella, was pregnant and soon expecting a child. The Proudlove family looked forward to the new baby's arrival.

The next morning, Thomas Cole hurried through the village to meet with vicar Proudlove. Only a few short blocks from the parish church, their meeting place was known as *Le Townhouse*. It was often used for meetings of the Manor Court of the Baron, church gatherings, and other village events. As Cole purposely strode down the lane, he thought of who else the vicar might have summoned: "Probably the other churchwardens, Thomas Billing, John Gare, Robert Abbey, Francis Billinge, and Edward Gare will join." Thomas Billing was one of Cole's closest friends in the village. For generations, the Billings had been the village's most prominent family. Cole and the others often served the Lord of the Manor, by administrating presentments at its biannual meetings, either as homage or jurors.

When Thomas unlatched the door of *Le Townhouse*, he stepped directly from Church Street into the rectangular building's first floor. In one corner, Proudlove was quietly talking with the other men sitting on a bench that rimmed the room. When he saw Thomas, he jumped to his feet. After the vicar embraced Thomas, everyone was invited to sit. As a fire glowed from the hearth, Proudlove asked them to assume the ancient prayer posture with palms up, indicating their submission to God.[1] The vicar opened the meeting with prayer:

---

[1] The *Orans* prayer posture was characteristic of early Christianity, whose adherents saw it as representing the posture of Christ on the Cross.

"O God, by whom the meek are guided in judgment, and light riseth up in darkness for the godly: Bless each one here and guide our conversation. Grant us, in all our doubts and uncertainties, the grace to ask what thou wouldst have us to do, that the Spirit of wisdom may save us from all false choices, and that in thy light we may see light, and in thy straight path may not stumble; through Jesus Christ our Lord. Amen."

As he looked in the men's eyes, the vicar surely wanted them to grasp and fully comprehend the significance of what he was about to say. But more importantly, he wanted to prepare them for what might happen next. He swore them to silence and admonished them to maintain the strictest confidentiality. With a sense of urgency, Proudlove launched into as much detail as he thought wise to share. He started with the capture of Martin Marprelate's secret press. Then, he recounted how three printers were arrested and dispatched to London. Proudlove's hearers had surely read at least some of the tracts. The vicar shared what happened to Northampton's vicar, Edmund Snape. When warned of an impending diocese visitation, Snape inadvertently left personal papers in books he hid at the home of Edmund Littleton, sometime vicar of Brixworth and another zealous Puritan. When diocesan representatives searched Littleton's house, they confiscated Snape's books which contained the incriminating evidence. Included was a detailed communication summary about *cla*sses in Warwickshire plus the names of a dozen participants.[2]

Proudlove wasn't completely sure, but suspected Snape had already been detained and summoned to London. Most certainly, the vicar gave his churchwardens enough background to understand the depth and breadth of the issues at hand. Then he paused and looked intently at each one. After a lengthy pause, he continued in a hushed tone. "Given my participation in the Daventry *Cla*ssis," he confessed, "we all must anticipate visitations from diocesan officials. I do not know God's timing in all this. But arrive they will." The vicar felt certain the officials would interrogate him and probably everyone in the room. It's even possible they would interrogate additional parishioners, as they had done in other parishes. That meant they all needed to be prepared. The churchwardens' attention was riveted on their vicar. It never waned.

With their full attention secured, the vicar discussed the likely interrogations at length. Then he patiently answered their questions, as best he could. When they finished, vicar Proudlove lifted a closing prayer. "I am most thankful, Lord, for these men. Watch over us and guide us, we pray. As it is written in Psalms:

Keepe thy tongue from evill, and thy lips, that they speake no guile.
Eschewe evill and doe good: seeke peace and follow after it.
The eyes of the Lord are upon the righteous, and his eares are open unto their crie.
But the face of the Lord is against them that doe evill, to cut off their remembrance from
    the earth.
The righteous crie, and the Lord heareth them, and delivereth them out of all their troubles.

---

2   Collinson, 404.

The Lord is neere unto them that are of a contrite heart and will save such as be afflicted in Spirite.

Great are the troubles of the righteous: but the Lord delivereth him out of them all.[3]

Assist us mercifully, O Lord, in these our supplications and prayers, grant us thy promised protection, and dispose the way of thy servants toward the attainment of everlasting salvation; that, among all the changes and chances of this mortal life, they may ever be defended by thy gracious and ready help; through Jesus Christ our Lord. Amen."

After tender embraces, they parted in silence and returned to their homes. Thank heavens for their conversation. Grave as it was, it proved timely.

St. Peter and St. Paul Parish Church in Weedon Bec.
With kind permission of Tony Johns, photographer. (2.1)

DIOCESE OFFICIAL AND THE CHURCHWARDENS

On 4 September 1589, a diocesan official appeared unannounced at Weedon Bec's parish church. When vicar Proudlove was not to be found, the official summoned the six churchwardens. When all had arrived, they were informed that, by virtue of their positions, they were required to swear an *ex-officio* oath and truthfully answer all questions asked. While many laymen might not have fully understood what this meant, these men did.

The six wardens remained silent. As Thomas Cole made visual contact with his friends, he eyed the official. Cole mentally reviewed the vicar's discussion. A dozen or more thoughts must have raced through Cole's mind. "What actions could the diocese take? What are the risks? What are my options? Could I be summoned to London . . . or imprisoned? What

---

[3] Psalm 34:13-19 (Geneva Bible 1599)

of my family?" As he felt tension in his upper body, he consciously relaxed his posture and strengthened his resolve. The bishop's surrogate waited and wondered, "How will they reply?" A test of wills had begun.

Archbishop Whitgift's examination process was reminiscent of the Spanish Inquisition for this very purpose. Those summoned were first required to swear an *ex-officio mero* oath. Whitgift knew they understood a breach of a religious oath was considered a mortal sin and perjury.[4] They must swear to tell the truth to all inquiries. But the oath would be administered before they knew what questions would be asked. The questions, of course, were worded to entrap them. After an *ex-officio* oath was sworn by examinees, their own testimonies could be used to prosecute them by self-incrimination. The official functioned not only as prosecutor but also as judge. Silence, or refusing to answer, was contempt of court. Examinees could jeopardize their standing with the church, their community, and even their livelihood. All risked suspension, imprisonment, or worse.

As Puritan lawyer James Morrice of Colchester would later argue, this interrogation method of self-incrimination violated English common law established in 1215. When noblemen forced King John to sign the Magna Carta, the Great Charter established the principle that everyone was subject to the law, including royalty. It guaranteed them protection of life, liberty, and property; freedom from unlawful searches and seizures; and the right to a jury trial. Later acts, however, such as the Act of Supremacy, conflicted with this common law of the land.[5] At the time, little did these six men realize how quickly the precedent they were modeling would gain strength in England. The outcry against the *ex-officio* oath became so great by the middle of the seventeenth century that the right against self-incrimination was established in common law. Nor could they and the Puritans who would follow their example imagine that two centuries later, what they were now preparing to do would influence the historical background for debates over the Fifth Amendment to the Constitution of the United States of America in 1791.[6]

---

[4] The accused would find themselves trapped between a breach of religious oath (taken extremely seriously in that era, a mortal sin and perjury), contempt of court for silence, or self-incrimination. The name derives from the questioner putting the accused on oath *ex-officio*, meaning by virtue of his office or position. See Jed Rubenfeld, *Revolution by Judiciary: the Structure of American Constitutional Law* (Cambridge: Harvard University Press, 2005). "*Ex-officio* oath." Viewed 29 October 2021. https// en.wikipedia.org/wiki/Ex_officio_oath/.

[5] Marion Gibson, *Possession, Puritanism and Print: Darrell, Harsnett, Shakespeare and the Elizabethan Exorcism Controversy* (Cambridge: Pickering & Chatto, 2015): 9-10.

[6] The Puritan refusals to swear the *ex-officio* oath and their influence on the development of the right against self-incrimination in England and the American colonies (specifically Plymouth Colony) is well-documented. See, for example, O. J. Rogge, "Levy: Origins of the Fifth Amendment," *Michigan Law Review*, Vol. 67, Issue 4 (1969). Part of the "Constitutional Law Commons" and the "Legal History Commons." https://repository.law.umich.edu/mlr/vol67/iss4/10. Leonard Levy, *Origins of the Fifth Amendment: The Right Against Self-Incrimination* (Oxford: Oxford University Press, 1968). On the use of this oath in Star Chamber proceedings and the relationship to the Fifth Amendment, see "Historical Background on Self-Incrimination," *Constitution Annotated: Analysis and Interpretation of the U. S. Constitution*. Viewed 8 February 2022. https://constitution.congress.gov/browse/essay/amdt5-4-1/ ALDE_00000864/. James Madison thought "the fifth resolution," that "no state shall violate the equal

When asked to affirm the *ex-officio* oath, Thomas Cole refused. The official asked, "Do you understand what refusing to do so means?"

Cole responded, "Yes, I do."

The official added, "Do you understand the consequence of what this choice means?"

Cole replied quietly, "Yes, I do understand." The official again asked him to affirm the oath. Cole firmly stated, "Again, sir, I refuse to take the oath."

The official replied, "If you refuse this oath, you will give me no choice but to ex-communicate you from the Church of England. I ask you again, will you affirm the *ex-officio* oath as churchwarden of the parish of Weedon Bec?"

Cole replied, "No sir, I do not affirm this oath."

In turn, this process was repeated five times for each remaining churchwarden. All six refused the *ex-officio* oath and stood firm in unanimous non-compliance.

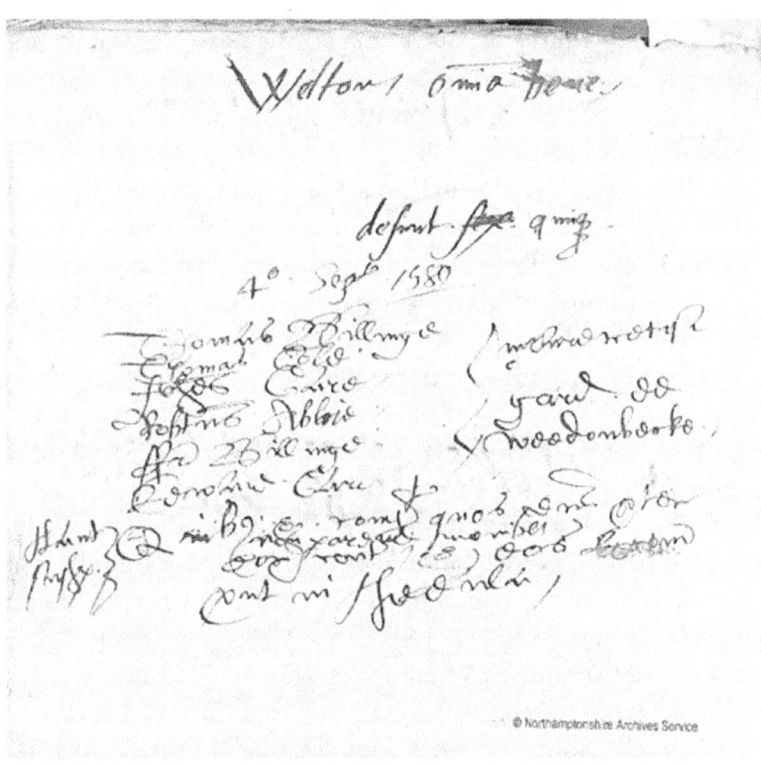

Weedon Bec Churchwardens' Excommunication.[7]
With kind permission of NRO. Sponsored by Scott L. Semans. (2.2)

---

rights of conscience …," was the most important amendment of all. See James R. Read, "James Madison," *The First Amendment Encyclopedia*. Viewed 8 February 2022. https://mtsu.edu/first-amendment/article/1220/james-madison.

[7] Northamptonshire Record Office, Correction Book, X609/23 fol. 96d. Hereinafter abbreviated as NRO. Recently, NRO has rebranded as Northamptonshire Archives.

In his correction book, the official noted the date, the names of the six, their positions, and his comments: "Six are lacking. They stand suspended. To whom, etc. they appeared, whom the Lord condemned as contumacious in not obeying their summonses, etc. Ex-communicated, just as in the schedule." For these six men, excommunication was considered the gravest of all ecclesiastical censures. Declared *out of communion*, they were banished from the parish church community. Though they were all leaders in their village, they risked sanctions from their fellow parishioners, friends, and even family. In typical villages, such forms of social ostracism typically included shunning, shaming, and loss of status within the community.

Two weeks later, the vicar's wife, Isabella, went into labor and bore her newest child, a daughter. Grace was baptized on 21 September by her father, William Proudlove. The proud parents now had six children. As William held his baby daughter in his arms, he most surely proclaimed, "What a lovely daughter God has blessed us with! Lord, protect my family from any harm. Be with me, whatever may come next." Proudlove knew it was only a matter of time before he, too, would be interrogated.

In gratitude, he lifted a prayer for his recently excommunicated churchwardens: "Thanks be to God for Thomas Cole, Thomas Billing, John Gare, Robert Abbey, Francis Billinge, and Edward Gare. Bless them, Lord. Watch over them and their families. Give them resolve and strength for the days ahead. May we all be found faithful to do thy will. Amen."

Early the following month, Proudlove received word that the seventh tract of *Martin Marprelate* had been distributed. With the three printers captured and detained in London, and printer Waldegrave headed north to Scotland, there would be no more. Diocesan officials were in pursuit of scores of Puritans to interrogate. Puritan clergy and their supporters were on notice.

Beginning in the fall of 1589 and continuing through the winter, the number of Weedon Bec's church parish register entries for baptisms, marriages, and burials declined noticeably. Perhaps the excommunicated churchwardens and their families attended other parish churches. That had occurred before, during the parish turmoil experienced before Proudlove's arrival in 1587, when it was noted that "more than twenty parishioners were attending elsewhere."[8]

This situation was not unique to Weedon Bec. The turmoil here was representative of what was happening in many English parishes throughout the realm at this critical juncture. This ecclesiastical turmoil had developed in the years before the *Martin Marprelate* tracts burst upon the scene and set the stage for William Proudlove, Thomas Cartwright, and the others. But even before this, five Puritans had been called to stand firm in the face of adversity, bravely face the consequences of whatever might befall them, and courageously sacrifice for actions they took, beliefs they held, and convictions they lived.

---

[8]   Shiels, 131.

FIVE PURITAN ZEALOTS

Throughout the 1580s, a growing chorus of Puritan voices progressively pushed Church of England leaders for Puritan reforms. In 1581, Robert Browne formed a Congregationalist church in Norwich located about one hundred miles northeast of London. Browne and his congregants, known as Brownists, withdrew from the Church of England. For that, he earned the nickname, *Troublechurch Browne*. Acknowledged as the first Separatist and Puritan zealot, he led his congregation into exile in Middleberg, Zeeland, in southwestern Netherlands. While there, Browne published *A Booke which sheweth the life and manners of all True Christians* at Middelburg in 1582. It set out his rationale for congregational independence.

After Archbishop Whitgift issued his Three Articles and subsequently demonstrated his intolerance for nonconformity, the growing Puritan movement bred conflict with ecclesiastical authorities. That same year, Browne published *A Treatise of Reformation without Tarrying for Any, and of the Wickedness of Those Preachers Which Will Not Reform Till the Magistrate Command or Compel Them*. In this tract, he laid out his concept of separation of Church and State.

Another leader in Browne's congregation, Robert Harrison, carried views in opposition to Browne, which resulted in Browne's forced exit from the congregation he started. It occurred in 1583, and he subsequently led a faithful group of followers to Scotland seeking to build up his congregation there. However, Browne was interrogated by local authorities to explain his writings and was effectively placed under house arrest. Essentially, the Scottish reception was less than he hoped for. In the summer of 1584, poor health and some despair undoubtedly drew Browne back to England. He began to write and publish again but was questioned and arrested. His family connections allowed for a negotiated release from jail. Still in poor health, he was allowed to return to his ancestral home in Stamford.

> By early spring of 1586, he had recovered enough to begin to preach without license again. He was brought up on charges to appear before Bishop Howard of Peterborough for his illegal preaching and writings. He ignored the summons and failed to appear, he was excommunicated. The Excommunication itself may have been the catalyst for his change of attitude. Or he may have found his personal freedom in England more important than willing to give a halfhearted recanting to Church authorities of his theological principles? The real reasons may never be known for certain.[9]

With Browne's change of attitude, he recanted his Puritan beliefs and sought reconciliation with the Church of England. At first, Puritans were distraught with Browne's unexpected change of heart. But other Puritan reformers stepped in to fill the gap and attracted the attention of ecclesiastical officials.

John Greenwood resigned as Wyham's vicar in Lincolnshire on 10 December 1583, then became vicar of All Saints, Rackheath, in Norfolk, located just five miles from the surviving

---

[9] "Brownists," *Exlibris*. Viewed 13 December 2021. http://www.exlibris.org/nonconform/engdis/brownists.html.

Brownist church of Norwich. Greenwood was most probably influenced by Robert Browne's teachings. He developed strong Puritan beliefs and, about September 1585, renounced his ordination as wholly unlawful. He resigned from All Saints, traveled to London, and joined another Separatist congregation there. By 1586, he led that congregation, known as the London Underground Church. This illegal Brownist-type congregation had its roots in secret meetings dating back to the late 1560s. Greenwood became the second Puritan zealot in this era.

Henry Barrowe, a lawyer, became the third notable zealous Puritan. Passing by a church in about 1583, he overheard a preacher whose words drew him inside. By the sermon's end, he converted to Puritanism. During the next three to four years, he associated with Independents and then joined John Greenwood in revitalizing the London Underground Church. Together, these two Puritans believed churches were to be made up of voluntarily committed believers, and the Church of England did not meet that standard. These congregations "met in fields in summer and house in winter, from 5 am, sometimes worshipping all day."[10] Henry Barrowe's "natural earnestness and eloquence made him conspicuous" as a leader in the congregation and to ecclesiastical authorities as well.[11]

On 8 October 1587 in the parish of St. Andrew-by-the-Wardrobe, a worship service at the house of one Henry Martin was raided. Greenwood was arrested along with twenty worshipers. On the 19th of November, Barrowe visited Greenwood in the Clink prison.[12] While there,

> Barrowe was detained by the gaoler and brought before Archbishop John Whitgift. He insisted on the illegality of this arrest, refused either to take the *ex officio* oath or to give bail for future appearance, and was committed to the Gatehouse Prison. After nearly six months' detention and several irregular examinations before the high commissioners, he and Greenwood were formally indicted at the Newgate Sessions in May 1588 under the 1581 Recusancy Act (originally directed against Roman Catholics). They were fined £260, then moved to the Fleet prison.[13]

After their lengthy imprisonment, totally unjust in Barrowe's view, he petitioned the queen. His request led to a fourth examination by the Privy Council, where "he maintained the principle of separatism, denouncing the prescribed ritual of the Church as 'a false worship,' and the bishops as oppressors and persecutors."[14]

At that examination on 18 March 1589, the Lord Chancellor asked Henry Barrowe, while pointing at Archbishop Whitgift: "What is that man?"

---

[10] "London Underground Church," *Wikipedia*. Viewed 13 December 2021. https://en.wikipedia.org/wiki/London_Underground_Church.

[11] "Barrowe, Henry," *1911 Encyclopaedia Britannica*. Viewed 13 Dec 2021. https://en.wikisource.org/wiki/1911_Encyclopaedia_Britannica/Barrowe_Henry.

[12] Located in Southwark very near London Bridge, this is where we derive the phrase "in the clink."

[13] "Henry Barrowe," *Wikipedia*. Viewed 10 September 2020. https://en.wikipedia.org/wiki/Henry_Barrowe. "Gaoler" is Medieval spelling for jailer.

[14] "Henry Barrowe," *Wikipedia*.

Barrow replied, "The Lord gave me the spirit of boldness, so that I answered: He is a monster, a miserable compound, I know not what to make [call] him: he is neither ecclesiastical nor civil, even that second beast spoken of in the Revelation."[15]

While still imprisoned in 1590, Greenwood and Barrowe wrote *An Answer to George Gifford's pretended Defence of Read Prayer*. Even in prison, "they turned the Fleet into a clandestine publishing house" that distributed pamphlets through their friends critical of their situation and the Church of England.[16] Their followers were known as Barrowists.

The fourth Puritan zealot, John Udall, a Kingston vicar, was "a man of excellent parts, great learning, genuine piety, and untarnished loyalty to Queen Elizabeth."[17] But as a Puritan, he suffered for his nonconformity. Brought before the Bishop of Winchester on 26 September 1586, Udall refused to swear the *ex-officio* oath until he was first able to see the articles for questioning. After much discussion, he was given thirty-six articles which contained charges from certain persons in his Kingston parish. On the 17th of October, Udall was brought before the High Commission at Lambeth Palace. It was convened by Archbishop Whitgift, the Bishops of Winchester and Hereford, Dr. Aubery, Dr. Lewin, Dr. Cosin, Mr. Hatwell, and others. Whitgift began the interrogation.

> W: You say, Christ, is the only archbishop. Why do you not call him arch-pastor and arch-shepherd?
>
> U: As I am at liberty to call the ministers of Christ by those titles given them by the Holy Ghost, as pastors, shepherds, and watchmen, so, I think, I may Jesus Christ.
>
> W: No, no; the archbishop was in your way, and it troubled you to think of him. But there will be an archbishop when you shall be no preacher at Kingston.[18]

After being deprived of his ministry, Udall was restored and allowed to continue preaching "for which he blessed and praised God and prayed that these troubles might be over-ruled for the advancement of God's glory, and the further prosperity of his church."[19] However in 1588, Udall was again suspended for nonconformity and deprived of his living.

He later published a pamphlet titled *Demonstration of the Truth that Discipline which Christ hath prescribed in his Word for the Government of his Church, in all Times and Places, until the end of the World*. Its dedication, "To the supposed governors of the Church of England, the archbishops, lord-bishops, archdeacons, and the rest of that order,"[20] was not complimentary to the Church of England and its leaders. Ecclesiastical authorities interviewed various men seeking to learn who was its author. The interviews yielded information that pointed to John Udall. Summoned to appear in court, witnesses swore depositions about Udall, but none appeared to testify. Therefore, Udall was not allowed

---

[15] Collinson, 243.
[16] Collinson, 412.
[17] Brook, 1.
[18] Brook, 2.
[19] Brook, 9.
[20] Brook, 14.

to question or confront his accusers. He denied authorship of the pamphlet but admitted to writing its dedication. Of the court's three articles against him, none were proven by a lawful court process. But Udall was imprisoned and deprived of his livelihood. His wife and children were denied access to visit him.

The fifth zealous Puritan of this group was the Welshman John Penry. He took his Bachelor of Arts degree at Cambridge in 1583, where his "fellow-collegians and intimate friends" were Henry Barrowe, John Udall, and John Greenwood. [21] Penry removed to Oxford and, in 1586, completed his Master of Arts degree. In 1587, Penry moved to Northampton and married Helen Godley. He drew the attention of the diocese when in one publication he stated that "reading homilies only, or any other books, was not preaching the word of God, and so the ordinary means of salvation was wanting."[22]

Employed in ministry, Penry participated in the Northampton *Classis*. During publication of the *Martin Marprelate* tracts, examinees identified Penry as one who asked Sir Richard Knightley to harbor the secret printing press at his estate and possibly authored at least some of the tracts. Although Penry emphatically denied authorship, authorities sought to arrest him, and he fled north to Scotland. While there, he prepared a petition for the queen if he should ever have a chance to present it. In part, Penry wrote:

> The last days of your reign are turned rather against Jesus Christ and his gospel, than to the maintenance of the same. I have great cause and complaint, *madam*, nay, the Lord and his church have cause to complain of your government, because we, your subjects, this day, are not permitted to serve our God, under your government according to his <u>word</u>, but are sold to be bondslaves, not only to our affections, to do what we will, so that we keep ourselves within the compass of established civil laws, but also to be servants to the *man of sin* (the pope) and his ordinances.[23]

One of Penry's opponents characterized him as, "a tolerable scholar, an edifying preacher, and a good man… But being of Welsh blood, and of a hot and restless head, he changed his course, and became a notorious anabaptist, and in some sort a Brownist, and a most bitter enemy to the Church of England."[24]

These five Puritan zealots—Browne, though he recanted, and the four who stepped in to take his place—represent some of many who preceded them. Puritans had long sought reforms of the Church of England. Beginning in the reign of Henry VIII, bolstered by influences from the European continent, supported by the availability of English translations of the Geneva Bible from 1560 onward, and emboldened with the new technology of printing presses, they accelerated their demands. With Henry's son Edward VI, they experienced Promises of reform. Then, they saw them dashed by his eldest daughter Mary I. With her death, Such Promises were somewhat reinstated by Elizabeth I, promoted by

---

[21] Samuel Hopkins, *The Puritans: or The Church, Court, and Parliament of England, during the Reigns of Edward VI and Queen Elizabeth*, in Three Volumes, Vol. 2 (Boston: Gould and Lincoln, 1861): 1.

[22] Brook, 48-9.

[23] Brook, 50.

[24] Brook, 48.

Archbishop Grindal, but finally dismantled by Archbishop Whitgift. Over several decades, Puritan reform efforts attracted controversy, like a magnet, almost every step of the way. The *Martin Marprelate* tracts were not the beginning of controversy. Rather, the tracts were the culmination of a long, hard road of reform attempts—primarily fought as a war of pamphlets before being fought in the courts of England.

PURITAN SUPPORTERS ON TRIAL

The infamous Court of the Star Chamber, widely feared because of the arbitrary and oppressive nature of its judgments and means of interrogation, was the setting for the legal battles that quickly embroiled the Puritan reformers. The Star Chamber "drew its authorization directly from the monarch and operated outside the procedures of the common-law courts, without juries and with judges drawn primarily from the royal council, supplemented in time by justices of the high court bench."[25] In essence, the Star Chamber Court operated outside of English common law as defined by the Magna Carta.

Queen Elizabeth empowered the Star Chamber Court to summon and judge those suspected of sedition or treason. Anyone suspected of harboring those responsible for printing inflammatory publications qualified. With Queen Elizabeth's mandate, the Star Chamber Court focused on the *Martin Marprelate* tract perpetrators and supporters. Archbishop John Whitgift's Canterbury colleague, Sir John Boys, served as legal adviser.[26]

A Northampton bookbinder, Henry Sharpe, who had helped with distributing the *Martin Marprelate* tracts, asked Sir Richard Knightley about his risk of interrogation. MP Knightley replied, "'Let me alone, the knaves dare not search my house: if they had, I would have cursed them, they know well enough.' But a servant Knightley had sent with copies of the new *Martin* to his brother-in-law [the Earl of] Hertford, revealed, while drunk, where the books had been printed. Sharpe confessed, despite Knightley's warning that 'surely they would hang him,' and Hatton warned Knightley that he was in danger."[27]

Sir Richard Knightley was elected to Parliament representing the shire of Northampton in 1588. Sir Christopher Hatton, the Lord Chancellor of England appointed in 1587, had supported the two Puritan candidates in Northamptonshire: Knightley and Sir Walter Mildmay.[28] Hatton controlled the patronage at Corfe Castle in Dorset, where he was constable and owned the manor. On 29 March 1589, Lord Chancellor Hatton opened Parliament, an honor placing him at the very pinnacle of the government.

---

[25] K.J. Kesselring and Natalie Mears, eds., *Star Chamber Matters: An Early Modern Court and Its Records* (London: University of London Press, 2021): 1.

[26] Collinson, 417.

[27] "Knightley, Sir Richard (1533-1615)," *The History of Parliament*. Viewed on 12 September 2020. https://www.historyofparliamentonline.org/.

[28] "Mildmay, Walter," History of Parliament. At Elizabeth's ascension, Mildmay came into prominence and was appointed chancellor of the Exchequer. For his remaining 30 years, he was one of Elizabeth's chief advisers. He died on 31 May 1589.

As Lord Chancellor, Sir Christopher Hatton also served as a judge on the highest court in England. Now, in September 1589, the Lord Chancellor faced a dilemma. His colleague, Sir Richard Knightley, had entangled himself in the controversy swirling around the *Martin Marprelate* tracts. Because of the uproar created by these incendiary tracts, Hatton could not shield Knightley from court action.

The Star Chamber. Courtesy of Yale Center for British Art. Public domain. (2.3)

The Star Chamber Court first issued a summons to interrogate a Mrs. Elizabeth Crane. Her country home in East Molesley, Surrey, was where Robert Waldegrave printed the first Martin Marprelate tract: The Epistle. Mrs. Crane, formerly Elizabeth Hussey, was the widow of Anthony Crane.[29] Mr. Crane, a supporter of Puritans beginning about 1572, served the Royal Household from 1578-1580 as Cofferer and Master of the Household. As such, he oversaw its domestic staff: the Royal Kitchens, pages, and footmen, to the housekeeper and staff. In this role, Anthony Crane served as a member of the Privy Council.

After Anthony Crane died on 16 August 1583, widow Crane continued with her support of Puritan writers and printers. After Robert Waldegrave's printing press was destroyed by Stationers' Company officials in May 1588, she permitted Waldegrave to bring a case of type, hidden under his cloak, to her London home. In late spring 1588, John Penry secretly obtained a new press for Robert Waldegrave which widow Crane allowed to be set up and operated in her country home, located directly across the River Thames from the queen's Hampton Court Palace. If the queen was in residence there, she could see widow Crane's home. One wonders if that was intentional.

---

[29] Born Elizabeth Hussey, she has been misattributed as the wife of Puritan minister, Nicholas Crane, who died in Newgate prison in about 1588. This corrects that misattribution.

In July 1588, John Udall's *Demonstration of Discipline* was printed there on the secret press. This pamphlet's subtitle, *A Demonstration of the truth of that Discipline, which Christ hath prescribed in His Word, for the government of His Church, in all times and places until the end of the world,* clearly laid out the Puritan position.[30]

In 1589, widow Crane married George Carleton, a lawyer, MP, and Puritan supporter. Unfortunately, Nicholas Tomkins, widow Crane's servant, betrayed his mistress when he swore to authorities on 15 February 1589 that John Penry and Robert Waldegrave were "about 3 weeks in her Howse in the Country after Midsommer [1588]."[31] With this discovery, the court, convinced it had the necessary evidence to examine her for seditious and treasonous Puritan activities, geared up for legal action.

When interrogated in the Star Chamber on 1 October 1589, the former widow Crane, now Mrs. Elizabeth Carleton,

> refused to answer upon oath to any question; either concerning herself, for that, as she said, she would not be her own hangman; or concerning others, for that she could not in her conscience be the accuser of others.

She also refused to consult a lawyer (even though her husband was one) or cooperate in any way. Elizabeth Carleton was heavily fined: £666 for contempt of court and an additional £500 for harboring the secret press. Facilitating the printing of the *Martin Marprelate* tracts was judged to be seditious and treasonous against Queen Elizabeth. Elizabeth Carleton was ordered imprisoned, probably in the Fleet, at the queen's pleasure. Her third husband, George Carleton, died in early January 1590. No decision had been reached in any proceedings which may have been instigated against him.

On 16 November 1589, Sir Richard Knightley was arrested and detained for "close examination."[32] So was his nephew, John Hales, along with Mr. and Mrs. Roger Wigston. Five Puritans who provided shelter for printing one or more of the *Martin Marprelate* tracts had been identified. One, John Penry, fled to Scotland. The other four awaited their trials while imprisoned in the Fleet. What was a London prison like? They were privately operated. The Fleet was among the most notorious.

> About the year 1586 . . . the suffering prisoners of the Fleet petitioned the Lords of the Council on the matter of certain grievous abuses in the management of the prison—abuses that were, indeed, never thoroughly corrected. It was the middleman system that had led to many evils.
>
> The warden, wishing to earn his money without trouble, had let the prison to two deputies. These men being poor, and greedy for money, had established an iniquitous system of bribery and extortion, inflicting constant fines and payments, and cruelly punishing all

---

[30] Edward Arber, ed., *Demonstration of Discipline* (Archibald Constable & Co., Westminster 1895).
[31] Hopkins, 295-6.
[32] Hopkins, 295-6

refractory prisoners who ventured to rebel, or even to remonstrate, stopping their exercise, and forbidding them to see their friends.

A commission was granted, but nothing satisfactory seems to have come from it, as we find, in 1593, another groan arising from the wretched prisoners of the Fleet, who preferred a bill to Parliament, reciting, in twenty-eight articles, the misdemeanours and even murders of the obnoxious deputy-warden. The warden's fees in the reign of Elizabeth, says Mr. Timbs, were—An archbishop, duke, or duchess, for his commitment fee, and the first week's "dyett," £21 10s.; a lord, spiritual or temporal, £10 5s. 10d.; a knight, £5; an esquire, £3 6s. 8d.; and even "a poor man in the wards, that hath *a part at the box*, to pay for his fee, having no dyett, 7s. 4d." The warden's charge for licence to a prisoner "to go abroad" was 20d. per diem.[33]

After imprisonment for three months while awaiting trial, Knightley, Hales, and Mr. and Mrs. Wigston were arraigned before the Star Chamber Court. On 13 February 1590, they were interrogated for their complicity with printing the *Martin Marprelate* tracts. John Hales, Sir Richard Knightley's nephew, denied any knowledge of what was being printed on the press. Hales swore he intended no malice toward the queen. Even so, the court fined him 1,000 marks (£666 13s. 4d.), and he served time in prison.

Mrs. Roger Wigston provided lively testimony. She "readily confessed that her zeal for the reformation in God's church" motivated her involvement but claimed that her husband didn't know anything about it, being "neither over curious nor meddlesome."[34] The court chastised Mr. Wigston for not controlling his wife and fined him £333. Mrs. Wigston was fined £1,000, and both spent time in prison.

Sir Richard Knightley also denied any knowledge of what was printed at his estate. His testimony, which carried plausibility, stated that during the time of the tracts' printing, he "had been conducting the trained bands to London for the army and was still occupied with his musters and local commissions." Knightley said he intended no malice toward the queen and asked for consideration for his "simple wit and weak capacity."[35] He was fined £2,000 and dismissed from the lieutenancy of the shire and the magistracy.

The fines in today's money are staggering. Mrs. Elizabeth Carleton fined £400,000 or USD $550,000; Sir Richard Knightley £700,000 or USD $960,000. The smallest fine was for Mr. Roger Wigston not controlling his wife: £116,000 or USD $160,000. Surely, these fines inflicted financial pain. But the prison experience was undoubtedly worse.

With the Puritan supporters dispatched, the court turned its attention to nonconformist clergymen. Vicar Daniel Wyght of Warwickshire, "one of the chief Puritan ministers . . . had his house forcibly entered, his study sacked, his papers seized, and he himself marched off to prison."[36] Wyght's Warwickshire *Classis* meeting minutes had unintentionally been included

---

[33] "Old New London," *British History*. Viewed 6 September 2020. https://www.british-history.ac.uk/old-new-london/vol2/pp404-416.

[34] Anna Castle, "The Marprelate Controversy, Part 2." Viewed 10 July 2017. https://www.annacastle.com/the-marprelate-controversy-part-ii/.

[35] Castle, "Marprelate Controversy."

[36] Hopkins, 371-72.

in Edmund Snape's books collected when Edmund Littleton's house was searched. "Seven other clergymen were arrested about the same time and committed to different prisons in and about London."[37] One was William Proudlove, vicar of Weedon Bec.

In the spring of 1590, the three *Martin Marprelate* tracts printers captured near Manchester were brought forward for examination. They had been imprisoned in the Tower since the end of August 1589. The notorious Tower was the scene of many executions due to actions deemed treasonous. It was well known, for either the threat or use of torture, to elicit prompt confessions. In the sixteenth and seventeenth centuries, the most common form of Tower torture was the rack.

Victims were laid out on the rack and pulled slowly by ropes attached to their hands and feet. Repeated racking increased the agony. Sometimes, the mere mention of racking was enough to gain a confession. This was likely the case for the three printers.

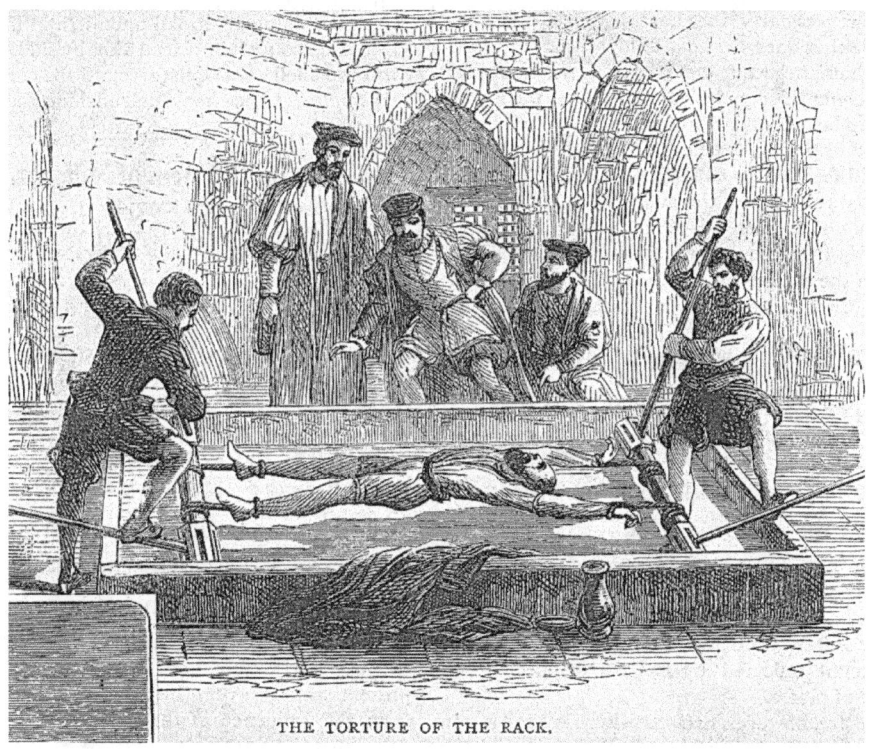

THE TORTURE OF THE RACK.

The Torture of the Rack. Wikimedia Commons. Public domain. (2.4)

John Hodgskins, the lead printer, "was tried at the court of the Queen's Bench for printing a book which contained 'a malicious intent against the queen' in violation of statute law. Hodgskins denied that the *Martin Marprelate* tracts contained any such malice towards [*sic*] Her Majesty. He was judged guilty of felony . . . [his assistant Valentine] Simms

---

[37] Brook, 151.

proofread Martins Jr. and Sr. . . . and testified 'fully and freely,' so he wasn't arraigned."[38] This was likely the case with printing assistant, Arthur Thomlin, as well. Following his felony conviction, John Hodgskins was moved from the Tower to another prison. Built in 1373,

> Marshalsea was a notorious prison in Southwark, just south of the River Thames. Although it housed a variety of prisoners, including men accused of crimes at sea and political figures charged with sedition . . . the Marshalsea court was a jurisdiction of the royal household. Known as the castle by inmates, the prison had a turreted lodge at the entrance, with a side room called the pound, where new prisoners would wait until a room was found for them.

> The front lodge led to a courtyard known as the park. This had been divided in two by a long narrow wall, so that prisoners from the common side could not be seen by those on the master's side, who preferred not to be distressed by the sight of abject poverty, especially when they might themselves be plunged into it at any moment. By all accounts, living conditions in the common side were horrific.

> Prisoners were regularly beaten with a "bull's pizzle" (a whip made from a bull's penis), or tortured with thumbscrews and a skullcap, a vice for the head that weighed 12 pounds (5.4 kg). What often finished them off was being forced to lie in the strong room, a windowless shed near the main sewer, next to piles of night soil and cadavers awaiting burial.[39]

PURITANS INTERROGATED IN THE HIGH COMMISSION COURT

The High Commission Court was the highest ecclesiastical court in the land. With the pursuit of *Martin Marprelate* tracts perpetrators, many participating Puritan vicars in *classes* or *conferences* had been identified. "In the course of the winter of 1589-90, the High Commissioners probably interrogated scores of preachers in an attempt to build up a fuller picture of the clandestine presbyterian organization of which they now had some knowledge."[40] Puritan ministers—which is how they referred to themselves as opposed to the term vicar—and their supporters were to be interrogated regarding three items:

1. Their knowledge of and subscription to the *Book of Discipline* draft;
2. its proposed Presbyterian church structure outside the bounds of the Church of England's structure; and
3. their involvement in *classis* and other unauthorized *conferences*.

During the early months of 1590, the Weedon Bec parish register entries dwindled significantly. The impact of the churchwardens' excommunications was noticeable. With a stable village population, baptisms, burials, and marriages should have continued at a

---

[38] Castle, "Marprelate Controversy."
[39] "Marshalsea," *Wikipedia*. Viewed 15 March 2019. https://en.wikipedia.org/wiki/Marshalsea.
[40] Collinson, 408.

normal pace. After a baptism on 26 April 1590, the registers stopped entirely. Why? Vicar Proudlove was either arrested or summoned and on his way to London. On 4 May 1590, a diocesan official noted in his visitation book, "William Proudlove, vicar, did not appear."[41] In fact, he was already in prison!

The vicar's wife, Isabella, was now home alone caring for her youngest child, Grace, aged seven months, and her five other children. To make matters more desperate, Isabella sensed she might be pregnant again. How would she possibly manage without her husband to provide and help care for the family? The family's head, its only provider, was in prison in London with his livelihood suspended. The Church of England no longer recognized Proudlove as the vicar of Weedon Bec.

On the 18th of June, a diocesan official visited the parish of Culworth (pronounced Cull-uth) near Weedon Bec. In his visitation book, he noted, "Andrew King, vicar, issued a citation for he osberveth not the booke of common prayer – in pryson."[42] One wonders if the official made any attempt to visit these two vicars' families and provide them with any form of Christian support. One can scarcely imagine the two vicars' thoughts while confined in a London prison.

As was the case for diocesan visitations and in the Star Chamber, Archbishop Whitgift's interrogation policy remained the same for the High Commission. "On each occasion the judge tendered a general oath, *ex-officio mero*, after which he would have assumed the role of prosecutor, presenting the examinee with a schedule of articles which assumed his guilt and which his oath would require him to answer."[43]

Because Edmund Snape's personal papers were confiscated during the hunt for the *Martin Marprelate* tracts' printing press, the Northampton All Saints vicar was a prime target of the High Commission. In 1590, "Snape had been examined on two occasions before the 11th of April . . . On the first occasion 'the issue was prison, the second close prison,' or so for Snape."[44] The term "close prison" describes a more confining environment than just prison by itself.

But not everyone who appeared before the court was, as it would be labeled today, a hostile witness. Some clergymen felt it was their ordained duty to testify fully and without reservation to ecclesiastical authorities about anything they knew or had observed. One such clergyman was John Johnson, Rector of Yelvertoft. Johnson previously served alongside Edmund Snape as Rector of All Saints, Northampton and testified openly about the Northampton *Classis*. Johnson

seems to have presented himself as an informer, in resentment at his censure by the Northampton *classis*. By April 11th, 1590, at least part of his evidence had been given, for on that day Edmund Snape wrote to his friends in Northamptonshire: "I would judge John

[41] NRO, Visitation Book, X610/24, Fol. 4d. Date: 4 May 1590.
[42] NRO, Visitation Book, Fol. 33. Date: 18 Jun 1590.
[43] Collinson, 409.
[44] Collinson, 409.

Johnson to have been the man, because (to my remembrance) persons and things of his time being mentioned, he only is not named.[45]

Johnson claimed that he had withdrawn from the *classis* at Northampton before the matter of the *Book of Discipline* was raised and could give no evidence about the nature of any subscription made to its terms.[46]

Another account of Johnson's testimony states:

Mr. Snape, Mr. Proudlove, & such others as were with him in the said two several meetings before specified . . . did agree to put the said articles & discipline in execution & practice so far as the present state of the Church of England now established would suffer & not enforce [it] to the contrary, that is to say till the magistrate did enjoin or enforce them to leave the practicing of the said discipline. And they did agree also to guide themselves by the said *Book of Discipline* and according to it with the same limitations.[47]

Another examinee, Edmund Littleton, a sometime vicar of Brixworth in Northampton, affirmed the *ex officio* oath and disclosed much information about the *classes*. His disclosure probably helped gain his release from prison. Likewise, "Richard Parker, the young vicar of Dedham, betrayed the names of several of his own associates."[48] They included Dr. Edmund Chapman of Dedham, Dr. Richard Crick of East Bergholt, Richard Dow of Stratton, and Rector William Tay of Peldon. Vicar Parker also revealed the existence of the Braintree Conference, when he named three Essex delegates: vicar Ezekiel Culverwell[49] of Felstead near London; vicar George Gifford of Maldon; and vicar Richard Rogers of Wethersfield.

Additional individuals discovered in vicar Edmund Snape's personal papers were also examined on the 16th of May. They included Edward Sharpe, Sir Richard Knightley's vicar at Fawsley, and "some of his own parishioners, and Johnson, for the second time."[50] In addition, Andrew King, vicar of Culworth, received a set of interrogatories designed to force him to self-incriminate, and then to condemn him upon his own confession. Though King refused the oath *ex-officio*, these two somewhat unique interrogatories are among many that were proposed to him and officially recorded.

1. Whether have you refused to use, or have you used in your sermons, the queen's majesty's whole title by law established under her, namely, defender of the faith, in all causes, and over all persons, as well ecclesiastical as civil, in these her realms and

---

[45] Collinson, 409.

[46] Shiels, 52.

[47] Shiels, 56.

[48] Collinson, 408.

[49] Ezekiel Culverwell, son of Nicholas Culverwell of London, haberdasher, educated at Emmanuel, and Rector of Great Stambridge, vicar of Felsted, in Essex. In 1583 he was suspended for nonconformity. Mass Hist Papers of the Winthrop Family Vol. 1, Folio 32.

[50] Collinson, 410.

dominions, and supreme governor next and immediately under God? For what cause have you so refused, or not used the said style? and were you admonished to use it?

2. Whether did you know or had heard before the 19th day of November, 1588, the said day was by and under her majesty's authority appointed to be solemnized and celebrated with thanksgiving unto God, for our happy deliverance from the intended invasion of the Spaniards? And did you that day, nevertheless, absent yourself from the parish church, and neither said divine service, preached, nor procured any other, then and there to do it? What was the cause, and what was your very true and only purpose and intent in so doing?

Imagine being required to recite Queen Elizabeth's complete title in a sermon. It starts: "Elizabeth by the Grace of God Queen of England France and Ireland, Defender of the Faith, et cetera." Also imagine being required as a minister to solemnize and celebrate the happy deliverance from the intended invasion of the Spanish Armada. These are some examples of how the highest officials in England controlled the queen's subjects, including its vicars. Of course, this was well before the concept of separation of Church and State was deemed acceptable. As court examinations continued, Puritan attorneys Nicholas Fuller and James Morrice hovered behind the accused ministers. The lawyers advised a strategy consistent with William Proudlove's advice to Thomas Cole and the other Weedon Bec churchwardens. The result? Most of the Puritan ministers refused to take the *ex-officio* oath,

Elizabeth I. Wikimedia Commons. Public domain. (2.5)

which blocked further proceedings since they could not convict without more evidence. However, the High Commission had the power to punish the ministers with contempt of court and with continuing imprisonment.

Despite these Puritans' refusal to testify, the court had already gained enough information about *classis*, *classes*, and *conferences* to set its sights on its highest profile Puritan reformer. On 20 May 1590, the High Commission summoned Thomas Cartwright. Because of his powerful supporters, Cartwright did not immediately appear. In his absence, the court continued its focus on those already detained.

On the 11th of July, the High Commission convicted Edmund Snape of offences against the Act of Uniformity and of contemptuously refusing the oath.[51] The court removed the former vicar of Northampton All Saints from his ecclesiastical offices and banished him from his clergy orders <u>for life</u>. Snape was again imprisoned.

---

[51] Collinson, 415.

Another Puritan apprehended, Thomas Stone, was known as a *pious divine*.[52] A leading member of the Kettering *Classis*, on the 27th of July, Stone was "brought before Attorney-General Popham and required to take the oath *ex-officio*."[53] Educated at Christ's Church in Oxford, Stone was a proctor at the university and the Rector of Warkton in Northamptonshire. Known as "a person of good learning and great worth, a zealous puritan, and a member of the *classis*, being sometimes chosen as moderator,"[54] Stone was presented with thirty-three articles. In his interrogation the following day, "He was examined . . . from six o'clock in the morning till seven at night."[55] The record provides detailed questions and summaries of some of his responses.

Who and how many assembled at their *classis*? Where, and when, and how often were they held? Stone answered with "the names of about forty ministers who attended these assemblies, though not all at one time; and that they held them in London, Cambridge, Northampton, and Kettering."

Who called these assemblies, by what authority, and in what manner? Stone stated that he knew not by whom they were called nor by what authority. He did state they were voluntary and communicated by letter or word of mouth.

Who were moderators in them, and what was their office? Stone answered that he only knew a single experience at Northampton when Mr. Johnson was admonished, and that either Mr. Snape or he moderated. He was not certain which.

What things were debated in those meetings or assemblies? Stone answered they were about "how far ministers might yield to subscribe unto the 'Book of Common Prayer,' rather than forego their ministry. The 'Book of Discipline' was often perused and discussed. Three petitions were agreed upon to be drawn up and presented, one to her majesty, another to the lords of the council, and another to the bishops. He also remembered discussing 'whether the books of Apocryphia might be warrantably read in public worship, as the canonical scriptures.'"

Were any censures exercised; what kinds, when, where, upon whom, by whom, and for what cause? Stone answered, "I never saw any censure exercised, excepting admonition once give to Mr. Johnson of Northampton, for improper conversation, to the scandal of his calling: nor was that used with any kind of authority, but by voluntary and mutual agreement, as well by him who was admonished, as him who gave the admonition."

Have any of the said defendants moved or persuaded any to refuse an oath, and in what case? Stone answered, "I never knew of any of the defendants to use words of persuasion to refuse any oath; only Mr. Snape sent me certain reasons gathered out of scripture which led

---

[52] Brook, 258.
[53] Brook, 259.
[54] Brook, 258-9.
[55] Collinson, 425.

him to refuse the oath *ex-officio*; which I am persuaded, he sent for no other purpose, than to declare that he refused to swear, not of contempt, but for conscience sake."[56]

From Stone's examination and previous interrogations, about eighty Puritan ministers and supporters were identified. Because of this, some of his Puritan colleagues held him responsible for their troubles. After Stone was released from prison and returned to his position at Warkton, he published a vindication of what he had done. It stated that "he thought it was unlawful to refuse an oath, when offered by a lawful magistrate; that having taken the oath, he was not at liberty to say nothing, much less to deliver an untruth; and he saw no probability, nor even possibility, of things being any longer concealed."[57] Meanwhile, many Puritan ministers languished in jail, enduring harsh conditions, where they most certainly searched Scripture for solace, consolation, and comfort. This New Testament Bible verse might have been a favored choice.

My brethren, count it exceeding joy, when ye fall into divers tentations [temptations], Knowing that the trying of your faith bringeth forth patience, And let patience have *her* perfect work, that ye may be perfect and entire, lacking nothing.[58]

As a result of the court's discoveries so far, diocesan activity accelerated in the county of Northampton. In Culworth, a new vicar, Edmund Rudierd, was installed on 19 August 1590.[59] He replaced vicar Andrew King, who was imprisoned in London. On the 1st of September, a diocesan visitation noted a discussion with the new vicar of Flowre, John Johnson.[60] Johnson's new parish church is a comfortable two-mile stroll along the path from Weedon Bec's parish church where William Proudlove had served. Johnson had testified in court, as had vicar Thomas Stone, as a friendly examinee just four months earlier. This suggests Johnson was transferred from the Northampton Parish to continue his livelihood in return for his testimony. The following month, another diocesan visit to Culworth's Edmund Rudierd occurred. It was noted he "did not appear."[61] What is most important about these notations is the significant increase in visitations. During this time of ecclesiastical turmoil, a normal pattern of annual visits increased to a rate of about once a month.

Meanwhile in London, Puritan delegates met secretly in *conference* to discuss the ramifications of the court's summons of Thomas Cartwright and his impending interrogatories. At a meeting held the week before Cartwright's arrival, delegates debated how he might be advised to answer and what the consequences might be. One delegate, Thomas Stone of Northampton, who earlier testified, which was not yet known by his fellow Puritans, encouraged Cartwright to make frank confession. Also debated was the merit of presenting a petition to the queen on behalf of those already in prison. Later in

---

[56] Brook, 259-60.
[57] Brook, 261.
[58] James 1: 2-4 (Geneva Bible 1599)
[59] CCEd. Variant spelling is Rudyard.
[60] NRO, Visitation Book, Fol. 33. Date: 1 Sep 1590.
[61] NRO, Visitation Book, Fol. 33. Date: 2 Oct 1590.

court, Thomas Stone identified the other delegates in attendance at this *conference*. He mentioned Cartwright, Chark, Travers, Egerton, Barber and Gardiner of London, Barbon [*sic*] and Fludd from Northamptonshire, Oxenbridge from Warwickshire, Gellibrand from Oxford, Culverwell for Essex, plus some others. Vicar Thomas Barber later confirmed some of them in his September court appearance.[62]

Finally, Thomas Cartwright surfaced in London in response to his May summons. His examination began on the 3rd of October in the consistory at St. Paul's Cathedral.[63] Court officials had changed the venue without notice. Obviously, they sought to minimize disruptions from Puritan supporters. Thirty-one articles were filed against Cartwright.[i] Four key charges were: 1) that he had forsaken and renounced his orders as a deacon of the Church of England; 2) that he had not followed the *Book of Common Prayer*; that he penned or procured to be penned, all or some part of the book, entitled *Disciplina Ecclesiae sacraverbo Dei descripta*; 3) he recommended the same to the judgment and censure of others; and 4) that he doth know who were the writers, printers, or dispersers of the writings under the name Martin Marprelate.

Cartwright refused the *ex-officio* oath and did not answer the articles. By late October, he was imprisoned in the Fleet. This was "a staggering blow for the Puritan cause."[64] The Puritans now faced an untenable situation. Most had been imprisoned for more than six months. The ministers' livelihoods had been stripped away with no apparent means to support their families. Without an intervention on their behalf, they had little hope of being released from prison. Accordingly, in December 1590 and January 1591, "the Puritan prisoners sent two petitions begging for their release to the High Commissioners. Both petitions were summarily rejected."[65]

Now even more desperate for freedom, the Puritan ministers solicited their godly friends in their congregations to petition Queen Elizabeth for deliverance. Edmund Snape, Edward Lord, Humfrey Fen, Daniel Wyght, and William Proudlove wrote to their congregations, suggesting that course of action. Banned for life the previous July and still in prison, Snape appealed to Northampton's mayor and to his former congregants to meet with Weedon Bec and Wolston, for "some pity may be had of us and our people."[66]

These petitions languished. As January 1591 ended, Archbishop Whitgift and Lord Chancellor Hatton had finally lost patience with the Puritan ministers. Unable to break their will, the High Commission had reached a legal stalemate. On 3 February 1591, Whitgift and Hatton drafted a document alleging these ministers acted with "certain seditious opinions,

---

[62] Collinson, 412.

[63] The Chapel of St Michael and St George, off the south aisle, was originally the consistory court in which cases of ecclesiastical law were heard. "St. Paul's Cathedral: History and Collections," *St. Paul's Cathedral*. Viewed 1 December 2021. https://www.stpauls.co.uk/history-collections/history/explore-the-cathedral/the-chapels.

[64] Collinson, 411.

[65] Collinson, 414.

[66] Collinson, 414.

practices, and intentions; and expressing their own opinions jointly, subject always to Her Majesty's most grave and excellent wisdom."

> These enormities being so weighty and aggravated with so intolerable disobedience in refusing to be examined upon oath, it seemeth unto us that this matter is of as great and dangerous consequence to the Commonwealth as anything that of long time hath happened.

> And therefore, for further discovery of their courses, and an exemplary punishment to the terror of others, it is proper to be brought to a speedy and public hearing (upon bill and interrogatories) in the Star-Chamber against some of the principal dealers; and the penalty thereof fit to be as grievous as by any order and precedent of that Court hath been, or may be, inflicted.

> And because, for misdemeanors of far less quality and danger, we find by precedents showed unto us, that banishment and condemnation to the galleys have been imposed, therefore, for many considerations we think perpetual banishment to be the most fit punishment in this case, so that it be into some such remote place as there shall be no danger of their return, nor of disturbance of the common quiet of the realm by their writings or otherwise.[67]

In early May 1591, Thomas Cartwright was again summoned by the High Commissioners. On a Saturday afternoon, the location was undisclosed "lest any that favored Mr. Cartwright's cause should come in."[68] Whisked away to the Bishop of London's palace, Cartwright's interrogation was "arranged without warning and with some secrecy in Alymer's house by St. Paul's."[69] The Bishop of London, John Alymer, again asked Cartwright to swear the *ex-officio* oath. Once again, Thomas Cartwright refused. Instead, he pleaded with the commissioners to relieve his suffering in prison from the gout and sciatica. His pleas were summarily dismissed. The bishop then chastised Cartwright with a long diatribe. Once again, after additional sparring with his adversary, Bishop Alymer demanded, "Take the oath." Cartwright replied,

> C: Before I come to the matter of the oath, let me be received to answer the grievous charges given partly against myself, and partly against myself and others; the charges uttered by Mr. Attorney, but especially those uttered by your lordship.
>
> A: Nay you shall not answer to anything but only to the oath, whether you will take it or no, to answer interrogatories under the Articles which you have seen.
>
> C: A hard course it is, my lord, to give *open* charges, and the same very grievous, such as your lordship hath but just now charged me withal, and yet to shut me up from all answer of them.
>
> A: Answer first touching the oath. Then shall you be admitted to answer the charges which I have brought.[70]

---

[67] Hopkins, 380-1.
[68] Hopkins, 383.
[69] Collinson, 416.
[70] Hopkins, 384-5.

After more back and forth, the debate with Cartwright reached its climax with both Dr. Bancroft and Bishop Alymer involved.

B: Authority you had none, and therefore could not use it.

C: We might have had ecclesiastical jurisdiction of reproof, suspension, excommunication, degradation—as we have been untruly charged to have done—had we *thought it lawful* for us to do so.

B: Take the oath, and then we will tell you wherein your answer is short and requireth addition.

C: So, then, an oath shall not make an end to the controversy?

B: Mr. Cartwright, think you thus to go away into the clouds? Or think you that you have to deal with men of so small judgment that we see not what is your drift? Do not we know from whom you draw your Discipline and church government? Do we not know their judgments and practice, which is to bring in further reformation by force and arms?

C: My meaning is not to hide myself in the clouds touching this matter, for it is one to which I have made a plain and direct denial. And if anything on this point of force and arms be doubtful, I will make it as plain, Mr. Doctor, as you can set it down. But I do now perceive that, if others of the Court be of like mind with yourself, all purgation of ourselves by oath will be in vain; for whatsoever we may depose, yet it will be answered that you known our drift well enough.

A: Mr. Cartwright, I ask you once again, will you take the oath?

C: I cannot.

A: Enter an act of that answer, Mr. Register.

C: Permit me to remind your lordship of your lordship's promise, that if I would first answer touching the oath (which I have done), I should be admitted to answer the charges given against me, which I am fully ready to do.

A: I have no leisure to hear your answer. If you would answer, do it by private letter.[71]

As the long debate neared its end, an exasperated Cartwright once again replied why he refused to affirm the oath. He exclaimed:

I lay the chief strength of my refusal upon the law of God; next upon the law of the land, which, in some men's judgment professing the skill of the laws, do out warrant such proceeding.[72]

Frustrated by their inability to break this Puritan's will and resolve, the High Commissioners "decided to transfer the trial of nine of the leaders to the more powerful Star Chamber." With the draft already prepared by Archbishop Whitgift and Hatton, the High Commission "referred both the persons and the cause" of these Puritans to the Star Chamber. This higher court had a "larger power to inflict punishment."[73]

---

[71] Hopkins, 388-90.
[72] Hopkins, 386.
[73] Hopkins, 380.

Introduced at the end of May, the bill contained thirty-four articles. It was taken into consideration led by Attorney-General Popham and Serjeant Puckering. As anticipated, the Star Chamber accepted the bill and proceeded to trial with grave concerns about the Puritan ministers. Even though the imprisoned Puritans "retained some powerful support in government circles," the venue shift indicated a significant escalation in what lay ahead.[74] Events were careening beyond what anyone anticipated. But the Puritans on trial kept their faith. With the stakes so high, they knew they needed God's grace and all His providential help available. Perhaps they prayed for God to perform a miracle, as the Apostle Paul and his disciple Silas experienced when imprisoned in Phillipi:

> Nowe at midnight Paul and Silas prayed and sung Psalmes unto God: and the prisoners heard them. And suddenly there was a great earthquake, so that the foundation of the prison was shaken; and by and by all the doors opened, and every man's bands were loosed.[75]

---

[74] Shiels, 59.
[75] Acts 16: 25-26 (Geneva Bible 1599)

CHAPTER 3

ON TRIAL IN THE STAR CHAMBER

On 13 May 1591, nine Puritans first appeared before the Star Chamber Court accompanied by their attorney, Nicolas Fuller, to hear the charges. Fuller "was a counsellor at law much employed by the Privy Council, and one of the most diligent Puritan lawyers."[1] As the Star Chamber Court presided at trial, this expanded council was, in effect, both judge and jury. Those judging the Puritans' fate consisted of Lord Chancellor Hatton, Lord Treasurer Buckhurst, Chancellor of the Exchequer Sir John Fortescue, Dr. Richard Bancroft, Dr. Richard Cosin, and Sir John Popham, Attorney General. While Archbishop John Whitgift was not a juror, as the queen's "favorite" he was a major influencer. With Lord Burghley absent, Sir Francis Knollys, a Privy Councillor, took notes for Burghley.

> The main charge against them was that they meant to overthrow the established government of the Church, and *by force* to bring in, in the room thereof, their own Discipline.[2]

> With attorney Fuller advising, the Puritans stood firm and resisted affirming the *ex-officio* oath. The questioning was suspended, but they were recalled for a second round on the 17th of May. On this, the last day of the Easter term, the Puritans steadfastly resisted and stood firm. Their second set of answers was judged to be "in many points as imperfect as before."[3]

As May ended, the Star Chamber Court judges were totally dissatisfied with the Puritans' answers. The court entered a formal bill against Cartwright and the eight Puritan ministers, including William Proudlove. They were charged with illegal assemblies, defamation of ecclesiastical governance, refusal to follow the established form of Common Prayer, guidelines for administering the sacraments, and refusing the oath *ex-officio*.

The Star Chamber Court expanded the list of interrogatories from those conducted previously by the High Commission Court. They required each of the imprisoned Puritans to submit sworn, truthful written responses to each interrogatory. This set the stage for another climactic round of courtroom drama and legal maneuvering. From the combined efforts of these English courts and their agents in the past year, more than eighty Puritans had been interrogated. Now, nine Puritans represented the entire movement. They were left to ponder their fate, write answers to the interrogatories, and pray for deliverance. For the moment, there was not much else they could do, as they awaited their next court appearance from their respective prison cells.

---

[1]   Collinson, 416-17, 519.
[2]   Hopkins, 382-3.
[3]   Collinson, 420.

In the Baliff's house of St. Katherines
    William Proudlove of Weedon Bec in Northamptonshire
    Edmund Snape of Northampton in Northamptonshire
    Melancton Jewell, of Thornebury in Devonshire

In the White Lion in Southwark
    Edward Lord of Wolston in Warwickshire

In the Fleet
    Thomas Cartwright of Warwickshire

In the Clink
    Humfrey Fen of Coventry in Warwickshire
    Andrew King of Culworth in Northamptonshire
    John Payne of Hanbury in Staffordshire
    Daniel Wyght of Stretton in Warwickshire

With apprehension and reflection, these nine Puritans considered their upcoming trials. What tribulations loomed ahead for these brave men? Only God knew. Three ministers, confined together in the Baliff's house of St. Katherines—William Proudlove, Edmund Snape, and Melancton Jewel—certainly would have met when at liberty in the garden to compare interrogatory notes. They no doubt searched Scripture carefully. And the same was likely true for the four prisoners in the Clink. As they prayed together, they would have found comfort and encouragement in these Bible verses.

> But before all these, they shall lay their hands on you, and persecute *you*, delivering you up to the assemblies, and into prisons, and bring you before Kings and rulers for my Name's sake. And this shall turn to you, for a testimonial. Lay it up therefore in your hearts, that ye cast not beforehand what ye shall answer. For I will give you a mouth, and wisdom where against all your adversaries shall not be able to speak nor resist.[4]

The original questions in the interrogatories no longer exist, but the Puritans' answers do. A designated court scribe recorded the details of the interrogatory responses, providing documentation of the court proceedings.[5] Two "lesser schedule" interrogatories were added without notice at the examination's beginning. Those were followed by forty-three "larger schedule" ones!

To convey the dynamics of the court process, original record transcriptions of primary source images are provided for the first two interrogatories along with a modernized and corrected translation. The italicized version is the original transcription, and the regular

---

[4] Luke 21:12-15 (Geneva Bible 1599)
[5] STAC 5A/56/1. All citations in this section are from this record set. Special acknowledgement to Simon Neal for photographing and transcribing these valuable primary sources.

font is a slightly modernized translation.[6] After the first two interrogatories, the original transcriptions are eliminated making it easier to follow each interrogatory's meaning.

On 8 June 1591, the Star Chamber Court began its examinations of the imprisoned Puritans. One at a time, they were called into court. First examined was Edward Lord. He was noted as "the late preacher of Wolston" in Warwickshire and "now prisoner in the White Lyon." Lord, after being sworn to truthfulness, responded to the first two lesser schedule Interrogatories:

> *He sayth That he hath not spoke[n] taught or preached anye such ~~matter in effecte words~~ matter as ~~ys be~~ is menc[i]oned in the Interrog[atory] to his nowe remembraunce ~~of him this def[endant]~~*

He sayeth that he hath not spoken taught or preached any such matter as is mentioned in the Interrogatory to his now remembrance.

> *This def[endant] sayth that the sev[er]all l[ett]res conteyned in the ~~lij^th and liij^th~~ 52 and 53 pages of the booke nowe shewed unto him this def[endant] att the tyme of this his exa[m] i[na]c[i]on be (as he verely thincketh in his Conscyence) of the proper handwriting of this def[endant] ~~And but~~ howbeit he doth take the 3 l[ett]re menc[i]oned in the ~~liiij^th~~ 54 page nowe shewed unto him ~~in the same page~~ not to be of his proper hande writing nor his l[ett]re but the iiij^th l[ett]re next following conteyned in the ~~lv^th~~ 55 page he thincketh in his Conscyence to be his owne l[ett]re and of his owne hande writinge And he also taketh the vth l[ett]re menc[i]oned in the ~~lvj^th~~ 56 page ~~allso~~ nowe shewed unto him to be also his l[ett]re and of his owne ~~proper~~ hand writing. Butt he sayth ~~allso~~ having l[ett]re menc[i]oned in the 57 ~~lvij^th~~ ~~Interr[ogatory]~~ page of the s[ai]d ~~same~~ booke shewed unto him as aforesaid is not ~~to be~~ his l[ett]re or of his handwriting as he thincketh verely in his conscience.*

This defendant sayeth that the several letters contained in the 52nd and 53rd pages of the book now showed unto him this defendant at the time of this his examination be (as he verily thinketh in his Conscience) of the proper handwriting of this defendant how be it in the 54th page now showed unto him not to be of his proper handwriting nor his letter but the 4th letter next following contained in the 55th page he thinketh in his Conscience to be his own letter and of his own handwriting And he also taketh the 5th letter mentioned in the 56th page now showed unto him to be also his letter and of his own handwriting. But he sayeth having letter mentioned in the 57th page of the said book showed unto him as aforesaid is not his letter or of his handwriting as he thinketh verily in his conscience.

As indicated, Edward Lord is shown a book of letters and notes with many pages. These are most likely taken from letters confiscated or notes taken from parties of interest interviewed by court agents investigating Puritan activities. In court, Lord's examination lasted the entire day. The court then recessed for one full day. Rather than report all of Lord's answers here, the second Puritan's responses to the same interrogatories are next included, with additional questions which add layers of new information. Throughout this section,

---

6   Author's Note: *The original transcription is included first* then the author's translation. Notice the crossed-out words indicating corrections to the Puritans' submissions and corrected during the interrogatory in court.

the process continues without repeating the same interrogatories until all examinations are completed.

On the 10th of June, the next Puritan examined is noted as Daniel Wyght, "the late preacher of Stretton" in Warwickshire and "now prisoner in the Clynke." Daniel Wyght is a Puritan of great interest to the Star Chamber Court. He moderated the Warwickshire *classis*. His notes, discovered by the court's agents in Edmund Snape's personal papers confiscated in the search for the printing press of the *Martin Marprelate* tracts, provided the court with much detail about the Puritan *classis*, *classes*, and *conferences*. The court likely considered Wyght one of the Puritan leaders of their cause. At the beginning of his examination, he is examined first with the same two questions contained in "the lesser schedule."

> To the <u>first</u> Interrogatory whereupon this defendant is appointed to be first examined which is contained in the lesser schedule he sayeth That for so much as the same Interrogatory doth contain matter clearly out of the Information in his understanding he thinketh not good by the favor of this honorable Court to make answer there unto.

In the second lesser-schedule interrogatory following, notice how much of original response submitted has been crossed out by the court scribe. This graphically shows how dynamic the court's interrogation was, and how each Puritan demanded accuracy in reporting his responses when changes were required. In addition, the brackets indicate words filled in by the transcriber to complete the words abbreviated by the scribe. As Daniel Wyght testifies, he looks directly at a book filled with letters and notes taken from previous interviews of those providing evidence about him and making corrections to them.

> *To the second Inter[rogatory] this def[endant] sayth that the l[ett]res conteyned in the 60 61 62 63 64 65 66 67 68 69 70 71 72 and 73 pages of the booke nowe shewed unto this def[endant] at the tyme of this his exa[m]i[n]ac[i]on be of his owne hand writing ~~but~~ And that the 74 page of the same booke is not of his said writing, ~~but~~ howbeit ~~thincketh sayth that~~ he sayth thatt the 75 page of the s[ai]d booke ~~is of his hand wr~~ and the first p[ar]te or syde of the page of paper quoted ys are both of the hand writing of this def[endant], but the first side of the 77 page is not of his handwriting ~~but confesseth~~ saying nev[er]theles that he had the same amongest his other writings but howe he came thereby or by whose delyvery he remembreth not, but the other syde therof is of his owne handwriting, ~~but~~ and the folded paper of the s[ai]d booke being quoted 78 is of his owne hand writing as hee verily thincketh in his Conscience ~~And this def[endant] sayth that the matters conteyned in the s[ai]d 60 and 61 pages of the s[ai]d booke were pryvately for theire better informac[i]on advysed and debated of by and betwixt this def[endant] Mr Cartwright Mr Fenne and Mr Lord and others whom he thincketh not good to nameand himself Bycause they are not named p[ar]tyes of the s[ai]d informac[i]on And~~ Butt for the tymes and occac[i]ons of the wryting of the same matters (otherwise then as yt appeareth by the thinges themselfes) this def[endant] doth not remember*

To the <u>second</u> Interrogatory this defendant sayeth that the letters contained in pages 60-73 of the book now showed unto this defendant at the time of this his examination be of his own handwriting And that the 74th page of the same book is not of his said writing, how be it he sayeth that the 75th page of the said book and the first part or side of the page of paper quoted us are both of the handwriting of this defendant, but the first side of the 77th page is not of his handwriting saying nevertheless that he had the same amongst his other writings but how he came thereby or by whose delivery he remember not, but the other side thereof is of his own handwriting, and the folded paper of the said book being quote 78th is of his own hand writing as he verily thinketh in his Conscience. But for the times and occasions of the writing of the same matters (otherwise then as it appeared by the things themselves) the defendant doth not remember.

The book pages shown to Wyght differ from those shown to the first Puritan, Edward Lord. A margin note indicates the interrogatories then continue with "the larger schedule."[7]

To the 1st Interrogatory contained in the same larger schedule This defendant denyeth that he this defendant or to his knowledge any other person or persons have taught affirmed or allowed any such matter as in mentioned in the Interrogatory.

To the 1st 2nd and 3rd Interrogatory this defendant sayeth that he hath not taught maintained or affirmed to his remembrance any such matter or matters as is or be mentioned in the same several Interrogatories And being asked whether he hath allowed of the same matters or not he sayeth for that the same matters be of judgement he is not to answer there unto.

To the 4th and 5th Interrogatories he forbeareth to answer for that the same several Interrogatories do not contain matter of facts saying that the same are matters of judgment only, and therefore not to be answered by this defendant.

To the 6th Interrogatory this defendant doth deny that he this defendant or to his knowledge any other person or persons have maintained taught or affirmed any such matter as is mentioned in the article.

To the 7th Interrogatory this defendant sayeth that albeit he taketh himself not bound to render what he hath taught affirmed or preached touching the matters in the Interrogatory mentioned yet for the satisfying of this honorable Court this defendant sayeth that he hath not taught maintained or affirmed any such matter as is mentioned in the Interrogatory, But whether in any letter or letters by him written any such matter of distinguishment of churches in this realm as is mentioned in the Interrogatory be Contained therein or not he taketh himself not bound to answer.

And so forth through the larger schedule, it continued for Daniel Wyght. After the 43rd interrogatory all participants—the court judges, advisors, and scribe; the Puritans and their advising attorneys; as well as any others involved in this courtroom drama—certainly needed another day of rest. Why? Because the Star Chamber Court next continued with their most sought-after Puritan examinee, Thomas Cartwright.

---

[7]   From this point forward throughout this section, the court Interrogatories continue with the slightly modernized translations.

On the 12th of June, Cartwright appeared in court. He was not designated as a preacher and was noted to be the "now prisoner in the Fleet." After declaring he was "not bound to answer" in response to interrogatories one through seven, he replied with a different tact and tone:

> To the 8th Interrogatory the defendant sayeth that he hath not in any sort propounded, treated of, debated or Concluded That if the Civil magistrate after all ordinary and sufficient means used by petitions and supplications etc. shall refuse to admit their discipline or government by pastors doctors elders and such like That then the ministers may allure the people unto it or otherwise put the same in practice or they may be able or use any means for the establishing thereof as is supposed by the article.

After denying any subversive actions as accused, Cartwright turns the question asked into an admonition. In essence, he chastises the authorities' lack of response to petitions and supplications made on behalf of the people the ministers serve. Cartwright then states that, without a negative response from ecclesiastical authorities, ministers may put into practice in their congregations and use any means for establishing what the interrogatory is trying to justify and promote. In other words, no response is a tacit approval for the Puritans to proceed with their desired reforms.

To the next two interrogatories, Cartwright declined to answer. But he did answer the following one partially.

> To the 11th Interrogatory this defendant sayeth That he hath seen a book or treatise so entitled or called as in mentioned in the Interrogatory But whether this that be now showed unto him at the time of this his examination be a true Copy or transcript thereof or not the defendant doth not know. And being examined when, where, and by whom the said treatise or any part thereof was devised penned corrected or reformed he sayeth that he is not bound to make any answer thereunto for that he is not particularly Charged therewith by the said information, and for that the same as charged upon diverse persons indefinitely by the said information saying further that the first offence wherewith this defendant is particularly charged by the said information is alleged by the same information to be done after the devising and setting down of the said book.

The next interrogatories probed Cartwright's participation in a conference on 30 September 1586. It is possible the court listed the wrong year. Cartwright was known to participate in September *conferences* at Cambridge in other years.

> To the 12th Interrogatory this defendant sayeth That he remembers since the last day of September in the 28th year of her Majesty's Reign that now is the time otherwise . . . he remembers not. This defendant assembled himself with others whom he is not bound to name as he thinketh to the end in a quiet and peaceable manner to treat and debate of the matter contained in the said book of discipline. But at what or how many places, or how often or with whom he did so assemble treat and debate this defendant thinketh himself not bound to answer upon Consideration had of the said information.

To the 13th Interrogatory this defendant sayeth that since the last day of September he approved and allowed of the said book in sort as doh appear by his subscription to the articles annexed as he remembered to the said book and no otherwise and this defendant did agree to the same articles and as he thinketh did subscribe also to the same articles. But as touching the referring or altering of the said book or any part thereof or for any further to the said Interrogatory this defendant taketh himself not bound to answer in respect the same be matters not to his charge by the said information.

To the 14th Interrogatory this defendant sayeth as he said to the Interrogatory next precedent. And further or more to this Interrogatory he taketh himself not bound to answer saying he sayeth further. That he did ask to put two points of the book of discipline in execution. That to follow the order of preachers set down in the said book of discipline, and the other to observe the order of meeting expressed also in the same book so far forth as the same might stand with the peace of the Church now established in England and the Laws of the land and not otherwise or further.

Cartwright's answer to the 14th interrogatory in his last sentence is very important. He stresses at the end that "the same book . . . might stand with the peace of the Church now established in England and the Laws of the land." He clearly states here that nothing he has done could be construed as seditious or treasonous without using those exact words.

Cartwright declined to answer the 15th Interrogatory claiming it was dependent upon his answer to the "next precedent," in others words the next interrogatory response.

To the 16th Interrogatory this defendant sayeth that the defendant hath put in practice the performance of the said two points mentioned in his answer to the fourteenth Interrogatory precedent so conveniently for the most part as the same might stand with the peace of the Church of England now established and also with the laws of the land how be it the . . . to testify their freedom in the use of the said two points he sayeth they carried from the orders contained in the chapters thereof and that in these things which they might very conveniently have performed And he sayeth that he did no otherwise perform the order of meeting them as his affairs did permit.

And further sayeth that it is true that it was set down in the said book of discipline That none should give voices in their assemblies but such as had first subscribed to the said discipline which he sayeth was set down as A matter of their judgment, only and that the establishing thereof was to be referred unto the authority of her majesty and the parliament, for Confirmation whereof he sayeth that the greater number of these that gave voices in the said meetings did to his knowledge never subscribe to the said discipline.

And also sayeth that there have not been any appeal or appeals made or seen of as intended to be made by any person or persons from any less assembly to a greater to the knowledge of the defendant And to all the rest of the pointes of the Interrogatories he leaveth to answer as taking . . . to be impertinent to the matters of offences wherewith he is particularly Charged by the said information.

In his answer, Cartwright reiterates and articulates four key principles as part of his rebuttal.

1. What he did "might stand with the peace of the Church of England;"
2. That it was within the "laws of the land;"
3. That they testified to "their freedom in the use of the said two points;" and
4. That what they did "carried from the orders."

The first point emphasized Cartwright's desire to work within the established Church. The second emphasized that what the Puritans were doing was legal under English common law. The third stated a narrow version of the concept of religious freedom. The fourth stressed that their actions were carried out because their calling and ordination as ministers was from God.

As his answers echoed throughout the Star Chamber, Thomas Cartwright articulated—perhaps for the first time—major themes for what became the Great Migration of Puritans to New England. This migration began in 1620 with the voyage of the *Mayflower* and lasted through 1640. A total of some 21,000 English subjects emigrated to the shores of America, with about 13,000 arriving between 1630-1640. Even more significant, Cartwright's four principles, articulated in 1591, resonate with and foreshadow founding principles used 185 years later in 1776 when the leaders of thirteen British Colonies in America declared their independence from the British Empire.

Cartwright's examination continued throughout the day.[8] By the similarities in the Puritans' answers and phrases duplicated by the three examinees so far, it is obvious there was coordination and preparation between them. And evidence of coordination in the Puritans' responses would continue. They seem to have made sure their answers were consistent and presented a unified stance.

Most likely, they were able to discuss each day's court appearances while at liberty in the prison yard or when visited by outsiders. In addition, their legal advisors certainly coached them on how best to answer these interrogatories. The Puritans walked a fine line of disclosing information truthfully that would not convict them of treasonous or seditious acts against her Majesty. They answered what they could and declined to answer everything else.

The following day, Humfrey Fen was sworn in and described as the "late preacher of Coventry and now prisoner in the Clink." As with Daniel Wyght, Fen was questioned with the lesser schedule questions first. He was shown a book, presumably the same one as in Wyght's interrogation. In the second interrogatory, he was questioned but shown different pages than Wyght, starting on page 45 through 49. Fen testified that two pages matched his handwriting but the other two did not.

For questions one through nine from the larger schedule of Interrogatories, Fen said they were not directly related to his charge and felt either not compelled to answer, or not bound to answer. The next few questions were answered congruently with Cartwright's

---

8   The entire set of Interrogatories of these nine Puritans is planned to be offered in a separate publication. Check with the author at https://wwwpassionategenealogist.org.

replies. Fen also did not answer two following Interrogatories. This reinforces the consistent pattern of the Puritans' answers. Fen's next answer illustrates his knowledge regarding the implementation of the concepts of Presbyterianism promoted by Cartwright.

> To the 19th Interrogatory this defendant doth deny that he this defendant or to his knowledge any of his fellow ministers did direct or put in use the authority or power of an eldership or presbytery or of any part thereof by pastors doctors elders deacons widows or any of them or by such like or by or under these or any other names or titles as is supposed by the article.

Fen's description of his sermons in the following two Interrogatories illustrates a typical Puritan worship service, and how it varied from Church of England services.

> To the 20th Interrogatory this defendant sayeth that before his sermons he did make a Confession of sins, and a prayer for the fruitful delivery and receiving of the word and after the sermon a blessing for the word delivered, and likewise A prayer for all estates, and ended with the Lord's prayer and so forth and no otherwise this defendant did ordinarily observe the order of the said book of discipline in that behalf.

> To the 21st Interrogatory this defendant deny that he this defendant did when he administered any of the sacraments put in use the form or order-prescribed in the Chapters of the same book *de reliquis liturgie officijs*[9] or any part there of or according to any part of the form prescribed or used in Geneva or in any other Church which they admitted such discipline by the prescript of any of the Chapters of the same book by the prescript or rule of any church admitting such discipline. That since the last day of September he approved and allowed of the said book in sort as doth appear by his subscription to the articles annexed as he remembered to the said book.

Then, Fen continued answering, or refusing to answer, until he finished his entire set of forty-five interrogatories. It was another exhausting day of courtroom drama.

On the 14th of June, Edmund Snape was sworn in as the "late preacher of Northampton and now prisoner in the Bailiffs house of St. Catherines [*sic*]." Snape's refusals to answer many Interrogatories used the same or similar phrases heard in previous testimonies: they were "matters of judgment, not of fact;" "impertinent to the matters charged upon him by the said information;" and he is "not bound to answer to this Interrogatory."

In response to later Interrogatories, Snape gave full statements to a few questions, but only to deny the action associated with the question which sought to entrap him.

> To the 28th Interrogatory This defendant sayeth that he this defendant did not in the year of our Lord God 1587 meet at any assembly or assemblies within the Towne or County of Cambridge to the purpose to Confer or treat of any matters of Church government And further or otherwise to the Interrogatory being particularly examined thereupon he thinketh himself not bound to answer.

---

9   Translation: of the rest of the liturgical offices.

In the next Interrogatory, he says he does not know of any assembly within the town or county of Cambridge where these matters mentioned were propounded, treated, or concluded. In the following two Interrogatories, he states he was not present at any assembly within or near the Town of Warwick in the year of our Lord God 1588 when and where the points mentioned in the 29th Interrogatory were treated the same. Then he emphatically states he is "not bound to answer" further on any of the final Interrogatories. Once Snape finished, the court concluded another full day of exhaustive examining. But the Star Chamber Court decided to pick up the pace.

On the following day, the 15th of June, the court moved swiftly and confidently. This is the first time multiple prisoners were examined on the same day. Andrew King, the "late preacher of Culworth from the County of Northampton and now prisoner in the Clink" was sworn in first to testify. He and William Proudlove, who was scheduled to testify next, had served in neighboring parishes and convened together in the Daventry *Classis*. That may explain why they were called to testify on the same day.

King's court appearance started with the two lesser schedule questions. He declined the first and answered the second. As did others before him, he testified he was not bound to answer any of the first nine Interrogatories in the larger schedule. In the 10th Interrogatory, he admitted meeting with some other ministers that last day of September. They considered how they could exhibit supplications to Her Majesty and Parliament. From there through the 32nd interrogatory, he replied many times he was "not bound to answer."

In the 33rd Interrogatory, King testified he had "not compiled any treatise in writing or print to set forth the ecclesiastical government in the said *Book of Discipline* draft or any part thereof." He chose not to answer the 34th. On the 35th, he denied that he "since the first day of November moved or persuaded any person or persons to embrace allow or submit themselves to that form of discipline ecclesiastical Comprised in the said *Book of Discipline* or any part as pretended by the article."

The final phrase "pretended by the article" is a bold statement. He is accusing the court—responsible for drawing up Interrogatories—of making up evidence. That surely indicates a Puritan who trusts God to protect him from all harm! That is the first time that phrase was used and was unique to King. After he finished his interrogatories, it was William Proudlove's turn.

William Proudlove was noted and sworn in as the "late preacher of Weedon within the County of Northampton and now prisoner in the Bayliff's House of St. Katherine's."[10] As had several before him, Proudlove declined to answer the lesser schedule's first two Interrogatories. In the larger-schedule Interrogatories, he also used similar words and phrases echoing previous testimonies before him. He stated he was "not bound to answer" the first three Interrogatories. Similarly, in the 4th and 5th Interrogatories, he was "not bound to answer" because they were "matters of the preamble of rehearsal, of judgment, and not of fact." That answer was unique to Proudlove. Like King before him, Proudlove made a

---

[10] The change of spelling for Katherine, instead of Catherine as was previously recorded, might indicate a different scribe notating the interrogations at this point.

courageous statement and put his faith in God's protection. What exactly did he mean by "the preamble of rehearsal?" One interpretation could be that he was accusing the Crown's officials of pre-judging the Puritans' guilt or innocence, rehearsing their approach, and therefore violating legal standards without judging the actual evidence. The addition "of judgment, not of fact" was an incredibly gutsy stance for a minister to take with the Star Chamber Court officials—some of the most powerful men in all of England!

As did his Puritan colleagues, Proudlove gave the same basic responses for the interrogatories six through twelve. He testified that he had considered the *Book of Discipline* matters but "did not subscribe nor submit himself" to it or any part of it nor did he "put any part into execution."

In the following interrogatory, Proudlove describes the pattern of his Weedon Bec worship services. These are what the Cole family and all their fellowship would have experienced.

> To the 20th Interrogatory He sayeth that he used before his sermon a Confession of . . . and a prayer of his fruitful delivery and receiving of the word, and a prayer of all estates after his sermon, but he sayeth that there is not any form of such prayers particularly described in the said book neither did this defendant use the same particulars in respect of anything contained in the said book or in respect of the prescript order or rule of the said book but only voluntarily. And further or otherwise he taketh himself not bound to answer.

Andrew King of Culworth had testified before Proudlove on this same interrogatory with a very similar worship service pattern, as did Humfrey Fen before them. All three Puritans were indeed reform-minded, godly ministers. Proudlove's examination continued:

> To the 22nd 23rd and 24th Interrogatories this defendant (under correction) leaves to answer, for that the matters mentioned in the Interrogatory are in the defendant's judgment indefinite and without certain limitation and besides are (as this defendant taketh them) not charged upon the defendant by the said information.

> To the 25th 26th and 27th Interrogatories this defendant under reformation taketh himself not bound to answer for that the matters therein supposed be not (in this defendant's understanding) laid unto his charge as matters of offence by the said information.

> To the 28th and 29th Interrogatories this defendant sayeth that he was never at any assembly or assemblies within the Towne or County of Cambridge to Confer or Treat of any the matters in either of these Interrogatories mentioned neither doth this defendant know of any such matters treated or debated of in any assembly within the Towne or County of Cambridge or be particularly mentioned in the said 29th Interrogatory.

> To the 30th and 31st Interrogatories this defendant sayeth that he was never in the assembly or assemblies within or near the Towne of Warwick to treat of any matters of discipline or Church government or of any the matters mentioned in the said 29th article And further to either of these Interrogatories he taketh himself not bound to answer.

To the 32nd Interrogatory this defendant (under reformation) taketh himself not bound to answer for that the matter of this Interrogatory is as he thinketh impertinent to the matters of offence wherewith this defendant is particularly charged by the said information.

To the 33rd Interrogatory this defendant sayeth that since the first day of November in the 30th year of her Majesty's Reign that now is he hath not written or printed anything to the advancing approving or setting fourth of the said manner of ecclesiastical government set forth in the said book of discipline or any part thereof But as touching what this defendant hath taught in that behalf for seeing as in the same his teaching there is no offence particularized in the said information he taketh himself by the favour of the said Court not bound to answer, neither doth he take himself bound to answer to the further privacy of this Interrogatory.

To the 34th Interrogatory (as the same is set down) this defendant taketh himself not bound to answer saying further that as he taketh it fully answered already to the information concerning the matter of this Interrogatory.

To the 35th Interrogatory this defendant sayeth that since the said first day of November he hath not moved or persuaded any person or persons to submit him or themselves to the said form of discipline ecclesiastical comprised in the said book of discipline or any parte thereof And further to the Interrogatory he taketh himself not bound to answer.

To the 36th Interrogatory this defendant sayeth That this defendant being Contented before her majesty's Comissioners ecclesiastical to answer unto the premises or some part of them this defendant was required by the said Comissioners to take his oath to answear to such articles as should be [ad]ministered to this defendant on her majesty's behalf concerning the matters for the which this defendant was so called before the said Comissioners And this defendant did refuse to take the same oath for such reasons as this defendant hath set down in his answer to the said information.

To the 37th Interrogatory this defendant (under reformation) taketh himself not bound to answer for that the Interrogatory doth not direct or tend to the effect of the Charge of the reformation in that behalf.

To the 38th Interrogatory this defendant sayeth that there was not any such supplication exhibited to her Majesty on the behalf of this defendant as is mentioned in this Interrogatory But this defendant sayeth that he this defendant sent out a letter to some of his hearers requesting them thereby to supplicate unto her Majesty for this defendant's enlargement[11] And further to this Interrogatory he taketh himself not bound to answer.

To the 39th Interrogatory this defendant sayeth as he said before to the Interrogatory next precedent And that he was not privy procuring nor consenting to the new writing of any

---

[11] "Enlargement" is a petition term often used by supplicants for increased liberty or a release from confinement.

petitions to be delivered to her Majesty neither did this defendant know of the new writing of any such petitions to be delivered to Her Majesty.

To the 40th Interrogatory this defendant for his own part doth deny the doing or Committing of any the offences in the same Interrogatory mentioned.

To the 41st Interrogatory this defendant of his own certain knowledge Cannot depose.

To the 42nd Interrogatory this defendant sayeth that he was not privy nor assenting to the matters of offence supposed by this Interrogatory.

To the 43rd Interrogatory he sayeth as he said before.

After William Proudlove's testimony concluded in the Star Chamber Court, the end of these examinations was in sight. The final two imprisoned Puritan ministers were examined the following day.

On the 16th of June, Melancton Jewell, the "late Preacher of Thornebury within the County of Devon and now prisoner in the Bayliff's house of St. Katherine," was first. He was followed by John Payne, the "late preacher of Hanbury within the County of Stafford, and now prisoner in the Clink."

These examinations revealed briefer answers than before. However, their answers were very much in line with those of their predecessors. They provide further indication of collaboration, coaching, and steadfastness on the part of the examinees and their advisors. Accusations were either denied, or the examinees declared they were not bound to answer. Why were these answers briefer than those before them? Perhaps they were not subjected to the same level of scrutiny by court officials. Or perhaps everyone was simply worn out by the experience. Or perhaps the prosecutors realized that their efforts would be in vain, having experienced the previous seven resolute Puritans before them. Regardless of the why, nine devout Puritans stood firm in the face of savvy inquisitors who grilled them relentlessly in the space of nine days. It must have been an intense experience for everyone.

In retrospect, the Star Chamber Court examiners did, in fact, extract relevant information from the Puritans. One also gets the sense that they were thwarted from obtaining as much information as they wanted. Certainly, everyone needed a break after this ordeal that ended on 16 June 1591. But that was not the end of it.

Three days later all nine Puritan ministers were recalled to the Star Chamber. All nine were re-examined on the same day! On the 19th of June, Thomas Cartwright was re-examined first. The scribe appeared challenged to keep up with the questioning. He crossed out numerous words and phrases to clarify the true meaning or intent of the interchange between Cartwright and his examiners, which Cartwright probably forced. Tension and frustration undoubtedly filled the room. It is obvious from the extensive crossed-out wording by the scribe.

To the third ~~Interr[ogatory] he sayeth~~ 4th, 5th. 9th. 10th, 11th, 13th, 15th and 23rd ~~xxiiij[th]~~ general Interrogatories this defendant being particularly re-examined thereunto (according to the …

of the judges) sayeth in everything as he said thereunto before upon his former examination, And otherwise or further to the same several Interrogatories of any of them he most humbly beseeches this honourable Court he may not be ~~Compelled~~ pressed to answer.

To the 24th general Interrogatory this defendant (being particularly re-examined thereupon) sayeth ~~in every~~ as before he hath said thereunto upon his former examination Adding thereunto nevertheless for the better satisfying of this honourable Court That he this defendant hath been in assemblies where ~~this poynte viz Thatt the ministry of suche in the Churche as are no preachers is no ministry~~ ~~was debated and treated of bar~~ ~~not concluded~~ all the pointes ~~poynted and~~ particularized in the Interrogatory (saving the last) were treated of and debated, but not answered or Concluded upon; And for the that last point which is touching the use of her Majesty's style in prayers at Sermons This defendant sayeth that he this defendant was not in any assembly or assemblies where ~~any such matters as be menc[i]oned in that~~ . . . ~~were~~ that point was debated treated of or concluded. And otherwise (then this) he most humbly prays this honourable Court that he may not be pressed to answer.

In the first half of examination, Cartwright continued to oblige the scribe to rewrite the record to satisfy Cartwright's attention to detail. Twice Cartwright required the phrase "compelled him to answer" be altered to read that the Court "pressed him to answer." For the second half of interrogatories, each question either received a denial or Cartwright refused to be pressured to answer. Cartwright's examination set the tone for the entire day. He was followed by Humfrey Fen who, in essence, refused to answer any re-examination question.

The third Puritan re-examined was Edmund Snape. His situation was different from the others, given that he was previously defrocked of his livelihood and suspended for life almost a year earlier. But as his re-examination unfolded, it was evident that his actions related directly to his support of the *Martin Marprelate* tracts and his oversight role in the *classes* and *conferences*. That made Snape unique among the nine. The Star Chamber Court could act on these charges where the High Commission Court could not. Once again, the large letter book was used in Snape's interrogatories. In the court's view, his re-examination provided irrefutable evidence of acts of sedition and treason.

Snape being Re-examined to the second special Interrogatory sayeth that the writings contained in the 83rd page of the book now showed unto this defendant at the time of this his Re-examination is not of the hand writing of this defendant, But the letter contained in the 84th page of the same book is of the defendant's handwriting and was written by this defendant upon such occasion as is mentioned in the same letter And the writing mentioned in the 85th page of the said book is (as this defendant taketh it of this defendant's own handwriting and that it was set down by this defendant upon some occasion of Conference by him said with sundry Brownists for their better satisfactions in the points debated betwixt them. And the letter mentioned in the 86th page of the same book is of the defendant's own handwriting And moreover this defendant sayeth that the letters contained in the 87th 88th and 89th pages of the said book be of the handwriting of this defendant and were written by him this defendant upon such occasions as are contained in the same several letters or writings And for the times when this defendant did so write the same letters or writings he referred himself to the several dates of the same letters or writings.

The examiners put forth evidence which Snape could not deny when his handwriting was identified. That he had discussed these issues with "sundry Brownists," the common term for Separatists, was important. In the other interrogatories presented to Snape, the examiners probed specific issues which he denied were discussed for purposes against her Majesty's reign. In his last statement, he directly denied any intent of sedition or treason. Throughout the rest of the examination, Snape repeated the same phrase multiple times: "I think it is not good to answer."

William Proudlove was next. He used the phrase "not good to answer" twice. To all other interrogatories, he denied that their purpose was against her Majesty's reign. As had Snape before him, Proudlove used the same phrase to deny any intent of sedition or treason.

In Daniel Wyght's re-examination, he stated the first few interrogatories were answered in his initial examination. But in two specific interrogatories, he revealed that he and three other Puritans on trial had participated in assemblies and collaborated on a paper.

> To the 10th Interrogatory this defendant sayeth that this defendant, Mr Cartwright, Mr Fenne [sic] and Mr Lord have been at diverse assemblies of ministers within these five years now past And that in the same assemblies the matter of discipline mentioned in the Interrogatory hath been treated and debated of amongst them, to the end nevertheless that the establishing thereof might be referred to her Majesty and the authority set over them before the same discipline should be put in practice And he sayeth that they gave notice thereof one to another by writing of letters and also by word of mouth when they met as occasion required And otherwise to the Interrogatory or to any part thereof he doth not answer.

> To the 24th Interrogatory he sayeth as before he hath said to the same Interrogatory Adding thereunto further That the matters contained in the paper of the defendants saide writing initialed *Acte Eventus Classiu Warwicensis*[12] and contained in the [*blank*] page of the said book showed unto him at the time of his last examination were propounded treated and debated of by this defendant, Mr Cartwright, Mr Fenne and Mr Lord as he thinketh and others whom he thinketh not good to name neither doth this defendant think good to set down the place where the same was so treated and debated of, but this defendant sayeth that the same was not debated or treated of in Warwick, neither were the same matters determined upon amongst them nor so much as allowed in judgment by them or any of them And otherwise to the Interrogatory or any parte thereof he thinketh not good to answer.

Wyght used the same phrase as did Proudlove multiple times: "I think it not good to answer." After Wyght finished, only one Interrogatory was required of the next Puritan.

> John Payne being re-examined to the first special Interrogatory upon the occasion of the writing of his letter sayeth That he took occasion to write the same letter to then tente[13]

---

[12] Translation: actual event Warwick *classis*, or actual meeting of the Warwick *classis*.

[13] "Tente" is a Medieval English term generally meaning to spread out a tent or pavilion for a tournament. It sometimes referred to securing a tentlike covering with ropes. "Middle English Compendium," *University*

that the said Mr Fludd should thereupon Confer with the learned preachers of London concerning the contents of this defendant's letter, and this defendant therewith affirm that he had not any disloyal, violent, or seditious meaning in the writing of the same letter.

After Payne, Melanchton Jewell declined to answer the only two Interrogatories presented to him. But following Jewell, Edward Lord started to answer the first three Interrogatories with statements reminiscent of Cartwright's answers.

Edward Lord being reexamined to the 3 general Interrogatories sayth that he hath not maintained or taught any such matter as is mentioned in the Interrogatory, but as touching what he hath allowed or doth allow thereof for that it is A matter of judgment and secret unto himself, he most humbly besecheth the honourable Corte he may not be pressed to answer.

After refusing to answer several following Interrogatories, Lord did answer the two final ones.

To the 23rd Interrogatory this defendant sayeth as he hath thereunto said upon his former examination Adding thereunto further that since the month of November in the 28th year of Her Majesty's Reign this defendant was at sundry meetings with certain ministers within the County of Warwick But at what place, or namely with what persons thereof did so assemble he this defendant thinketh not good to answer.

To the 24th Interrogatory concerning the general points of the first part of the same Interrogatory this defendant sayeth as he hath already said upon his former examination And further sayeth that in the assemblies before mentioned in which this defendant hath been present with other ministers of his own Country as aforesaid all the said particular pointes in the Interrogatory (saving only the last point for the use of her Majesty's style) and treated of in the same their assemblies were debated And upon such treaty and debate thereof had This defendant and the said other ministers left the resolution of each man's own private judgment thereof to himself, without any conclusion had thereupon But to the said last point That is to say concerning the use of her Majesty's style in their prayers at Sermons, This defendant thereunto sayeth that that point was not in debate treated or spoke amongst them And further or otherwise to the Interrogatory he thinketh not good to answer.

As summer was about to start in London, enough daylight remained to shed light on whatever he was about to say. Once again, the phrase "thinketh not good to answer" was used to close off this Puritan's testimony.

One final Puritan remained: Andrew King. To the first set of interrogatories, King reiterated he had already answered them in his initial examination. Then,

---

of Michigan Library. Viewed on 10 January 2023. https://quod.lib.unich.edu/middle-english-dictionary/dictionary/MED44838. In effect, Payne says he was attempting to spread the net broadly to establish support and consensus among the London preachers.

To the 10th Interrogatory the defendant sayeth as he said before upon his former examination to the same Interrogatory And that within these seven years now last past this defendant Mr Prowdlove [*sic*] and sometimes Mr Snape and diverse other ministers whose names he thinketh not good in Conscience to set down did at sundry places within this realm (which places also he thinketh not good to mention) assemble themselves to the purpose mentioned in his former answer to the same Interrogatory. And this defendant sayeth that they assembled themselves as aforesaid upon notice and advertisement of them . . . by messages and by word of mouth set where they met And further to the Interrogatory he thinketh not good to answer, more than before to the same Interrogatory he hath already answered.

King's answer to this 10th Interrogatory revealed information about both Proudlove and Snape that was not previously known. King, Proudlove, and sometimes Snape and diverse other ministers had met in assemblies set up by advertisement, word of mouth, or message in sundry places. His statement confirms the close working relationship between him and Proudlove, certainly fostered by the proximity of their parishes. And at times other ministers, including Snape, participated with them in these assemblies. The rest of King's responses resulted in no further information.

That was it. Nine Puritans re-examined in one day by the most powerful court in all of England. The result? From a legal standpoint, it seemed to be a stalemate with no clear winner. Apart from Snape, not proven were the charges of sedition and treason by the Puritans against her Majesty Queen Elizabeth.

However, the nine Puritans were still imprisoned. Was it worth the effort?

CHAPTER 4

NINE IN NEVER-NEVER LAND

DIOCESE VISITATIONS

Two weeks after the inconclusive outcome from the Star Chamber Court trials, diocesan officials expanded their investigation in Weedon Bec Parish. On 2 July 1591, an official arrived and recorded:

> Thomas Billinge of Wedonbecke: There issues a citation for absenting himself from the church. The same against John Gare and his wife of the same: There issued a citation, as above, and for carrying away the town "fyrrs" that the churchwardens had provided for the repair of the church. The same against Robert Toy and the maid servant of Mr Prowdlove [*sic*] and the maid servant of Thomas Gare of the same: There issues a citation upon a crime. They appeared and acknowledged the same, etc. [Margin]: Anne Ley and Ursula Peysnole.[1]

> The diocesan official returned in two weeks. On the 16th of July, he again noted: the same against Thomas Billinge of Wedonbeck: There issued *vijs et modiis*[2] for absenting himself from the church. The same against Robert Toy, Anne Ley and Ursula Peysnole of the same: To purge themselves, except for Toy, etc.[3]

Eleven days later, on the 27th of July, he again noted "the same against Thomas Billinge of Wedonbeck: There issued a s' for absenting himself from church."[4] Within one month, three visitations was an extraordinary number. Two years earlier, a single annual visit appeared to be normal. This increased level of diocesan activity in Weedon Bec corresponds precisely with William Proudlove's post-Star Chamber trial dates in London. During the court trials, Proudlove was identified as the "past preacher of Weedon Bec." Now, he is referred to as "Mister Proudlove." Except for Robert Toy, the other men listed are excommunicated churchwardens or their family members. Twenty-two months after Thomas Cole and the five other excommunicated churchwardens refused to swear the *ex-officio* oath, the family members of Billinge and Gare are noted to be absent from church along with a maid servant.

---

1. NRO. *Correction Book*, X610/24: Fol. 107. Date: 2 Jul 1591.
2. "Lat. In the ecclesiastical courts, service of a decree or citation viis et modis, i. e., by all "ways and means" likely to affect the party with knowledge of its contents, is equivalent to substituted service in the temporal courts, and is opposed to personal service. Phillim. Ecc. Law, 1258, 1283." "Viis et Modis Definition and Legal Meaning," *The Law Dictionary*. Viewed 30 August 2021. https://thelawdictionary.org/viis-et-modis/.
3. NRO, Fol. 108d. Date: 16 Jul 1591.
4. NRO. Fol. 109d. Date: 27 Jul 1591.

The official's listing of Mr. Proudlove's maid servant, probably Anne Ley or possibly Ursula Peysnole, begs another question. What is the status of William Proudlove's family? When Weedon Bec's vicar was arrested and imprisoned more than a year prior, Proudlove's wife, Isabella, had already sensed she was pregnant. During his imprisonment, she gave birth to a boy named William. But with another mouth to feed, how did she manage a household of seven without her husband? How could they possibly afford a maid servant?

The fact is the village's most prominent families stepped in to support the defrocked vicar's family. As the Bible directs Christians: "Do right to the poor and fatherless; do justice to the poor and needy. Deliver the poor and needy; save them from the hand of the wicked."[5] In an extraordinary gesture, "John Billinge, Thomas Cole, and Thomas Gare surrendered . . . *Le Townehouse* to the use of William Proudlove during his natural life." These three men plus Thomas Billinge turned over their rights to this town meeting place to gain William Proudlove and his family's admittance and lifetime use of the *Le Townhouse* tenement.[6] The transcribed record is in endnote.[ii]

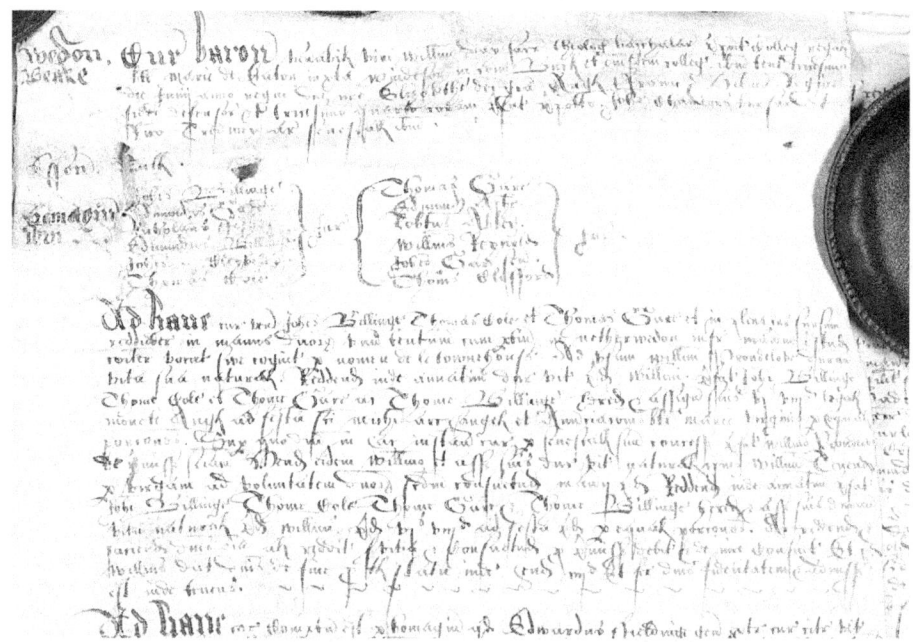

John Billinge, Thomas Cole, and Thomas Gare surrendered Le Townhouse, 1591-2.
Reproduced with kind permission of Eton College Archives, image 6.
Sponsored by John and Patricia Donohoe. (4.1)

---

5   Psalm 82:3-4 (Geneva Bible 1599)
6   Eton College Archives. "Weedon Bec Manor Court Records." ECR 27/232, 1591-2. "Thomas Bylllinge, Thomas Cole, John Gare and John Byllinge assign Le Townhouse to William Proudlove. Weedon Bec Manor Court of the Baron Presentment 1591-2 — Tenement is the term for a leased space owned by the Lord or the Manor. Fees were collected, typically once or twice a year, at Court Baron presentments. Tenants were required to report all changes, transactions, or disputes to the court. In this record, there are three separate presentments.

Meanwhile in London, the reform-minded Puritans remained in prison. Owing to their earlier petitions, they had achieved some rights and privileges, including the access of friends and "liberty of the house and garden."[7] When the Star Chamber trials finished in June, "all the petitioners except Mr. Cartwright had liberty granted by the archbishop to leave their prisons on Sundays to attend public worship, and on any other day of the week, if any one of them should allege a special cause of business," though they were required to post a bond of twenty pounds each to ensure their return to their prisons at the end of the day.[8] Of course, the ministers would have needed charity from their supporters, since they had been deprived of their livelihoods.

The manor court records show that William Proudlove personally appeared at the Weedon Bec presentment. He agreed to be responsible for payment to the Court Baron of 3s 4d twice a year for his right to live in *Le Townhouse*. He paid a small fealty for that privilege.[9]

When one considers the logistics of the vicar attending, this is remarkable. Weedon Bec is some seventy-five miles northwest of London. No coach service, let alone trains, existed in the early 1590s between those two locations. However, Weedon Bec is located on Watling Street, the original Roman Road. Today, it follows one of England's major thoroughfares: the A4 Highway.

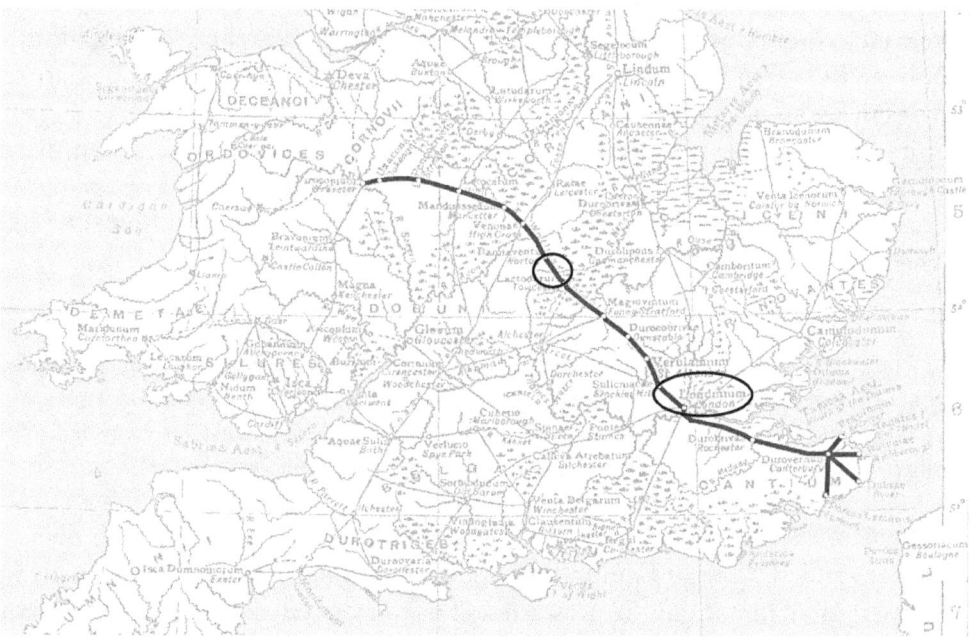

Locations of Weedon Bec and London: Watling Street on the Old Roman Road.[10] (4.2)

---

7   Collinson, 412.
8   Samuel Hopkins, *The Puritans or The Church, Court, and Parliament of England During the Reigns of Edward VI and Queen Elizabeth, in 3 Volumes* (Boston: 1861): Vol. 3, 396.
9   Fealty is a legal court term used for fines or other court required fees.
10 "1911 Watling Street," *Wikimedia Commons*. Public Domain. Viewed 8 January 2022. https://commons. wikimedia.org/wiki/File:1911Watling_Street.

In the 1590s, this trip would usually take a few days. It may be that Proudlove was granted liberty from prison for an extraordinary amount of time to accomplish this task. If so, it would have required a bond payment of at least £100, possibly more. An imprisoned, unemployed vicar would have needed to rely upon his friends and supporters' charity for such an expense. This is the most probable explanation for Proudlove's personal appearance at a Weedon Bec court baron presentment in 1591-2.[11]

When Thomas Cartwright's liberties were denied in London, he appealed by letter to Lady Russell, a relative of the Lord Treasurer, Sir William Cecil. On 13 August 1591, Cartwright wrote:

> The fame that ariseth from your favor . . . hath no more steadiness that the voice which is committee to the air, or writing engraven upon the water . . . I beseech your honorable mediation . . . especially toward the Lord Treasurer . . . We thought the suit of ministers (some of whom have preached the Gospel thirty years of her Majesty's reign) upon reasonable bail to return to their homes would not have been refused. Being refused herein, I know not what we should make suit for. . . . There is no ease so small, but we would gladly and thankfully embrace.[12]

Cartwright's reference to "some of whom have preached the Gospel thirty years of her Majesty's reign" corresponds almost exactly to when William Proudlove started his ministry in 1562. Lady Russell did, in fact, plead with her relative for consideration of Cartwright's situation—but without success.

Despite granting the prisoners some liberties, court officials were not finished. Additional examinations of more Puritan clergymen were conducted. They hoped to extract details that would conclusively prove their most grievous claims and charges of sedition against the imprisoned nine Puritans.

> In August, attempts were made to discover more about the St. John's *Conference* of 1589 from Henry Alvey and William Perkins. In early September, Thomas Barber, suspended preacher of Bow and a leading London *Classis* member, made a full and valuable deposition. Later in the month Edmund Littleton, Anthony Nutter and Hercules Clevely added a few details to what was known of the movement in the Midlands.[13]

But even with these and subsequent examinations of Snape's parishioners from Northampton, and of Thomas Edmunds and John Johnson in October, none yielded proof of subversive Puritan intentions the prosecutors hoped to ascertain. That forced the court to conclude: 1) the Puritans did not persuade others to put in practice the *Book of Discipline*

---

[11] Weedon Bec Court Baron manor courts were held typically twice per year on the 25th of March, Lady's Day, and the 29th of September. The September date is most probable for this event.

[12] Hopkins, 396.

[13] Hopkins, 426.

without consent of authorities; 2) they did not attempt to subvert the authority of Parliament and Queen Elizabeth; and 3) they did not undermine the authority of ecclesiastical courts.[14]

When the Lord Chancellor, Sir Christopher Hatton, died on 20 November 1591, his absence altered the Puritans' case trajectory. In December, the nine Puritan prisoners sent a petition to Lord Burghley, Sir William Cecil, requesting a release from prison on bail. On the 12th of December, Attorney General Popham sent Burghley "a moderately confident opinion of how the case stood." Popham expressed satisfaction that the Puritans had shown the right "to exercise their Book of Discipline in so far as this might be done with the peace of the Church and law of the land." But Sir William Cecil deemed Popham's response too optimistic for such a complex and difficult situation. The petition was denied, and the case "drifted into stalemate."[15] A subsequent appeal to Sir Frances Knollys, a senior member of the Privy Council, "opened the way for an appearance before the Privy Council, when the cold of January increased their chance of a merciful reception."[16]

In April, the Council sent seven of the prisoners another schedule of interrogatories. Why seven and not all nine? The Council had already concluded that two imprisoned Puritans, John Payne and Melancton Jewell, "played no significant part in the conference movement."[17] Since the interrogatories were nearly the same as ones answered the previous June, Edmund Snape and William Proudlove "persisted in their denial that they had ever subscribed to the Book."[18] Proudlove insisted that the meetings were "voluntary and informal . . . nevertheless even he promised that he would not 'hereafter in such sort meet in conference.'"[19]

> As a result of this interview the prisoners signed a submission which contained a most important statement on their classical meetings. They still insisted that these assemblies had been innocent and profitable but understanding that "such prescript and set meetings" were offensive to her Majesty and their lordships, they regretted that they had provoked this displeasure and promised thereafter to "avoid the occasion of offence." They added that their submission would have been made earlier if the archbishop had not confronted them with yet another lengthy collection of interrogatories.[20]

Following their signed submissions, the prisoners in the Clink and the White Lion "were allowed on a bail of forty pounds to go to church on Sundays [and] were permitted to leave their prisons on one other day in the week to conduct their necessary business." The defrocked Northampton minister banned from his ministry for life, Edmund Snape, "asked Whitgift for similar privileges, to go once a week into the fields or gardens for the sake of this health, and to go into the city to look after the affairs of his brother and of his

---

14 Collinson, 426.
15 Collinson, 427.
16 Collinson, 428-9.
17 Collinson, 501, footnote 39.
18 Collinson, 429.
19 Collinson, 430.
20 Collinson, 428-9.

invalid wife." Another minister "had 'continually voided blood by urine' since October, and he bore the additional burden of a 'poor lame wife and seven small children.'"[21] This description may match William Proudlove's family. But even small improvements in their prison liberties would have been a blessing.

Yet, the Puritan ministers remained imprisoned and deprived of their livelihoods. Cartwright also remained imprisoned, but the court had no control over his Warwick hospital livelihood. Undaunted by all they had endured, another more extensive and carefully crafted petition outlined their case. Addressed and sent to Lord Burghley, Sir William Cecil, it requested Queen Elizabeth to grant them "enlargement," a term used for clemency sometimes in relation to posting a bond. The Puritans' appeal contained heartfelt pleas, questions, statements, requests, and admonitions.

> Our exceeding heavy and distressed estate as most dutiful subjects . . . as men trained up in the schools of learning . . . as Ministers of the Gospel . . . We know not what misinformation to some of Her Majesty's Ecclesiastical Commissions . . . most of our houses have been raided by Officers, our studies, books and private papers rifled. . . .

> We humbly prayed . . . as by the Word of God is due to the Ministers of the same; by which Word they are not to be provided against, but upon, accusation, and the same confirmed by testimony of two or three witnesses. Moreover, also we prayed such favor, as dutiful subjects by the law of this land.

> By which law this proceeding is declared to those most expert and best learned cannot escape the danger of capricious interrogatories of it, that it standeth not with the right order of justice, or good equity, and encourageth untrue accusations and presentments which might be maliciously conspired and kept secret and unrevealed until time might be expired.

After an extensive series of ecclesiastical and legal points, the Puritans closed their appeal with this request.

> Weigh our case, and according to the equities and important consequence thereof, to become an honorable means for us unto our most gracious and sovereign Prince. That her highness displeasure being appeased she may in her accustomed clemency, understanding our case . . . grant us her gracious relief.

Your Honours most humble Suppliants prisoners:

Andrew King	*Daniel Wyght*
John Payne	*Thomas Cartwright*
Humfrey Fen	*Edward Lord*
Edmund Snape	*Melancton Jewell*

William Proudlove

---

[21] Collinson, 429.

Unfortunately, it is not known how Lord Burghley replied to this petition. It was filed in Burghley's palace in May 1592. But it is believed to have been received earlier or concurrently with another petition which was dated April 1592. Frustrated by their ongoing predicament, the nine Puritans acted quickly and "resolved at last to address a petition to the queen herself. They wrote up the following Declaration, containing a full answer to the several Charges brought against them."[22] Because this Declaration starts with a reference to the "above-mentioned Puritan Ministers imprisoned," one may conclude it was connected to the previous petition. These brave and courageous Puritans signed their names to their Declaration, defending their actions directly to Queen Elizabeth I.

Signatures of Nine Puritans' Petition to Queen Elizabeth, 1592.
With kind permission of the British Library.
Sponsored by the American Society of Genealogists. (4.3)

A Letter of the above-mention'd Puritan Ministers imprisoned, to her Majesty, in Vindication of their Innocency. Dated April 1592. May it please your excellent Majesty,

There is nothing, right gracious Sovereign, next to the saving mercy of Almighty God, that can be more comfortable than your Highness's favour, as to all other your faithful and dutiful Subjects, for to us your Majesty's most humble Supplicants, who are by our Calling Ministers of God's holy Word; and by our present Condition now, and of long time, prisoners in divers Prisons in and about the City of London, for which Cause our most humble Suit is, that it may please your most excellent Majesty, graciously to understand our necessary Answer to such grievous Charges as we hear to be informed against us, which if they were true, might be just cause of withdrawing forever from us your Highness's gracious Protection and Favour which above all other earthly Things we most desire to enjoy.

The Reason of our Trouble is a suspicion that we should be guilty of many heinous Crimes; but these supposed Crimes we have not been charged with in any due and ordinary court Proceeding, by open Accusation and Witnesses. But being called up to London by authority of some of your Majesty's Commissioners in Causes Ecclesiastical, we have been required by them to take an Oath of Inquisition or Office, as it is called; for not taking whereof we were

---

[22] Daniel Neal, *History of the Puritans,* Vol. I (Dublin: Brice Edmond, Bookseller, 1755): 412.

first committed to Prison, and since have continued there a long time, notwithstanding, that all of us save one have been deprived of our Livings and degraded of our Ministry.

Wherefore, for that the Oath is the next and immediate Cause of our Trouble, we have made our Answer first to that, and then after also to the Crimes that are suggested and secretly informed against us. [23]

As promised, these brave Puritans analyze and refute accusations in seven categories: the Oath; Schism; Rebellion; Supremacy; Excommunication; Conferences; and Singularity. Significantly, they begin with:

THE OATH

The *Declaration*, written to Queen Elizabeth I, acknowledges their respect for authority. They earnestly "desire to show themselves as becoming of their calling, examples of that obedience to Magistrates in all things that they have taught others." However, they draw a line in the sand (to coin a phrase) when it comes to ultimate authority, which rests in "the word of God." They will not take "the name of God in vain," nor will they risk "ensnaring [their] consciences" by taking an oath "without limitation." Here they are referring to the many demands they have faced to swear an *ex-officio* oath. In their refusal to swear to answer all questions put to them fully and truthfully, before knowing the questions, they are repudiating this demand for self-incrimination as contrary to the word of God.

> We . . . desire, that the oath which is tendered us, were such, as we might lawfully take by the word of God. For that we take it not, . . . we are charged of contempt of authority, which not for fear only, but of conscience, and duty to the ordinance of Almighty God, we regard with all dutiful respect; but (as the Lord Our God knoweth) the fear of ensnaring our consciences, and of taking the name of God in vain. For the oath . . . is without limitation of any certain matter, infinite, and general to answer whatsoever shall be demanded of us, of which kind of oath we find neither rule not example in the word of God.

SCHISM

Here, the Puritans directly address the charge that they have condemned the Church of England and refuse to be "in communion with it." They call these charges "secret informations" that are "suggested and secretly informed against us." This alludes to information from witnesses they are not privy to and were not allowed to publicly question in trial examinations. In essence, they are claiming the right to confront their accusers directly and to have knowledge of all the charges and evidence against them. They continue:

---

[23]   British Museum. MS72 f137v and MS72 f138r – the Declaration's entire original source document was transcribed, translated, and compared by the author from a secondary source: Neal, 412-19.

Which things if they were true we were of all men living the most unthankful; first to Almighty God, and next to your excellent Majesty by whose blessed means we are partakers of that happy liberty of the profession of the Gospel, and of the true service of God, that by your Highness gracious government, with all your loyal and dutiful subjects, we do enjoy.

Wherefore we most humbly beseech your excellent Majesty, to understand, that we acknowledge unfeignedly as in the sight of God, that this our Church as it is by Your Highness Lawes and authority established amongst us, having that faith possessed, and taught publicly in it, that was agreed of in the Convocation held in the year 1562, and such form of public prayer and administration of the Sacraments, as in the first year of your Majesty's gracious reign was established, notwithstanding any thing that may need to be revisited and further reformed, to be a true visible Church of Christ, from the holy communion whereof by way of schism, it is not lawful to depart.

Our whole life may show evident proof hereof. For always before the time of our trouble, we have lived in the daily communion of it, not only as private men, but at the time of our restraint, and in any years before, preached and exercised our ministry in the same : and at this present, most earnestly beseech all authority that is set over us, especially your excellent Majesty, that we may so provide to serve God and your Highness all the days of our life.

Concluding this section, the Puritans collectively deny the charges that they have any intent to undermine Queen Elizabeth's authority. In fact, they stress, their whole lives show evident proof of their desire to "serve God and your Highness all the days of our life."

REBELLION

In this category, they reject any suggestion that they practiced or tried to foment rebellious actions against the Church. They stress their abhorrence of these accusations, "judg[ing] it most unlawful and damnable by the word of God to rebel, and by force of arms, or any violent means, to seek redress thereof." They declare their intent to reform, not overthrow, the Church through "peaceable means" of speech and protest.

Another crime suggested against us, is, that we should practice or purpose rebelliously to procure such further reformation of our Church, as we desire, by violent and undutiful means.

Whereunto our answer is, that as we think it not lawful to make a schism in the Church for anything that we esteem needful to be reformed in it: so do we in all simplicity and sincerity of heart in the presence of Almighty God (to whom all secrets are known) and of your excellent Majesty, to whom the sword is given of God for just vengeance and punishment of transgressors, that for procuring of reformation of anything that we desire to be redressed in the state of our Church, we judge it most unlawful and damnable by the word of God to rebel, and by force of arms, or any violent means, to seek redress thereof.

And moreover, that we never intended to use or procure any other means for the furtherance of such reformation, than only prayer to Almighty God, and most humble suite to Your excellent Majesty and other in authority; which such like dutiful and peaceable means, as might give information of this our suite; and of the reasons moving as thereunto.

SUPREMACY

Here, the Puritans return to the issue of ultimate sovereignty. They claim the third Crime, impeaching her Majesty's supremacy, is "misinformed" against them. They have taken the Oath of Supremacy "as occasion hath required," and acknowledge the right of Crown and Parliament to enact civil and ecclesiastical regulations. But their stance is firm. Monarchical sovereignty and power are limited in this crucial way: they are "next and immediately *under God* [emphasis added]." Their ultimate allegiance is to a Higher Authority.

> A third Crime misinformed against us, is, that we impeach your Majesty's Supremacy. For Answer whereunto, we unfeignedly protest (God being witness that we speak the Truth herein from our Hearts) that we acknowledge your Highness' Sovereignty and supreme Power, next and immediately under God, over all Persons, and in all Causes, as well Ecclesiastical, as Civil, in as large and ample Manner, as it is agnized [acknowledged] by the high Court of Parliament in the Statue of Recognition, and is set down in the Oath of Supremacy enacted by the same and as it is further declared both in your Majesty's Injunctions, and also in the Articles of Religion agreed in the Convocation, and in sundry Books of learned Men of our Nation, published and allowed by public Authority.

> We add yet also hereunto, that we acknowledge the form as fully as ever it was in old Time acknowledged by the Prophets to belong to the virtuous Kings of Judea, and as all the reformed Churches in Christendom; do acknowledge the same in their Sovereign Princes in the Confessions of their Faith exhibited unto them, as they are set down in a Book named *the Harmony of Confessions*, and the Observations annexed thereunto.

> Besides this our unfeignedly Protestation, our true and simple meaning herein may appear by the whole former Course of our Lives, wherein it cannot be showed, that ever we made question of it, and more particularly both by our public Doctrine, declaring the same; and by taking of the Oath of Supremacy, as Occasion hath required: and finally by this, that if we be not thus sufficiently purged we are now also ready to take it again; that there may remain no manner of doubt or suspicion off our most faithful and dutiful allegiance in this behalf.

EXCOMMUNICATION

With regard to the penalty of excommunication, they do not deny its legitimacy in certain cases when in line with the word of God. But this "Censure" in their case was not only undeserved but unjust. It aimed to deprive them of their office and calling, and their right to speak freely through preaching, prayer, and ministry. It also deprived parishioners of "spiritual comforts," the sacraments, and Christian fellowship.

> A branch of this charge it is, that hath been adversely devised against us, concerning the persons subject to excommunication, and the power thereof how far it extendeth. Touching

the former whereof our answer is, that we hold in it nothing diverse from the word of God, or from the judgment of the Church of Christ, since the beginning of it to this present age.

We add yet further that we judge no otherwise herein, then all the reformed Churches that are this day in the Christian World, nor then our own English Church, both always heretofore hath judged of it, and doth still at this present, as in any appear both by the Articles of Religion, agreed by the Convocation and by a book of homilies allowed by the same, and also by sundry other books of greatest credit and authority in our Church which is, That the word of God, the Sacraments, the power of binding and loosing, are all the ordinances of Almighty God, gratuitously ordained for the comfort and salvation of the whole Church, and that therefore no part or member of it, is to be denied the comfortable and wholesome aide and benefit thereof, for the furtherance of their Faith, and (as need maybe require) of their Repentance; to the forgiveness of their sins, and the salvation of their souls.

For the other point, how far this Censure extendeth, we profess, that it depriveth a Man only of spiritual Comforts, as of being Partaker of the Lord's Table, and being present at the public Prayers of the Church, and such like, without taking away either Liberty, Goods, Lands, Government, private or public whatsoever or any other civil or earthly Commodity of this Life.

Wherefore from our Hearts we detest and abhor, the intolerable Presumption of the Bishop of Rome, taking upon him, in such Cases, to depose Sovereign Princes from their highest Seats of supreme Government, and discharging their Subjects from that dutiful Obedience that by the Laws of God they ought to perform.

CONFERENCES

Here, they address the objections leveled against their independent meetings—the *classis*, *classes*, and *conferences*. First, "Conferences of the Ministers" are nothing unusual, and have been allowed to confer on a variety of topics for a "long Time." Their meetings were convened not for the purpose of Schism, but to discuss matters of particular importance and relevance to them. They deny they exercised any ecclesiastical powers such as ordaining ministers or excommunications. In essence, they claim the right, "common [to the] Affairs of Men," to associate freely with "their acquaintance[s] and friends."

> There remain that two things objected against us, whereof one is of our Conferences, wherein we have been charged to have given Orders and made Ministers, and to have administered the Censures of the Church, and finally to have exercised Ecclesiastical Jurisdiction.

> To which Suggestion we answer, that indeed of long Time we have used as other Ministers have done, as we think, in most Parts of the Land, to meet sometimes and confer together, which being granted to our good and dutiful Subjects upon occasion to resort and meet together, we esteem it was lawful for us so to do.

> For besides the common Affairs of all Men, which may give them just Cause to meet with their Acquaintance and Friends, mutually to communicate for their Comfort and Help

one with another, Men professing Learning have more necessary and special use of such Conferences for their furtherance in such Knowledge as they profess.

In which regard learned men of all professions have of their Colleges and houses, whereunto they may resort, for enjoying such comport and benefit. But of such as profess learning, ministers of the word, have sundry great and necessary causes so to do more than other, because of the manifold Knowledge both of Divinity, and also of diverse Tongues and Sciences, that are of great use, for the better enabling of them for their Ministry.

In which respect, the Conferences of the Ministers were allowed by many Bishops within their Dioceses, and to our Knowledge never disallowed or forbidden by any. Some late Years also have given us more special Cause of conferring together, wherein Jesuits, Seminaries, and other Heretics, sought to seduce many, and wherein also some Schismatics condemned the whole State of our Church, as no part of the true visible Church of Christ, and therefore refused to have any Part or Communion with it: upon which Occasion it was needful for us to advise of the best Way and Means we could to keep the People that we had charge to instruct from such damnable Errors.

Further also particularly because some reckoned us to have part with their Schism and reported us to agree in nothing, but to differ one from another in the Reformation that we desire: We had special Cause to confer together, that we might set down some things touching such matters, which at all times whensoever we should be demanded, might be our true and just Defense, both to clear us from partaking with the Schism, and to witness for us, that we agreed in the Reformation that we desire. And for those causes we acknowledge, as the occasions required, to have used for some years, to meet and confer together.

But as touching the Thing surmised of our Meetings, that we exercise in them all ecclesiastical Jurisdiction in making Ministers, in confirming and excommunicating, in ordaining Constitutions and Orders upon such Censures to bind any, we protest before God and his holy Angels, that we never exercised any part of such Jurisdiction, nor had any Purpose agreed amongst us to exercise the same, before we should by public Law be authorized thereunto.

Further also touching such our Meetings, we affirm that they were only of ministers (saving in some parts where a schoolmaster two or three desirous to train themselves to the ministry joined with us) and the same but of six or seven, or like small number in a Conference, without any deed or appearance that might be offensive to any. And this is our just answer touching our Conferences.

SINGULARITY

Finally, the Puritan ministers address the charges surrounding their involvement with the revised *Book of Discipline*. They do not deny the importance of ecclesiastical authority. But they stress their desire for church governing structure and discipline practices of the "primitive," ancient Church. They affirm, yet again, their hope and objective of reform within the Church of England, not separation from it.

The other point that we are charged with is Singularity, which although it be not subject to any Punishment of Law yet is suggested against us by such as favor not our most humble Desire of a further Reformation, to disgrace us, and to make us odious both with other, and chiefly with your excellent Majesty.

Wherein our answer is that the Discipline of the primitive Church, which we desire is ancient and so acknowledged by the *Book of Common Prayer* established by your Majesty in the first year of your happy reign in these words. That there was a godly Discipline in the primitive Church, instead whereof until the said Discipline may be restored again (which Thing is much to be wished) it is thought convenient to use such a Form of Commination[24] as is prescribed.

Further also, if it please your Majesty with favor to understand it from us, we are ready to show, it in such points of ecclesiastical discipline of our Church, which we desire most humbly may be reformed, we hold no singular or private Opinion, but the Truth of the word of God, acknowledged to be such, by all the best Churches and writers, of ancient time, and of this present age.

Thus have we declared (Right Gracious Sovereign) truly and sincerely, as we will answer it to God and to your Majesty upon our allegiance, what judgment we are of, concerning the matters informed against us: and further testify, upon like bond and consumed of our duty, that no minister within this land, desiring a further reformation, with whom we have had any private Acquaintance or Conference or these Matters (whatsoever may be otherwise informed) is of any other Mind or Opinion in these Causes that have been mentioned. By which Declaration, if (according to our earnest Prayers to Almighty God) your Majesty shall clearly discern us, to stand free from all such matter as we are charged with, our most humble suite is, that your Majesty's gracious favor (which is more dear and precious to us then our lives) may be extended unto us.

In conclusion, the nine Puritans ask that:

We may enjoy the comfortable Liberty of our Persons and Ministry, as we did before our Troubles which if by your Highness's special Mercy and Goodness we may obtain, we promise and vow to Almighty God, and your excellent Majesty, to behave ourselves in a peaceable and dutiful way in every respect, as may give no just Cause of your Highness's Offence, but according to our Callings, both in Doctrine and Example as heretofore, for always hereafter to teach due Obedience to your Majesty among other parts of holy Doctrine; and to pray for your Majesty's long and blessed Reign over us, etc.

There was no immediate response from the monarch or her representatives. After many exhaustive appeals, the nine faithful Puritans remained imprisoned. Though removed from their families, their homes, and their churches, their resolve—based on faith—held firm. Their prison walls might contain their bodies but not their spirits. After two years of

---

[24] Definition: a threat of punishment or vengeance. a denunciation. In the Church of England, a penitential office read on Ash Wednesday in which God's anger and judgments are proclaimed against sinners. "Commination," *Dictionary.com* Viewed 25 January 2022. https://www.dictionary.com/browse/commination.

confinement, they continued their reliance upon God's Promises, as they kept the word of God close to their hearts. They certainly would have meditated on this Scripture:

> But as we were allowed of God, that the Gospel should be committed unto us, so we speak, not as they that please men, but God, which approveth our hearts. Neither yet did we ever use flattering words, as ye know, nor did we mask to cover up greed, as God is record. Neither sought we praise of men, neither of you, nor of others, when we might have been chargeable, as the Apostles of Christ.[25]

NOTEWORTHY PURITANS BEYOND THE NINE

The nine imprisoned Puritans were not alone. After Queen Elizabeth called a new Parliament on 19 February 1592, more significant developments brought an upsurge in Puritan activity. A crescendo of events was building to a clash of epic proportions.

John Udall, one of five zealous Puritans whose writings were viewed as seditious before the *Martin Marprelate* tracts, was imprisoned for almost two years and sentenced to death. When informed of Udall's death sentence in 1591, King James VI of Scotland, later to be King of England, wrote a letter on his behalf—but all for naught. In March 1592, Sir Walter Raleigh, a member of Parliament, intervened with authorities on behalf of Udall. Raleigh arranged for Udall to swear loyalty to the queen and accept exile. Archbishop Whitgift received the papers. After some delay, the Turkey Company of Merchant Adventurers offered Udall a position in Syria contingent upon a quick release. The queen signed the pardon in June. On the 15th of June, Udall informed Sergeant Puckering of his acceptance. Tragically, John Udall fell ill and died in prison. He never achieved his liberty.

> His death was attributed to the cruel and illegal usage to which he had been subjected, and he was long remembered and honoured as a martyr by those who shared his religious convictions. He was buried in the churchyard of St. George's, Southwark. He was survived by his wife and son Ephraim.[26]

That summer of 1592 brought the return, temporarily, of three of the other five zealous Puritans to the London area. The Puritan congregation known as the London Underground Church had continued meeting in secret after its pastor John Greenwood, Henry Barrowe, and John Penry—along with nineteen other worshipers—were arrested in October 1587. Most were still imprisoned in Newgate or the Clink.

When several of the members, including Greenwood, were released from prison in July 1592, he joyfully rejoined the church, which elected him as teacher and Puritan minister Francis Johnson as pastor. Johnson had joined the London Underground Church after ministering at an English church in Middelburg, Netherlands.

---

[25] 1 Thessalonians 2:4-6 (Geneva Bible 1599)

[26] "Dictionary of National Biography, 1885-1900/Udall, John," *Dictionary of National Biography, 1885-1900,* Volume 58/ Viewed 22 January 2022. https://en.wikisource.org/wiki/Dictionary_of_National_Biography,_1885-1900/Udall, John.

In September, Henry Barrowe was freed from prison and active in the church. The next month, John Penry joined the congregation. Before his escape to Scotland in November 1589, Penry was one of the most sought-after figures in connection with seditious and treasonable acts. Thought to have authored some of the *Martin Marprelate* tracts, Penry had been labeled "the most wanted Puritan in England."[27]

In December 1592, authorities again arrested John Greenwood, along with minister Francis Johnson and elder Daniel Studley. This church had formally chosen elders and deacons to serve their congregants, as described in Cartwright's Presbyterian model of governance. The Church of England's *Book of Discipline* forbade this action, which was subject to censure and worse if discovered. John Penry remained at large.

While much occurred in and around London, the activity was not limited geographically. In the East Midlands and specifically in Weedon Bec, diocesan activity continued unabated. During the six months from November 1592 through April 1593, the following corrections by diocesan officials were noted:

21 Nov 1592	Weedonbecke: John Cleveley, Edward Gare, churchwardens there, present John Gare the younger will not suffer his child to be baptized, the children be a quarter old, and not frequenting their parish church. The same against Thomas Billinge of the same: for not frequenting his parish church.
Dec 1592	The same against John Gare the younger and his wife of Wedonbecke: There issued *vijs et modiis* against John and a citation his wife, as they will not suffer their child to be baptized till it be a quarter old and not frequenting the parish church.
	The same against Thomas Billinge and his wife of the same: There issued an excommunication.
16 Dec 1592	The same against John Gare and his wife of Wedonbecke: There issued an excommunication against John and *vijs et modiis* against his wife.
	The same against Thomas Billinge and his wife of the same: There issued an excommunication.
9 Jan 1592/3	The same against John Gare and his wife of Wedonbeck: There issued an excommunication.
	The same against Thomas Billinge and his wife of Wedonbeck: They stand excommunicated.
24 Jan 1592/3	The same against John Gare and his wife of Wedonbeck: They stand excommunicated.
	The same against Thomas Billinge and his wife excommunicated
7 Feb 1592/3	Same against John Gare and his wife of Wedonbeck: They stand excommunicated.
	The same against Thomas Billinge and his wife of the same: They stand excommunicated.[28]

---

27 Stephen Tomkins, *The Journey to the Mayflower* (London & New York: Hodder & Stoughton, 2020): 207.
28 NRO, *Correction Book*, X610/24: Fol.107, 108d, 109d, 113, 125, 129, 131d, 136, 139.

About a week later in London, another Puritan tragedy caused an uproar. On Friday, 16 February 1593, Roger Rippon, of Southwark, died in Newgate prison. Rippon was among those arrested at an illegal gathering of the London Underground Church and had been imprisoned for five years. In a procession protesting Rippon's death in early March, his coffin was carried through the streets of London while church members and supporters chanted in a public display of defiance. The crowd left Rippon's coffin on the doorstep of Justice Richard Young's house. Young was an officer in the Court of High Commission. The coffin's engraved inscription expressed their sentiments about his tragic death.

> This is the corps[e] of Roger Ripponn, a servant of Christ, and Her Majestie's faithfull subject, who is the last of 16 or 17 which that great enne[m]ye of God, the Archbishop of Canterbury, with the Highe Commissioners, have murdere[d] in Newgate within theise 5 yeares for the testimony of Jesus Christ.

> His soule is now with the Lord and his bloud cryeth for spedy vengeance against that great ennemy of the sainctes and against Mr. Richard Younge, who in this and many the like poynts hath abused his power for the upholding of the Romishe Antichriste, prelacy and priesthood.[29]

Infuriated and incensed, officials searched for those associated with the protest and arrested fifty-six people. Only one admitted to taking part in the procession.

When the new Parliament convened in late February 1593, Queen Elizabeth declared all matters of State should be referred to herself and her Privy Council. She further declared all matters relating to the Church should be referred to herself and her Bishops. She asserted her belief in her God-given right as absolute sovereign in all those areas of governance. In effect, Queen Elizabeth warned Parliament to stay out of all things pertaining to the relationship of Church and State. Yet, the Puritans maintained many bold and zealous advocates in both houses of Parliament. In fact, three attorneys who had assisted the nine imprisoned Puritans and others, Robert Beale, Nicholas Fuller, and James Morrice, were present and visible in their lobbying efforts.

On the second full day of business, the 27th of February, Morrice "asked the House to consider three 'matters of very great weight and importance'—the *ex-officio* oath, an 'ungodly and intolerable inquisition'; Whitgift's articles, 'a lawless subscription'; and the oath of ecclesiastical obedience required of excommunicated persons before absolution."[30] Morrice's attack on the church courts' abuses, which he personally witnessed, resulted in his imprisonment. He was confined in the Tower for eight weeks while the debates raged without him. Meanwhile, back in Weedon Bec, the same diocesan visitations occurred with the same results.

---

29 Albert Peel, ed., *The Notebook of John Penry 1593* (London: Royal Historical Society, 1944): xx.

30 "History of Parliament/Morice, James," *History of Parliament.* Viewed 8 January 2022. https://www. historyofparliamentonline.org/volume/1558-1603/member/morice-james-1539-97.

23 Feb 1592/3	Same against John Gare and his wife excommunicated
	Same against Thomas Billinge and his wife excommunicated
9 Mar 1592/3	Same against John Gare and his wife excommunicated
	Same against Thomas Billinge and his wife excommunicated
23 Mar 1593	Same against John Gare and his wife excommunicated
	Same against Thomas Billinge and his wife excommunicated
6 Apr 1593	Same against John Gare and his wife excommunicated
	Same against Thomas Billinge and his wife excommunicated
27 Apr 1593	Same against John Gare and his wife excommunicated[31]

Also in April, Dr. Goodman, the Dean of Westminster, and others examined prisoners suspected of being Barrowists over a period of three days. Among them were those arrested from London Underground Church services. One prisoner examined exemplifies the plight of so many others.

George Collier, aged thirty-seven, a haberdasher of the London parish, St. Martens at Ludgate, stated he was committed by the Bishop of London and imprisoned. Collier said he was incarcerated with Greenwood, Crane, and others of the Underground Church. He testified he had never been examined until now during his five-year incarceration! When offered liberty from prison in exchange for returning to his former parish church that he attended before his involvement with the London Underground Church, Collier responded that "he will not."[32] Such was the faith of a committed Puritan.

During this period, Parliament vigorously debated the proposed *Act against Seditious Sectaries* sponsored by supporters of Archbishop John Whitgift. It gave ecclesiastical authorities greater powers to "imprison, banish and even execute suspected separatists."[33] The new proposal employed, as a template, a precursor act used to prosecute Catholic Papists and expanded it to include Puritanism a punishable offence—even with death.

While Parliament debated, Archbishop Whitgift moved aggressively to punish his highest profile prisoners. Both Henry Barrowe and John Greenwood had either stated in examinations or wrote publications that likened the Archbishop to the Antichrist—the highest possible condemnation of the highest-ranking ecclesiastical authority in all of England. Whether or not Whitgift was motivated by revenge, Barrowe and Greenwood were charged with "devising and circulating seditious books." They were tried in March 1593 and sentenced to death under the Seditious Words and Rumours Act of 1581. John Penry petitioned Parliament to protest his colleagues' arrest, treatment in prison, and conviction. While still hiding from authorities, Penry asked three women to deliver the document. The women were arrested. As the debate dragged on, Whitgift took no chances on what Parliament might do. He proceeded with orders to execute the two prominent Puritans. "After two reprieves, one at the foot of the gallows, the two Puritan leaders, John

---

[31] NRO, *Correction Book*, X610/24: Fol. 144, 146d, 150, 153, 155d.
[32] British Museum. 1 Harl. MS. 421, fol. 133-34 verso, B. II. 1. "Early English Dissenters."
[33] "Puritanism in the Elizabethan Age," British Broadcasting Corporation. Viewed 1 September 2021. https://www.bbc.co.uk/bitesize/guides/z9qpjty/revision/3.

Greenwood and Henry Barrowe, were hanged on the 6th of April 1593."[34] Two days later, after almost two months of debate, Parliament passed the Seditious Sectaries Act of 1593. It effectively outlawed Puritanism.

After the executions of Barrowe and Greenwood, Queen Elizabeth quizzed the Earl of Cumberland, "What end make they?"

He replied, "A very Godly end; and prayed for your Majesty and the State."

Elizabeth also sought out the opinion of John Whitgift, Archbishop of Canterbury, with a similar question: "What, in your very conscience, think you of these two men, Barrow[e] and Greenwood?"

Whitgift replied, "I think, your Highness, that they were servants of God but dangerous to the State."[35]

Elizabeth exclaimed, "Alas! Shall we put the servants of God to death!"[36]

Henry Barrowe and John Greenwood, stained glass memorial in
Emmanuel United Reformed Church, Cambridge. Wikimedia Commons. Public domain. (4.4)

---

[34] "1911 Encyclopædia Britannica/Greenwood, John," 1911 Encyclopædia Britannica. Vol. 12. Viewed 8 January 2022. https://en.wikisource.org/wiki/1911_Encyclopaedia_Britannica/Greenwood,_John.

[35] Hopkins, 541-2.

[36] Hopkins, 542.

After Elizabeth's acknowledgement that Barrowe and Greenwood were servants of God, and perhaps having been affected by the nine Puritans' petition, her heart softened. Whatever the catalyst, she changed her mind. "The High Commission abated their persecution of the Presbyterian Puritans."[37] But there were still unresolved matters. A few Puritans and their supporters remained imprisoned.

John Hodgkins, a printer of the *Martin Marprelate* tracts, had been incarcerated since August 1589. He was one who received the queen's mercy and was released. But others were still sought to face ecclesiastical authorities. The most prominent Puritan fugitive was John Penry.

John Penry was seized in May in London's Stepney Parish through information provided by the vicar. Authorities rejoiced when they finally arrested him. The Star Chamber's attention immediately turned to prosecution. He was indicted "for seditious words and rumers [*sic*] uttered against the queen's most excellent majesty, tending to the stirring up of rebellion among her subjects."[38] When examined, Penry was asked what he disliked about the Church of England. He answered, "I dislike:

1. The false ecclesiastical officers.
2. The manner of calling those officers.
3. A great part of the works wherein these false officers are employed.
4. Their maintenance or livings.

All of which I will be bound to prove, by the Lord's assistance, to be derived, not from Jesus Christ, but from antichrist. Therefore, as I cannot be partaker of those holy things of God, except under the power of antichrist, and by bearing those marks by which he is known; I am bound to seek the comfort of the word and sacraments where I may have them without submitting to any other ecclesiastical government than that which is derived from Jesus Christ.[39]

Penry was convicted on 21 May 1593 and sentenced to death by Lord Chief Justice Popham. The next day, Penry wrote an additional appeal. In it, he defended and attached his previously drafted private writings.

Unfinished and perfectly secret . . . even in these writings . . . he had shewn his duty and true loyalty to the queen, nor had he ever the most secret thought to the contrary . . . that secret, confused and unadvised observations are brought against me, even to the spilling of my blood.

Though I be condemned as a felon, or as a traitor to my natural sovereign, I thank God, that heaven and earth shall not be able to convict me of it . . . And I thank God, that whensoever the end of my days comes, and I expect not to live to the end of this week, I shall die Queen

---

[37] Hopkins, 578-9.
[38] Brook, 52.
[39] Brook, 53.

Elizabeth's most faithful subject, in the consciences of mine enemies . . . Subscribed with the heart and hand that never devised or wrote anything to the discredit or defamation of my sovereign, Queen Elizabeth. This I take on my death, as I hope to live hereafter.

Thus preparing myself, not so much for an unjust verdict, and an undeserved doom in this life, as for that blessed crown of glory, which, of the great mercy of my God, is ready for me in heaven, I humbly commit your lordship into the hand of our righteous Lord. In great haste, from close prison, this 22d of the fifth month, May, 1593. Your lordship's most humble servant in the Lord, John Penry. [40]

Penry also interceded for his family, asking that "the merciful Lord, who relieves the widow and the fatherless, will reward my desolate orphans and friendless widow, whom I leave behind me, and even hear their cry, for he is merciful."[41] His wife, Helen, presented a petition for clemency which was denied. Penry was executed by hanging on 29 May 1593. He left his poor widow, Helen, with four children. The eldest child was not more than four years old.

Upon news of Penry's execution, adversaries of the Puritans published their own considered and predictive evaluations of the events of the winter of 1592 through the spring of 1593. With John Udall's death in prison and the executions of John Penry, John Greenwood, and Henry Barrowe, "the neck of the plots of the fiery nonconformists was broken, and their brags were turned into prayers and tears, as the only means for Christian subjects." Another stated, "The pressing of the law thus closed, struck terror into the party, and made the dissenters of all sorts, less enterprising against the government."[42]

After the turmoil of trials and tribulations, of interrogatories and imprisonment, the Puritans' antagonists believed they had been broken. Her Majesty, the Privy Council, the Courts of the High Commission and Star Chamber, and the Archbishop of Canterbury were satisfied that the Puritan Movement was no longer viable and required no further harsh or vindictive sentences to defend the Church.

Puritan supporters, previously tried in the Star Chamber—Mrs. Elizabeth Crane now Mrs. Carleton, Sir Richard Knightley, John Hales, plus Mr. and Mrs. Roger Wigston—had their fines abated, either partially or entirely. But the most significant change was Elizabeth's declaration that "during her reign care was taken that no more Protestants should be put to death for their religion."[43]

In early summer of 1593, the nine Puritan prisoners—Andrew King, John Payne, Humfrey Fen, Edmund Snape, Daniel Wyght, Thomas Cartwright, Edward Lord, Melancton Jewell, and William Proudlove—were released from prison. But only John Payne and Melancton Jewell were freed without conditions. Edmund Snape's lifetime ministry ban was reduced to a decade with his time already served in prison credited. But Snape and

---

[40] Brook, 61-3.
[41] Brook, 61-2.
[42] Brook, 66.
[43] Hopkins, 542.

the others were required to remain in London awaiting further ecclesiastical direction. For these nine faithful Puritans, God had at last fulfilled one of his *Promises*. As it is written in Scripture:

> Blessed is he whose hope is in the Lord his God, which made heaven and earth, the sea, and all that therein is: which keepeth his fidelitie for ever: Which executeth iustice for the oppressed: which giveth bread to the hungry: the Lord loseth the prisoners.[44]

While they awaited further instructions, the remaining Puritan ministers lingered in London, some of them teaching and ministering in secret. Like-minded Puritan supporters and congregations, eager to hear their stories, arranged meetings. As the Bible records:

> The wicked flee when no man pursueth, but the righteous are bold as a lion.[45]

---

[44] Psalm 146:6-7 (Geneva Bible 1599)
[45] Proverbs 28:1 (King James Version)

CLOSING COMMENTARY ON PURITANS

Starting some three decades earlier—near the beginning of Proudlove's ministry—and especially in the period of the nine zealous reformers' challenges from ecclesiastical authorities—the Puritans developed and articulated principles and took actions that would resonate long after the events of the 1580s and early 1590s. They consistently appealed to the use of their own conscience as the arbiter of their choices and behavior. They refused to allow external authorities—including a monarch and her representatives—to dictate their opinions, beliefs, and decisions. That they claimed the validity of their "own private judgment" was bold and courageous indeed!

The nine Puritans held firm to these values throughout their interrogations and series of trials. In their *Declaration* they developed them further, expressing principles that sound familiar to us today and that foreshadowed rights that found their way into American founding documents: freedom of religion and association; freedom of speech and the press; the right to self-government and to confront accusers; freedom from self-incrimination and from unreasonable search and seizure; the right to peaceful protest; and the appeal to God as the highest authority.

If evaluations of the Puritan Movement's demise had been accurate, history would need to be rewritten. What happened after these climactic events reveals a much different story. In fact, Puritanism was not suppressed by the defeat of the *classis, classes,* and *conferences.* "The *classes* were . . . of central importance, for their members shared the same concern of all puritans for the reform of parish life."[46] Even though a Presbyterian structure was not implemented, a solid Biblical foundation was strengthened in congregations led by Puritan ministers. The focal point of reform became congregational worship, which regained central importance in the hearts and minds of Puritans and their congregants.

While the template for church government and discipline promoted by Thomas Cartwright did not win the battle, it would later be revived when Puritans' expectations for their long-hoped-for Promises were rekindled at the beginning of the reign of King James I, who succeeded Elizabeth I in 1603. As W. J. Shiels notes: "The activities of the presbyterian party in the 1580s were not the climax to the history of Elizabethan puritanism . . . but rather a turning point."[47]

What was achieved by the brave and committed Puritans standing firm throughout their ordeal, trials, and tribulations—Thomas Cole and his fellow excommunicated churchwardens, the Puritan ministers gathering in clandestine meetings, those who were involved in producing and distributing pamphlets and tracts, their Puritan supporters, and the nine courageous and zealous Puritans on trial for their very lives—was a profound change of direction, in government and society as well as religion.

Theirs was just the beginning of the story.

---

[46] Shiels, 66.
[47] Shiels, 66.

ENDNOTES

CHAPTER 2

[i]   Charges against Thomas Cartwright were:

1.   That Mr. Cartwright, being lawfully made deacon according to the church of England, hath forsaken and renounced the same.

2.   That, to shew his contempt of this calling, he hath obtained a new ordination in foreign parts, not according to the laws ecclesiastical of this realm.

3.   That, by virtue of this vocation, he hath established at Antwerp and Middleburg, a certain presbytery and eldership ecclesiastical.

4.   That, by the said eldership, certain persons, being Englishmen, were ordained to be ministers, not according to the laws ecclesiastical of this realm.

5.   That his eldership, so established, hath used ecclesiastical censures.

6.   That the said Thomas Cartwright, in his public ministry there, hath not used the Book of Common Prayer, but conformed to some of the foreign churches.

7.   That since his return from beyond seas, he hath promised, to the utmost of his power, to promote the peace of the church.

8.   That he, having no ministry in this church, and without any license, hath taken upon him to preach at Warwick and other places.

9.   That at sundry times, he hath shewed his dislike of the government of this church, and various parts of the liturgy; and hath persuaded others to do the same.

10. That he hath traduced and spoken against the bishops, and other governors of this church.

11. That he hath such hatred against them, he hath prayed publicly to this effect: 'Because they who ought to be pillars in the church, do ben themselves against Christ, and his truth, O Lord, give us grace, and pwer, all as one man, to set ourselves against them.'

12. That at sundry times and places he hath spoken against the laws, government, orders, prayers, and ceremonies of the church.

13. That preaching at the baptism of one of Job [sic] Throgmonton's children, he spoke much in justification of government by the eldership in every congregation.

14. That he could not endure those who defended the laws, government, and orders of the church.

15. That in his sermons at Warwick and elsewhere, he hath often delivered many frivolous and indiscreet positions.

16. That by his persuasions, sundry persons refused to give thanks after child- birth, according to the order prescribed.

17. That at sundry times, when he communicated at the Lord supper, he sate, or stood up on his feet, and persuaded others to do the same.

18. That before the Bishop he spoke in justification of these things; And declared the *Book of Common Prayer* was not established by law.

19. That in contempt of the ecclesiastical authority, he hath preached since he was under the sentence of suspension.

20. That his man-servant having a bastard child fathered upon him, he caused him to perform penance, taking upon him the authority of the ordinary.

21. That he and some others have kept diverse public fasts, and have invited more to join them, without the authority of the queen.

22. That since he came to Warwick, he hath cost much faction, by distinguishing the people into *godly* and *profane*.

23. That he doth know who were the writers, printers, or dispersers of the writings under the name Martin Marprelate.

24. That being asked his opinion of these books, he insinuated, that as the bishops would not amend by grave writings, it was meat they should be dealt with to their great shame and reproach.

25. That he penned or procured to be penned, all or some of part of the book, entitled *Disciplina Ecclesiae sacraverbo Dei descripta*; and he recommended the same to the judgment and censure of others.

26. That the said Thomas Cartwright and sundry others have met in assemblies, termed synod's, in London, Oxford, Cambridge, Warwickshire, Northamptonshire, &c.

27. That at such synods, it has been concluded, that all ministers should subscribe the said Book of Discipline and be governed by it.

28. That at such synods, a moderator was by him and them chosen, according to the order of the said book.

29. That at such assemblies, he did, with others, dispute upon certain articles, and set down their determinations.

30. That he, with others, in an assembly at Cambridge, did conclude upon certain decrees, which were afterwards considered an allowed at Warwick.

31. That all the proceedings of such meetings have been set down, from time to time, by the said Thomas Cartwright and others.

CHAPTER 4

ii Court Baron 1591-1592 (membrane 1)
Homage: John Billinge, Edmund Billinge and Thomas Cole
Presentments: John Byllynge and Thomas Cole

> At this court there came John Billinge, Thomas Cole and Thomas Gare and in full court they surrendered into the hands of the lords one tenement with appurtenances in Netherwedon within this manor commonly called or known by the name of "le townehouse." To the use of William Proudelove during his natural life. Paying thereupon yearly during the life of the aforesaid William to the aforesaid John Billinge, Thomas Cole and Thomas Gare and Thomas Billinge, their heirs and assigns 6s 8d of lawful money of England at the feasts of St. Michael the Archangel and the Annunciation of the Blessed Virgin Mary by equal portions. Upon which the lords in this instant court by their steward granted to the aforesaid William Proudlove seisin of the premises. To have to the same William and his assigns during the natural life of the same William. To hold by the rod at the will of the lords according to the custom of the aforesaid manor, paying thereupon yearly to the aforesaid John Billinge, Thomas Cole, Thomas Gare and Thomas Billinge, their heirs and assigns during the natural life of the aforesaid William the aforesaid 6s 8d at the aforesaid feasts by equal portions. And paying and doing to the lords all other rents, services and customs due for the premises and lawfully accustomed. And the aforesaid William gives to the lords as a fine for having such his estate thereof 4d. And he did fealty to the lords and is admitted as tenant thereof.

SECTION TWO

PLAGUES

CHAPTER 5

PLAGUES RAVAGE SOUTHWARK'S FAMILIES

PROUDLOVE CROSSES LONDON BRIDGE

In August 1593, William Proudlove stepped onto the north end of London Bridge and headed south across River Thames. Since Roman times, London Bridge was the only crossing of the mighty river between north and south. As he glanced left, he stopped in his tracks. Proudlove exclaimed, to no one in particular, "What a sight for sore eyes! I am so thankful, Lord." He watched the scene, absolutely mesmerized by the moment. The morning summer sun glistened on the river as sunlight danced across its waves. After more than two years confined, with its associated trials and tribulations, Proudlove and his Puritan minister colleagues were free of their prison walls at last!

The river bustled with activity. As he looked eastward to his left, sailing ships lay at anchor in the river loading cargo of all sorts destined for distant ports. Watermen shuttled cargo and passengers to and from both sides of the river and to the anchored ships. Ever since the defeat of the Spanish Armada five years before, the amount of trade and commerce had increased exponentially. London was now a major distribution point for goods to and from foreign destinations.

London, London Bridge, and Southwark in 1593.
Wikimedia Commons. Public domain. (5.1)

As Proudlove looked west and to his right, small craft powered by watermen shuttled single or small groups of passengers to and from one bank to the other. As he strolled alongside diverse shops that lined the bridge, Proudlove peered into shop windows. Shops, operated by merchants and tradesmen, beckoned customers with gold, spices, dyed cloth, sweet treats, tailored clothing, and many other goods presenting opportunities many only dreamed of. The cacophony of sounds and sights tickled his senses. He thought to himself, "How long has it been since I have seen and experienced such activity?" The sights, sounds,

103

and smells were overwhelming. For the first time in a long time, they made him feel alive again deep down in his bones. It was a good feeling!

As Proudlove walked through the arched gate framing the bridge's southside entrance, he stopped, turned around, and looked up. He could see stakes atop the Traitors' Gate. Since Henry VIII's reign, severed heads atop each stake graphically signaled the fate of those who attempted treason or seditious acts against the Crown. Strategically placed for all who entered London from the south via the only entry across River Thames, they served as a stark reminder of the Monarch's power. Proudlove likely thought, "There, but for the grace of God, one of those could have been mine!"

Traitors' Gate. Wikimedia Commons. Public domain. (5.2)

Even though Proudlove would rather have been at home in Weedon Bec with his family, he had no choice but to be in London now. When the Puritans were released from their jail cells following their legal standoff, the court imposed restrictions on most of them. Thomas Cartwright had already resumed his hospital work in Warwick. He agreed to return to London when summoned within twenty days for any reason whatsoever. Melancton Jewell and John Payne had been released to resume their livelihoods. The others—Edward Lord, Daniel Wyght, Humfrey Fen, and the Northampton group: Edmund Snape, Andrew King, and William Proudlove—were required to stay in London pending further dispensation of their cases. But those restrictions presented these ministers with community and outreach opportunities. Not only could Proudlove and his fellow Puritans walk in the liberty of their surroundings, but they could expand their knowledge of what God was doing in the network of unsanctioned Puritan communities.

When Proudlove stepped off London Bridge heading south, he entered a separate district with an environment quite different than that of the north bank of the Thames. Even though Southwarke, pronounced "suth-uck," was considered part of the burgeoning metropolis, it was a distinct entity governed by authorities independent of the City of London. That distinction contributed to a more flexible and sometimes lackadaisical approach toward controlling its commerce and entertainment district.

On his left, he noted St. Olave's church tower alongside the river's eastward bank. Looking across the Thames, Proudlove spotted the infamous Tower prison complex dominating the northern riverbank and its surroundings. He recalled terrifying stories he heard in prison. The notorious use of the rack to extract prisoner confessions was nothing short of barbaric. Crowds rimmed the square to view public executions designed to stifle oppositionists to her Majesty's policies. Gruesome details of executions held in and near there were vividly recounted by the general populace.

St. Olave's Church and the Tower. Wikimedia Commons. Public domain. (5.3)

As he viewed and compared the two edifices, William pondered them. "How ironic. On one side, Church. On the other, State. In view of all that has transpired in the last two years, I wonder where this contentious relationship will lead." While he intended no disrespect to Queen Elizabeth, he believed with all his heart the Church was governed by a higher authority: Almighty God.

He recalled how brutal the monarchy had been in its fight to maintain control and power over its subjects. The Traitors' Gate was one example. His two years in prison with his Puritan colleagues was another. Even stronger evidence was provided by the prison deaths of Roger Rippon and John Udall, plus the executions of martyrs John Greenwood, Henry Barrowe, and John Penry. These godly men, all Puritans, died in the first half of this year of our Lord, 1593.

As Proudlove glanced right along the south bankside to the west, he spotted the second-largest church in the London area, St. Saviour's, which loomed above the river. He thought it odd that it was so close to St. Olave's. They were just a brief five-minute walk apart. But he dismissed it as justified by London's large burgeoning population.

ENGLAND'S DOMINANT METROPOLIS: LONDON AND THE BOROUGH

London in the late sixteenth century, where nine Puritans found themselves in 1593, was by far England's dominant city. In 1558, at the beginning of Elizabeth I's reign, its estimated population was 50,000. But the city was still mostly encased in its Roman-era walls on the north bankside of River Thames.

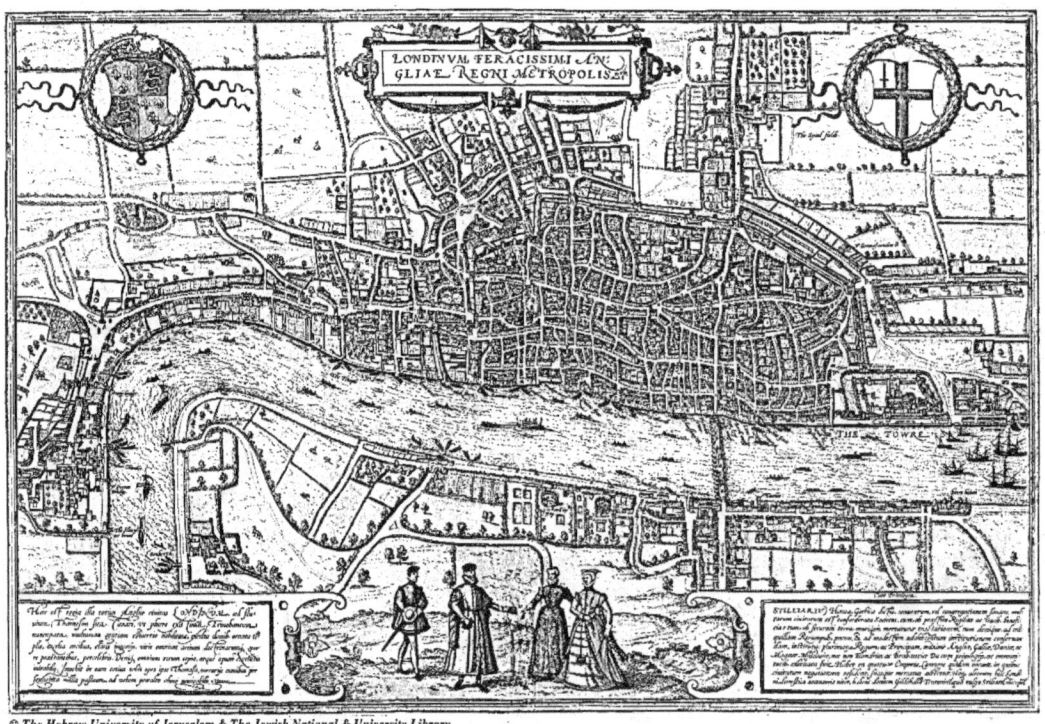

© The Hebrew University of Jerusalem & The Jewish National & University Library

London, 1560. With kind permission of Hebrew University of Jerusalem. (5.4)

Ships laden with cargo, either to be delivered to London or bound for foreign ports, lay anchored to the east of London Bridge. Smaller watercraft navigated River Thames with cargo to load or unload from the anchored ships, or with passengers to deliver to the north bankside, London proper, or to its south bankside district.

Southwark derived its name from London's defensive position established by King Alfred in the ninth century. Ever since the first bridge was constructed across River Thames, Southwark had been an important command post and road junction approaching London from the south. As the Domesday Book recorded in 1086, its name was *Sudweca,* meaning "southern defensive work," which eventually contracted to south-warke.

From early Saxon times, Old Southwarke—traditionally known as *The Borough*—was, and still is, a market town. The pilgrim route to Canterbury, as described by Geoffrey Chaucer in his *Canterbury Tales*, started from the Tabard Inn near the southern entrance to London Bridge.[1] In medieval times, *The Borough* was granted a charter of autonomy which allowed it to function outside of traditional hierarchical oversight—free from normal shire governance as well as ecclesiastical hundreds.[2] When the county of Kent introduced hop growing in the fifteenth century, the area's brewing industry grew rapidly. Water drawn from the Thames was considered peculiarly good for that purpose.

In 1509, the Bishop of Winchester and the Prior of St. Mary Overies granted a license to Southwark's brewers to pass with their carts "from ye Borough of Southwark until the Themmys . . . to fetch water . . . to brew with" so long as the brewers made no claim to the passage as a highway.[3] This license was renewed by later bishops and certainly helped proliferate alehouses and inns in the area.

Not surprisingly, this district attracted other forms of entertainment. By their very nature, they received less oversight from local authorities than those overseen by Crown officials in London proper. Southwark fostered "a haven for criminals and prostitutes" and created conditions rife for outbreaks of plagues.[4]

PLAGUES

From medieval times through the Renaissance, plagues regularly ravaged greater London's population. The first recorded plague in 1348-9 killed an estimated 30,000 Londoners. As this plague swept first through Europe and then into England, an estimated 50-60% of the population of Europe died.[5] Since black spots often appeared on victims' bodies, and usually brought death within a week of the onset of symptoms, the label Black Death was applied. The ever-present knowledge that anyone could be swept away by this gruesome disease at any moment frequently was depicted as "the Dance of Death."

---

[1] That thoroughfare is known as High Street today.

[2] A hundred was a division of a shire (county) which was used for administrative, military, and judicial purposes. It was introduced by the Saxons before the 12th century and was used until the 19th century. Originally, a hundred had enough land to sustain approximately one hundred households headed by a hundred-man or hundred eolder (elder). Within each hundred, there was a meeting place where the men of the hundred discussed local issues, and judicial trials were enacted. All hundreds were divided into tithings, which contained ten households,
"England Jurisdictions," *Wikipedia*. Viewed on 1 December 2022. https://www.familysearch.org/en/wiki/England_Jurisdictions.

[3] Hereinafter, Southwarke will be Southwark as it is known today.

[4] "Survey of London: Volume 22, Bankside (The Parishes of St. Saviour and Christchurch Southwark)," *British History Online*. Viewed on 8 September 2022. https://www.british-history.ac.uk/survey-london/vol22/pp78-80.

[5] Ole Jørgen Benedictow, *The Black Death, 1346-1353: The Complete History* (Suffolk UK: Boydell Press, 2018).

Michael Wolgemut, *The Dance of Death*, 1493. Public domain. (5.5) Anton Koberger, 1493

After the first recorded outbreak of plague, significant waves repeatedly wreaked havoc on London and other parts of England from 1361 until the Great Plague of 1665.[6] The disease was typically carried by rodents infected by flea bites—especially from black rats. When a victim died of the plague, its fleas found new hosts, including humans.

Human victims experienced painful swellings of lymph nodes. Known as buboes, they would attack victims' armpits, legs, neck, or groin. They suffered high fevers, delirium, vomiting, muscular pains, bruises, blisters, coughing up blood from the lungs, and mental disorientation. Once identified, houses would be bolted on the outside and locked from the inside. Plague victims were not allowed out nor anyone allowed in. The result was typically a death sentence. After infected, 60-80% of its victims died, most within two to four days. Plagues also spread quickly within households. In worst-case scenarios, entire families were wiped out—a painful and terrifying death experience.

In one particularly severe outbreak, the Plague of 1563, more than 20,000 souls perished in greater London—estimated to be 24% of its population. Another 60,000 lives were lost throughout England. Queen Elizabeth prohibited imports of all foreign goods, which dramatically impacted the economy. Terrified of the plague, she moved her entire

---

6   Compiled by Brian Williams in 1996 as part of "The Cycles of Plague," dissertation for a BA (Hons) degree at the University of Hull, England. Viewed on 4 February 2022. https://urbanrim.org.uk /plague.

court to Windsor Castle. As an extra protection measure, she erected gallows as a warning for those coming from London—they would be hanged.

Due to labor shortages, the dead were sometimes abandoned in homes until someone was available to drag corpses outside. Plague victims' corpses were thrown on carts and buried in often hastily reopened grave-pits about twenty feet deep, with widths expanded as necessary. Burial yards proliferated in rural areas adjacent to River Thames—including Southwark, already an area rife with disease.

Carts Full of Dead to Bury, London Plague. Public domain. (5.6)

LONDON'S GROWTH IN POPULATION AND COMMERCE

Despite plagues ravaging its residents and disrupting trade, London's population grew rapidly—as did its economic opportunities. The largest trading center in England, London's area merchants sold fine English wool, made from sheep in Wales, to Antwerp textile manufacturers where it was woven into cloth. Spices from foreign parts flowed into the country and were resold by wholesale grocers.[7] By the middle of the sixteenth century, England was a major trading power—directed by its monarchs and their favored merchants.

---

[7] Over time, grossers morphed to "grocers." Hereinafter, the modern spelling, grocers, will be used.

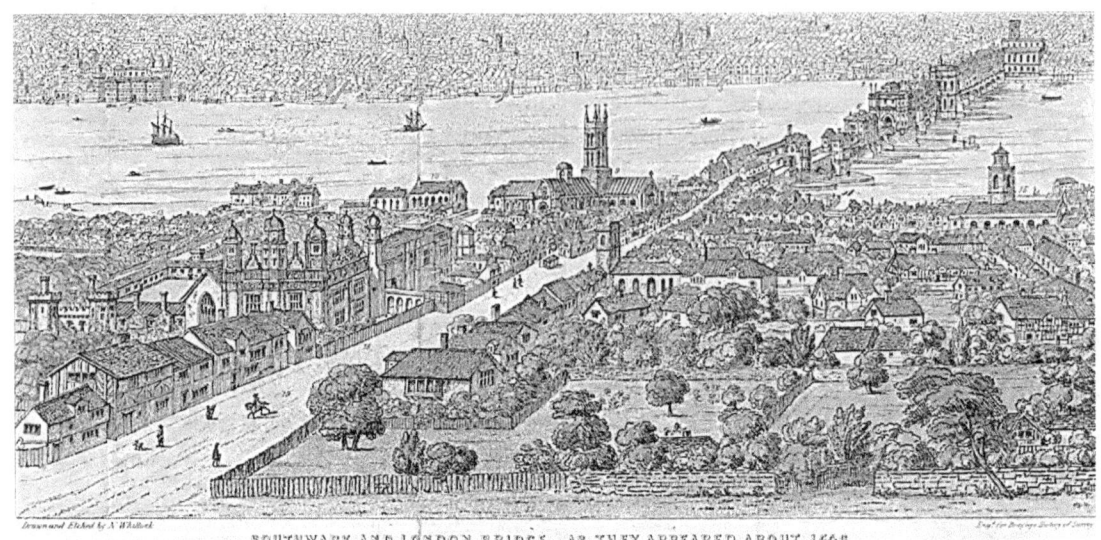

SOUTHWARK AND LONDON BRIDGE AS THEY APPEARED ABOUT 1546.

Southwark and London Bridge. Courtesy of Yale Center for British Art.[8]
Creative Commons. Public domain. (5.7)

From Henry VIII's death in January 1547, through the religious turmoil that followed during the reigns of Edward VI, Mary I, and into Elizabeth I's reign starting in 1558, the growth of England's commerce and trading continued unabated. As favored merchants expanded their business interests, the rapid expansion in trade and commerce led to the rise of a wealthy and powerful merchant class. While the nobility still held dominant power and favor from the Crown, the emerging merchant class steadily gained influence in England and on the Continent.

London became a magnet for immigrants seeking opportunities. But London's growth in commerce also encouraged a continuous stream of young men to move from their villages to the capital city for apprenticeships and work. Given the traditional inheritance pattern of English families—the eldest son inherited any property or tenant rights from his father—younger sons would often seek their livelihoods away from their home villages. These trends furthered London's long history of blended ethnic populations. Despite the ongoing threats of plagues, London's metropolitan area grew rapidly with an ongoing influx of new residents. These forces fueled a housing boom. Supply and demand reduced the size of affordable houses in greater London for laborers and created denser population centers. Lower-order families, including an increasing number of immigrants, were often forced to live in small shacks with dirt floors. This bred the term "dirt poor."

When Antwerp fell to Spanish forces on 17 August 1585, a high percentage of its merchants migrated north to Amsterdam and London.[9] Antwerp Delftware pottery

---

[8] From the *Long View of London from Bankside*, engraving by Wenceslaus Hollar, 1647. It depicts views in 1546 looking northward from Southwark. At the top right, London Bridge angles across River Thames as it enters London proper.

[9] "Fall of Antwerp," *Wikipedia*. Viewed on 31 January 2022. https://en.wikipedia.org/wiki/Fall_of_Antwerp.

manufacturers followed their brethren and relocated to Southwark. They built kilns for its manufacture adjacent to St. Saviour's Parish church. In particular, London was an attractive relocation target for Antwerp clothing manufacturers wanting to be near the source of fine dyed cloth. The resulting economic boom boosted dyers' livelihoods and attracted more commerce. Other trades benefited as well including carpenters, coopers, felt makers, grocers, haberdashers, joiners, watermen, and many others.

Unfortunately, cleanliness and infrastructure needs did not keep up with the demand of a growing population. No sewage system existed in Elizabethan London. Waste was dumped into River Thames. As a tidal river, it acted as a natural sewer. With the English habit of bathing only once a year in May, dirty and increasingly filthy conditions afflicted both London and Southwark. The area was littered with—and became known for—its poorer, run-down districts. But with the area's burgeoning population, entertainment was sought out as families' fortunes improved.

LONDON'S ENTERTAINMENT DISTRICTS

By the mid-1580s, the first permanent theatres appeared in Shoreditch, a district east of London's city boundary. Their success and profitability quickly convinced impresarios, playwrights, and actors that "people clearly liked going to a play, and they especially liked going to a new play. The pressure was on for anyone who had the skills to write new material as fast as they could."[10] As audience demand grew, actors and playwrights sought out additional opportunities to reach untapped audiences. They found the perfect setting and conditions on the south bankside of River Thames.

As an independent borough, Southwark was able to become London's extended entertainment district. In 1587, its first playhouse theatre, The Rose, opened with a capacity for 2,000 theatregoers. Established by Philip Henslowe, it soon became a popular place of entertainment for Londoners of all social ranks. Watermen's businesses boomed as they shuttled Londoners to the south bankside for popular plays of the day.

With the growing demand, The Rose offered as many as six different plays a week. It added new plays into the mix and extended runs of the most popular productions. Christopher Marlowe and William Shakespeare, two of the finest writers of the Elizabethan age, worked at The Rose. Anyone with a penny could see a play, and audiences grew. Since theatres were outside London's jurisdictional boundaries, playwrights and actors pushed the boundaries of good taste, as they are prone to do, and got away with more than the queen's watchmen would have preferred. With The Rose's success, a rival venue, built by Francis Langley, opened in 1595. Described as the finest and biggest of London's theatres, the Swan had a capacity for 3,000 spectators.

---

[10] Ruth Goodman, *How to Be a Tudor: A Dawn-to-Dusk Guide to Tudor Life* (New York: Liveright Publications, 2017): 223.

1595 Sketch of Swan's stage, Aernout van Buchel.
Wikimedia Commons. Public domain: (5.8)

The Swan Theatre was located in the manor of Paris Gardens, on the west end of the Bankside district of Southwark . . . at the northeast corner of the Paris Garden estate nearest to London Bridge . . . four hundred and twenty-six feet from the river's edge. Playgoers could arrive also by water landing at the Paris Garden Stairs or the Falcon Stairs, both short walking distances from the theatre.[11]

Southwark's theatres attracted large crowds and theatregoers who frequented shops, alehouses, and its other diversions. But as popular as theatres were, Southwark's most popular entertainment venues were established well before its theatres.

---

[11] "The Swan (Theatre)," *Wikipedia*, Viewed on 21 June 2021. https://en.wikipedia.org/wiki/The_Swan_ (theatre).

BLOOD SPORTS

Blood sports included cockfighting, bull baiting, and bear baiting. With traditions established earlier in parishes and market towns throughout England, "blood sports might be sponsored by the parish as money-raising events."[12] Cockfighting was the earliest blood sport and quite popular. General admission cost a penny, while two pence secured close-in seating along with gambling opportunities.

Bull baiting offered the spectacle of a bull moving freely about the arena while being attacked by armed men on foot or horseback A later version featured a tethered bull pitted against a pack of dogs. Bulls killed in these battles were sold to local butchers. By 1594, Edward Alleyn, the most famous actor of his time, acquired a part interest in the nearby bear-baiting arena along with his father-in-law, Philip Henslowe, which yielded a handsome profit.

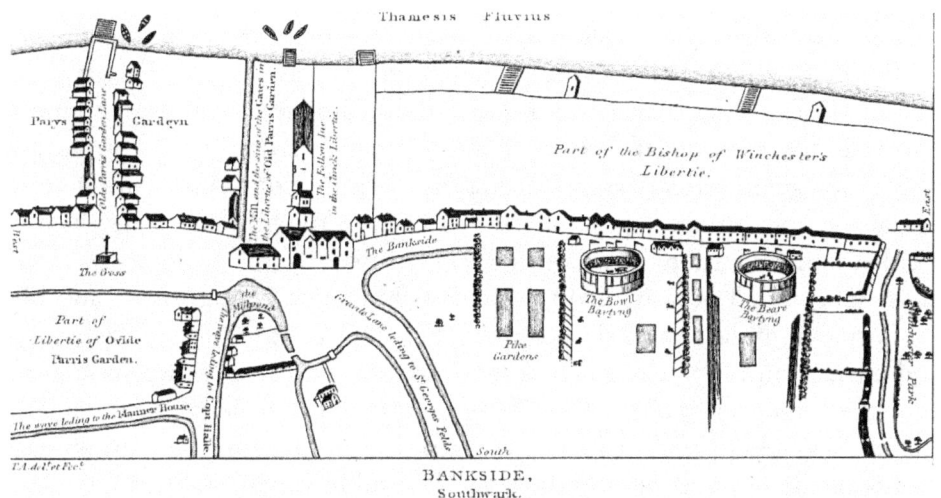

Bankside, Southwark. Bull, and Bear Baiting Arenas.
Wikimedia Commons. Public domain. (5.9)

Bear baiting closely resembled bull baiting but without the excuse of tenderizing the meat for human consumption. The exoticism provided as much of a draw as the blood-sport element. Bears were expensive beasts, and their owners were not keen to lose them. The baiting . . . though violent, was rarely permitted to result in fatalities for the bears—dogs were a little more expendable . . . The bears were sometimes trained to "dance." An inventory of the bear garden . . . in 1590 listed five "great bears" and four others. The great bears [were] performing animals who had to stand their turn in the ring; the "others" may well have been female breeding stock.

---

[12] Goodman, 215.

The crowds who flocked of an afternoon to the bear gardens on the edge of the city were large, boisterous, and very socially mixed. Bear baiting was popular with noble lords and humble carters alike. Visiting ambassadors were as likely to be among the throng as visiting sailors from the Port of London. Prostitutes, con men, pickpockets, and fast-food sellers all congregated to seek their respective customers, rubbing shoulders with, if not the actual noblemen themselves, at least with their bodyguard of menservants around them.[13]

Southwark's entertainment district of theatres, inns, alehouses, spas, country resorts, blood sport arenas, and houses of ill-repute served visitors and locals alike. It ensured the area was always busy, crowded, unsafe, and unhealthy.

Proudlove Visits a Southwark Puritan Gathering

This was the environment in which William Proudlove found himself on this Sabbath day in August 1593. As he entered this bustling borough, he contemplated the past several years' events—both their challenges and victories. He observed the borough's conditions and considered the relationship between Church and State. This day, he felt particularly convinced of God's calling him here. Though a hotbed of secular and economic activity, Southwark was also a center of Puritan support. Several parishes here—St. Saviour's, St. Olave's, St, George's, and St. Mary Magdalene, Bermondsey—had Puritan traditions. Members of the London Underground Church lived in the borough. They held worship services either in fields or homes on both sides of the river.

Today, William had been invited to attend a Puritan gathering. As he and his fellow at-liberty Puritan ministers awaited news from their appeals to remove restrictions on their travel and associations, they circulated around London, meeting with diverse groups like these throughout the metropolitan area. Without any formal or sanctioned role, Proudlove would share his stories of trials, tribulations, and deliverance with this Puritan group. He would undoubtedly recount the promises God had fulfilled while he was imprisoned and on trial. Certainly, he would tie his experiences to the word of God. As he was prone to do, he paused and prayed,

> "Most gracious God, I am most blessed and thankful for the liberty I now enjoy. Guide my steps and my words today. Use me, I pray, as thou wilt, and always for thy glory, Father, Son, and Holy Spirit. Amen."

As William strode past an unassuming dyer's shop, occupied by a family he did not know, there was no reason for it to attract his attention. The upstairs living quarters' street-facing window revealed nothing of interest or kinship behind the curtain. But William sensed there was something significant in God's plan for this family. And as he was soon to be reminded, God works in mysterious ways. What this Puritan minister could not then know, was that this household—members of the Henry Yates family—was in a life and death

---

[13] Goodman, 217-18.

struggle battling the plague currently ravaging London and Southwark. If he had known, he most surely would have stopped to pray for them.

Unbeknownst to him, this was also the home of a family that would play a key role in the Puritan cause, one of whose descendants would share their lives with descendants of his friend and Weedon Bec churchwarden, Thomas Cole. Their daughter, Jane, was destined to benefit from Proudlove's steadfast faithfulness to God's Promises and his resistance to ecclesiastical authorities during his trials and tribulations. And she was destined to find God's Promises—not only in England, but also in America.

THE FAMILY YATES

Henry Yates learned his trade as an apprentice, a common path for young men of the time. A typical apprenticeship in the late sixteenth century lasted seven years, often followed by a three-year period of honing and perfecting the craft with the goal of attaining the status of master. Apprentices started as young as fourteen, and almost always by age eighteen. In return for his labor, the apprentice received room and board along with his training, most often living with the master's family. It was hard work, with long days and few days off.[i]

After Henry completed the necessary instruction and preparation, probably in the late 1570s, he settled in the Southwark parish of St. Olave's to ply his trade and raise a family. When Henry married Alice, she was probably between eighteen and twenty years old. Sometimes brides married at a younger age due to a family's need, perhaps as early as fourteen. Most likely, Henry was a few years older than Alice. At this time, men most often married only when they were able to support a wife, ranging in age from their early to late twenties.

As a freeman citizen, Henry Yates was entitled to enjoy the privileges and benefits of guild membership. His trade was dyeing cloth—a living consisting of staining clothing or other fabrics with color. "Dyer" is derived from the Latin "dire," meaning awful, fearful, and threatening. The cloth manufacturing industry, which Yates served, was booming, partially due to the influx of Antwerp cloth manufacturers relocating to Southwark in the mid to late 1580s.

Throughout the 1580s, Henry and Alice Yates' family grew rapidly—a sign of prosperity. Two boys, Thomas the eldest and his brother John, plus two girls, Alice and Margaret, are not shown in the parish registers which started in March 1583. These four children were most likely born before that date. The Yates family baptisms recorded in St. Olave's Parish registers were Nathaniel, on 24 November 1583; Henry, on 8 November 1584; and Jane, on 5 February 1587.[14]

Three days after Jane's baptism, a major event rocked England. Queen Elizabeth had approved the execution of her cousin, Mary Queen of Scots. Aged forty-four, Mary was an heir to the English throne through her Tudor grandmother, Margaret, Henry VIII's older sister. On 8 February 1587, the executioner beheaded Mary at Fotheringhay Castle in Northamptonshire.

---

[14] St. Olave's Parish Registers (1583-1627)

The following year, another major event determined England's future course. Elizabeth's spies had uncovered the plot of a planned Spanish invasion of England. In 1588, the English Royal Navy, led by Francis Drake and Lord Charles Howard, assembled forty warships and several dozen armed merchant vessels. On the 31st of July, the English flotilla engaged the Spanish Armada off Plymouth. Over the next several days, the English harassed the Spanish as its fleet plied the English Channel and anchored off Calais, France. They planned to rendezvous with 30,000 troops commanded by the Duke of Parma and protect their invasion of England.

After a nine-hour battle, the Armada fled into the open sea having lost some 2,000 men. Bad weather blew them off course and into the North Sea. They abandoned the invasion attempt and made an ill-advised decision to head north and circumvent Britain to return to Spain. As they passed Scotland and the west coast of the island of Eire, storms ravaged the Armada. Spanish ships sunk in squalls, ran aground, or were dashed on rocks. When the Armada arrived at its home port, it had lost almost half its ships and an estimated 15,000 men.

The Spanish Armada's destruction was heralded as a great naval triumph. The truth is the Armada's defeat happened more by weather than by the skill of the English navy. But it elevated England's status as a naval power and bolstered its exploration efforts. In turn, that emboldened the Crown's expansionist desires, including the colonization of North America. Queen Elizabeth appointed a day of celebration and thanksgiving unto God for deliverance from the Spanish in November 1588. The Yates family most certainly attended the church service in St. Olave's Parish that day of solemn commemoration. They no doubt joined their fellow parishioners and offered praise and thanksgiving to God for England's great victory. But within a year, the family's fortunes would be forever changed.

As spring approached, Alice Yates gave birth to the newest member of the family, a daughter, Ursula. She was baptized on 2 March 1589. Daughter Jane, aged two, was mobile enough to explore the family's cramped living quarters upstairs above her father's downstairs shop. As most toddlers, Jane was curious and thrilled with her new baby sister. Her older sister, Margaret, and two older brothers now had someone else to help their mum. By the spring of 1589, Henry and Alice Yates' family of ten engaged a household servant, William—another sign of prosperity.

Unfortunately, Ursula died after only three months of life. She was buried on the 30th of May.[15] The loss of a child for any family is tragic but not uncommon for the time. Infant death was a fact of life. "At the end of the sixteenth century, one in eight children died within the first year of life and fully one-quarter of those born never reach age 10."[16] Despite the loss of baby Ursula, the family looked forward to a prosperous future.

Two and a half years later, Henry and Alice Yates lost two more children. Samuell was buried on 15 April 1592.[17] Six months later, John, a young lad about age nine, was buried on the 10th of October. The Yates' family mourned the deaths of three children within

---

[15] William E. Cole, "Jane Clarke: A Strong Woman: The English Origins of William Collier's Wife." (*The Mayflower Descendant*, Vol. 69, no. 1 (2021)): 57.

[16] Bucholz and Key, 163.

[17] Most likely a stillborn baby since no baptism was found.

three and a half years. By age five, Jane, had already lost three siblings and observed death first-hand. But she still had five surviving siblings. Unfortunately, the worst was yet to come.

Ten months later, another major plague hit metropolitan London hard in the late summer of 1593. The plague wreaked havoc on Henry and Alice Yates' family. Daughter Alice died first and was buried on 5 August 1593. The family's father, Henry, must already have contracted the disease from his daughter. He quickly realized the urgent need to set his affairs in order and wrote his will the same day his daughter was buried.[ii] Henry Yates was buried three days later, on the 8th of August. But that was not the end of it for the family— even more tragedy followed. The next day, son Nathaniel was buried. The family's servant, William, was buried on the 23rd of August. And the next day, Alice Yates lost her eldest son, Thomas. This horrendous plague devastated the Yates' family within three weeks.

In late August 1593, the only Yates family survivors were widow Alice, son Henry, and two daughters, Margaret and Jane. To make matters even more dire, Alice was seven months pregnant. If William Proudlove had recognized their need, he most surely would have stopped and ministered to them.

Understandably devastated by their losses, widow Alice Yates and her three children observed first-hand the horrible plague symptoms inflicting pain, agony, and suffering on their father and siblings. But even more tragedy was ahead. John Bell, a witness to the writing of Alice Yates' husband's will, died and was buried on the 6th of September. Even worse, Alice's eldest daughter Margaret, age nine, also perished. Her burial was unrecorded. One can scarce imagine the challenge the poor overextended vicar faced trying to keep up with so many burials during the Plague of 1593. Throughout greater London, many families saw losses similar to what the family Yates experienced. But it was particularly acute in Southwark. And its epicenter was St. Olave's Parish.

The following month, widow Alice Yates gave birth to a healthy baby daughter as her young daughter, Jane, helped. Baptized on the 14th of October, the parish scribe listed Margaret as the daughter of Henry Yates, dyer—two months after his death. As Alice nursed and cradled her newborn, she certainly felt strongly mixed emotions. She had named Margaret after her eldest daughter, who died just weeks before. While Alice wanted to rejoice and praise God for her healthy baby daughter, she found herself lacking. With no husband, no visible means of support, and with three children—her babe in arms, Margaret; her daughter Jane, not yet six years old; and her son Henry, age eight—she desperately needed to remarry. As overwhelming emotions coursed through her mind and body, she caught herself in a moment of despair. Alice breathed out a heavy sigh. Then she fell to her knees and turned to the Lord in prayer.

> "O God, Father of mercies and giver of comfort: I am so weary. But thy word teaches that in returning and rest we shall be saved, in quietness and confidence shall be our strength. By the might of thy Spirit, lift us—me and my family—I pray, to thy presence, where we may be still and know that thou art God. Amen."

A month later, another freeman dyer in St. Olave's Parish, John Arnold, lost his wife, Elizabeth. On the 23rd of November, she was buried in the parish's burial ground. Perhaps

God meant to bring these two together, both grieving the loss of their spouses. Two months later, on 24 January 1594, widow Alice Yates joined widower John Arnold in holy matrimony in St. Olave's Parish—the second marriage for each.[18]

Coping with the loss of their spouses, John and Alice's marriage brought into their union the house she inherited from her husband, two daughters, and a son. But with the support of her new husband, John, and by the grace of God, Alice Yates Arnold once again looked forward to what the Lord had in store for her new life. Even the cold, dreary winter days and long nights in 1594 looked brighter than they had in a long time. And the following month, Jane Yates celebrated her seventh birthday. The young, wide-eyed lass was growing up rapidly.

THE PLAGUE'S SILVER LINING

After William Proudlove shared, taught, and preached in Southwark in the summer of 1593, similar Puritan gatherings continued into the autumn, despite the epidemic proportions of the plague. On the 3rd of October, when Proudlove and his colleagues still in the city were summoned to meet with court officials, they "asked to be excused in view of the plague then raging in London."[19] When word arrived that their request was granted, the Puritans rejoiced. Edward Lord, Daniel Wyght, Humfrey Fen, and the Northampton group of Edmund Snape, Andrew King, and William Proudlove shouted praises aloud for God's goodness and providence.

At last, the remaining six Puritans were free to exit London and begin to rebuild their lives that had been disrupted for the past three years. Proudlove praised God for his liberty and anticipated reuniting with his family. He missed them so much and ached to embrace them all.

LIBERTY AT LAST

With the Puritans' liberty granted, their supporters sprang into action. They coordinated logistics quickly and arranged for their transportation home to their families. Thomas Cartwright had returned to his duties at the Warwick hospital. Edmund Snape had already arrived home safely in Northampton. Melanchton Jewel and Edward Lord, previously released, had returned to their parishes.

Today was the day for William Proudlove and Andrew King. During the past three and a half years, the two former vicars had shared so much during their trials and tribulations. Their return would reunite them with family, friends, and hopefully their livelihoods. Early in the morning, a coachman waited to collect them from their accommodations for their long journey home—Andrew King returning to Culworth, and William Proudlove to Weedon Bec. These two men were up early and eagerly clamored into the coach.

---

[18] St. Olave's Parish Registers (1583-1627)
[19] Collinson, 430 footnote 41.

Private coaches were first introduced in England in 1565. Dutchman Guylliam Boonen presented one to Queen Elizabeth. Not much more than springless carts, they became popular with the gentry in the sixteenth century's final decade. As one observer noted, "now of late years the use of coaches, brought out of Germany, is taken up and made so common . . . for the world runs on wheels with many whose parents were glad to go on foot."[20]

As Proudlove and King settled into their seats, the driver estimated the travel would take two, maybe three, overnight stops. Any travel hardships would be nothing compared to their experiences in prison. Gratefulness exuded from their hearts and lips when their restrictions were finally eliminated. At last, they were free—after three and a half long years! Now, in October 1593, they were beginning the journey home to be reunited with their families and resume their lives.

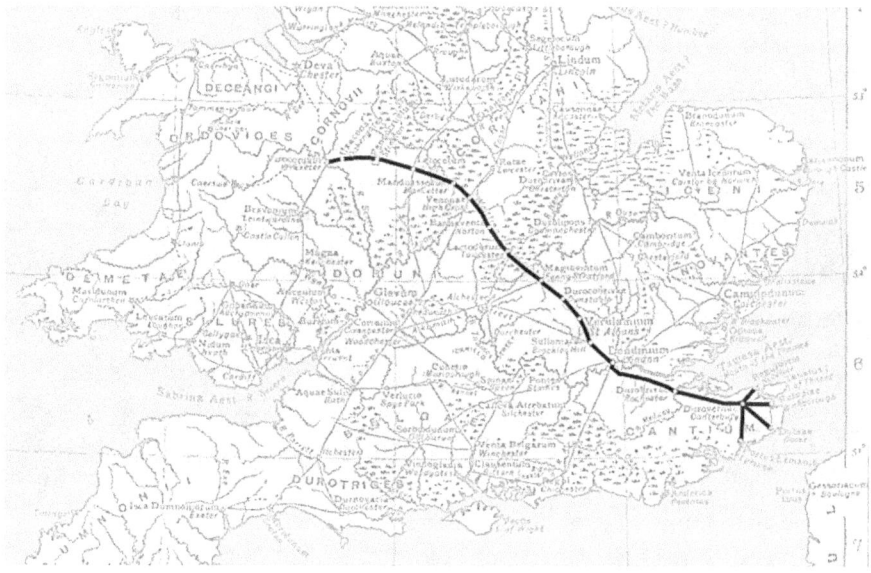

Watling Road [Old Roman Road]. Public domain. (5.10)

As the grimy neighborhoods and pungent smells of London receded into the background, the coachman traveled northwest on the old Roman Road—now Watling Road.[21] One of the few roadways acceptable for this type of travel, the open terrain was a welcome sight for their sore eyes. They rejoiced for the freedom and luxury of riding in a coach compared to their prison cells. Proudlove and King suspected that Sir Richard Knightley had made these arrangements and paid for the coach. Deprived of their livelihoods, they never could have obtained such a luxurious blessing on their own. Smiling at each other, they burst into antiphonal prayers, praising God for fulfilling his promises of protection and blessing them with such provisions.

---

[20] Edwin A. Pratt, *A History of Inland Transportation and Communication in England* (London: Kegan Paul, 1912): 38.

[21] Image of "1911 Watling Street" *Wikimedia Commons*.

Despite countless bumps, ruts, and jostles, time passed quickly as they recounted their experiences in London's courts and prisons. For more than three years, stances the nine Puritans took based on their consciences had helped them all stand firm in the faith. Facing powerful men intent on imposing penalties even greater than prison, they collaborated with each other and attorneys to craft their testimonies and appeals. After courageously signing a petition directed to Queen Elizabeth I, they finally received some liberties—albeit with restrictions. They temporarily gained enough freedom to visit Puritan gatherings with believers eager to hear their stories and learn from their experiences. With the Plague of 1593 raging in London, they were at last on their way home.

Once outside of London, the landscape's beauty glistened as it always did in the fall. Proudlove and King breathed in deeply. The fresh air reminded them of God's life-giving breath and this part of Creation: the beautiful countryside of Northamptonshire.

Northamptonshire Countryside. Courtesy of William E. Cole. (5.11)

As nightfall approached, their coachman pulled into an inn. There, they would have supper and spend the night. As Proudlove lay on the rough-hewn bed, he reflected on the pain he endured during nearly three and a half years away from his family. He eagerly anticipated seeing them once again. "I wonder how it will feel to embrace my wife. And the children—how much have they grown?" William had been arrested when his young daughter, Grace, was an infant. "The other children, how much have they changed?" Overwhelmed with thoughts and emotions, he breathed out a sigh and took a moment to compose himself. With a clear head, he offered the Lord his nightly evening prayer.

"Most gracious God, I am truly thankful for the blessings of the day that is past, and I humbly beseech thy merciful protection through the coming night. Bring us in safety to the morning hours; through him who died and rose again for us, thy Son our Savior Jesus Christ. Amen."

Fortunately, the Lord gave him a restful night's sleep and, after another day's ride, the next one as well. As the morning of the third day flowed into afternoon, the men's excitement grew as the English Midlands countryside became more familiar. When the church tower of Weedon Bec came into view, Proudlove's heart leaped and his mind raced in anticipation of embracing his loved ones.

Weedon Bec Church in Autumn. Courtesy of William E. Cole. (5.12)

Just a few blocks beyond the church tower, the coachman stopped in the heart of the village. Proudlove embraced his traveling companion and said goodbye. His Puritan colleague, Andrew King, former vicar of Culworth, would travel on with the coachman to his village—thirteen miles away.

Eagerly, Proudlove clamored down from the coach, stepped up from Church Street, unlatched the door to *Le Townhouse*, and leapt into the waiting arms of his wife, Isabella. The sweetness of her kiss and passionate embrace embedded a memory he would cherish for the rest of his life. With tears of joy streaming down his face, his children formed a circle around him, anxiously tugging on him as they awaited their father's kisses. His spirit warmed in a way he had not felt in such a long time. He realized how blessed he was for the support of his family!

William exclaimed to his children, "How much you have grown!" His two eldest boys, John and Thomas, were not quite teenagers. Three younger daughters were growing up rapidly: Elizabeth, 9; Ellen, 6; and Grace, almost 4. His youngest son, William, just a toddler holding his mother's hand, had been born a few months after his father's arrest. Proudlove reached out to his namesake and swooped him up in his arms. He had last seen his family in 1591, when given liberty to attend the Court Baron presentment where his family was granted the privilege to occupy *Le Townhouse*. Proudlove fell to his knees surrounded by his family. He gave God thanks for the love of his family, and the home given to him through the generosity of Thomas Cole, Thomas Billinge, John Gare, and John Billinge.

"Almighty God, heavenly Father, we give thee most humble and hearty thanks for all thy goodness and loving-kindness. We bless thee for our creation, preservation, and all the blessings of this life; but above all for thy inestimable love. Direct us, O Lord, in all our doings with thy most gracious favor, and further us with thy continual help; that in all our works begun, continued, and ended in thee, we may glorify thy holy Name, and finally, by thy mercy, obtain everlasting life; through Jesus Christ our Lord. Amen."

As the nights lengthened and temperatures dropped, the two downstairs fireplaces of *Le Townhouse* warmed the Proudlove family. The embers glowed, as they basked in the joyful blessings of being together. With autumn's transition toward winter, snow settled on the village in December 1593. With prayers remaining on their lips, they looked forward to God's direction on where William would next be called to serve.

Weedon Bec Church in Winter. Courtesy of William E. Cole.[22] (5.13)

---

[22] Special thanks to Julia Johns, photographer of this image.

CHAPTER 6

A COLE FAMILY OF NORTHAMPTONSHIRE

CHURCH AND FAMILY DISRUPTIONS IN WEEDON BEC

When Thomas Cole heard the news of William Proudlove's return from London, he rejoiced. The lives of the former churchwarden and his wife had been dramatically disrupted ever since their excommunication in 1589-90. When his vicar was imprisoned in May 1590 and experienced the trials and tribulations in London, the Coles and their fellow village parishioners steadfastly supported Proudlove, his wife, and his family as best they could. In addition to the families Cole, Billinge, and Gare gifting *Le Townhouse* to Proudlove in 1591, the villagers worked determinedly for their vicar's release from prison. They jointly sent petitions with other Northampton parishes on behalf of Proudlove and Edmund Snape.[1] In Weedon Bec, "a third of the congregation were absenting themselves from the parish."[2]

On 2 October 1590, four new Weedon Bec churchwardens were selected and noted in a visitation by diocesan officials. They also noted that the "churchwardens there present the glass windows and churchyard wall is out of repair, which have both surplice and book, but cannot come by them. Item, the wife of Robert Muscott was buried without a minister and there a minister procured to be present."[iii]

Things went somewhat more smoothly in the neighboring village of Culworth. On 6 Nov 1590, four churchwardens there stated they had only one service in three months during the vicar's default—Andrew King, Proudlove's friend and fellow Puritan colleague was detained in prison at that time. The bishop had replaced the former vicar, King, with Edmund Rudierd some three months before.[3] After a transitional time, vicar Rudierd integrated well into parish life and conducted baptisms for several of his own children.

But in Weedon Bec, parishioners steadfastly petitioned the bishop for Proudlove's reinstatement. When the bishop sent replacement vicars, the remaining parishioners protested. They adamantly resisted returning to the traditional liturgy—unprecedented actions within the Church of England. The bishop attempted to set the rebellious parishioners straight multiple times. A new vicar, Randolf Wade, was presented on 2 December 1591 and deprived the same day. The same occurred for his replacement— vicar William Cherington—also presented and deprived on 27 January 1592.[4] Continued visitations by diocesan authorities, recorded once or twice monthly, named a few prominent Weedon Bec parishioners absenting themselves from church including Thomas Billinge and

---

[1] Collinson, 414.

[2] Shiels, 131.

[3] CCEd. "Edmund Rudierd," variant spelling is Rudyerd. He was presented and installed on 19 August 1590.

[4] CCEd, "Randolf Wade." "William Cherington."

his wife, Alice, and John Gare and his wife. Both couples were excommunicated and issued citations through April 1593.[iv]

During these disruptive years, the parishioners who left hoped to worship undisturbed by diocesan authorities. Thomas Cole, his wife, and family visited extended family in nearby villages. When Thomas was warmly welcomed in Pitsford, a village thirteen miles northeast of Weedon Bec, it appears he served there as a churchwarden in 1592 and 1593.[5] Helped by his family and friends, Cole maintained his tenancy rights in Weedon Bec and kept abreast about ongoing Weedon Bec efforts to free the imprisoned Puritan ministers during this tumultuous time.

When Proudlove finally regained his liberty in October 1593, the villagers celebrated. But when he was not reinstated, parishioners were greatly disappointed, as was Proudlove since he remained deprived of his livelihood. Along with Andrew King, neither of the former vicars was reinstated. With the status of their ordinations unchanged, they were officially restrained from formal contact with parishioners. They were forbidden from preaching, leading small group studies, engaging in normal pastoral care for their parishioners, and presiding over sacraments in the Church of England including communion, baptisms, marriages, burials, or any other sanctioned parish activities. But these ministers had steadfastly maintained in the trials that they had done nothing wrong and were directed—with no intended disrespect to her Majesty the Queen—by an even higher power, Almighty God.[6]

Given this climate of religious chaos, one can imagine non-sanctioned Puritan gatherings may have been held in Weedon Bec's *Le Townhouse* after Proudlove's return in autumn 1593—perhaps similar to those in which he had participated in Southwark the previous summer. No wonder his loyal churchwarden, Thomas Cole, rejoiced when he heard of his return. He may even have participated in unsanctioned meetings.

Despite his personal trials and tribulations, Thomas never lost faith and was grateful for God's goodness. He often lifted prayers of thanksgiving for his many blessings. When he was able to see Proudlove in person, he had asked him for a special favor. Thomas asked William to make inquiries for his son, John Cole. A smile formed on Thomas' face as he thought about John finding work on a Culworth farm with Proudlove's help and Andrew King's connections. Thomas smiled because he believed there was more to it than just his son's livelihood—much more. He was quite sure his son was smitten with a daughter of the family who owned the farm. Thomas was grateful his son and heir may have found his mate. With that thought, he immediately lifted a special prayer of gratefulness for William Proudlove and Andrew King. His grateful remembrance of these blessings rekindled thoughts of his own family's history.

---

5 Pitsford Parish Registers (1560-1686)
6 More information on this subject is detailed in chapters 1-3.

HISTORICAL CONTEXT FOR THE COLE FAMILY

Thomas recalled how his father explained the dynamic events that reshaped England's villages and property rights to him as a young lad—developments that had greatly influenced the lives of his grandfather and his father, and indeed his own. After Henry VIII declared himself Supreme Head of the Church of England in 1531, he moved steadily to separate the Church of England from the authority of Pope Clement VII. The 1534 Act of Supremacy confirmed King Henry's status of sovereignty over the Church of England and required those of noble rank to swear an oath recognizing it.

Henry next moved to confiscate Catholic abbeys in England. In 1536, the Act of Suppression closed small monasteries with an income of less than £200 a year. After Pope Paul III excommunicated Henry over the annulment of his marriage with Catherine of Aragon in 1533, a second Suppression Act in 1539 dissolved larger monasteries and religious houses. In essence, these combined acts confiscated all Catholic property in England and Wales—its churches, abbeys, other buildings, land, and money—and transferred their ownership to the Crown. These acts enabled King Henry to reward faithful subjects with property, making them Lords of the Manor.

But more than a century earlier, in 1414, King Henry V had ordered that "'Alien Priories', as they were called, be taken over, and the income transferred to the Crown."[7] This started England's acquisition of French property. On 11 October 1440, Henry VI affixed his seal to establish *Kynge's College of Our Ladye of Eton besyde Windesore* with the appointment of two faculty members. Its purpose was to provide free education

Eton College. Wikimedia Commons. Public domain. (6.1)

to seventy poor boys who would go on to King's College, Cambridge, which he founded 1441. The Foundation Charter is stored in the school's archives among other treasures.[8] The

---

[7]   "A Short History of Weedon Bec," *Weedon Bec History*. Viewed on 4 August 2019. blisworth.org.uk/images/Canal/rumbold.htm. Eton College - By David Loggan – St. Louis Public Library - Steedman Architectural Collection Description page, Public domain. https://commons.wikimedia.org/w/index.php?curid=18911071.

[8]   "Eton College," *Eton College*. Viewed on 20 August 2022. https://catalogue.etoncollege.com/ecr-39-03. "In about 1472 the Manor was granted by Henry VI to the newly formed Eton College, who remained

earliest documents stored in the archive pre-date its founding. Eton College—near Windsor Castle (the home away from home of the royal family)[9]—along with its provost and fellows were granted manorial rights and homage as Lords of the Manor over Weedon Bec, which became one of the funding sources for the school.

In 1508, Henry VII affirmed that Weedon Bec Manor Courts were to be held "twice per year. . . . Law Day would be with previous customs of the whole lordship which were written in 1157 by Henry II . . . on the Thursday after Hock Tuesday and the Thursday next after St. Martin's day."[10] Hock Tuesday, the second Tuesday after Easter, represents the massacre of the Danes by King Ethelred in 1002. St. Martin's Day celebrates the day Saint Martin was buried in the Netherlands on the evening of 11 November.

Throughout England, a governance system ensured the manorial courts' primary purpose was to preserve the lord's financial interests. Customs of the manor regulated tenants' rights and privileges. While some variance occurred from place to place, standard practices and procedures directed the court to settle disputes or complaints about tenants' tenures and prosecute those who failed to render proper services due to the lord. Tenants were required to seek permission to sublet, exchange lands, or include property in a will. A tenant's right to hold property was written on the manor court rolls and a copy was provided to the tenant—hence the name copyhold.

Since Medieval times, English manors followed a fundamental formula that enabled a village's sustainable agriculture for its

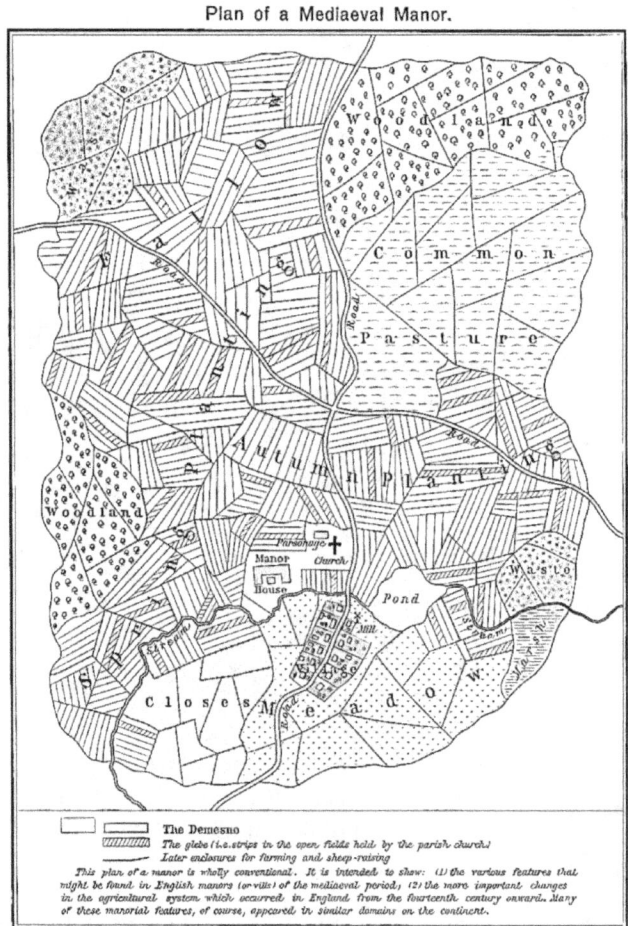

Plan of a Mediaeval Manor.

The Demesne
The glebe (i.e. strips in the open fields held by the parish church)
Later enclosures for farming and sheep-raising

This plan of a manor is wholly conventional. It is intended to show: (1) the various features that might be found in English manors (or vills) of the mediaeval period; (2) the more important changes in the agricultural system which occurred in England from the fourteenth century onward. Many of these manorial features, of course, appeared in similar domains on the continent.

William R. Shepherd, Historical Atlas, New York, Henry Holt Co., 1923. Wikimedia Commons. Public domain. (6.2)

Lords of the Manor until changes in the law relating to leasehold property in the 1920s."

[9] By 1110, Henry I had domestic quarters within the Castle, and his grandson Henry II converted the Castle into a palace in the late 12th century.

[10] Bridges, 451.

tenants and protected their livelihoods through the regulation of trades. The Lord of the Manor wanted villagers to be successful and continue their land leases and pass them along to their heirs. This supervision created stability for the villagers and for the Lord of the Manor.

At manorial court meetings, formal ceremonies dictated the court's procedures in the same order. The Jury, or Homage,[11] was made up of tenants who owed fealty to the Lord of the Manor. They were first called and sworn in to determine injuries, trespasses, debts, and other actions. Second, Essoins were listed—the names of tenants who have sent apologies for their absence.

Third, Presentments followed. Similar to a court action, reports or accusations were made to the steward by other manorial officials. Jurors made decisions based on the customs of the manor. Persons accused could produce witnesses prepared to swear to the truth of his story. If judged guilty, personal property could be seized, or the offender would be required to find personal pledges who would suffer penalties if the offender failed to attend the next court to submit to the court's ruling.

Outgoing tenants surrendered property to the lord, and new tenants were admitted by the Rod.[12] This refers to a stick, or rod, carried by the steward which the tenant touched in the formal admission ceremony. Monies payable to conclude a case or transaction were noted as Fines (or *amercements*). Heriot was a payment exacted by the lord on the death of a tenant. An heir who wished to take over the property had to surrender his best beast or a payment.[13] A final action, Fealty, was to swear allegiance to the Lord of the Manor or higher authority.

Cole Family's Arrival in Weedon Bec

As Thomas recounted the blessings of the autumn of 1593, he thought back to the time his family first came to Weedon Bec, some fifty years earlier. Since his father, John, was not the eldest son, he would not inherit tenancy rights from his father, William Cole. Thomas' grandfather, William, was well established in the village of Long Buckby, about five miles north of Weedon Bec. Cole paid taxes there in 1524.[14] It is likely that William and his wife, Alice, had lived there since at least the late fifteenth century.

William's son, John, was born there no later than 1513.[15] John married there, but his wife's name is unknown. Thomas Cole was their eldest son. But without tenancy rights in Long Buckby, about five miles north of Weedon Bec, John Cole needed an opportunity

---

[11] Latin *homagium*.

[12] Latin *pervirgam*.

[13] "The Court Baron," *Herts Memories*. Viewed on 7 July 2022. https://www.hertsmemories.org.uk/content/herts-history/places/manors/the-court-baron. "The Court Baron manorial court held for the tenants" by Sue Flood and Carol Futers. Manorial courts declined in the 17th century, were somewhat obsolete in the 18th century, and officially disbanded in 1922.

[14] E179 tax roll "Long Buckby."

[15] Additional research has attempted to locate previous Cole generations. Possible connections exist, but no proven ties have yet to be found up.

to acquire tenant rights in another village. When John was at least thirty years old,[v] he brought blacksmith trade tools with him to Weedon Bec. He hoped they might lead to an apprenticeship opportunity, allowing him to save money, gain tenancy rights, and become a husbandman.[16] That was John's desire—to acquire tenant property rights and create a better life for his family.

In 1550, John achieved his goal. Summoned to his first Court of the Baron meeting, John settled in on *Le Townhouse's* bench. He observed the swearing-in ceremony of homage and selection of jurors for the day. In charge of the court were three Billinge men: Edward, William, and Richard. As both John and Thomas would discover, the Billinge family was the most prominent and influential in the village, and had been, since the early fourteenth century.[17]

John Cole was called for the first presentment. They explained the local procedures, and he was sworn in. This simple and straightforward presentment granted Cole a land tenancy of a "certain close, lying in Small Acre" enclosed at the time of the commission.[vi]

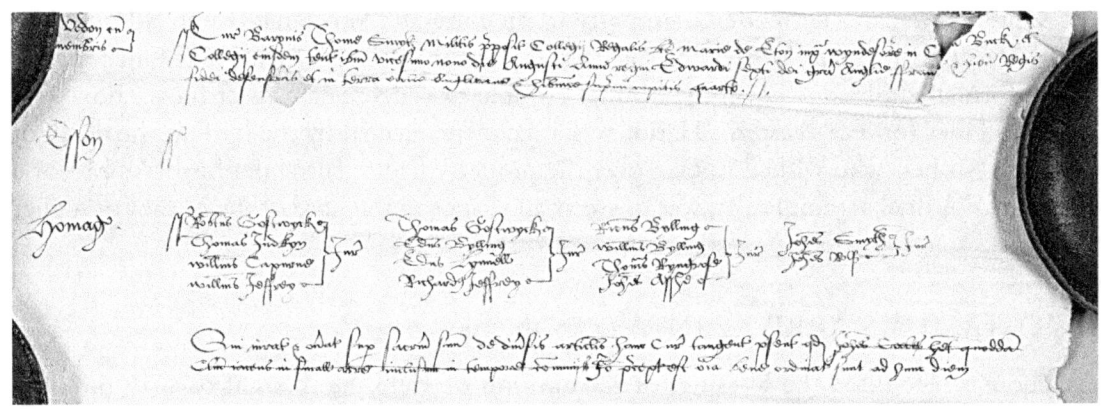

John Cole, 1550 Manor Court. His presentment is the two bottom lines, after the Homage names. Reproduced with kind permission of Eton College Archives, image 17. Sponsored by Anne Cole Linscott and James Stuart Cole in memory of their father, Charles Henry Cole, Jr. (6.3)

Throughout the following decade, John appeared often at manorial court meetings. In 1551, John was presented that he had "encroached upon the waste of the lords near to his house in length a yard by estimation and in width at one end three yards, and at the other end one foot."[18] As a result, John was fined.[vii] Thomas smiled at that thought. His father seemed to have a knack for controversy.

---

[16] In English society, a yeoman is a commoner—a freeholder under the rank of a gentleman—and a step above a husbandman. Both yeomen and husbandmen would be considered farmers by today's standards.

[17] Variant spellings are many including Byllynge, Byllinge, Billynge, Billinge, Byllyng, Bylling, Billing. Hereinafter, Billinge.

[18] Eton College Archives, ECR27_228, 1550, John Cole. Hereinafter abbreviated Eton. Cole personal archive image 17. Several Cole spelling variations exist in these records. They include Coole, Cooles,

A second court presentment involved him that day, more complicated than the first. It generated more work for court officials than normal. Thomas again smiled at the memory. The case recorded a transaction involving a home and three parcels of land from John's neighbor, Richard Campyon. But it had not accounted for a debt owed to Cole by the son of his neighbor. The recorded presentment was then crossed through—which meant cancelled.

It is found at this court by the homage that Richard Campyon out of court in the presence of Richard Waw and Thomas Judkyn, by the hands of Thomas Clyfford, bailiff of the lords, surrendered into the hands of the lords one messuage and two virgates of land in Overwedon, and a meadow pertaining to the same messuage called Too Yerd Land Mede in Over Wedon, to the use and behoof of John Cole, his executors and assigns for the term and throughout a term of 20 years from the feast of St Michael the archangel next following. Whereupon there befalls to the lords as a heriot according to the custom of the manor 5s. Upon which there came the aforesaid John Coole and he took out of the hands of the lords the aforesaid messuage, two virgates of land and meadow called Too Yerd Land Meade with appurtenances, and he seeks to be thereupon admitted.

The court then corrected its record—accommodating the debt owed to Cole by his neighbor's son, John Campyon.

And for the aforesaid last ten years he John Coole [*sic*] will pay nothing to the aforesaid Richard Campyon, his heirs and assigns, because he lent to the aforesaid John Campyon £20 before the date of this court. Therefore, the same John Coole [*sic*], his executors and assigns will then enjoy and have the aforesaid tenement during the aforesaid ten last years in satisfaction of the aforesaid £20, saving, nevertheless, to the lords the rents, customs and services thereupon previously due and lawfully accustomed. And he will hand over a heriot after a surrender or any decease according to the custom of the manor. And the aforesaid John Cole gives to the lord as a fine for having such estate thereof one horse at the value of [blank], and he did fealty and is admitted as tenant thereof.[19]

Thomas recalled another noteworthy episode that left an indelible impression on him. On 1 April 1552, John Cole again appeared before the court. He and a dozen other men were presented for using hand mills, known as querns. This practice undermined the village

Cowle, and Colles. But it is confirmed there was only one John Cole at this time. The variant spellings all describe the same man, John Cole. Cole will be used unless it is in an original source document cited. "Waste of the lords" refers to the time before enclosures in England, when a portion of land was categorized as *common* or *waste*. *Common* land was under the control of the lord of the manor, but certain rights on the land such as pasture, pannage, or estovers were held variously by certain nearby properties, or (occasionally) *in gross* by all manorial tenants. *Waste* was land without value as a farm strip—often very narrow areas (typically less than a yard wide) in awkward locations (such as cliff edges, or inconveniently shaped manorial borders), but also bare rock, and so forth. *Waste* was not officially used by anyone, and so was often farmed by landless peasants. "Inclosure Acts," *Wikipedia*. Viewed on 15 October 2021. https://en.wikipedia.org/wiki/Inclosure_Acts.
19 Eton, ECR27_229, 1551, John Cole.

miller's business and the Court Baron's income.[viii] One quern typically required two people to operate. One turned the handle and the other poured in the grain, which often served

several families. Even with a village miller, some "families may have preferred to have the ability to grind grain for themselves on short notice."[20]

Prized by wealthier households and coveted throughout the region, these valuable and ancient hand mill tools originated in the Middle East. After newer versions spread into medieval Europe, they finally reached the shores of England. By the sixteenth century, a manufacturing facility in Southwark churned out large quantities for London traders to sell throughout England's

Women at the Quern by Moses Griffin. Wikimedia Commons. Public domain. (6.4)

countryside villages to tenant farmers—men like John Cole.

John Cole, Illegal Mill and Quern fines, 1552. Reproduced with kind permission of Eton College Archives, image 14. Sponsored by Ronald E. Benson. (6.5)

The Weedon Bec Court Baron officials sworn in that day were again the three Byllyng men: Edward, Richard, and Henry. They received Cole's sworn testimony under oath, plus a

---

20 "Quern," *Medieval London*. Viewed on 20 March 2020. https://medievallondon.ace.fordham.edu/exhibits/show/medieval-london-objects-3/quern.

payment of 16d for relief in the full court. Besides himself, Cole testified that twelve men "are suitors to this court," have defaulted, and are each "in mercy" for payment of a fine of 2d.[ix]

Three of the twelve men were not Weedon Bec villagers. They were prominent men from nearby villages and market towns who likely owned or controlled village land. Peter Colles, a gentleman from Preston Capes, slightly more than five miles southeast from Weedon Bec, descended from an ancestral line of Colles dating back to the early fifteenth century. Others included men from the Fawsley Manor near Preston Capes, and John Clarke who resided in Wolfuncote, a town to the west of Daventry that straddled the border of the shires of Northampton and Warwick.

As Thomas recalled his father's testimony, John did fealty and was admitted as a tenant. He also named thirteen men, including himself.[x] They testified that they

> have hand-mills called "querns" and exercise the same to the detriment of the liberty of the lords there. Therefore, they are ordered to destroy the same before the next court or to agree with the lords for the same to be occupied and make a fine, under pain. Upon which it is ordered that anyone, who after this will have or occupy any hand-mill, will pay to the miller yearly as his fine thereof 12d.
>
> Affeerers: William Jeffrey and Edmund Bylling, sworn.[21]

Thomas knew how difficult it was for his father to testify against some of his neighbors and friends. But John continued to be active in property acquisition. On 22 September 1553, John Cole of Weedon, husbandman, personally replied to Robert Gostwyck that "he was prepared to pay tithe for meadow at 6d for each yardland. He had agreed and paid a tithe for ½ acre of oats and ½ acre of barley."[22]

Four months later, John Cole's neighbor, Richard Campyon, asked John to witness his will. Richard named him co-executor along with Campyon's wife, Sybell, in the early 1550s. Campyon fit the profile of a small farmer. His will gave his son, John, a bequest of animals. Campyon's will probate occurred in January 1554.[23]

However, another earlier presentment involved John Cole and Valentine Brothers. Brothers surrendered land he received from William Capron to the "use and behoof of Thomas Lovett, his heirs and assigns."[xi] Thomas Lovett V, a prominent and wealthy man, lived in Astwell, five miles west of Culworth, and eighteen miles from Weedon Bec. Lovett was about thirty years old and first became High Sheriff of Northamptonshire in 1552. Thomas Lovett II had married Joan Billing. The Billings might have been Lovett's connection to Weedon Bec.

> At this court there came Thomas Lovet [sic], esquire, and he took of the lord by his steward from the handing over of William Dobson, bursar of the aforesaid college on this occasion,

---

[21] Eton, ECR27_230, 1552, John Cole. Upon oath, affeerers settled and moderated fines in courts.

[22] *Witness Statements from Deanery and Chapter Records at Peterborough. 16th and 17th Centuries.*

[23] NRO, "Will of Richard Campion" proven on 10 January 1554. A variant spelling for Campion is Campyon.

all those lands and tenements, lying in Upper Wedon, now in the tenure of John Cole. To have and to hold to the aforesaid Thomas Lovet [*sic*], his heirs and assigns at the will of the lords according to the custom of the manor by the rent of 22s 4d, suit of court and other services, etc. And he gave to the lord as a fine for his entry thereof, just as appears in the margin. And he did fealty to the lord and is admitted as tenant thereof.

Lovett's receipt of this property, handed over directly from Eton College's bursar, reinforces his stature. However, John Cole did not give up on his claim. The property rights were reversed when Cole paid a £10 Fine and Heriot of 5s. The court then restated the presentment's outcome.

At this court there came the said Thomas Lovet [*sic*] and he surrendered into the hands of the lords all those lands and tenements in the tenure of the said John Cole, aforesaid, with appurtenances, lying in Upperwedon, aforesaid, to the use and behoof of the same John Coole [*sic*]. To whom the lord granted seisin and possession thereof. To have to him, his heirs and assigns at the will of the lord according to the custom of the manor by the rent of 22s 4d a year, suit of court and other services, etc. And he gave as a fine [blank]. And his fealty is respited etc.[24]

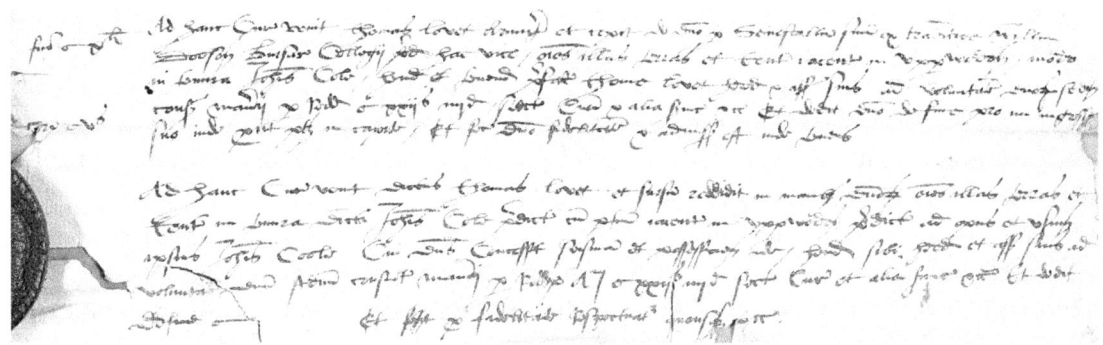

Thomas Lovett and John Cole, 1552. Reproduced with kind permission of
Eton College Archives, image 13. Sponsored by Michael John Cole. (6.6)

Thomas recalled other significant events his father related to him in his youth that marked his memory. When Henry VIII died in 1547, his son, Edward VI, was only nine—close to Thomas' age. But Edward VI as England's king embraced Puritanism. Unfortunately, his reign was cut short when he died as a teenager in 1553. His death ushered in the reign of Mary I. Henry VIII's eldest daughter had remained Catholic and took steady steps to revert England back to Roman Catholicism. Known as Bloody Mary, she authorized harsh measures for those who refused to renounce Protestantism and re-embrace Catholicism.

---

[24] Eton, ECR27_230, 1552, Thomas Lovett and John Cole.

Labeled heretics, more than 300 were burned at the stake. It was during this Marian Persecution that William Proudlove was ordained to begin his ministry in 1555.

In 1557, Thomas recalled his first appearance at a Court Baron meeting. He and his wife, Joan, received land tenancy rights from Thomas Billinge.

Thomas Billing, Thomas and Joan Cole, 1557. Reproduced with kind permission of Eton College Archives, image 11. Sponsored by William E. Cole, in memory of his father, Harold Myron Cole. (6.7)

At this court there came Thomas Byllyng and in full court he surrendered into the hands of the lord according to the custom of the aforesaid manor three roods of pasture . . . To the use and behoof of Thomas Coole [sic] and Joan his wife and the issue lawfully begotten between them. To which same Thomas and Joan the lord by his steward granted in this instant court seisin thereof by the rod . . . And he gives to the lord as a fine, just as appears in the margin, and the aforesaid Thomas Cole did fealty, and they are admitted as tenants thereof in the aforesaid form. [25]

The following year, Queen Mary's reign ended abruptly, when she died of uterine cancer. Her younger sister, Elizabeth, was crowned queen. From the beginning of her reign, Elizabeth I steadfastly signaled the end of Catholic practices as England reverted to its former religion—Protestantism. All Protestants, and especially Puritans, rejoiced at the Promises of the return of their faith.

The Earliest Proof of Coles' Passings

Sometime before December 1561, John Cole's father, William, passed. William Cole named his son and heir, John, to be executor of his will. In it, William bequeathed some personal items to his namesake grandson, William.[26] Sometime later, William Cole's son, John, prepared his own will.

---

[25] Eton, ECR27_231, 1557, Thomas Billing Thomas Cole. Author's theory: Thomas married the daughter of Thomas Byllyng, Joan, and this land was granted to him, perhaps as a wedding present.

[26] William Cole's will is referenced in court documents and John Cole's will, but it has not yet been discovered.

Will of John Cole, 1561, with kind permission of Northamptonshire Archives Service. Sponsored by John Anholm Cole, in memory of his father, Jeffrey Anholm Cole.[27] (6.8)

In the name of God, Amen. On the 7th of December 1561, I, John Cole, of Weedon Bec in the County of Northamptonshire being sick in body yet whole of mind (thanks be to Almighty God) do make my last will and testament in manner and form following. First, I bequeath my soul to Almighty God, trusting him to be Protector of my Body, which is to buried in the Parish Churchyard of Weedon Bec.

- Item - I give and bequeath to Thomas Cole, my son, 1 malt quern and a spade.
- Item - I give to William Cole, 4 sheep.
- Item to John Cole - 20marcs [of money] to be paid within 6 years after my decease by Thomas Cole, his brother.
- Item to Helen, my daughter, 20 marcs.
- Item to Agnes Chilleys, my wife's daughter, £5 and another £5 that I owe her from her father's will.
- Item to Henry Cole £6 13s 4d and 20 of my best ewes. Also my best cart or else 4 marcs of money, also a plough with all its appurtenances, 3 harrows, 1 garner to use for malt, a new step satt [unidentified], a lead, a salt trough and all of the timber boards in the stable and cow shed.

---

27   NRO (Northampton Record Office), "Will of John Cole," 1561 Book 3, No 55. Probate given 5th May 1562. Translated into modern English by Nicola Waddington.

- Item to Robert Cole my son £6 13s 4d and a pair of [black]smith's bellows; a nansylde / nanfylde [unidentified] and all the rest of my fowls [chickens] It is to work with a cow and 6 sheep [exact meaning unclear].
- Item to John Gibbs £6 13s 4d.
- Item to Edmund Kinge £6 13s 4d.
- Item to John Gibbs £6 13s 4d.
- Item to Margery Kinge £6 13s 4d.
- Item to Agnes Cole £6 13s 4d.
- Item to Alice Cole £6 13s 4d.
- Item to every one of my grandchildren - one sheep.
- Item to William Cole - all the items given to him by his grandfather's will, being a nanfylde, a pair of Smiths bellows, an iron tourne for a greenstone, two great hammers, a vice, a beckhorne, a heifer, a carte and 4 ounce pieces of pewter.
- Item to Margaret my wife the residue of my goods not yet bequeathed.
- I make Margaret my wife my Executrix.

Witnesses: Robert Reynolds, Thomas Cole, John Billing and other men.[xii]

John Cole first listed three sons, Thomas, William, John, and a daughter, Helen, who are children with his first wife. Then he listed the daughter of Margaret, Agnes Chilleys, who was from Margaret's marriage before John. He then listed two sons, Henry and Robert, from his marriage with Margaret. It is not clear who the other individuals receiving bequeaths are. The two Cole females listed, Agnes and Alice, could be additional daughters, nieces, or grandchildren.[28]

A month later, John Cole surrendered "out of court" his messuage which he then inhabited on the 16th day of January. John specified his son, Henry, and Henry's heirs "lawfully begotten" to receive tenancy rights. His eldest son and heir, Thomas, had already received tenancy rights in 1557 from Thomas Billinge. John specified his other son, Robert, as a backup heir to Henry, if Henry lacked such issue of male heirs. This most likely means Henry did not have any male heirs as of that date. John designated his widow, Margaret, and Henry's mother to enjoy a moiety[29] of the premises of both Henry and Thomas for the term of her life. After her decease, those premises would revert to Henry and Thomas separately.[xiii]

John Cole perished sometime between 16 January 1562 and his will probate, dated 5 May 1562. At the following Court of the Baron 1561-2 presentment, much about the relationship between Margaret Cole and two of her sons was revealed. As was very clear to those attending the Court of the Baron meeting, Thomas and Margaret Cole's relationship was strained. In fact, Thomas was not Margaret's son. She was his stepmother. Thomas Cole was John Cole's eldest son by his first wife. When John Cole married Margaret, she was in possession of a messuage called Lovettes, three virgates of land, four virgates of meadow, and

---

[28] Further research is required.
[29] Meaning of moiety is half.

one close with appurtenances. Thomas Cole currently inhabited that property which was granted by the Rod to Margaret at the meeting.

John Cole, deceased, Margaret Cole, Thomas Cole, Henry Cole, 1562. Reproduced with kind permission of Eton College Archives, image 18. Sponsored by Stephen Dandridge Cole. (6.9)

To have and to hold the moiety of all and singular the aforesaid premises with their appurtenances to the aforesaid Margaret and her assigns for her dower for the term of her life according to the custom of the aforesaid manor, with remainder thereof after her decease to the aforesaid Thomas and Henry Cole, their heirs and assigns, of the lord by the rod at the will of the lord according to the custom of the aforesaid manor by the ancient rents, customs and services thereupon previously due and accustomed. And she gives to the lord as a fine [blank] and she made fealty and was admitted as tenant of the premises.

It is decreed and ordered at this court by the homage between the aforesaid Margaret Cole, widow, on the one part, and Thomas Cole, aforesaid, on the other part (with their assent and consent) in this manner, viz that if the aforesaid Margaret or anyone else for her or in her name violently or voluptuously enters into the same part of those lands or tenements which came by partition to the aforesaid Thomas by the surrender of his father, to disturb, molest or vex the same Thomas or his assigns at any time during the natural life of the aforesaid Margaret, that then the same Margaret is to forfeit and pay to the lord for each time so doing a trespass £10.

And similarly that, if the same Thomas, or anyone else for him or in his name, violently or voluptuously enters into the same part of those lands or tenements, which lately by partition were coming to the aforesaid Margaret for her dower [after] the death of the aforesaid John Cole, late her husband, to disturb, molest or vex the same Margaret or her assigns at any time during her life, that then the same Thomas is to forfeit and pay to the lord for every time so making a trespass £10.[30]

PURITAN CONNECTIONS TO WEEDON BEC

In 1562, the probate date of John Cole's will and the beginning of John Ringrose's ministry in Weedon Bec coincide closely. Just eleven days later, Ringrose was instituted by the Church of England as its parish vicar.[31] While he may or may not have known John Cole, he ministered to his family and descendants for the next quarter of a century. Since Ringrose was a known Puritan, it indicates a Puritan foundation for John Cole's descendants and particularly his son, Thomas.

This same year, the bishop also appointed William Proudlove to serve the nearby parish of Fawsley.[32] Supported by Sir Richard Knightley's patronage, the Knightley family controlled some 850 acres. Richard would later be elected a Member of Parliament representing Northamptonshire. His well-known support of Puritans would later bring him into direct conflict with ecclesiastical authorities. These two appointments marked the beginning of Puritan traditions in the village of Weedon Bec. Puritan vicars, John Ringrose and William Proudlove, would create them for their parishioners, profoundly impacting them for years to come.

MORE MANOR COURT PRESENTMENTS

After his father's death, Thomas Cole gained more and more prominence in the village. By 1573, he served in responsible positions in Court Baron meetings. That year, Thomas oversaw a suit as Homage. It included his stepmother, Margaret. While the suit's details were not recorded, it appears somewhat parallel in format of a suit nearly twenty years prior regarding John Cole's use of quern hand mills. This presentment lists nineteen villagers in default—including three women—with fines and pardons specified.

Court Baron 1573 Homage: Thomas Cole

Who say upon their oath that John Goodman [3d], John Gare [3d], Edward Fysher [3d], Henry Judkyn [3d], John Packer [pardoned], John Smythe [3d], William Bedford [pardoned], Thomas Caswell

---

[30] Eton, ECR27_232, 1561-2, (membrane 27), John Cole deceased, Margaret Cole, Thomas Cole, Henry Cole. Translation by Simon Neal.

[31] CCEd, "John Ringrose."

[32] "William Proudlove," *Bible Study Tools*. Viewed on 2 January 2020. https://www.biblestudytools.com/history/brook-lives-puritans-volume-1/william-proudlove.html.

[3d], William Sherman [under age], Henry Mariotte [3d], Ralph Gudgyon [pardoned], Ralph Blount [3d], Edmund Lynnell [3d], Richard Wawe [sick], Thomas Brynknel [3d], Margaret Cole [pardoned], Anne Clyfforde [pardoned], Richard Clerke [3d] and Anne Wheatley [3d] owe suit at this court and at this day have made default. Therefore, they are in mercy, just as appears upon their names.[33]

In this same court, Thomas Cole, and three other villagers—John Billinge, Thomas Billinge, and Thomas Gare—appeared together in a presentment. They jointly took possession of a cottage with appurtenances which came to be known as *Le Townhouse* "for the use and behoof of the vill of Wedon." Eighteen years later, it was to become the residence of William Proudlove's family.

> At this court there came John Byllynge [sic], Thomas Cole, Thomas Byllynge [sic] and Thomas Gare and they took of the lord of this manor one cottage, lying between the lands of Thomas Gare on the south side and the tenement of Richard Wawe on the west. To have and to hold the aforesaid cottage with appurtenances to the aforesaid John Byllynge [sic], Thomas Cole, Thomas Byllynge [sic] and Thomas Gare and the heirs and assigns of the same John Byllynge [sic], Thomas Colle [sic], Thomas Byllynge [sic] and Thomas Gare forever, according to the custom of the aforesaid manor, to the use and behoof of the vill of Wedon, aforesaid. Paying thereupon for the premises to the lord 4d a year, and also paying and doing all other customs and services for the premises due and accustomed. For which same purchase the aforesaid John Byllynge [sic], Thomas Cole, Thomas Byllynge [sic] and Thomas Gare gave to the lords £4. And they did fealty and were admitted as tenants thereof. And it is agreed that, if the inhabitants of Wedon, aforesaid, do not pay to the aforesaid John Byllinge [sic], Thomas Cole, Thomas Byllynge [sic] and Thomas Gare the aforesaid £4 before the feast of St James the apostle next, that then the aforesaid John, Thomas Cole, Thomas Billinge and Thomas Gare and their heirs will enjoy the aforesaid tenements to their own uses.

Three years later, three of these men oversaw the court proceedings. Henry Cole, Thomas' stepbrother, was summoned but notified the court he would be absent (Essoin).

Court Baron 1576-77 (membrane 15)
Homage: Thomas Cole, John Byllynge, and Thomas Byllynge
Essoins: Henry Cole[34]

At this court it is found by the homage that Thomas Billinge out of court after the last court surrendered into the hands of the lords by the hands of John Clifford, bailiff of the aforesaid manor, in the presence of Thomas Cole and William Reynoldes, customary tenants of the aforesaid manor, bearing witness to this, one "le lay" called "a lay," lying in Wedon, aforesaid, in a certain field called Water Furlonge, adjoining to the land of a certain Anne Wheatley, and also one rood of "ley," lying in Whitewell in Wedon, adjoining to the land of the aforesaid Anne, now in the occupation of the aforesaid Anne or her assigns. To the use and behoof of the aforesaid Anne, her heirs and assigns forever. Upon which, the lords

---

[33] Eton, ECR27_232, 1573, Margaret Cole.
[34] Essoins is defined to be a summoned individual who notified the court of his absence beforehand.

by their steward granted seisin of the premises to the aforesaid Anne. To have to the same Anne, her heirs and assigns forever. To hold by the rod at the will of the lords according to the custom of the aforesaid manor by the rents, services and customs due for the premises and lawfully accustomed. And he gives to the lords as a fine for having such estate thereof 12d. And the fealty and admission are respited, because he was not at this court.[35]

In 1581-2, Henry Cole joined the Court Baron proceedings in a leadership role along with his stepbrother, Thomas, and two other well-known men in administrative roles for these court presentments as Homage: John Billinge, Thomas Billinge, Thomas Cole, and Henry Cole. A few years later in 1585-6, the two Cole stepbrothers oversee presentments involving Thomas Billinge, Thomas Cole, Richard Wawe, the baliff of the manor, and Henry Marrette.[xiv]

SECOND COLE WILL

When William Proudlove became vicar of Weedon Bec Parish in 1587, Margaret Cole was the Cole family's matriarch. Her husband, John, passed away twenty-six years earlier. While her relationship with stepson, Thomas, was strained, the family was united in support of Proudlove's Puritan teaching. She became close with Proudlove as did her stepson. But by the end of the following year in failing health, she documented her last wishes. She asked vicar William Proudlove to witness her will.

Will of Margaret Cole, 1588, with kind permission of Northamptonshire Archives Service. Sponsored by Claire Diane Jaynes, in memory of her mother, Diane Cole Semans. (6.10)

---

[35] Eton, ECR27_232, 1576, Membrane 15, Thomas Cole Thomas Billing.

"In the Name of God Amen. The fifte day of December in the yere of | our Lord God 1588 I Margarett Cole of Wedonbeck in the countie of North[ampton] | widow being sick in bodie but of whole minde and p[er]fect memorie thanks and | praise be geven to allmightie God do constitute and make my | Testa[me]nt containing herein my last will in maner and forme following. First | I bequeath my soule to almightie God and my bodie to be buryed in the | churchyard of Wedonbeck aforesaid."

- To her son Robert Cole a selection of livestock and household items and 20 shillings which William Kyble owed her.
- To her daughter Jone Batson plates and sheets.
- To the daughter of Jone, Anne Pampion, a heyfar.
- To her grandson Thomas Fowkes [son of her daughter Agnes Fowkes] a heyfar.
- To her daughter Alex Muscott, a cow.
- To the daughter of Alex Muscott, Jone, a pair of sheets.
- To her son Henry Cole, the residue and he is made Executor....

Witnesses: William Proudlove vicar of Weedon Bec, George Batson, Alex Billinge, Agnes Fowkes, Alex Muscott. [36]

With her will finished, Margaret's soul rested, and her Lord took her home. As her family gathered in the blustery cold of winter, Margaret's burial service was conducted by William Proudlove on 7 December 1588.[37] As her mortal body was lowered into the grave next to her husband in the parish churchyard, Proudlove offered a prayer.

"Almighty God, Father of mercies and giver of comfort: We give thee thanks for giving our sister Margaret to us, her family and friends, to know and to love as a companion on our earthly pilgrimage. In thy great compassion, console us who mourn. Give us faith to see in death the gate of eternal life, so that in quiet confidence we may continue our course on earth, knowing the consolation of thy love; until, by thy call, we are reunited with those who have gone before. Through Jesus Christ our Lord, Amen."

While Margaret Cole's burial marked the end of the first-generation Cole family in the village, more generations of the family would remain prominent in this East Midland village well into the eighteenth century. As for William Proudlove, who presided over many burials since he began his ministry in 1555 during the Marian Persecutions, he would continue to impact subsequent generations of Coles for another decade and a half.

The fact is, in ways none of them could imagine at the time, the Cole family was destined, not only to thrive here, but to extend its reach outward dramatically in the next century—first to London and then to America. While these *Puritans* faced an uncertain future challenged by *Plagues*, it was also one filled with *Promises*.

---

[36] Northampton Record Office, "Will of Margaret Cole," Ref: 1st series, Book V, f. 315. Probate given on 23 Jan 1588/9. Note the same will is repeated in different handwriting at ref: Series C&D, Book C, MF 83.
[37] Weedon Bec Parish Registers (1588-1665)

CHAPTER 7

NEW BEGINNINGS FOR FAMILIES COLE, ARNOLD, AND COLLIER

Anxious to catch up with his former vicar, Thomas Cole hurried through the village's streets to see him. As he reached *Le Townhouse* on a crisp November day in 1593, he knocked, unlatched the door, and pushed it wide open. When William Proudlove saw Thomas' smiling face, he warmly hugged him. Their long-lasting embrace warmed their hearts and stirred their souls. After William described the details and circumstances of his return from London, Thomas proceeded with his agenda. He told him of his son's need for a suitable partner to share his life and heart.

Before Proudlove's extended absence, he had been impressed with Thomas' son, John. William thought he might be a great catch for a young maiden of marrying age. He recalled thinking, "If such a maiden latched onto John, might he perform their marriage ceremony?" But after three and a half years away, so much had changed. Even though he was home again in Weedon Bec, he was still deprived of his livelihood as a minister.

When they finished their meeting, Proudlove contacted his Puritan colleague in Culworth, Andrew King. He told him about John Cole, son of his former churchwarden. King knew everyone in his village and promised to help. One of his former parishioners stood out in his mind. He owned a large farm in a nearby hamlet and could always use an extra hand. As is the case for the faithful, God had already led the way. The farm's owner approached King, his former vicar. He needed to find suitable husbands for his three daughters. King recommended that he meet with John Cole.

John had been running more and more of his father's properties in Weedon Bec whenever Thomas was away. During those trying times for the Cole family, God tested their faith and perseverance. In addition to Thomas Cole's excommunication in 1589, the continued parish upheaval and petitions for Proudlove's release, Thomas experienced two other painful losses in his life.

First, his fellow excommunicated churchwarden and close friend, Thomas Billinge, died, leaving his wife, Alice, a widow.[1] As a longtime friend, Thomas consoled her as best he could. She apparently had family in other parishes and spent time away with extended visits to family and friends.

Second, Thomas experienced his most painful loss when his wife and John's mother, Joan, died. Losing his faithful wife of more than thirty years stung him deeply. The pain and loneliness challenged his faith. He turned often to the Bible's book of Job. Searching for answers, he cried out, "God, is my faith being tested as Job's was?" But the void he felt

---

[1] No record of his burial has been found. It is estimated to be 1591-3.

was deep. Instinctively, he knew he needed another church and community to help him cope with his trials and tribulations. On visits to neighboring parish churches, he searched for spiritual guidance. A warm greeting by the parish vicar in Pitsford, some thirteen miles northeast of Weedon Bec, encouraged Thomas, and his preaching touched him. He felt welcome and stayed. With kinfolk in the community, it appears he served there as a churchwarden in 1592 and 1593.

With full confidence in his son, Thomas charged John with the care of his property, animals, and crops. He returned occasionally to check back with his son and farm, but the change of scenery was cleansing and renewing for him. But now that his former vicar had returned, Thomas sensed God's will and his readiness to rejoin his longtime home and community.

His son had more than proven his worth. Thomas was pleased how well John ran the farm operations, worked with horses and other beasts, and tended the crops. Thomas thought, "It's no surprise. He has done so his entire life." In fact, John was particularly adept with horses. Thomas surmised that his son was the equal of any man in this shire—well known for its fine tradition of equine husbandry. When Proudlove relayed King's recommendation to Thomas, John Cole excitedly anticipated exploring the opportunity.

Near Culworth in the hamlet of Cotton,[2] a substantial farm produced wool from an extensive herd of sheep. When John Cole arrived, the farm's owner discussed its operations and extensive scope. He saw sheep numbering more than one hundred, pigs, chickens, a few boars, and horses. Fields of hay were harvested each year to feed them all. Many storage areas and outbuildings supplied what was needed. John was impressed with what he saw and heard firsthand.

The farm's owner and family patriarch, William Gardyner,[3] was equally impressed with this young man. He sensed a maturity far beyond his years. He anxiously introduced John at the messuage to his family. His wife, Margaret,[4] welcomed him warmly. Their son, Thomas, shook hands with a firm grip, and their three daughters, Frances,[5] Mary, and Martha smiled broadly. John's impression of the two younger girls was that they were somewhat shy. But from their first encounter, John's attraction to the family's eldest daughter, Frances, appeared mutual. His visit ended with an offer from the family patriarch. A responsible position with room and board was readily accepted. When his eyes met those of Frances, he felt something he'd never felt before.

As often happened, living with a family could lead to a marriage proposal. Not long after, John asked William Gardyner and his wife, Margaret, for their daughter's hand in marriage. They gladly agreed. Since it was common practice to marry in the bride's parish, the couple certainly discussed how the ecclesiastical turmoil had affected families in both Weedon Bec and Culworth. At this moment, neither William Proudlove nor Andrew

---

[2] Variant spelling is Coton; will use Cotton hereafter.
[3] Variant spellings include Gardiner, Gardener, Gardner, and Gardinar. Genealogical evidence is provided later in the chapter.
[4] Variant spelling, Margarett; will use Margaret hereafter.
[5] Variant spelling Fraunces, will use Frances hereafter.

King was sanctioned by the Church of England to perform marriages. However, John and Frances had both grown up in their churches with ministers they knew and trusted. It is quite probable, again given the turmoil of this time, that the couple asked them to bless their marriage. If so, it would have been celebrated on the family farm sometime between late 1593 and no later than June 1594.[6] Frances' two sisters, Mary and Martha, her brother, Thomas, and her parents, plus members of the Cole family, likely witnessed the ceremonial blessings.[xv] Afterwards, John and Frances Cole stayed on the family farm. As John continued to work with his father-in-law, William, his mother-in-law, Margaret, thanked God for the blessings of having her eldest daughter, her new son-in-law, and her other children staying close by.

But God's work was not yet completed with the family. The two longtime friends, Thomas Cole and Alice Billinge, had remained in touch. They had both experienced the pain of excommunication, separation from their community, and shared the loss of their respective spouses. They recognized that their individual loneliness would be mitigated if they shared their elder years. On 3 December 1594, widower Thomas Cole married Alice Billinge, the widow of Thomas, in Fawsley Parish.[7] Now, they were a comfortable couple living together.[xvi]

Not long after their marriage, the elder Coles were thrilled when they received the blessed news that John and Frances were expecting their first child. On 20 March 1595, Nathaniel Cole was baptized in Culworth Parish's church.[8] When the proud grandfather, Thomas, arrived at the Cotton farm, he swept his first grandson into his arms as the family watched. He kissed the baby boy and beamed a smile from ear to ear. Witnessed by the other grandparents, William and Margaret, Thomas' wife, Alice, and the proud parents, John and Frances, they all shed tears of joy.

With three generations of Coles together for the first time—grandfather, father, and newborn son—everyone mentally etched the moment in their memories. John was particularly grateful that God blessed his father with the joy of cradling his first grandson in his arms. As Thomas asked for God's blessing on the child, John closed his eyes and listened intently to his father's prayer.

> "Watch over thy child, O Lord, as his days increase. Bless and guide him wherever he may be. Strengthen him when he stands; comfort him when discouraged or sorrowful; raise him up if he fall; and in his heart may thy peace which passeth understanding abide all the days of his life. Through Jesus Christ our Lord, Amen."

Later in the year, Culworth's former vicar, Andrew King, accepted a school headmaster position in Chessam at Woburn Manor, Buckinghamshire. A market town located

---

[6] With no parish records extant for marriages in Culworth before 1610 or in Weedon Bec before October 1594, this is unverified. The marriage date proposed corresponds with Proudlove and King's return to their villages and the birth of the Cole's first child.

[7] Fawsley Parish Registers (1585-1660)

[8] Culworth Parish Registers (1563-1709)

twenty-five miles northeast of London, Chessam had a long history of nonconformity and a Puritan tradition. King was licensed to serve there on 1 December 1595. After four and a half years of being deprived of their livelihoods, Proudlove prayed for his friend and colleague that King would thrive, be blessed, and serve God there effectively.[xvii]

That same month, the Weedon Bec parish records resumed to keep track of baptisms, marriages, and burials. One of the early records, on 13 December 1595, notes "a son of William Proudlove was buried."[9] An unknown official or churchwarden kept track of these events. The son, although unidentified by name, was Proudlove's namesake, William—born while he was in prison. While Proudlove would have been allowed to attend the graveside burial, he was banned from officiating. For the former vicar, it was a doubly sad experience. Still deprived of his livelihood more than two years after obtaining liberty, he watched and listened as a standard Scripture verse from the *Book of Common Prayer* was recited by a replacement who didn't even know his son's name. "The Lord giveth, the Lord taketh away. Blessed be the name of the Lord. Amen."[10] After his son's burial, William Proudlove wiped away tears, comforted his wife Isabella, and hugged his other children at graveside.

During the past year, Weedon Bec's parishioners had kept up the pressure on the diocese through their unprecedented absence and petitioned the bishop for Proudlove's reinstatement. In October 1594, the parish records resumed briefly when four events were recorded, but again stopped abruptly. Finally, the former vicar was reinstated to his orders in the Church of England. On 26 May 1596, William Proudlove was installed and given the new title as perpetual vicar.[11] He also received the vicarage, which was valued at £11 annually.[xviii]

After his faithfulness through trials and tribulations, God blessed his calling with renewed energy and hope for the future. William praised God for his deliverance and for the parishioners he loved so dearly. Rejoicing for the blessing of serving them once again, he lifted his voice in prayer:

> "O good and merciful God, by thy grace we have been called into this goodly fellowship of faith. Bless thy people, and grant that thy word may be truly preached and truly heard, and thy Sacraments faithfully administered and faithfully received. By thy Spirit, fashion our lives according to the example of thy Son, that we may show the power of thy love to all among whom we live. Through Jesus Christ our Lord, Amen."

Once again, his preaching and Bible studies stimulated his parishioners. Word traveled quickly of his reinstatement, and previously absent villagers filled the church pews once again. He administered Sacraments previously forbidden to him. The parish registers brimmed with familiar surnames including Billinge, Clevely, Clyfford, Gare, Wawe, and Cole.

While Proudlove had agreed to conform to church practices of the Church of England, there were occasional issues. On 24 September 1596, a diocesan visit recorded that he was

---

9 Weedon Bec Parish Registers (1588-1665)
10 Prayer inscription is found in a nearby church for a young child who lived briefly in 1606.
11 CCEd, "William Proudlove."

presented for not catechising properly. It also noted that Henry Cole, Thomas' stepbrother, was presented "for not paying the level . . . [the tithe of] the church." [12] Despite minor infractions, the diocese generally refrained from disturbing Weedon Bec's parish vicar and leaders. In 1597, Proudlove appointed Henry Cole and Robert Abby as churchwardens. Thomas Gare and Robert Judkin were also mentioned.[xix]

Proudlove's ministry again thrived as he recorded significant events in his parishioners' lives—christenings, marriages, and burials. Eleven months after his reinstatement, William and Isabella Proudlove celebrated the birth of another son. They named him after the son they buried sixteen months earlier. The parish register reads, "William Proudlove, the sonne of Mr. William Proudlove, vicar of Wedonbecke was baptized the twenty-seventh of April, 1597."[13] With an overflowing and thankful heart, William prayed.

> "Almighty and everlasting God, may thy fatherly hand ever be over thy servant, William. So lead him in the knowledge and obedience of thy word that he may gladly and heartily serve thee all the days of his life. Through Jesus Christ our Lord, Amen."

As the end of the sixteenth century approached in Culworth, John and Frances Cole were blessed again. In early April 1599, Frances' mother, Margaret, and her sisters assisted with the birth of Frances' second son, Zacheus, at the Gardyner farm. As was customary, infant Zacheus Cole was baptized promptly in the Culworth Parish church on the 8th of April.[14]

Thomas Cole and his wife, Alice, arrived soon to celebrate the newborn with the growing Cole family. John and Frances were most pleased when Thomas and Alice married. Their companionship was wonderful to behold. As Thomas held his newborn grandson, John was particularly grateful today that God blessed his father with the double joy of cradling his newest grandson in his arms while conversing with his other grandson, Nathaniel, aged four. While Thomas held baby Zacheus, John Cole prayed for his second son.

> "Almighty God, heavenly Father, thou hast blessed us with the joy and care of this child. Give us calm strength and patient wisdom as we bring him up, that we may teach him to love whatever is just and true and good, following the example of our Savior Jesus Christ. Amen."

After ending his prayer, John Cole gazed directly in his father's eyes and smiled broadly. With two sons, John felt his father was pleased the Cole name was secure for another generation. His beaming smile etched another three-generation Cole image into the minds of grandfather, father, and grandson, Nathaniel, along with everyone else in the room.

Throughout the visit, John observed his father carefully. In conversation, John felt his father wasn't as sharp as normal. His movements seemed labored. John sensed his father was slowing down and perhaps failing in health. After Thomas and Alice left, John shared his

---

[12] NRO Reference: X610/26, Correction book. Dated: Sep 1594-Oct 1597.
[13] Weedon Bec Parish Registers (1588-1665)
[14] Culworth Parish Registers (1563-1709)

perceptions with his wife. Frances said she had observed the same. They discussed seriously what Thomas' passing might mean for their young family and for Frances' parents, William and Margaret Gardyner.

Living and working the farm with her parents, the past few years had mightily blessed John and Frances. They could see how much William and Margaret cherished watching their grandson, Nathaniel, grow up. Baby Zacheus now presented that same opportunity. But John Cole anticipated what was ahead. When his father was called to his heavenly home to be with his Lord and Saviour, Jesus Christ, John knew he and Frances would have a choice to make.

When Thomas returned home to Weedon Bec, he also recognized his deteriorating health. Thomas paused and thanked the Lord for his full life. But he decided it was time to arrange his affairs. Thomas and his wife, Alice, discussed a plan to present to the court baron.

On 14 July 1599, Thomas Cole surrendered half of his home and subleased it to Henry Cole, his stepbrother. They agreed to a 21-year lease beginning that very day.[xx] Henry would pay forty shillings annually to Thomas Cole or his heirs. The other half of the home and attached property would be retained for Alice for the remainder of her life. Her annual lease would be only one pence—the manor's customary fee for a widow.

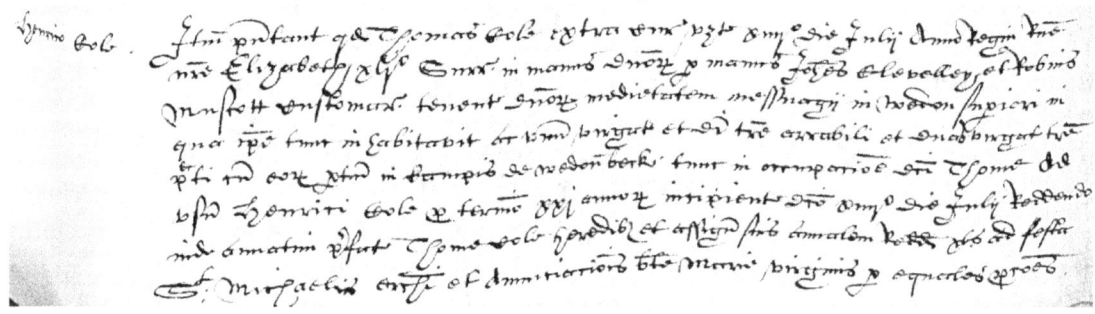

Henry and Thomas Cole, 1599. Reproduced with kind permission of Eton College Archives, image 3.[15] Sponsored by American Society of Genealogists. (7.1)

Thomas' preparation was indeed timely. A little over a week later, Thomas Cole breathed out his last breath. On the 24th of July, Weedon Bec's vicar, William Proudlove, presided at Thomas' burial service. He prayed:

"Almighty God, our Father in heaven, before whom live all who die in the Lord: Receive our brother Thomas into the courts of thy heavenly dwelling place. Let his heart and soul now ring out in joy to thee, O Lord, the living God, and the God of those who live. This we ask through Christ our Lord. Amen."

As Thomas Cole's mortal body was lowered into his burial plot in the Weedon Bec parish churchyard, young Nathaniel grasped the concept of death. He understood he would no longer sit on his grandfather Cole's lap. His death was final.

---

[15] Eton, ECR27_266, 1599, Thomas and Henry Cole. Translations are by Simon Neal.

For vicar Proudlove, Thomas' burial brought forth a flood of memories. He remembered the first time he met Thomas, twelve years earlier in 1587. When he stepped into the chaos in Weedon Bec's parish, Thomas' support helped him stabilize the parishioners and begin their spiritual growth. He recalled witnessing the will of Thomas' stepmother, Margaret, and her burial the following day in December 1588. And he painfully recalled the trying times of the *Martin Marprelate* tracts followed by Thomas Cole's excommunication in 1589. The vicar winced as he remembered his own arrest, imprisonment, and trials in London beginning in 1590. But he also recounted how many blessings the gifting of *Le Townhouse* meant for him and his family in 1591. After his continued tribulations in London ended in October 1593, he recalled how Thomas was among the first to celebrate his return to Weedon Bec. Even during nearly three more years of his deprived livelihood, Thomas continued his support, until his vicar was finally reinstated in 1596. William realized, now that he was finally reinstated in his calling, how much God had taught him and tested his faith.

At that moment, William was overcome with gratefulness by how much Thomas Cole had supported him in his ministry. And unlike young Nathaniel Cole, William knew Thomas' death and burial was not final. While his mortal body had in fact died, William knew it was the beginning of Thomas' eternal life in heaven.

Later that year, three related presentments were recorded in the Court Baron Roll. First:

> At this court there came Alice, relict of Thomas Cole, and she seeks his dower of a moiety of one messuage and virgate and a half of land with appurtenances, of which the said Thomas died seised according to the custom of the manor. To which same Alice the lords granted seisin by the rod of a moiety of the premises according to the custom of the manor. To have and to hold to the same Alice for the term of her life at the will of the lords according to the custom of the manor by the rents and services thereupon previously due and accustomed, and she gave to the lords a fine of 1d, just as is the custom, she made featly and was admitted thereupon.[16]

Alice, widow of Thomas Cole, 1599. Reproduced with kind permission of Eton College Archives, image 5. Sponsored by John and Patricia Donohoe. (7.2)

---

16   Eton, ECR27_266, 1599, Alice, widow of Thomas Cole.

As Thomas had directed in his estate plan shortly before his death, his widow, Alice, did indeed receive the messuage and attached property for her use during the remainder of her life. This was a customary way for the court to support widows and she paid only one pence to complete the transaction. Second:

> At this court there came John Cole, son and heir of Thomas Cole, deceased, and he seeks to be admitted tenant to a moiety of a messuage . . . and to one cottage . . . of which the said Thomas died seised according to the custom of the manor. . . . And he gave to the lords for his relief 5s 9d, he did fealty and was admitted as tenant thereof.[17]

John Cole, son and heir of Thomas Cole, 1599. Reproduced with kind permission of Eton College Archives, image 4. Sponsored by David Charles Cole. (7.3)

As Thomas' heir, John Cole's fee required a substantially higher amount of money than did the widow, Alice, John's stepmother. Third:

> The homage present upon their oath that Thomas Cole, who held to him and his heirs of the lords at the will of the lords according to the custom of the manor a moiety of one messuage . . . and one cottage . . . has died since the last court thereupon seised. And that John Coles is his son and heir, whereupon there befalls to the lord in the name of relief according to custom.[18]

John Cole received the Court Baron's approval to occupy half the messuage and one cottage. The homage documented the passage of the tenancy rights from Thomas Cole to his son and heir. John paid five shillings and nine pence and was admitted as a tenant. This formalized his return to the village of his birth with his wife, Frances, and two young sons—Nathaniel, not quite five, and Zacheus, aged three months. His return marked the third-generation Cole family to live in Weedon Bec, raise a family, and work the land: 1) John's grandfather, his namesake who had arrived in the village in 1543; 2) John's father,

---

[17] Eton, ECR27_266, 1599, John, son of Thomas Cole.
[18] Eton, ECR27_266, 1599, John Cole Thomas Cole.

Thomas, the heir of the elder John Cole; and 3) now John himself, his father's heir. He felt doubly blessed that the Puritan vicar, William Proudlove, who was his minister as a youthful lad, would once again guide his family's walk with the Lord.

For John Cole's family, this village was their new home. John was pleased to return to his ancestral home. But his son, Nathaniel, no doubt missed his grandparents, Margaret and William Gardyner, who remained on their farm in Cotton. That was the only home Nathaniel had ever known.

But he was happy his grandmother, Alice, was here. In his four-year-old eyes, everything stimulated him. New surroundings presented new adventures. New chores were required of him. Plus, his parents gave him greater responsibilities in the home for his younger brother. He eagerly explored the farm, the animals, and the fields of crops. In his new village, new playmates beckoned him to meet and play with them. Yes indeed, there was much to learn about in his new surroundings!

Southwark's Family Arnold Prospers

In the closing years of the sixteenth century, Alice Arnold kept her household properly set up and stocked, while husband John worked tirelessly and diligently to build his dyer business and provide for his family. But Alice also brought into the marriage her knowledge and experience of working with her first husband, Henry Yates, in his dyer business. She became a support and partner with John, assisting him with administrative tasks in their enterprise. God blessed them, and Southwark's Arnold family prospered. Alice also poured herself into raising up her three children. The older two, Henry and Jane, constantly absorbed the sights and sounds of Southwark's St. Olave's Parish with child-like fascination but were wise beyond their years. With their church facing the River Thames and almost abutting London Bridge, the sights, sounds, and smells of Southwark were always stimulating.

London Bridge from St. Olave's Stairs. Public domain. (7.4)

London's exploding population approached 200,000 souls as the sixteenth century drew to its close. Its growth appeared unstoppable, even with recurring plagues. The age of exploration was at hand. As the center of trade for all England, London prospered. Its prosperity acted like a magnet attracting immigrants from many countries, mixing their languages and dialects, and demanding new products and more services.

Spain's violent attempts to reimpose Catholicism in the Netherlands where Protestantism was spreading rapidly spurred an exodus of Dutch merchants in the last quarter of the sixteenth century, which in turn created an influx of experienced traders settling in London. As London's shops expanded to meet the needs and wants of its fast-growing population, both banksides of the river, north and south, bustled with seemingly unending activity. As people prospered, they had more money to enjoy occasional entertainment diversions. Southwark's theatres and its blood sports, including cockfighting, bull baiting, and bear baiting, attracted huge crowds.

As Alice's two children peered at the river's activity, watermen shuttled passengers to and from the north and south banksides of River Thames. Jane and her older brother Henry strained to see ships laden with goods, heading for foreign ports as they traversed and plied the waterway. They imagined where the ships were headed and what adventurers beckoned the brave traders and mariners.

LONDON, 1593. By JOHN NORDEN.

London, 1593. By John Norden. Public domain. (7.5)

Southwark's growth presented many opportunities which greatly benefited John Arnold's business. By the beginning of the seventeenth century, his hard work paid off handsomely. On 25 April 1600, John Arnold of the parish of St. Olave's and Anthony Smyth of the parish of St. Saviour's in the Borough of Southwark were appointed grocer collectors for the "fift and sixt fifteenes and tenths, nowe due." A bond of £73 was taken for them.

In witness whereof we have here unto sett our hands and seales on the 25th day of Aprill and in the 42nd yeare of the Raigne of our Soureraigne Ladie Elizabeth by the grace of God of England Fraunce and Ireland Queene defender of the Faiyth etc" and submitted by "E. Bowyar and Rychard Lyntton to the right honorable Sir Thomas Knight Lord Keeper of the Great Seale of England.[19]

A great honor, his selection entrusted him with a heightened level of responsibility and visibility in his community. Alice and her children felt very proud of him.

WILLIAM COLLIER STARTS APPRENTICESHIP

In the summer of 1601, teenager William Collier looked feverishly across London Bridge to get his bearings. As he peered southward across River Thames, he mentally exclaimed, "How different it is here. I've not seen anything like this anywhere else!" The sights, sounds, and smells of Southwark could be overwhelming for any lad. Across the river, he spotted three theatres rising above the modest buildings on the south bankside. The Globe Theatre with its Shakespeare plays now competed directly with the Swan and Rose, and indirectly with Edward Alleyn's Bear Baiting Arena. Tempting sights and sounds beckoned the unwary. As he stepped off London Bridge's southern gateway and entered his new surroundings, William thought to himself, "Here, there are opportunities aplenty!"

As most lads of his age, Collier might have been tempted by Southwark's available forms of entertainment. The Globe enticed theatregoers with plays crafted by Shakespeare and others. Blood sports drew throngs of large crowds and filled brewhouses. Many young men found difficulty choosing between attending cockfighting, bull baiting, or the bear baiting arena owned by the famous actor, Edward Alleyn. A few found their way into houses of ill-repute.

At age eighteen, Collier was about to begin a new chapter in his life. His grocer's apprenticeship opportunity had finally arrived. William imagined his future occupation. What would becoming a wholesale merchant, a grocer, be like? Exciting images flooded his mind with the hopes and promises of many opportunities. Southwark was the center for the importation of spices—a booming trade. Imports of all kinds came from distant shores, and London was the distribution point for all of England.

Collier's master, William Russell, was well-established in his grocer business. From August 1593 through August 1598, Russell paid annual taxes in Southwark's Boroughside of £3, which increased to £4 through August 1600.[xxi] Russell's ever-increasing share of taxes

---

[19] SP 46/22/87.

helped to fill the Crown's ever-expanding need to fund Elizabeth's reign, her colonization ambitions, and external wars.[20]

As Russell's apprentice, Collier would receive room and board in return for his labor and learning the trade of grocer from his master, an eight-year commitment for him. As he began his apprenticeship on 25 July 1601, William Collier believed that when he proved himself worthy, as his reward he would become a freeman in London. If all went as he hoped, he would accomplish that goal by the time he reached his mid-twenties. Two days later, he was presented to the Grocer's Guild and paid a fee of 2s 8d.[21] As most apprentices felt starting out, the Promises of a bright future excited him.

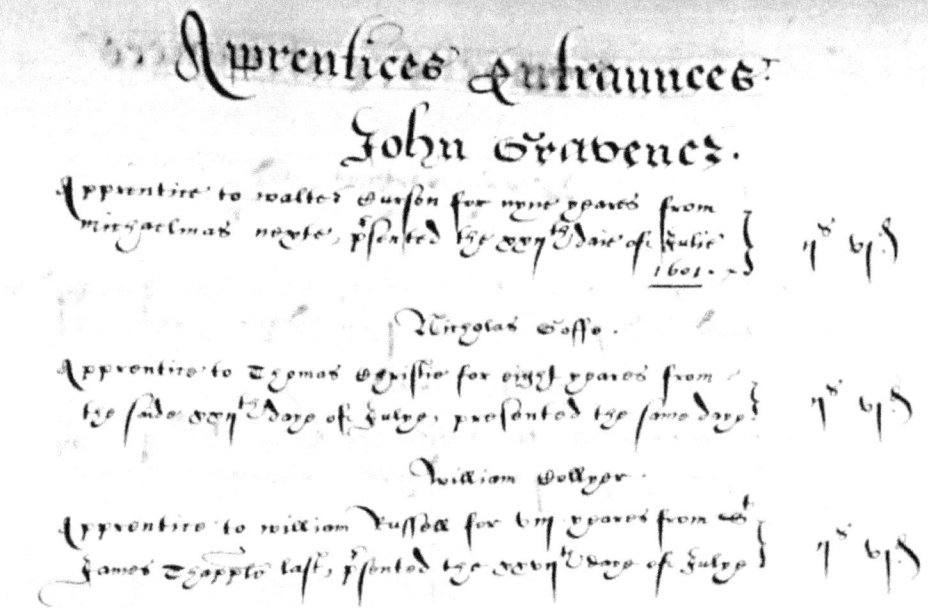

William Collier, Grocer's apprentice, 1601. Reproduced with kind permission of the Grocers' Company of London. Sponsored by Scott L. Semans. (7.6)

Even as a teenager, Collier possessed characteristics and qualities that would set him apart from his peers. A focused determination to work hard and learn the trade motivated him to excel. He watched carefully and listened to his master, which grounded him in the fundamentals of his trade. His good head for numbers and ability to absorb information quickly yielded a natural business sense. His curious nature about how things worked, and why certain things caused other things to happen, gave him an edge and set him apart from his peers. Perhaps more than anything else, his faith in God granted him an inner strength.

---

[20] William Russell came from a prominent Gloucester family. His brother, Thomas, served as a MP. In William Shakespeare's will, he bequeathed £5 to Thomas Russell. In Southwark, William Russell served as a member of the Sewer Commission.

[21] Grocers' Guild, Wardens' Accounts, 1601-1611. MS11571/9 Folio 12. Guildhall Library, London. Variant spelling is Collyer. Hereinafter spelled Collier.

His maturity shone beyond his years, and William Collier eagerly looked forward to this new chapter in his life.

New Beginnings in Weedon Bec

As the seventeenth century dawned on Weedon Bec, the futures of the Cole and Proudlove families were filled with Promises. William and Isabella Proudlove celebrated two more baptisms—son Elias on 24 February 1600 and daughter Martha on 22 January 1602.[22] Two months later, John and Frances Cole welcomed their third son, Job. When vicar Proudlove baptized him on 21 March 1602, the Cole's eldest son, Nathaniel, now seven, and Zacheus, not quite three, were thrilled to help raise their baby brother.

As encouraged by their Puritan vicar, John and Frances used biblical names with each one of their children. This Puritan practice emphasized a family's faith—a visible sign indicating their children were set apart by God. In this, Puritans followed a tradition similar to that of the ancient Israelites. Puritan ministers encouraged this practice in England as early as 1560.[xxii]

John and Frances chose to name their first-born Nathaniel—meaning "God has given." Several minor characters with variant spellings are in the Old Testament. The New Testament features Nathaniel, an apostle of Jesus. Nathaniel is thought to be another name for the apostle Bartholomew. Zacheus is well-known from the New Testament Gospel of Luke. He was a tax collector in Jericho who climbed a sycamore tree to see Jesus and gave half his possessions to charity. Job is an Old Testament icon known as a righteous man tested by God. He endured many hardships and emerged faithful.[23]

John Cole felt secure in the choice he and Frances made to return to Weedon Bec. Blessed by his right of inheritance, his father's good farmland provided well for his wife, Frances, and his growing Cole family. As eldest son Nathaniel worked the land alongside his father, the family thrived. With five hungry mouths to feed, John and Frances thanked God daily for his merciful bounty. They gratefully acknowledged the Lord's multitude of blessings richly poured out on them, and no doubt took the Old Testament leader Joshua's declaration, "As for me and my house, we will serve the Lord," as the family motto.

Unexpected Changes

1602 brought unforeseen developments which affected the entire village of Weedon Bec. William Proudlove received a new calling. Word came that another parish needed a minister. The village of Chippenham in Wiltshire suffered the resignation of vicar White in May. With sadness, perpetual vicar William Proudlove bid farewell to his Weedon Bec parishioners who had faithfully supported him during the past fifteen tumultuous years. By autumn, he was serving as Chippenham's vicar.

Once again, Weedon Bec parishioners confronted the loss of their revered vicar, the one for whom they had worked so hard to gain his reinstatement. The bishop quickly appointed

---

[22] Weedon Bec Parish Registers (1588-1665)
[23] "Job," *Behind the Name*. Viewed on 1 June 2017. https://www.behindthename.com/name/job.

as his replacement the vicar of the adjacent parish of Flore, Dr. Leonard Hutton. He would serve both parishes. On 24 September 1602, Dr. Hutton was instituted as Weedon Bec's vicar and received the vicarage as well.[xxiii] For Hutton, it was an easy half-hour stroll between the two parish churches.

Foot Path from Weedon Bec to Flore's Parish Church. Courtesy of William E. Cole, in memory of his mother, Beatrice Rosamond "Kay" Cole. (7.7)

But even greater disruptions were in store for English villagers throughout the country. Rumors were already circulating that their queen's days might be numbered. Elizabeth's tight circle of advisors and servants observed her decline. In her headstrong way, Elizabeth "seemed determined to defy and to belie infirmity by a great show of ability in walking, and even by dancing in presence of her own and foreign courtiers."[24]

But Elizabeth became melancholy and sought to conceal her infirmities. Her step was increasingly feeble as her strength waned. She became despondent and described her condition as "a great horror of darkness." In June 1602, she told the French ambassador she "was weary of life." In January 1603, she removed to Richmond, complaining that her "heart was sad and heavy."[25] Elizabeth named her cousin, James VI, King of Scotland, to be her successor. James Stuart, the son of Mary Queen of Scots whom Elizabeth had ordered beheaded to eliminate any threat of Mary deposing the English monarch, would unify the kingdoms of England and Scotland—the first unification since the thirteenth century.[xxiv]

On the 10th of March, Elizabeth's servants found her unresponsive and thought she was dead. But Elizabeth rallied. Two weeks later, with Archbishop of Canterbury John Whitgift attending her, England's longest reigning monarch of forty-five years died at three o'clock in the morning at age seventy. As her subjects mourned the loss of their queen, Elizabeth's cousin, James VI, King of Scotland, was proclaimed James I, King of England and Scotland, the very same day—24 March 1603.

---

24 Hopkins, 639.
25 Hopkins, 640.

Plague Delays King James' Coronation

Given the presence of the plague, James Stuart was in no hurry to arrive in London. It started in 1602 but lingered on. The epidemic had not yet reached its major proportions. But its devastation was just getting ready to unleash itself on England. This plague would disrupt and reshape the lives of many families once again.

As soon as James was declared king, Puritans acted quickly in hopes of further reforms. With the change of monarchs and the fact that Scotland was steeped in Presbyterianism, Puritans' hopes for the fulfilled promises of reforms that Elizabeth had not embraced were rekindled. But James took his time traveling from Scotland.

In April 1603, the *Millenary Petition* was presented to James while he was still in transit to London. With claims that it was signed by 1,000 Puritan ministers,[26] the petition's drafters outlined reforms they sought in the Church of England. Signing the cross during Baptism, the use of a ring for marriage, the rite of confirmation, and ministers' wearing of surplices were among the many objectionable practices. They sought more substantive changes in church government and *The Book of Common Prayer,* as well as a new translation of the Bible.

James saw no reason to attend Elizabeth I's funeral. After she authorized his mother's execution, James no doubt felt animosity for Elizabeth. Sixteen years earlier, the beheading of Mary Queen of Scots took place after her lengthy imprisonment in Northamptonshire. When James Stuart arrived in

JAMES I *King of Great Britain, France, & Ireland, &c*

James I. Courtesy of National Portrait Gallery, Smithsonian. Public domain. (7.8)

London on the 7th of May—nine days after Elizabeth's funeral on the 28th of April—he wasted no time setting up his government and planning his coronation.

On his coronation day, James Stuart united the two kingdoms of Scotland and England, with his wife Anne, the daughter of Denmark's king, by his side. He was the first Scottish king to be crowned in over three-hundred years seated on the Stone of Scone, which was contained within the English Coronation Chair.[xxv] James VI, King of Scotland and Ireland, officially became James I, King of England and Ireland, as Scotland merged with England. King James was crowned by the Archbishop of Canterbury, John Whitgift. The date was 25 July 1603.

---

[26] Latin *millenarius,* "of a thousand."

PLAGUE STRIKES SOUTHWARK

In Southwark, across River Thames from the royal festivities, Alice Yates Arnold and her daughter Jane experienced another sorrowful loss. The very same day as James I's coronation, Alice Yates Arnold buried her youngest daughter, Margaret, aged nine. As St. Olave's curate. James Bamford led the graveside service in the parish churchyard, Jane Yates, aged sixteen, tearfully bade farewell to her only surviving sister.

Jane painfully recalled her terrible experience at age six, when she witnessed her father's death and burial, plus the deaths of all except two siblings in the Plague of 1593. Now, the Plague of 1603 robbed her of her sister Margaret. The church's parish register recorded Margaret's burial as the daughter of Henry Yates, a dyer, who died nearly a decade before.[27] In England, during the late sixteenth and early seventeenth centuries, death was all too commonplace.

Under terms of her father's will, Jane Yates inherited her sister's bequest as had happened with her previously deceased siblings. Jane's dowry now totaled £122—which made her a desirable match for a man seeking a wife.[28]

Through his guild membership, John Arnold knew an eligible freeman dyer in Southwark's St. Olave's Parish, Thomas Clarke. From a business point of view, John felt Thomas was an excellent match for Jane. Her mother, Alice, agreed. Most marriages were arranged to build alliances between families to improve their status and enhance their prospects. Rarely would children deny their parents' wishes on this matter.

To escape the plague ravaging Southwark's population, Thomas Clarke and Jane Yates sought and obtained a special license for permission to marry outside their parish from the bishop. Two months after her sister Margaret's death, on 27 September 1603, Jane Yates (aged sixteen years and seven months) married Thomas Clarke "by Licence from St. Olave's in St. Benet's Gracechurch Parish."[29] Located across the River Thames from their home parish, their marriage was recorded by a vicar who did not know the young couple. Had it not been for the special license, no one in St Benet's Gracechurch Parish would have known that Jane and Thomas could legally marry.[30] This parish included one of its most famous parishioners, actor and playwright William Shakespeare.

---

[27] St. Olave's Parish Registers (1583–1627). The record was written and indexed as Gates.

[28] Value in 2017 equals £16,500 or approximately $21,870. "UK Historical Currency Converter," *The National Archives*. Viewed on 25 June 2017. https://www.nationalarchives.gov.uk/currency-converter/.

[29] St. Benet Gracechurch Parish Registers (1558–1730). "London, England, Church of England Baptisms, Marriages and Burials, 1538–1812." [Hereinafter St. Benet Gracechurch Parish Registers (1558–1730)] Jane Yates' maiden name is recorded as Gates. In greater London—given diverse county dialects and immigrants from other countries—Yates and Gates can be heard as almost the same depending on the speaker and listener.

[30] For marriages in the Church of England, a public announcement must be made weeks before the wedding. This announcement for people who know the couple is normally made by banns read in the bride's parish and the groom's parish. In three circumstances, banns are not possible if: 1) one party is under the age of 16; 2) the couple is closely related (i.e. first cousins); or 3) the couple is marrying outside their home parish.

A NEW VICAR IN ST. SAVIOUR'S PARISH

William Collier's master, William Russell, and his family attended worship services only a five-minute walk from St. Olave's Parish church where the Arnold family worshiped. St. Saviour's Parish church was the second largest church in greater London and loomed over nearby London Bridge. Only St. Paul's Cathedral across the river was larger and more prominent.

Russell, his wife, Anne, and his children were devoted worshipers. By the late sixteenth century, after the dissolution of the abbeys, their church fell into disrepair. Its adjacent buildings had been filled with small manufacturing shops, including one that made querns for distribution throughout England and kilns that fired the Delftware made by Dutch immigrants.

But in the late sixteenth and early seventeenth centuries, perhaps fueled by the success of grocers like Russell and other merchants, the parishioners took an aggressive stance and bought the church from the Crown. The nearby theatres and blood-sport arenas attracted large crowds who frequented nearby brewhouses and other merchants. The area adjacent to the church was undergoing a renaissance.

William Russell served his church in various capacities and supported it financially. But most important, St. Saviour's had a long history of Puritan leanings.

St. Saviour's Parish Church in Southwark. Public domain. Courtesy of Tony Sharp, Historian. (7.9)

Those Puritan affinities were on distinct display one December evening in 1603, when an upcoming parish event was discussed around the Russell family supper table. Since all apprentices attended Sunday services with their masters' families, William Collier listened carefully as Master Russell discussed church news. The church's vestry was looking forward to the presentation of a new vicar at the next worship service. His reputation preceded him. It created quite a stir filled with much anticipation and speculation.

One parishioner said the new vicar possessed a fiery personality. Another said he was known to be a zealous Puritan in the late 1580s and early 1590s. Many elderly parishioners remembered the upheaval caused by the *Martin Marprelate* tracts. A select few vividly remembered the trials and tribulations of nine Puritans who stood in defiance of the queen's authority over the Church of England. It was rumored he might have been one of them and supposedly signed his name to a petition sent directly to her majesty, Queen Elizabeth. Another rumor said his actions led to his loss of orders from the Church of England for ten years! One parishioner relayed a story he heard about his refusal to baptize an infant because his name wasn't biblical. What was known for sure, is that the new vicar came from Northampton, a hotbed of Puritanism in its day.

St. Saviour's Parish was, in fact, the new vicar's first assignment since his reinstatement in the Church of England. Whether any of his new parishioners knew it or not, the new vicar, Edmund Snape, had, in fact, stood trial alongside two fellow Puritans, Andrew King and William Proudlove, in the highest court in England—the Star Chamber.

In attendance on Sunday at St. Saviour's with William Russell and his family, William Collier heard a Puritan preach the word of God with a Puritan perspective. This preaching moved and stimulated William in ways he'd never felt before. Something stirred deep within his soul. He wanted more. He faithfully attended services and soaked up Puritan teachings with enthusiasm. Snape's Puritan messages stirred and convicted him about his faith. He acquired his own copy of a Geneva Bible and read it regularly. Along with applying himself to learning his trade, he also thirsted to learn more about God. His spirit was inspired!

KING JAMES PRESIDES AT HAMPTON COURT CONFERENCE

In response to the *Millenary Petition* received from the Puritans in April, James I announced the Hampton Court Conference, to be held in November 1603. But the plague delayed it until January 1604, when James I personally presided over the conference to ensure its proper direction. In a reduced role, Archbishop John Whitgift represented eight bishops who were unable to be present. Other Church of England bishops and four Puritan spokesmen, representing those supporting the petition, attended the conference. Some thirty Puritans—not invited—gathered nearby to pray, debate among themselves, and wait for news of the conference outcomes. Many in this group were the more vocal and assertive Puritans who were most likely purposely excluded.

James rejected most of the Puritans' demands. Most adamantly, he rejected any change in the episcopal form of church government. When confronted, he declared emphatically the principle he had learned in Scotland: "No bishop, no king." The conference signaled James' directives for the Church of England—and his intended sovereignty over it. Few changes were accepted, and virtually none the Puritans desired. The only substantive change authorized was for a new version of the Bible. When completed, it would carry the name of its major benefactor: King James.

Across England, Puritans were disheartened about the lack of results from the Hampton Court Conference. Once again, they felt promises of further reforms had just disappeared.

The following month, Archbishop Whitgift died at Lambeth Palace. While he received customary accolades from the Church of England, Puritans across England were relieved they would not again face his opposition or wrath. Those included Snape, who rejoiced that his longtime nemesis, John Whitgift, would no longer oppose him.

For more than twenty years as Archbishop of Canterbury, Whitgift held fast to practices of the Church of England opposed by the Puritans. After his death, one Puritan wrote a scathingly sarcastic poem about Whitgift as an epitaph and tacked it onto the funeral hearse.[xxvi]

As encouraged by Whitgift's passing as some Puritans were, most were more distraught by the lack of reforms that emerged from the Hampton Court Conference. In fact, one

Puritan minister concluded that staying in the Church of England and working for reform was no longer an option. This associate vicar was John Robinson of St. Andrews Parish in Norwich. He refused to swear allegiance to the new *Book of Canons* as required by the archbishop. That same year when "Archbishop Richard Bancroft launched his purge of Puritan preachers," Robinson believed a submission "would violate his conscience."[31] As had happened to many of the Puritan ministers imprisoned in the early 1590s, Robinson was suspended from his ministry. This was his moment of separation from the Church of England.

When Robinson returned home with his family to his village of Sturton in Lincolnshire, he discovered another defrocked Separatist preacher, John Smyth, who led a growing congregation in the nearby town of Gainsborough. In 1607, Robinson joined the nearby Scrooby separatist congregation and became co-pastor with Richard Clyfton. Meeting at the manor of Edward Winslow, Robinson also met a young William Bradford. In mysterious ways, God orchestrated the meeting of these men. It's unlikely they realized then just how far God's calling would take them—far beyond the shores of England.

PLAGUE STRIKES THE ENGLISH COUNTRYSIDE

The Plague of 1603 continued unabated through the winter and spread from London into the East Midlands. Weedon Bec villagers were not spared. John and Frances Cole's middle son, Zacheus, a young lad not quite four, died and was buried on 22 January 1604. The grieving couple—along with their sons, Nathaniel at age nine and young Job, who was not quite three and would not have fully comprehended what just happened—watched as their brother's lifeless body was lowered into the burial site.

Weedon Bec Parish Church Graveyard. Courtesy of William E. Cole,
in memory of his grandmother, Mary Jane "Jennie" McLeod. (7.10)

---

[31] Rod Gragg, *The Pilgrim Chronicles: An Eyewitness History of the Pilgrims and the Founding of Plymouth Colony* (Washington D.C., Regeny Publishing, 2014): 54.

Vicar Hutton prayed for everyone affected by the Cole lad's death.

"O merciful Father, thou hast taught us in thy holy word that thou dost not willingly afflict or grieve the children of men. Look with pity upon the sorrows of thy servants. Remember us, O Lord, in mercy; nourish our souls in patience; comfort us with a sense of thy goodness; lift up thy countenance upon us and give us thy peace. Through Jesus Christ our Lord, Amen."

While Nathaniel cried at the loss of his brother, Zacheus, John and Frances tearfully praised God for sparing their other two sons. But the plague persisted—it was not yet finished with this family. Three months later, God took away their youngest child. Job was buried in April 1604. With heavy hearts at their painful loss, the family certainly recalled the Bible's story of Job. Frances and Nathaniel fell to their knees sobbing as John cried out, "Lord, how much more will we be asked to endure?"

They also received disturbing news from Frances' sister, Mary. She and her husband, Edward Launden, lived in the village of Pitsford, thirteen miles northeast of Weedon Bec. She sent news that five of their kin died in the plague. Indeed, it inflicted a heavy toll on the region.

MORE RELIGIOUS TURMOIL IN WEEDON BEC

From the time of William Proudlove's reinstatement in 1596 until his departure in 1602, ecclesiastical authorities had received only praises from Weedon Bec parishioners. But by 1604, a diocesan visitation recorded discontent.

Churchwardens presented certain of their neighbours for resorting to other churches "because we have not any minister among us of good report." The wardens clearly had some sympathy with the godly who had by now long experience in the cause, four of those presented in 1604 came from families first reported in 1584—the families of Wawe, Cole, Gare, and Billing.[32]

On 26 February 1605, vicar Hutton resigned from Weedon Bec. He had never been fully embraced by the village parishioners. On 27 March 1605, his replacement, Robert Smith, was formally instituted as perpetual vicar.[33] Vicar Smith proved to be an excellent match for Weedon Bec's parishioners. Their belief and faith consistently supported Puritan ministers for more than forty years and resisted any others.

ANOTHER COLE CHILD ON THE WAY

Not long afterward, Frances Cole told her husband she was pregnant again. John threw his arms around her, embraced her with a lingering hug, and kissed her warmly. With all his

---

[32] Shiels, 133, footnote 3.
[33] CCEd, "Robert Smith."

heart, John Cole believed God was providing them with another gift—not only to him and Frances, but to his son Nathaniel as well. He was distraught over the losses of his younger brothers. John knew his son would relish another opportunity to shepherd, care for, and assist a younger sibling with learning the required skills for the family and the farm. John Cole knew he would be a big help to his mother. He prayed quietly to himself, "We give thee thanks, O Lord. We are most grateful for your promises and blessings!"

When Frances Cole bore another healthy son, the village celebrated with the joyous couple. Everyone rejoiced at his birth and praised God. John and Frances named him, Zacheus, after their first son lost in the Plague of 1604. But for some reason, the baptism of the second Zacheus was not recorded in the parish registers.

It might have been simply missed in transition from one vicar to the next. Or it might be explained by a dramatic series of events that were about to unfold—events that would directly impact the lives of John and Frances Cole, their extended family, and their close friends in the years ahead.

CHAPTER 8

PLAGUED BY TRANSITIONS, TRIALS, AND TESTING

By the middle of the seventeenth century's first decade, Frances Cole's parents, William and Margaret Gardyner, became increasingly burdened by the demands of running their farm in Cotton. Even with servants, the crop planting and harvesting, their livestock, and all the equipment necessary to run; the farm had become too much for them.

Their daughter Frances and her husband, John Cole, had removed from the farm to Weedon Bec with their boys. Daughter Martha had married Nicolas Kymbell and lived nearby in Culworth. Their other daughter, Mary, had married Edward Launden and lived in Pitsford, some thirteen miles away. Despite years of stored-up family memories, William and Margaret agreed with their children: it was time for them to shed the encumbrances of farming. William and Margaret's grandchildren were plentiful. More were on the way. Time was precious, and they wished to enjoy the freedom to be with them more often. A time of transition was at hand. But such transitions are never easy.

William Gardyner formally transferred the ownership and responsibility for running the farm to his only son and heir, Thomas. He and his wife, a daughter of Thomas Atkins from Culworth, took responsibility for the farm and messuage while his parents continued living with them.[1] Thomas granted his father "sufficient convenient chamber meate drinke and other necessaires according to his degree age and falling and one annuitie of ten poundes per annum" for the remainder of his life.[2] This act established conditions for his parents to remain there without their previous responsibilities and still derive income for their old-age needs from the goods and chattels of the farm.

Unfortunately, Thomas Gardyner, a Merchant of the Staple of England, overextended himself financially.[3] He solicited loans with friends and neighbors using the farm's land and its messuage as collateral. While he acquired a few loans, they still weren't enough to make ends meet. Thomas was approached by a neighbor, Martin Wright, who told him of his son's interest in acquiring the mortgage for Gardyner's farm and messuage. Wright's son,

---

[1] Messuage was the term then used to designate a dwelling house with its outbuildings and land assigned to its use. Atkins is the surname with a variant of Adkins. The daughter's forename is not listed in records found.

[2] C2/Jas1/W18/62 Int. 1-21.

[3] Merchants of the Staple were English merchants who controlled the export of English wool from the late thirteenth century through the sixteenth century. With the growth of English manufacturing in the sixteenth century and after, more wool was used domestically, and the Staplers became less important as the export trade diminished.

William, worked in London as a councillor.[4] He hailed from the village of Trafford, located five miles west of Culworth near Chipping Warden, with a secondary address in London at Clement's Inn in Westminster. Ultimately, Thomas Gardyner entered into a mortgage agreement signed by Martin Wright, on behalf of his son, William, who held the mortgage on the messuage and property. But Thomas was still overextended and soon found himself in arrears on both his loan and mortgage payments. William Wright threatened to foreclose on the mortgage. Concerned about his parents' future needs, Thomas decided to act to protect his parents' security.

On 3 May 1606, Thomas Gardyner met in London with Simon Gardyner.[5] Thomas told Simon he had mortgaged the farm and house to William Wright. Together, they drafted a deed of gift for the all the moveable and unmoveable goods and chattels of Gardyner's farm. The deed provided for "better relief and maintenance of his parents in their old age."[6] Unfortunately, Thomas did not consult with a councillor about this transaction. Simon and Thomas then met in the Franchurche Street office of a scrivener, Mr. Frithe.[7] Frithe wrote the document as instructed and sealed the deed of gift in an envelope for safekeeping. The following month, Simon Gardyner retrieved the envelope, traveled to Culworth, and delivered it to William Gardyner at his farmhouse—a few days before the 24th of June, the feast day of St. John Baptiste. Thomas Gardyner absented himself from the farm and left for parts unknown. Perhaps the weight of responsibility and financial pressure were too much for him.

When notified of Thomas' absence, John Cole traveled to Culworth to discuss his brother-in-law's departure, the deed of gift to his father-in-law, and other urgent matters. William Wright had foreclosed on the property and intended to take possession of the farm. As John heard the details from his father-in-law, he wondered aloud, "Given the situation, what might be the best course of action?" His father-in-law wanted to enlist the help of John and another son-in-law, Edward Launden, to clear out the Gardyner household, the farm's goods and chattels including its livestock, and the harvested crops. William would arrange for his third son-in-law, Nicholas Kymbell, and for Richard Gardyner to store everything temporarily until sales could be arranged.[8]

As John considered the complexity of clearing out the family's house and farm, he hoped they had thought of and discussed everything needed for the project at hand. This would prove to be quite an undertaking, much beyond what any of them imagined—and with unexpected consequences.

Just after the 18th of October, St. Luke's day, John, with the help of his brother-in-law, Nicholas Kymbell, and Anthony Foxe, both of Culworth, branded the cattle, including

---

[4] The common term for an attorney.

[5] The relationship, if any, of Simon Gardyner, Woolwinder of All Hallows Sayinges Parish to William Gardyner is unknown.

[6] C2/Jas1/W18/62 Int. 4.

[7] A scrivener functions like a Notary Public in modern times.

[8] Relationship between William and Richard Gardyner is unknown; perhaps a brother or cousin.

sheep, pigs, horses, and boars with a mark belonging to his father-in-law.[9] John also separated out the livestock which belonged to his brother-in-law's own brand. He thought to himself, "How could Thomas simply abandon his problems, obligations, and family?" When the task was completed, John directed his servant and one of his father-in-law's servants to drive "diverse sheepe, horses, and beastes branded" to John's land in Weedon Bec for his use, and for the use of his brother-in-law, Edward Launden.[10]

In early November, John and Frances Cole returned to the family farm. They came in their wagon with a team of four horses to help oversee this complex project's last phases. Her parents, William and Margaret, greeted them with hugs and kisses and tears in their eyes. William said, "We are so grateful for your help and coordination of everything. You are an answer to our prayers."

On the 12th of November in dawn's early light, John Cole's servant, William Cowper of Weedon Bec, hitched up another of Cole's wagons to a four-horse team. John Cosford of Watford joined him, and they set off for Culworth. After the thirteen-mile ride, they were greeted by John and Frances with her parents, William and Margaret. John Cole introduced them to the large group gathered, which included Thomas Gardyner's wife and several local villagers—Anthony Foxe, John Kemble, and Margarett Kemble.[11] Others assembled were Richard Shepard, John Branfield of Weedon, John Lawe, and one known only as "olde Robert."[12]

The last to arrive was John Cole's brother-in-law, Edward Launden. He had traveled the farthest. His village, Pitsford, was northeast of Weedon Bec and double the distance Cole traveled. John greeted Edward warmly and thanked him for joining in the work ahead. At least fifteen people had been enlisted to help with the logistically challenging and complex project.[xxvii]

William Gardyner reiterated how grateful he and Margaret were for everyone's assistance. With the crew's full attention, John Cole went over the plan and logistics for removing and carrying away all the goods and household items. John realized it would be too much to fetch everything right away and agreed to sell his cart and team of horses to his father-in-law for £20. John also wanted his father-in-law to "be assured of a team to do any necessary business."[13] Witnessed by everyone there, William gave his son-in-law, John, six pence in earnest money. The time for action was at hand. The next step was to enter the messuage now occupied by Martin Wright's servants.

As Edward Launden, John and Frances Cole, William Cowper, and John Cosford entered the messuage, Martin Wright's servants were there setting up. They listened as John and Edward explained their intent to remove the household stuff, goods, and the harvested crops which were granted to William by a deed of gift made by his son, Thomas. When one of Wright's servants advised them to refrain from carrying away the goods, Edward

---

[9] The term cattle in this era applied broadly to farm animals.

[10] C2/Jas1/W18/62 John Cole Int. 12.

[11] Possible parents of Nicholas Kymbell.

[12] John Lawe, variant spelling Lowe, old Robert is probably Robert Brynckoe.

[13] C2/Jas1/W18/62 John Cole Int. 9.

and John emphasized that their brother-in-law, Thomas, had granted and sold the goods to William Gardyner. When the servant objected, Cole asserted, "The law is open on this issue. We will let the law determine who has best right to the goods."[14]

Upon leaving the messuage, the crew of laborers had grown and now included servants of William Gardyner and Edward Launden. Cole and Launden instructed the crew to start removing the household stuff and goods in or about the messuage. After those were secured, they also separated the cattle, harvested corn, hay, carts, ploughs, timber, wood, seacoles, hovells, hovell posts, pails, planks, racks, and mangers, and cleared the yards and backsides belonging to their father-in-law, William.[15]

When the labor crew finished loading the wagons, they left, carrying the household goods and chattels away. They deposited part of them in the nearby yard of Nicholas Kymbell, John's brother-in-law. The larger part of the goods was deposited in a little close on Richard Gardyner's property.[16] As darkness descended, the group departed. They likely collapsed and fell asleep quickly, exhausted from a hard day's work.

In the days following, John set about helping his father-in-law sell the goods and chattels from the farm. Part of the goods were sold to pay a debt owed to Anthony Plante of the village of Mooreton. When Anthony challenged John about the legality of paying the debt with these goods, John reiterated exactly what he told the servants of Martin Wright. "The law is open on this issue. We will let the law determine who has best right to the goods."

In addition, William Gardyner sold 120 sheep to Roger Drewrie for 100 marks; a "rick of hay" for about £5; five or six beasts to Anthony Fox for about £12; and other beasts for about £20.[17] William then gifted a deed for all his remaining goods, cattle, and chattles to his sons-in-law, Edward Launden and John Cole.

About the 20th of November, William and Margaret Gardyner bade farewell to their farm and home of many years. Memories pulsed through their minds as they recalled their children growing up and marrying. While sad about the change, they looked forward to less pressure from the farm. Edward hitched up one team of horses with his wagon, and John hitched up the other one. Once the wagons were fully loaded, it was time to go. As William and Margaret departed with two of their sons-in-law and daughter, Frances, they took one long lingering glance back at the home and farm they were leaving behind. With a few teary eyes, they turned their heads and looked back no more. They realized the need of leaving the past behind and looking forward to their new life.

Initially, William and Margaret planned to stay at their daughters' homes in Weedon Bec and Pitsford. They stayed first with the Coles in Weedon Bec, where major blessings awaited. The grandparents could hardly wait to see their grandchildren—Nathaniel Cole,

---

14 STAC 8/304/20 Edward Launden Int. 15.
15 Seacoles were probably fuel from a type of coal, and hovells means sheds.
16 "Close" is a shortened term for enclosure, also spelled inclosure. It defined crop or pastureland individually managed which formerly was communal land.
17 C2/Jas1/W18/62 [Membrane 2] 12 June 1607.

age twelve, and baby Zachary.[18] After a brief stay, Edward drove his cart and team of horses along with his in-laws, his goods, and livestock on to Pitsford. The grandparents looked forward to hugging two more Launden grandchildren: Thomas, almost four, and Alice, who was just about a year and a half old. As they were traveling to his home, Edward Launden thought about how much he had to share with his wife, Martha. The events of the last two weeks had required hard work. How would he describe her parents' last days on the family farm? Meanwhile, William and Margaret Gardyner wondered what their future would be like. Their plan was to alternate staying with their children and grandchildren in the months and years ahead.

COMPLAINTS FILED

The Cotton farm's new owner, William Wright, and his father, Martin, were unable to locate the farm's seller, Thomas Gardyner. He had vanished. Sometime around or after the clearance of the goods and chattels from the farm, a fire erupted at the farm's messuage. Wright speculated the fire was deliberately set. Unfortunately, but not unexpectedly, Wright aggressively disputed Thomas Gardyner's version of the farm's purchase agreement. His version of what happened when the farm was cleared was dramatically different as well.

From his office in London, councillor William Wright, Esq., gentleman, filed multiple suits in English courts against Thomas Gardyner, his father, William Gardyner, and anyone else he could identify. In his initial filings, he asked the court's indulgence to allow him to add names of people and details of their exact involvement that he did not initially know, and to add them to the court case after the original filing was made. Perhaps because of his professional standing in the courts of London, his request was granted.

Councillor Wright wasted no time in taking legal action. He filed complaints in the regional market town of Banbary in Oxfordshire, followed rapidly by another suit in the Court of Common Please at Westminster. Wright alleged:

> Whereas Thomas Gardner [*sic*] of Cullworth, Northants, merchant of the staple of England, being lawfully possessed of one farm or tenement and of diverse lands thereunto belonging of the yearly value of £30, situate and being in Cullworth, for term of diverse years yet to come and unexpired, and of and in a flock of 200 sheep, 30 horses, etc, and of sundry other goods and chattels upon the same farm to the value of £1,000 at least, and the same did use, enjoy, possess and employ as his own proper goods and chattels, and kept his family to the number of 12 persons thereupon.

> And being so possessed, and standing indebted in the sum of £300 unto the said orator, and in sundry great sums of money to diverse others of the king's subjects, for which the said orator and other the creditors of the said Thomas Gardner had impleaded the said Gardner in the Court of Common Pleas at Westminster and elsewhere, the said Thomas Gardner (thereupon having a very unconscionable purpose and intent to defeat and defraud the said

---

18   The Cole family often referred to him as Zachary, instead of his formal given name, Zacheus. This may have been a way to differentiate him in their minds from the one who perished.

orator and other his said creditors, and to keep, use and occupy in his own possession and to his own use and benefit.[19]

Apparently, Wright found no restitution in either of the lower courts. In February 1607, he lashed out at what he viewed as a despicable conspiracy by Thomas Gardyner, his parents, and other family members. Wright chose to file complaints in two additional London courts. Why would he do that? Two complaints filed in the different courts served two different purposes.

The Court of Chancery was an equity court, presided over by the Lord Chancellor and his deputies, as opposed to a common law court. It promised merciful justice beyond common law courts' strict rules, which enabled it to hear more complex presentments.[20]

The Court of the Star Chamber presided over criminal cases. But in specific situations, it also exercised some civil jurisdiction. If violence or other serious charges including sedition or treason were alleged, the Court of the Star Chamber might accept the case. And because of the circumstances and details of Wright's case, there was a reasonable chance that some allegations were fabricated.[21]

---

[19] STAC 8/302/4. This filing describes the previous court cases that were unable to be located. They could be pursued in future research efforts. But William Wright's previous legal claims with him and other creditors against Thomas Gardner were to no avail. They occurred sometime after November 1606 and before February 1607.

[20] "Chancery Equity Suits," The National Archives. Viewed on 30 June 2022. https://www.nationalarchives. gov.uk/. The Court of Chancery was used by all walks of life, from laboureres and bricklayers to peers of the realm. People turned to the court because it promised a merciful justice not bound by the strict rules of common law courts (which included the Court of King's Bench) and was able to hear more complicated problems.

[21] "The Court of the Star Chamber," The National Archives. "The Court of Star Chamber. . . had effectively been the judicial arm of the Kings Council. . . The court presided over criminal cases for the most part but did exercise some civil jurisdiction. The kinds of cases brought before the court . . . every case needed to allege violence for the court to hear the case (there is a reasonable chance that some allegations were fabricated)."
From Simon Neal, AGRA: "STAC cases involved some sort of violence whereas Chancery did not. Whether or not it's the same case being moved from court to court, I don't know. It must have been rather expensive to bring two suits in two separate courts at the same time."
From Amanda Bevan, Head of Legal Records for the National Archives (TNA), replied it was "standard for litigants to pursue different aspects of a case in multiple courts, consecutively or concurrently – because each court can provide a remedy for a bit of the whole problem. You might for example have a case about land, but you don't have the deed – you might go to Chancery for discovery of the document. Then you can maybe go to Common Pleas or King's Bench, who will send the case down to be heard in the country at the assizes, before a local jury. But your opponent has suborned members of the jury, who include several of his tenants, and you go to Star Chamber, to allege perjury by the jurors and subornation of perjury by your opponent."

DETAILS OF THE BILL OF COMPLAINT FILED IN THE COURT OF THE STAR CHAMBER

In his complaint, William Wright spared no one even remotely connected to his case. Only the complainant and one defendant, Simon Gardyner, are known to be from London. His complaint named a long list of defendants.

> William Wright of the Inner Temple, London, gentleman, versus William Gardner [sic], Thomas Gardner, Simon Gardner, John Cole, Margaret Gardner, Margaret Kimbell [sic], William Cowper, John Cosford, Anne Cole, Edward Landen, Daniel Wattes, Francis Cole, John Brodefeild, John Lawe, Robert Brinckoe, John Casewell, Thomas Gennings, Nicholas Kimbell, John Kimbell, Anthony Fox, Thomas Hawkes, Luke Dunckeley and Thomas Aris.[22]

With filings in multiple courts operating concurrently, defendants were required to answer interrogatories and make depositions. Since Wright did not need a solicitor to represent him, he incurred no additional legal fees—just his time and energy. The defendants, if summoned to London and examined in person under sworn oath, would incur onerous expenses and travel time to appear in court seventy miles or more from their homes. By horse, wagon, or coach, a one-way trip would take about three days and possibly more. Wright's legal strategy guaranteed an exhaustive process where defendants would expend time, money, energy, and emotional strain during the trials and testing that would follow. At the heart of Wright's complaint were serious accusations. He alleged that Thomas Gardyner

> did in or about the first day of May in the third [sic] year of his [James'] reign of England the 38th as king of Scotland, confer and practice with William Gardner of Cullworth (natural father to the said Thomas Gardner), John Cole of Weedon, Northants, (who not long before had married one of the sisters of the said Thomas Gardner), how and by what means he might effect and bring to pass his unconscionable purpose therein.

> Whereupon it was unlawfully complotted, practiced, concluded and agreed between the said Thomas Gardner, William Gardener and John Cole, that the said Thomas Gardner should make unto him the said William Gardner a deed of gift of all his goods and chattels, and that notwithstanding, the said deed of gift, he the said Thomas Gardner, should as well keep the said fraudulent deed of gift as also possess and enjoy the said goods and chattels to his own use.

---

22 STAC 8/302/4, STAC 8/304/20, and C2/Jas1/W18/62. Primary Source documents were reviewed, photographed, transcribed, and translated or summarized by Simon Neal. Gardyner is the family's surname original spelling, Gardner and Gardiner are variant spellings. Gardyner will be used in normal text, and Gardner in quoted cases will be left as is. Kymbell is the family's surname. A variant spelling is Kimbell. Kymbell will be used in normal text, and Kimbell will be left as in quoted cases. Launden is the family's surname. Landen is a variant spelling in the court cases cited and will be left as is in case records.

As had happened before to another Weedon Bec villager, vicar William Proudlove, more than fifteen years earlier, John Cole was about to be summoned, deposed, and examined in London's courts.

FILINGS IN THE STAR CHAMBER AND COURT DRAMA

William Wright filed allegations against Thomas Gardyner, his father, William, and William's sons-in-law—Edward Launden of Pitsford, John Cole of Weedon Bec, Nicholas Kymbell of Culworth—and others. Wright alleged he bought not only Gardyner's messuage and farm in the hamlet of Cotton in Culworth from Thomas Gardyner but also its goods and chattels. This claim contradicted the validity of the deed of gift, dated 3 May 1606, from Thomas Gardyner for the benefit of his parents, William and Margaret Gardyner.

> At the instant and earnest request of Thomas Gardyner . . . he became obligated for the payment of £1600. On the first day of June last past [1606], Gardyner granted 160 sheep, 20 beasts, a crop of corn, hay, and sundry implements of his Culworth household to Wright.[23]

Wright further claimed a conspiracy employed by the Gardyner family. They attempted to defraud him. His language left no doubt about his opinion of the family members. He first attacked three Gardyner men, Thomas, William, and Simon, and then singled out John Cole and Edward Launden with derogatory, perhaps outlandish descriptions.

> Setting apart all fear of God, without fear or due regard for your highest laws and ordinances, in the month of October last past [1606] . . . their devilish and unconscionable practices and designs, made and procured an antedated writing on the 3rd day of May.

> Afterwards, Thomas and William Gardyner, having consorted with one John Cole, an unnatural and un-graceless person who not long before had grievously beaten his own natural father, expelled him out of his house, and all that he had. Cole then engaged nine others (naming among them his brothers-in-law, Nicholas Kymbell and Edward Launden) and diverse other riotous persons, numbering twenty-two, in unlawful assemblies for riotous purposes, appareled and attired in the habit of women, obtained four carts and four teams of horses on 18 November 1606. They were arrayed and weaponed in a war-like manner with swords, daggers, bows and arrows, Bills, pick staffs, pitchforks, handguns and cavaliers, and other weapons as well.

Wright here likens the actions of the defendants to a coordinated military operation, which included some of the men disguising themselves in women's clothing.

> Cole, Launden, and Gardyner did, very riotously and unlawfully, enter my principal dwelling house, break down, and carry away all the glass, wainscot doors, partitions, flowers,

---

[23] STAC 8/304/20. This entire section is excerpted from the primary source Complaint filed by Wright with its serious allegations against those involved. The author has excerpted and modernized the translation from the original transcription done by Simon Neal.

rakes, planks, mangers, outhouses, hovels, hovel posts, pails, hedges, and mounds, in and about the messuage, its backsides, and orchards.

Cole and Launden, in like riotous and unlawful manner not only caried away, out and from the barns, hovels, and yards of my messuage, one hundred cartloads of barley, unthreshed in the straw, twenty cartloads of winter corn unthreshed in the straw, forty loads of peas and beans unthreshed in the straw, ten cartloads of oats, unthreshed in the straw, one hundred loads of hay, and twenty loads of bedding, bedsteads, pewter, brass and other household stuff, and implements of household, and thirty stocks of bees.

But they also carried and took away, out of the fields of Cullworth, two hundred sheep, twenty beasts, and twenty horses all which goods, corn, grain, hay, cattle, household stuff and other premises, so violently taken, and carried away as aforesaid were the proper goods of your said subject, and by him bought of the said Thomas Gardner as aforesaid.

The amount of crops, household goods, and animals Wright claims were taken is staggering. With such "riotous and unlawful manner" of the perpetrators, one can see why the Star Chamber would be prone to try this case. And if that were not enough to get the court's attention:

John Cole, and other riotous persons, most maliciously purposing, and wickedly intending, of further spoils, and almost utter undoing, without the fear of God, and your highness' laws and ordinances aforesaid, about the twentieth day of November last past did set on fire, or caused to be set on fire, one of my messuages in Cullworth, which I had also purchased from Thomas Gardner. It was burnt down to the ground, and thereby divers other houses, next adjoining put in great and imminent danger to have been burnt to the great astonishment, and fear of all the inhabitants of Cullworth as also of sundry others, inhabitants in other towns adjoining it. From whence five hundred persons at least, came to help quench the fire. Some beams of timber and principal parts of the house, not being wholly burnt, Cole and Landen, and other riotous persons came with their carts and horse teams and carried away the same and converted them to their own use, to the great fear, grief and admiration of all the beholders.

"Maliciously purposing and wickedly intending . . . without the fear of God" are certainly descriptive! But intentionally setting fire to the family home and farm sounds outrageous. That the fire "put in great and imminent danger . . . all the inhabitants of Cullworth . . . also . . . inhabitants in other town adjoining it" begs a question. Are there historical accounts of such a fire? One would think there would have been. But none has been found.

After which Cole and Landen, fearing that for such their outrageous wrongs, they should be either be questioned and punished, according to your highness' laws, they moved William Gardner that he would save them harmless for the same, in respect (as they pretended) they had done that they did for his good for that all men utterly disliking and abhorring their wicked, and malicious manner of proceedings, and obtaining, and getting of the goods.

Cole, Landen, and other riotous persons entered into a new consultation. It was agreed that Cole and Landen should forthwith go next market day to the next market town and make a proclamation of the sale of the said goods, which accordingly they did on the four and twentieth day of November. They came into Banbury, being an ancient, and great Burrow, and market town, in your highness County of Oxon'.

Then and there, Cole and Landen, contrary to your highness laws and without any lawful authority or custom to warrant the same, at the high crosse there in the presence and hearing of at the least five hundred persons proclaimed the sale of the goods, so wrongfully and riotously gotten, and obtained. But the fame and report of their wickedness following them wheresoever they went, so that they failed of their purpose. Very few or none ever came to contract for, or to buy any of the said goods.

Whereupon Cole and Landen were at last constrained to divide the said goods, and cattle and so each party to carry, drive, and take away his share, and part, in which division. While driving away, many differences growing between the riotous persons, especially between Cole and Landen. After many opprobrious [scornful, excoriating] words, the two men fell to blows and brawled, which were, with much difficulty, quieted.

If, in fact, such a fight between these two brothers-in-law happened as described, there must have been eyewitnesses. But such an altercation surely met the definition of violence necessary for the Star Chamber to hear this case. Councillor Wright then closed his complaint with a summary appeal.

In consideration of, and for as much as the riots, routes, unlawful assemblies, deceits. frauds, antedating of deeds unwarranted, making of proclamations and other misdemeanors aforesaid, are not only against the statutes, laws, and ordinances of this your highness Realm of England, therefore requires that some severe and exemplary punishment may be inflicted upon the said lewd and notorious offenders according to the due course of your highness' laws commanding them and every of them thereby at a certain day, and under a certain pain therein to be limited to be and personally to appear before your Majesty's most honorable privy council in your highness' honorable Court of Star Chamber at Westminster.

End of Complaint

If that were not enough, Wright filed an additional complaint in the Chancery Court on the 16th of May.[24] In it, he made similar and parallel allegations to the complaint he already filed in the Star Chamber. Wright, the orator, leveled accusations at his defendants, continuing to use inflammatory words such as "defraud" and "fraudulent" several times.

As he detailed his grievances, he alleged substantial financial harm caused by Thomas Gardyner's actions. Wright also alleged that Thomas Gardyner had absconded with the money and was in hiding. Gardyner's brother-in-law, Edward Launden testified that

---

[24] C2/Jas1/W18/62.

Thomas was apparently bankrupt and had disappeared. He "lurks and hides himself in places far remote and unknown to the said orator."[xxviii]

THE STAR CHAMBER COURT ACTS ON ALLEGATIONS

Based on Wright's allegations, the Star Chamber drew up twenty-one interrogatories. They required two individuals, Simon Gardyner and John Cole, to submit their answers to specified interrogatories regarding Wright's allegations in writing to the court. On 7 May 1607, the joint answers of John Cole and Simon Gardyner, defendants, were submitted. As an eyewitness to pertinent events, Simon Gardyner answered twelve specific interrogatories as required.[25]

On 22 May 1607, the clerk of the court examined him in London. Gardyner confirmed the deed of gift details of the goods and chattels of the Cotton farm in Culworth from Thomas Gardyner to his father, William Gardyner. In detailed testimony, he affirmed witnessing the scrivener's writing the deed and sealing it in an envelope on 3 May 1606. He confirmed that he personally delivered the deed a month later to William at his Cotton farm. He testified the deed was

> made bona fide and for the better relief and mayneten[a]nce of the s[ai]d Will[ia]m Gardyner and his wyef in their olde age, and not in trust. He did not know the value of the deed but stated it was for "alle the goodes and Chattles of the s[ai]d Tho[mas] Gardyner moveable and unmoveable, and that the same deed was absolute and not uppo[n] condyc[i]on to the knowledge or understanding of this def[endan]t."[26]

In response to most details contained in the other interrogatories, Gardyner claimed no direct knowledge. Over the next six days, the court's second witness readied himself for his examination.

As John Cole prepared, he recalled an evening in late August 1589 when William Proudlove, Weedon Bec's former vicar, returned his father's horse after meeting with other Puritan vicars. He remembered how urgent Proudlove's voice sounded when he relayed the importance of meeting with his father and other churchwardens the following day to discuss serious matters. His father's detailed story about his confrontation with a diocesan official riveted John's attention. When Thomas Cole and the others refused to swear the required *ex-officio* oath, it caused their immediate excommunication from the Church of England. Firsthand, John saw the immediate impact on his parents and other villagers. All that and more led to his vicar's imprisonment, and trials in London during three subsequent years.

John pondered his situation. "My vicar endured three years of confinement and six years deprived of his livelihood. Lord, what test of faith is before me now?" Silently, John Cole sat and contemplated that question. He instinctively knew how mentally sharp and

---

[25] STAC 8/302/4 Int. 1,2,3,4,5,6,7,8,9,10,11, and 19. Simon Gardyner's testimony transcribed by Simon Neal.

[26] STAC 8/302/4 Simon Gardyner. Int. 5.

prepared he needed to be when his turn arrived. He would likely face the same type of Star Chamber inquisition that William Proudlove faced fifteen years earlier.

STAR CHAMBER COURT DRAMA WITH JOHN COLE

On the 28th of May, the court clerk noted, "John Cole of Weedon in the streete w[i] thin the Countye of North[ampton] yeoman sworne and examined."[27] Required to answer all twenty-one interrogatories, Cole confirmed what he had seen or heard regarding the deed of gift between two of his relatives. In the first nineteen interrogatories, John's testimony corroborated Simon Gardyner's sworn testimony about John's father-in-law, William Gardyner, and his brother-in-law, Thomas Gardyner, with no substantive variations. John recounted details of being asked to help clear out his father-in-law's farm. He testified about his involvement in the branding of livestock, and the activities leading up to and the days following in which he helped remove and dispose of its goods and chattels. However, in the final two interrogatories, John emphatically denied any conspiracy and refuted specific allegations made by William Wright.[28]

> 20. ITEM what and how manye proclamation or proclamations did you, or any other by your meanes, or with our knowledge make in Cullworth or in Banburye in the Countye of Oxon [Oxfordshire] or elsewhere touching the calling togeather of any persons for the buying or selling of the said cattell, goodes and householdstuffe, or any of them; and what are the names and surnames of such person or persons as made such proclamation or proclamations or by what Commission or other authority did you they or any of them make the same; and what number of the said goodes and cattell have you the said William Gardner and Edward Landen or any of you solde and to whom and for what somme or sommes of money have you the said William Gardner and Edward Landen or any of you solde them or any of them.

Cole vehemently denied making any proclamations in Culworth or Banbury regarding the sale of any items mentioned. He did provide details of what was sold, to whom, and at approximately what cost. But the final interrogatory crossed a line with John.

> 21. ITEM whether did not you (att any time heretofore) wound, beate or stricke your own natural father; and whether did you not expel or putt him out of or from his dwellinge house, or any parte threeof or one of or from his land or living or any parte thereof.

Cole passionately denied these charges of abusing his father-in-law. He emphasized they were totally untrue. Despite John Cole's impassioned pleas and absolute denials of all allegations, there were no further questions and his examination ended.

---

27 STAC 8/302/4 John Cole Int 1-21.

28 For more information and transcriptions detailing these court cases, contact the author through his website: https://www.passionategenealogist.org.

In less than three weeks, John Cole testified to another complaint on the same matter in a different court. Just as the Star Chamber required, Simon Gardyner and John Cole, defendants, jointly answered to the Bill of Complaint filed by William Wright in the Chancery Court. They again prepared their responses and submitted them in advance. Their sworn testimony is contained in the court record titled "The Joint and several answers of John Cole and Symon Gardner defendants for their part to the Bill of Complaint of William Wright gent, Complainant."[29]

CHANCERY COURT DRAMA

As John Cole awaited the call to provide his testimony under examination on the 12th of June, he fidgeted in his chair and bowed his head in silent contemplation and prayer.

> "Almighty and everliving God, source of all wisdom and understanding: I am most thankful that thou art present now and preparing me for the inquisition I now face. While the trials of the Star Chamber tested me mightily, I've learned much. Guide my words and thoughts in this next test to perceive what is right. And grant both the courage to pursue it and the grace to accomplish it, to thy glory. Amen."

When it was his turn to testify, John rose from his chair and swore an oath to speak truthfully. Deliberately, he paused, gathered his thoughts, and then responded to the complaint. He looked directly at the clerk of the court, who would scribe his remarks for the judges and was one of the most prominent men in King James' inner circle, and emphatically declared:

> I, John Cole of Weedon Bec, vigorously defend myself against this bill of Complaint of William Wright, gentleman and Complainant. This bill of complaints against me is mere malice which the Complainant has caused me needless and excessive charges and expenses in the law. Its exceptions, uncertainties, insufficient evidence which has many imperfections. The multiplicity of suits I have endured without any just cause intends, to cause me decay, utter overthrow as he hath no regard for the truth. I beseech this honorable court and humbly pray for due consideration.

His words echoed throughout the courtroom in language laced with strong words and phrases that certainly caught the clerk's attention. He voiced his displeasure at the proceedings. "The multiplicity of suits I have endured without any just cause intends, to cause me decay, utter overthrow as he hath no regard for the truth." After expressing his disapproval, John continued with his understanding of pertinent facts.

---

[29] C2/Jas1/W18/62 [Membrane 2] 12 June 1607. While the court scribe recorded what John Cole said in third person detailed testimony, the author restated this section in the first-person as if John is addressing the court rather than as it was recorded. This first-person account reveals how John Cole refuted allegations and conducted himself in court. He appears to be as passionate as his ninth great-grandson, this author, is known to be. This is the beginning of the proceedings in Chancery Court.

Nevertheless, I declare the Truth and full answer to the Complainant's bill: Thomas Gardyner about two years ago lawfully seized the messuages, cottages, and premises which are situated near and adjoining the messuage where the Complainant doth inhabit and dwell. The complainant, as it should seem, thirsted after the said messuage and the lands belonging to Thomas.

I have credibly heard and think it to be very true, that the Complainant did entice Thomas Gardyner to lend him certain sums of money at such times as he had occasion of need—and by such alluring means—Thomas Gardyner at several times borrowed several times from the Complainant. When Thomas Gardyner failed to pay the money owed at the day fixed at last, about the 25th of November 1606, the Complainant enforced the mortgage of the said premises for his security of repayment.

Without hesitation, he continued and directly addressed allegations of a conspiracy.

To the conspiracy charge regarding myself and Thomas Gardyner, or any others, I did not, nor did I, with any persons named in this bill, confederate[30] to disinherit the Complainant of the said premises. Nor did I or we secretly, or at times unknown, enter the principal messuage and take possession of all the Conveyau[n]ces, deeds, writings, and evidences or the mortgages, deed of gift, or other papers concerning the same. Nor did I or any others— to my knowledge—secretly or otherwise enter the messuage or by any means take possession of any deeds, evidence, or writings concerning the said premises.

Then, he asked a rhetorical question.

Howbeit, I say, that in or about the month of November last (before the Compl[ainant] h[e]ld poss[essi]on of the said premises) William Gardner possessed one box with certain writings therin (as this I taketh it) and delivered the box with the writings therein tied fast to me, and wished and requested me to convey the said box and writings to my dwelling house at Weedon in the County of Northamptonshire? And when Thomas Gardyner requested the box tied fast, I delivered it over upon his request. It is he who now hath it in his custody. But whether the writings in the box did in any way concern the said premises, I certainly do not know. This is the cause of the Complainant to sue, vex, or trouble me in this honorable Court.

Cole used strong language including, to "sue, vex, or trouble me," which emphasized his displeasure. Then, he refuted Wright's claim of the value of the property and the conditions of its sale.

I further say on my behalf, that I deny and traverse that w[i]thout that deed the said premises in the bill menc[i]oned were not above the yearlie value of Twentie poundes. I also refute the Compl[ainan]t was solicited p[er]suaded or importuned by Thomas Gardner to purchase the property in the manner and form as by this bill is surmised and w[i]thout that the Compl[ainan]t had no notice or knowledge that there were rents or annuities granted before

---

[30] At this time, confederate means to conspire.

he purchased the same or that it is material to this defense if the said Thomas Gardner did make any the supposed premises in the bill menc[i]oned.

John categorically denied advising his brother-in-law to secretly depart and hide himself and all conspiracy allegations.

And w[i]thout that, I was acquainted w[i]th anie the Confederacies in the bill menc[i]oned and against him objected (if any such were) in the manner and form as by the bill is suggested (and w[i]thout that) that I, by any the unlawful means in the bill menc[i]oned, had and obtained any of the evidence, or writing in the bill menc[i]oned or doth detained the same in manner and form as by bill is declared.

That Thomas Gardner, by my persuasion or advice, secretly departed from his dwelling house and hid himself in unknown places is denied. Or that I set forth or published any titles or estates in fee simple or inheritance or for times or years of the premises, or that I or any other of the said defendants (to my knowledge) have made to me or themselves or any secret of fraudulent estates or the said premises in manner and form as by bill is pretended. And I deny it.

Or that I do Claim or make any title to the said premises or do detain any conveyance or writing thereunto belonging and rightfully belonging to the Compl[ainant] in manner and form as by bill is showed and alleged, I deny.

And what that that any other thing or matter material Contained in the said Compl[ainan]ts bill and against me objected and not herein Confessed and avoided traversed and denied or otherwise sufficiently answered is true in manner and form as the Compl[ainan]t by bill most untruly alleged and suggested.

After his forthright testimony, John Cole concluded with a promise and a pledge:

And which matters I will aver and prove as this honourable Court shall see. . . and humbly pray to be dismissed with my good costs for my wrongful vexacion and charges herein most unjustly sustained.

After his dismissal from the session, John was quite worked up. He replayed his testimony in his head. He felt he had spoken plainly, clearly, and truthfully. Now it was up to the court to decide. But it was also near the end of this court's regular session. Summer would soon arrive. That likely meant no conclusion would be reached now nor a verdict rendered at this time.

BOTH COURTS ADJOURN FOR THE SUMMER

As was its custom, the Chancery Court adjourned without concluding its case and suspended operations until hearings resumed in autumn. The Star Chamber Court planned to call additional witnesses to testify in the autumn session and did the same. Perhaps the Chancery Court judges wanted to follow the Star Chamber's lead after the additional witnesses testified. Or perhaps William Wright pulled weight with the judges more than the accused defendants from the East Midlands did. Whatever the reasons, the judges sent a clear message—they were not yet satisfied.

Regardless of the reasons, further answers and examinations would be required of John Cole in the Chancery Court in a few months. Both courts' sessions ended for the summer without resolving either case. Additional testimony from other key witnesses would be required during the Star Chamber court's autumn session.

When John finally arrived home in the summer of 1607 after his trials and testing, he first kissed his wife and embraced his two sons. Frances had kept the household running smoothly in his absence. Nathaniel, now twelve years old, competently handled the farming chores and caring for their animals. John thought, "What a fine lad my eldest son has become. He is such a help to his mother and blossoming as my heir. Someday, whatever we have will be his." Their young toddler son, Zachary, had grown much during his father's absence. But he was not yet walking steadily on his own.

John attempted to quickly set aside the trials and testing he faced in London and reveled in once again being with his family. He had missed them so. Now they were fully together again and would be throughout the summer. After he opened their first meal in prayer, John thought how blessed he was as they again broke bread and ate together as a family.

Their long days of summer were filled with working their land, preparing for the harvest, and enjoying their time with Frances' parents, William and Margaret, who often stayed with them. The doting grandparents loved their two grandsons, Nathaniel and Zachery. However, both John and Frances noticed her father's continuing decline in health. The stressful move away from their longtime home, the Cotton farm near Culworth, had been traumatic. As much as they could, they shielded her parents from the ongoing trials and testing that John was experiencing. It helped that their extended family was once again worshiping in the comfort surroundings of their village's parish church.

John had developed a strong relationship with the new vicar Smith and embraced his Puritan teachings and studies, just as he had done with vicar Proudlove in earlier years. John shared his London trials and testing experiences with his vicar and received wise spiritual guidance and counsel.

As the summer harvest concluded, John realized how quickly the time passed. Too soon, he would return to London, and he made the most of his break with his wife and family. But he would be required to leave them to testify again at the Chancery Court.

Both Court Cases Resume

As summer turned to autumn, the London courts resumed both cases. The Star Chamber issued subpoenas to four key eyewitnesses to the events in William Wright's complaint. They were deposed to answer some or all of twenty-seven interrogatories. On 31 October 1607, depositions were taken from Edward Launden, identified as a yeoman from Pitsford in the county of Northampton, Nicholas Kymbell of Culworth, John Cofford of Watford, a husbandman, and William Cowper of Weedon Bec. Most of these new depositions confirmed information previously disclosed while some expanded the judges' understanding of pertinent events.[31]

DEPOSITION OF EDWARD LAUNDEN IN THE STAR CHAMBER

John Cole's brother-in-law, Edward Launden, confirmed his understanding of pertinent facts. His testimony confirmed the previous testimonies of Simon Gardyner and John regarding the deed of gift to Thomas Gardyner and when it occurred. He added that he believed the deed was made in good faith, contrary to any claims by Wright in the Bill of Complaint. He stated that immediately after the deed was made, William Gardyner started to use the goods as his own.

Launden further stated that Thomas Gardner had mortgaged to the Complainant, William Wright, his messuage and lands, as specified in the Bill of Complaint, and Thomas and William remained living in the same messuage.

Edward disclosed more information about his father-in-law's situation and motivation to remove the property's goods and chattels when he did. Since the Gardyners could not pay the mortgage, they were supposed to yield up the property to the complainant. When Wright would not give them more time, William Gardyner decided to remove the goods from the farm before Wright took possession. Otherwise, he feared he would not be able to collect them. He feared being accused of trespassing. That is when his father-in-law resolved to remove the goods and chattels of and from the messuage and land before Wright was to enter by virtue of not paying his mortgage.

Edward stated that Gardyner wished him to help, having married his daughter. Accordingly, at or about the time of the pretended riot alleged in the Bill of Complaint, Launden did lawfully, as he conceived it, and in peaceable manner help remove the goods and chattels. He added they were far inferior both in quantity and in value to the proportion mentioned in the Bill of Complaint regarding the house and lands. About the deed of gift mentioned and made by William Gardener to him and John Cole, he said they both did marry two daughters of Gardener. He further disclosed that his father-in-law

> being of great age and by reason thereof very unfit and unable to use and dispose of his stocke and goodes was desirous to putt over the same to this defendant and the sayd Cole being his sonne in lawes and to take some security from them that they should make him some competent allowens of necessaries for his maintenans [maintenance] and thereupon the sayd William Gardner made to the sayd John [sic] Cole and this defendant a deed of gift of his goodes and this defendant and the sayd Cole did thereupon covenaunt and agree to make a certen allowans to the sayd William Gardener for and towards his maintenans in such sort as between them was agreed on.

Edward Launden conceived the deed of gift was lawfully made and bona fide for the considerations stated and "not upon any such cause nor fraude as in the sayd Bill of

---

[31] STAC 8/304/20 folio 39.

Complaint is alleaged." He further stated that there was no "unlawfull publishing of two several fraudulent deeds of gift or either of them made by Thomas Gardener [*sic*] to William Gardner."

To setting on fire or causing to be set on fire the messuage claimed or "making of any proclamation for the sale of the sayd goodes or taking or contriving of any fraudulent or unlawfull deed of gift," and

> as to all and singular the Ryots, unlawfull assemblies and other offences and misdemeanours examinable in this most honourable Court wherewith I am charged by the sayd Bill of Complaint – I am not, of any of them guilty, in manner and forme as in the sayd Bill of Complaint is set forth and declared.[32]

In the twenty-second interrogatory concerning Thomas Gardyner, his brother-in-law, whose subsequent departure was not captured in other records, Edward swore

> about the xx[th] of No[vember] last past and the s[ai]d Will[ia]m Gardyner after his making of the s[ai]d deed of guifte unto the s[ai]d John Cole and me yd dep[ar]te secrettly in an Eveninge from his then dwelling howse and ever sythence that tyme dyd absente himself from the same and afterwards came sometymes to thee howsee of him this def[endan]t and sometymes to the howsee of the s[ai]d Cole and sometymes went to other places. And when hee so came to this dep[onen]ts howse and those other howses and places he dyd repayre to the churche to heare devyne s[er]vyce.

> And I say that the s[ai]d Will[ia]m Gardyner and his wyef have byn mayneteyned and kepte all the charges of the s[ai]d Cole and this dep[onen]t sithence their dep[ar]ted from their late dwelling howse in Cullworth afores[ai]d.

To the twenty-third interrogatory, Launden added

> Tho[mas] Gardyner above a yeere sythence secrettly dep[ar]ted from his said dwelling howse in Cullworthe afores[ai]d and is become banckrupte and refusethe to paye the s[ai]d Compl[ainan]t or anye of his Creditors their due debtes or anye p[ar]te of them. And I sayI have heard that the Tho[mas] Gardyner hath changed his name and that he lyeth and wandreth secrettlie up and downe in places unknowen.

The facts that Thomas Gardyner disappeared, is bankrupt, has changed his name, and is living in places unknown are significant. They may better explain the motivations of the Complainant, William Wright, as to why he is making these allegations of conspiracy. It is most likely his attempt to recover money he lost in his failed attempts to find his primary culprit, Thomas Gardyner.

To the twenty-sixth interrogatory about his brother-in-law, John Cole, Launden answered that he and John did "sell and convert to our owne uses all the goodes and cattle to us Conveyed by the s[ai]d Will[ia]m Gardyner as afores[ai]d." As an eyewitness, he added that John Cole

---

32 Restated in first-person by the author.

did in quiet and peaceable manner. . . help to carry away part of the goods and chattels. . . and by the strength thereof and of two or three other horse teams of the proper goodes of the said William . . . as Lawful it was for him and them to doe as these defendents verilie think.

Edward Launden's examination closed after he expressed his displeasure about this complaint, with strong opinions about the alleged financial losses claimed by the complainant.

By all which it may evidentlie appear unto this honorable Court how unjustlie maliciouslie and wrongfully those defendents are sed vexed and trowbled in this behalf.

And further these defendents saye denie and ... withat that the said messuages cottages and other the lands in the bill mentioned are not about the yearlier value of Twentie poundes by yeare at the uttermost or that the Complainant was drawne to purchase the same and without that the Complainant became bound for the defendant Thomas Gardner for the somme of one thousand and six hundred poundes due debt or that the Complainant hath gaien securitie for three hundred and twenty poundes in manner and forme as by bill is sett forth.

Three final depositions were less extensive. John Cofford and William Cowper confirmed they were present at the removing of Willian Gardener's goods and chattels.[33] For their part, they testified they did help and assist, but all the actions were "done only in peacible sort and lawfully as these defendants thinke." They also stated they were not guilty as charged by the Complaint in any number and form of any other actions claimed by the Bill. Then, William Gardyner's son-in-law, Nicholas Kymbell, testified.

For his part . . . as to all and singular the Ryots, routes, unlawfull assemblies, publishing of fraudulent deeds making of proclamations without warrant setting or causing to be sett on fire any house or houses and all and every other the misdemeanours and offences examinable in this honourable Court wherewith he this defendant is Charged by the sayd Bill he is not of them nor any of them guilty in manner and form as in the same Bill is supposed.

All which matters they these | defendants are ready to aver and prove as this honourable court shall award and pray to be dismissed out of the same with their reasonable costs damages and | expenses by them in this behalf most wrongfully susteyned.

Signed by Thomas Coventry[34]

Even with the preponderance of evidence gathered in this court, another trial in another court resumed and required more testing of John Cole three weeks later.

---

[33] Cosford is a variant spelling.
[34] Thomas Coventry is most likely the clerk of the court who took the deposition.

JOHN COLE RETURNS TO FACE THE CHANCERY COURT JUDGES

Less than a month later, it was John's turn to testify in the Chancery Court case. On 21 November 1607, he reiterated his previous testimony and provided more details.

I do not acknowledge or confess any of the said matters in the said Bill of Complaint specified touching the said defendant to be true in such manner and form as herein the same are contained. I further answer and more certain declare the truth—that a long time before any suits were commenced by the said Complainant against me and the other defendants touching the matters now in variance betwixt them, I did receive one deed being a Counterpane[35] of an Intaile of the said Messuage and the other said premises as I then took it, made by William Gardner unto the said Thomas Gardyner being my brother-in-law which the said William Gardiner delivered him when he dwelt in the said Messuage which was to show unto Counsel to be advised thereupon the which as I take it under favor of this honourable Courte was lawful for me to do.

Also, at one other time being at the said Messuage, I took into my hands one other writing which was, as I then took it to be, another Counterpane of a Conveyance made of the said premises by the said Thomas Gardiner unto the said Complainant which I afterwards delivered unto Thomas Atkins, Thomas Gardyner's father-in-law, to be kept to his use which was likewise before this suite commenced.

Which two said deeds or writings were all the Evidences deeds or writings that I possessed at any time or took into my hands coming to the said Messuage, concerning the said premises or any other lands that the said complainant hath purchased, saving only the said Box of writings in the said report mentioned which was delivered to me by the said William Gardiner the which said Box I delivered very shortly after I was served with process into this honourable Court and long before I knew the cause why or wherefore I was so served unto the said Thomas Gardner my Brother-in-law the which he the father so did because I thought the same Box and the writings therein contained, did of right appertain and belong unto him, but what were the contents of the same writings I knew not because I never opened the said Box all which matters I will be ready to averre and prove as this honourable Court shall award and doth most humbly pray as before in my said former answer I hath already prayed to be dismissed hence with my reasonable costs and charges most wrongfully sustained. [36]

[Signature of] Mr Ritche[37]

---

[35] Counterpane in this medieval legal usage meant a document stating the rules covering the disposition or transfer of property or land. (The literal definition of counterpane was a bedspread or decorative cloth; first used in fifteenth century.)

[36] C2/Jas1/W/18/62 [Membrane 3] "The further answers of John Cole." This is the final court record available.

[37] C2/Jas1/W/18/62 [Membrane 3] Mr Ritche, presumably the clerk of the court, recorded the testimony in the third person, which the author translated into first-person testimony. This is the final court record available.

Afterwards, John prayed one more time that the trials and testing were at last finished.[38] The allegations of William Wright, his being away from his family, enduring the writing of the depositions, the courts' examinations, and the overall London experience had weighed heavily on him. Finally, and thankfully, John Cole and the others were found not guilty and pardoned from any wrongdoing. He was free to return home. With late fall transitioning into winter, John gratefully anticipated his return to Weedon Bec as the end of 1607 approached.

DOUBLE BLESSINGS AND A LOSS

As winter settled in over the village, Weedon Bec's vicar Robert Smith asked to speak with John. His father-in-law, William Gardyner, had conversed with him many times after worship services. He often repeated how grateful he was and blessed for John's help and support over the past two years. After summarizing those conversations, vicar Smith looked directly in John's eyes and said, "John, I believe God has set you apart for his purposes. Will you serve him and our parish as a churchwarden?"

As images from the past flashed through his mind, John remembered a similar episode nineteen years before when his father, Thomas, was honored in the same way by vicar William Proudlove. John replied, "Vicar Smith, I am honored and humbly accept your invitation. I will serve the parish and our Lord alongside you." In that capacity, he signed the parish register at the bottom of the page below the last entry made in February 1608.

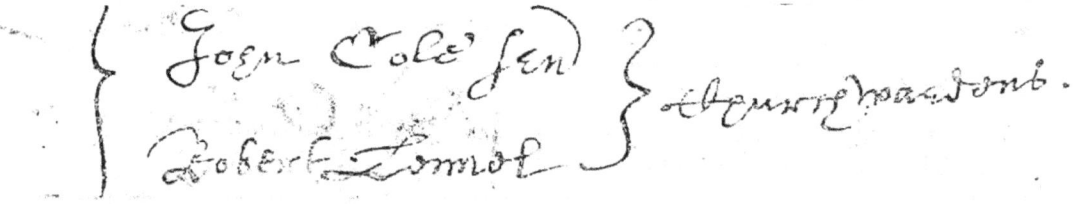

Signatures of John Cole, (Senior) elder, Robert Lemol, the churchwardens.[39] (8.1)

When John shared the good news with Frances, she hugged him. Then she kissed him tenderly, gently pulled away, and looked directly in his eyes. She softly whispered, "I am so proud of you, my dear husband. I love you! I know our soon-to-be-born child will love you too." John gleefully exclaimed, "How blessed we are! I love you, my dear wife!"

Two months later, as they previously had done with young Zacheus, the proud Cole parents named their newborn son after their young son who died in 1604. The second

---

[38] The Star Chamber and Chancery Courts most often did not record their final judgements. No further court records are known to exist. But a later Star Chamber court case, STAC/109/3 "Suit of John Cowper" filed by William Wright was also discovered and reviewed. It involved John Cowper, who may have been the father of John Cole's servant, William. It states that the defendants were pardoned two years prior from any wrongdoing in this matter. It appears William Wright tenaciously clung to his allegations.

[39] Weedon Bec Parish Registers (1588-1665).

Job Cole's baptism was recorded on 1 May 1608.[40] Following this time—plagued by the transition, trials, and testing—naming him Job made perfect sense.

In the Old Testament story of Job, an ancient man tormented by Satan remained steadfast in his faith in God through many serious tests. The root meaning of Job's name in Hebrew is "persecuted." After all that John and Frances experienced during the past two years, they knew that, for Christians, persecution builds endurance and yields righteousness—the characteristic that the biblical book of Job uses to describe him.[41]

Together, John and Frances had certainly endured hardships and tragedies while remaining faithful to God. Once again, the Cole family thanked God for blessing them. Job now joined Zachary, aged two, his elder brother, Nathaniel, now thirteen, and his parents to make a family of three boys and two parents. They smiled as Frances' father, William Gardyner—despite his weak and failing condition—cradled his infant grandson in his arms and talked with his teenage grandson about what a fine young man Nathaniel was becoming. Ever since he and his wife, Margaret, left their farm, they stayed with the Coles often and attended Weedon Bec's worship services. Before long, John was performing his normal duties as a churchwarden. On the 25th of May, a church official recorded these details during a visitation.

> Weedon Bec: Robert Lynnell and John Cole, churchwardens, present that Henry Wilkinson, a butcher, dresses meat usually upon the Sabbath day, as the fame goeth, and that he dressed a calf upon Easter Day last. Item they present that the wife of John Chambers for abusing Thomas Woodruffe, being overseers for the highway, calling him 'burson knave, snub nose knave and olde knave' and such like words, and for a common scold among her neighbours. Item, they present Ellen Caswell, widow, for a very common scold and a dissentious person, and John Gare and William Rodhowse for standing excommunicate, and so hath done by the space of these two years, Item, that John Davie was married to Anne Earndell about St James tide last past, but where, they certainly know not, and that his wife was brought to bed about Christmas next after, and the child was baptised before it died.[42]

Three weeks later, the Cole family experienced a loss they knew was coming. Frances' father, William Gardyner, died. On 12 June 1608, Vicar Smith led the parish churchyard graveside service for William Gardyner, father of Frances Cole and husband of Margaret. As the Cole family gathered at the burial site, John put his arm around his wife's shoulders as she comforted her mum, Margaret. Teenager Nathaniel watched closely as his grandfather's mortal body descended into a grave in the parish churchyard.[43] With his grandfather laid to rest, Nathaniel listened intently to vicar Smith's prayer offering eternal hope.

---

40 Weedon Bec Parish Registers (1588-1665). This corrects the author's previous article that mis-stated the baptism date of Job Cole as 6 May 1608. "The English Origins of Job, John, Daniel, and Ruth Cole," (*The Mayflower Descendant*, Vol. 69, no. 1 (2021)).
41 "Job," *Behind the Name*.
42 NRO, Western Deaneries, Correction Book no. 40, visitation 6,
43 Weedon Bec Parish Register, mis-indexed as Cardiner on Ancestry.com.

The Cole Family Life Returns to Normal

As the Cole's family life returned to a more normal state, farming and caring for their animals consumed the summer months. John continued performing his church duties as churchwarden. At harvest time, he diverted his attention away from the farm temporarily. In his responsibilities, he was drawn into a minor controversy—this time with a village parishioner.

> Date: 10 Oct 1608 Weedon Bec: The same present Ellen Caswell for a very common scold and a dissentious person. Stands excommunicated, etc. On 8 Oct 1608 before the lord chancellor at his chambers in Northampton, the lord absolved her, because she alleges that John Cole, one of the churchwardens, does deny that he ever presented her, etc. The said John Cole affirmed in force of oath that he does not know of himself her to be a common scold, and the lord decreed that, if Richard Marriatt and Nicholas Willkins, the new churchwardens, will certify him that she is no scold before the next court, then she should be dismissed, etc.[44]

During another regular diocese visitation that winter, John and a fellow churchwarden presented two parishioners for disciplinary action on 3 January 1609.

> Weedon Bec: Robert Linnell [sic] and John Coles [sic], churchwardens, present that Henry Hollis, gentleman, and Mary Banbury have lived incontinently so that the said Mary is with child.[45]

Clearly the range of issues occupying a seventeenth-century churchwarden's discretion and judgment were broad and varied. By then, John and Frances' oldest boy Nathaniel, a lad of fouteen, had grown to be a big help to his father, tending the crops and animals. Young Zachary, about three, kept Frances busy as did her baby Job, at seven months.

The Cole family's routine settled into one of regular seasonal changes. The next two harvests went smoothly. Their life was good, and everyone seemed happy and blessed. During the harvest season of 1610, Frances pulled John aside one evening. "John, we are to have another child. If God blesses us with a boy, we shall name him after you." In the spring, Frances bore a son, and they named him, John. On 28 March 1611, John Cole was baptized in Weedon Bec's parish church by vicar Robert Smith.[46] With him, the family grew to four boys and two parents: six mouths to feed. They were faithful parishioners, and the family was known and respected in the village. But there would be one more addition.

During the summer growing season in 1614, Frances came again to her husband. "John, I have news." He asked, "What is it, my dear wife?" As he searched her face for a clue, it suddenly dawned on him. "Darling, are you pregnant again? Am I right?" She nodded. John cupped Frances' face in his hands and kissed her. He held her in a tight embrace. John spoke

---

[44] NRO, Correction Book, Folio 592.
[45] NRO, Correction Book, Folio 342.
[46] Weedon Bec Parish Registers (1558-1665)

a quiet exclamation, "Even at our greatly advanced age, we will be parents. God has blessed us once again!" Frances was about forty. In December, their fifth son, Daniel, was born. With vicar Smith presiding, Daniel Cole was baptized at the parish church baptismal font. The date was 26 December 1614.[47]

Throughout the winter months of 1615, the warm embers glowed in their fireplace. Infant Daniel rested in his mother's arms. Zachary, almost eight, played with Job, nearly five, and John, who would be four in the spring. The boys rolled on the floor and climbed on each other's backs. Nathaniel, who turned twenty in January, read in a corner quietly. The family had recently acquired a new Bible—the King James version. He also chatted with his father about the spring planting season ahead. When needed, he intervened from his chair to reprimand or oversee his younger brothers. John and Frances' family now numbered seven with five boys. They counted their blessings daily.

Horse Breeding and Horse Thieves

With their farm properties and Nathaniel's help, John developed good agricultural and management techniques. But he also developed an avid interest in raising horses and other animals. He had learned much, not only from his father, Thomas, but also his father-in-law, William Gardyner. When John and Frances married, John's responsibilities on his father-in-law's large farm in Cotton taught him much as a young man in his twenties. He learned crop raising and animal husbandry techniques.

When he brought his family back to Weedon Bec and inherited his father's tenancy rights in 1599, he expanded his farming interests. By 1606, John demonstrated his horsemanship abilities with the four teams of horses and carts used to help clear his in-laws' farm. As a result, they added to their collection of animals, and John developed his keen interest in horses even further.

As London and England's population burgeoned during Elizabeth I's reign, the demand for good horses increased and transportation options proliferated. An informal horse census was conducted on the road between Shoreditch, just outside the north boundary of London, and Enfield, about fourteen and a half miles north [23 km]. On one morning, 2,200 horses traveled that road.

But hundreds of years before Queen Elizabeth's reign, beginning in the Middle Ages and extending geographically throughout the Isle of Britain, horses were coveted by the nobility. England's long tradition of horsemanship and racing was well-entrenched in the upper rungs of society. The first documented "horse race meeting" occurred in 1174 documented by William Fitzstephen at a St. Bartholomew's horse fair in London.[48] Henry VII passed several laws regarding horse breeding, which led to better record keeping. His son, Henry VIII, was an accomplished horseman. The first record of a trophy being given out was in

---

[47] Weedon Bec Parish Registers (1588-1665)

[48] "History of British Horse Racing," *Gambling Sites*. Viewed on 1 November 2022. https://www.gamblingsites.com/horse-racing/uk-ireland/history/.

1512 in Chester. It consisted of a wooden bat covered in flowers. The oldest horse race, the Kiplingcotes Derby at the East Riding of Yorkshire, was run in 1519.

During the reign of King James, widespread ownership of horses in England outstripped continental Europe. In 1605, he discovered Newmarket and established public horse racing in England. He imported quality animals and aimed to develop new, lighter, and faster types of horses.[49] With the growing popularity of all things related to horses, Gervase Markham published *Cavalarice, or The English Horseman* in 1617.[50]

> Contanying all the art of horse-manship, as much as is necessary for any man to understand, whether hee be a horse-breeder, horse-ryder, horse-hunter, horse-runner, horse-ambler, horse-farrier, horse=keeper, coachman, smith, or sadler: together with the discovery of the subtil trade or mystery or horse-coursers, and an explanation of the excellency of a horses understanding.

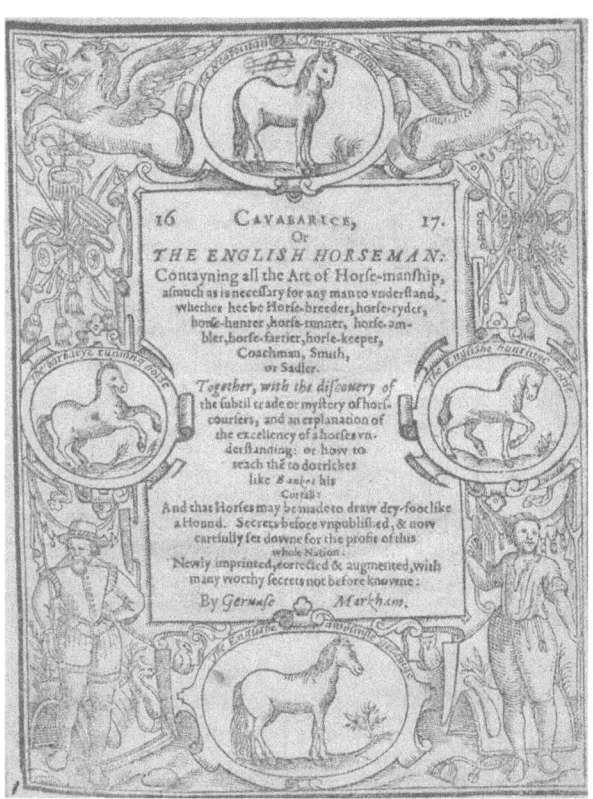

Public domain. (8.2)

This landmark book captured and promoted techniques for raising and breeding horses. At that time, farmers raised and used pack horses, farm horses, and cart horses. But they also bred horses for saddling and driving. In his tome, Markham gave instructions and recommendations for cross breeding the animals for more specialized purposes. It's likely John Cole acquired a copy, read it, and applied the recommended techniques.

These factors increased the popularity and use of horses beyond farming and extended to widespread travel uses. Horses could be hired. Another common practice developed for the convenience it offered. A traveler would often simply buy a horse for a particular journey and sell it upon arrival at his destination.[51]

As with most advances, there are often downside risks. Criminals find

---

[49] J. Wortley Axe, *The Horse: Its Treatment in Health and Disease, with a complete guide to breeding, training, and management* (London: Gresham Publishing, 1907): 544.

[50] Gervase Markham, *Cavalarice, Or the English Horseman* (London: printed by Edw. Allde for Edward White, 1617).

[51] Peter Edwards. *The Horse Trade of Tudor and Stuart England* (Cambridge: University Press, 2004).

opportunities to take advantage of unsuspecting law-abiding citizens. As horses proliferated, so did horse thieves. Two Weedon Bec villagers, including a familiar churchwarden, arrived in London at Whitechapel. While inside conducting their business, Lawrence Wade of Whitechapel and William Raye stole their horses, "a white gelding and a grey nag, each worth £4, belonging to Robert Lennell [*sic*] and Martin Billinge, on 2 January 1617/8."[52]

John Cole's love of horses, raising and breeding them, was recognized in the village. Neighbors consulted with him on the breeding techniques he employed. He was happy to share something he so enjoyed. But most importantly, John passed those skills along to his sons. They made good use of their tenancy property.

Cole Family Special Treat

Something genealogists dream to walk where their ancestors did. This author has done that.

Author William E. Cole in front of Cole Land in Weedon Bec, September 2018. (8.3)

As a special Cole family treat, a modern Weedon Bec map follows. In it, the circled numbers 1 through 7 designate locations where the Cole family raised their crops, cared for and raised their animals, and lived. The map legend indicates place names found in Cole records associated with those locations in the sixteenth and early seventeenth centuries.[53]

---

[52] Sessions of the Peace and Gaol Delivery, on 14 and 15 January, 15 James I A.D. 1617–18. (H.M. Stationery Office, London, 1942), Sess. Roll 562/69, 71–6, 157–61. P.R.B. 1/119. G.D.R. 2/136d, 137, 138d. Viewed on 20 September 2021.

[53] Special thanks to Julia Johns and David Hall for helping our research team identify the locations of Cole property as indicated in the Eton College Archives' Weedon Bec Manor Court records. David Hall holds the map's copyright and gave the author permission to use it in his publications and presentations. Hall is the author of *Open Fields of Northamptonshire* (Northampton: Northamptonshire Record Society, 1995).

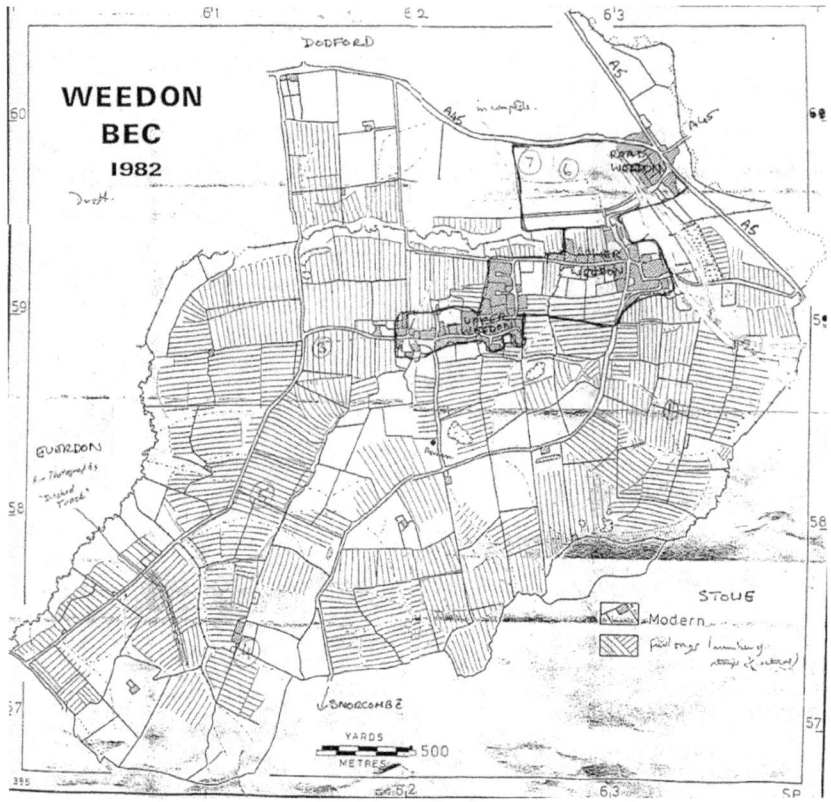

Seven Cole Lands Designated in the 16th – 17th centuries. Permission granted by David Hall. Sponsored by Dave and Tamara Hollars. (8.4)

Map Legend

Field toward Stowe:
1. Cherry Pit Hole
2. Nether Nine Acres

Field toward Everdon:
1. Water Furlong
2. Outwoods
3. Broadfurlong (*the area marked covers fields now called Longlands and Big Grounds so might possibly be Broad Furlong*)

Field towards Dodford:
1. Middle Furlong
2. The Downes

The Quality Book mentions Coles Hedge Furlong in the Field toward Stowe and Coles Leys towards Dodford.

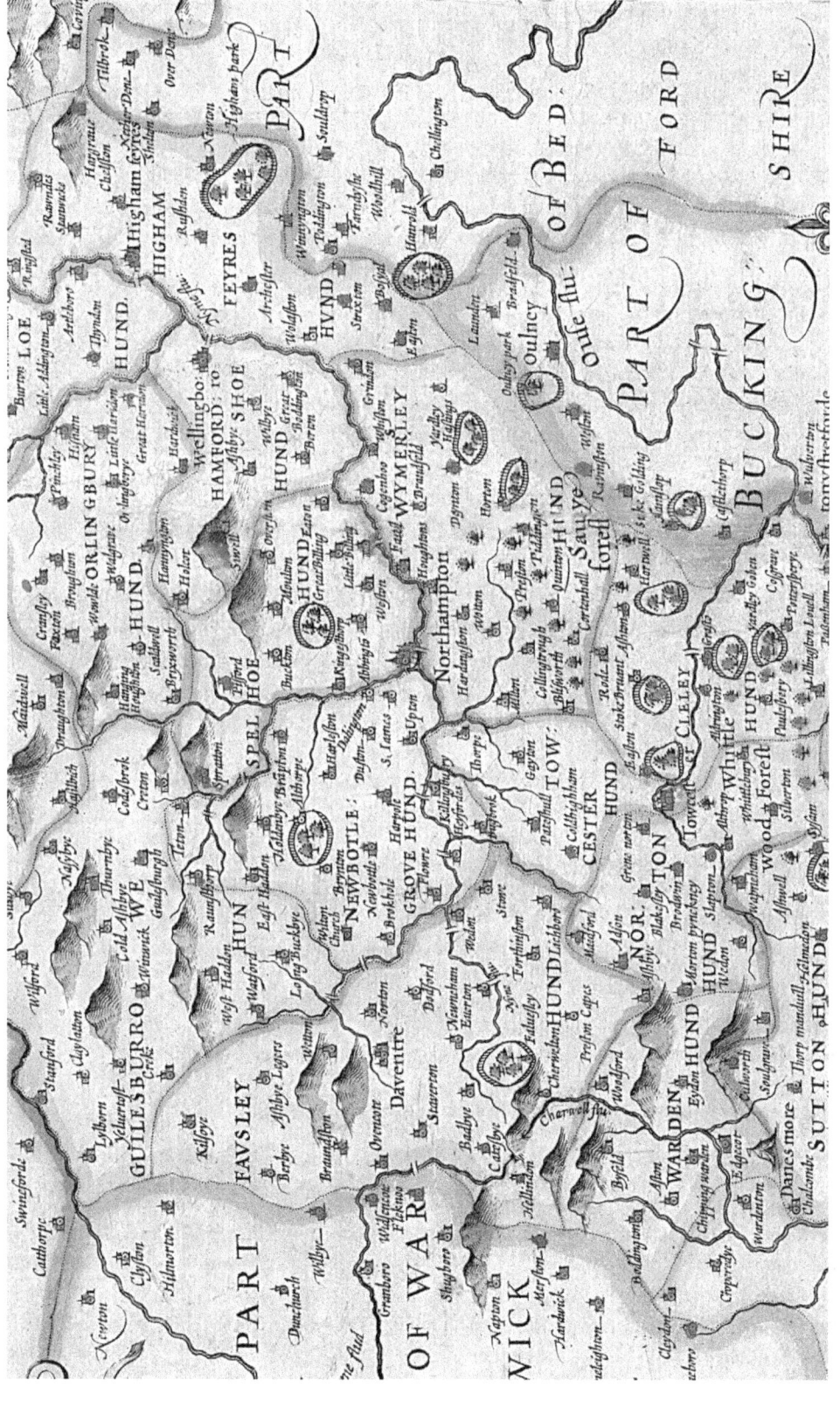

Northamptonshire, John Speed, 1610.

With kind permission of Unique Maps Co. https://uniquemaps.co/.

With highest recommendation. https://uniquemaps.co/. Sponsored by Jerrine A. Stanbury. (8.5)

ENDNOTES

CHAPTER 5

[i]   Melissa Snell, a historical researcher and author with a Middle Ages and Renaissance period focus, provided an apprenticeships' overview during this time. "The Learning Years of Medieval Childhood: Schooling, University, and Apprenticeship in the Middle Ages," *ThoughtCo*. Viewed on 9 July 2020. https://www.thoughtco.com/medieval-child-the-learning-years-1789122

> London apprenticeships usually began in the teens and lasted from seven to ten years. Sons of master craftsmen were by Guild law automatically accepted. Many [apprentices] were supplied from outlying villages in substantial numbers, supplementing labor forces that dwindled from diseases such as the plague and other factors of city living. The destiny of an apprentice was usually determined by the connections his family had. For example, a young man whose father had a haberdasher for a friend might be apprenticed to that haberdasher, or perhaps to another haberdasher in the same guild. The connection might be through a godparent or neighbor instead of a blood relative. Affluent families had more affluent connections, and a wealthy Londoner's son was more likely than a country boy to find himself learning the goldsmith trade.

> The relationship between master and apprentice was as significant as that between parent and offspring. Apprentices lived in their master's house or shop; they usually ate with the master's family, often wore clothes provided by the master, and were subject to the master's discipline. Living in such close proximity, the apprentice could and often did form close emotional bonds with this foster family and might even marry the boss's daughter. Whether or not they married into the family, apprentices were often remembered in their masters' wills.

> The apprentices were there to learn and the primary purpose the master had taken them into his home was to teach them; so learning all the skills associated with the craft was what occupied most of their time. Some masters might take advantage of the free labor and assign menial tasks to the young worker and teach him the secrets of the craft only slowly, but this was not all that common.

> An affluent crafts master would have servants to perform the unskilled tasks he needed to be done in the shop; and, the sooner he taught his apprentice the skills of the trade, the sooner his apprentice could help him properly in the business. It was the last hidden "mysteries" of the trade that might take some time to acquire.

[ii]   Excerpts from the will of Henry Yates of the Parish of St Olave's in Surrey, dyer.

1. His body is to be buried in the New Churchyard.
2. To his mother, Margaret Yates, £10, which the testator lent to his brother, William Yates.
3. He lists bequests to his children: Sons: (eldest) Thomas £13 6/8; Nathaniel £13 6/8; Henry £13 6/8; Daughters: Jane £13 6/8; Margaret £13 6/8.
4. To his unborn child that his wife carries £13 6/8 if it survives. If any child dies, then their portion is equally divided between the other siblings.

5. To his wife, Alice Yates, their dwelling house for the term of her natural life as long as she dies before the lease expires. The 'Comodity' that remains about the house is left to the children.
6. Full Executrix is wife, Alice.

Henry Yates' probate was recorded on the 11th of August. "Comodity" probably means household goods. New Churchyard was a new burial ground set aside for plague victims and was not the parish churchyard.

CHAPTER 6

iii NRO Diocesan Visitation book (report 13a) Transcriptions by Simon Neal.
Folio 58d - 2 Oct 1590
Wedonbecke:

William Renioldes	}
Edmund Gare	}
Richard Roffe	}churchwardens
Thomas Greeneocke	}

Folio 72 - 6 Nov 1590
Brackley deanery:
Culworth:

William Wattes, Nicholas Aris, John White, Robert Shryve, churchwardens, present that they had one service this three months in the vicar's default.

Wedonbecke:

The churchwardens there present the glass windows and churchyard wall is out of repair, which have both surplice and book, but cannot come by them. Item, the wife of Robert Muscott was buried without a minister and there a minister procured to be present.

iv NRO diocesan Visitation book Transcriptions by Simon Neal.
Folio 87 - 5 Dec 1590

The same against Robert Muskett of Wedonbecke:

There issued a citation: his wife was buried without a minister and there not a minister to procured to be present he sitteth in the church and doeth neither rise nor move his hat at any time during divine service, being warned thereof, etc.

Folio 107 - 2 Jul 1591

The same against Thomas Billinge of Wedonbecke: There issues a citation for absenting himself from the church.

The same against John Gare and his wife of the same: There issued a citation, as above, and for carrying away the town 'fyrrs' that the churchwardens had provided for the repair of the church.

The same against Robert Toy and the maid servant of Mr Prowdlove and the maid servant of Thomas Gare of the same: There issues a citation upon a crime. They appeared and acknowledged the fame, etc.

[Margin]: Anne Ley and Ursula Peysnole.

Folio 108d - 16 Jul 1591

The same against Thomas Billinge of Wedonbeck: There issued 'vijs et modiis' for absenting himself from the church.

The same against Robert Toy, Anne Ley and Ursula Peysnole of the same: To purge themselves, except for Toy, etc.

Folio 109d - 27 Jul 1591

The same against Thomas Billinge of Wedonbeck: There issued a s' for absenting himself from church.

Folio 113 - 21 Nov 1592

Wedonbecke: John Cleveley, Edward Gare, churchwardens there, present John Gare the younger will not suffer his child to be baptized, the children be a quarter old, and not frequenting their parish church.

The same against Thomas Billinge of the same: for not frequenting his parish church.

Folio 125 - Dec 1592

The same against John Gare the younger and his wife of Wedonbecke: There issued "*vijs et modiis*" against John and a citation his wife, as they will not suffer their child to be baptized till it be a quarter old and not frequenting their parish church.

The same against Thomas Billinge and his wife of the same: There issues 'vijs et modiis' against Thomas and a citation against his wife.

Folio 129 - 16 Dec 1592

The same against John Gare and his wife of Wedonbecke: There issued an excommunication against John and '*viijs et modiis*' against his wife.

The same against Thomas Billinge and his wife of the same: There issued an excommunication.

Folio 131d - 9 Jan 1592/93

The same against John Gare and his wife of Wedonbeck: There issued an excommunication.

The same against Thomas Billinge and his wife of the same: There issued an excommunication.

Folio 136 - 24 Jan 1592/93

The same against John Gare and his wife of Wedonbeck: They stand excommunicated.

The same against Thomas Billinge and his wife of the same: They stand excommunicated.

Folio 139 - 7 Feb 1592/93

The same against John Gare and his wife of Wedonbeck: They stand excommunicated.

The same against Thomas Billinge and his wife of the same: They stand excommunicated.

Folio 144 - 23 Feb 1592/93

The same against John Gare and his wife of Wedonbeck: They stand excommunicated.

The same against Thomas Billinge and his wife of the same: They stand excommunicated.

Folio 146d - 9 Mar 1592/93

The same against John Gare and his wife of Wedonbeck: There issued a citation, as above.

The same against Thomas Billinge and his wife of the same: There issued a citation, as above.

Folio 150 - 23 Mar 1592/93

The same against John Gare and his wife of Wedonbeck: They stand excommunicated.

The same against Thomas Billinge and his wife of the same: They stand excommunicated.

Folio 153 - 6 Apr 1593

The same against John Gare and his wife of Wedonbeck: They stand excommunicated.

The same against Thomas Billinge and his wife of the same: They stand excommunicated.

Folio 155d - 27 Apr 1593

The same against John Gare and his wife of Wedonbeck: They stand excommunicated.

The same against Thomas Billinge and his wife of the same: They stand excommunicated.

[v] A special thanks and acknowledgement to Julia Johns of the Weedon Bec Historical Society. After attending this author's presentation in Northampton, England in September 2018, she located the following record from *Witness Statements from Deanery and Chapter Records at Peterborough. 16th and 17th Centuries*. The village, Bugbie, is known to be Long Buckby.

Cause tithes: 22nd Sept 1553 John Cole of Wedon, husbandmen; had lived there 10 years, before that at Bugbie where he was born. Aged 40 or more. Personal response by: John Cole in reply to Robert Gostwyck. He was prepared to pay tithe for meadow at 6d for each yardland. He had agreed and paid a tithe for ½ acre of oats and ½ acre of barley.

[vi] Eton, ECR27_228, 1550, John Cole. Note: several Cole spelling variations exist in these records. They include Coole, Cooles, Cowle, and Colles. But it is confirmed there was only one John Cole at this time. The variant spellings all describe the same man, John Cole.

Who, sworn and charged upon their oath about diverse articles touching this court, present that John Cooles has a certain close, lying in Small Acre, enclosed at the time of the commission. Therefore, it is ordered that everything is well ordered at this day.

[vii] Eton, ECR27_229, 1551, John Cole fine.

[viii] English Mill Law et al, Chpt 9 p 305

From the late twelfth century onward in England, mills and their incomes were increasingly regarded as valuable assets which needed to be protected from encroachment, alienation, and competition. Mills became entrenched as a customary right of manorial lords. Because querns were common in France and Weedon Bec was established by the French Abbey of Bec, their overseers imposed similar obligations on their English tenants with 'a simple act of proclamation, followed by a decade or two of customary usage.' This announcement gave the Court Baron right to protect its mill's value—making the use of quern mills inappropriate or even illegal. In most situations, the offenders were ordered to destroy their mills before the next court. If they continued using or simply possessing one, an annual fine payable to the miller was imposed. 'Lords had the right to confiscate household querns, as well as any grain which they had milled at any establishment not belonging to the lord, along with the horse used to carry it, and there are many documented cases of lords doing precisely that.'

ix Wolfhampcote's parish in Rugby borough includes the old village, plus the nearby village of Flecknoe, and the small hamlets of Sawbridge and Nethercote.

x Alphabetical listing by surname of thirteen men fined in Weedon Bec Court Baron Presentment in 1552:
Bylling, Edmund;
Capurne, William;
Coole, John [*sic*];
Corbet, William;
Gare, John;
Gostwyck, Thomas;
Jeffrey, John;
Jeffrey, William;
Judkyn, Thomas;
Leedes, William [alias Kyrby];
Lynnell, ?John;
Lynnell, Robert;
Wawe, Richard.

xi Eton, ECR27_230, 1552, John Cole, 2nd entry.

At this court there came Valentine Brothers and in full court he surrendered into the hands of the lords three acres of meadow with appurtenances, lying in one close called Betwex the Towns, which the aforesaid Valentine lately had from the surrender of William Capron. To the use and behoof of Thomas Lovett, his heirs and assigns. And the bailiff of the lords is ordered to summon the aforesaid Thomas Knyghtley to be here before the next court to make a fine with the lord for the things before granted, etc.

It is found at this court by the homage that after the last court held here Valentine Brothers and Anne his wife, and the same Anne having been examined alone by the steward out of court, in the presence of Robert Lynnell, Thomas Judkyn, Thomas Clyfford, Thomas Ryngrose, William Corbett and John Cole, they surrendered into the hands of the lords one messuage and one cottage and six virgates of land with appurtenances in Wedon, aforesaid, to the use of Thomas Lovett, his heirs and assigns. Whereupon there befalls to the lord as a heriot 5s. And the bailiff is ordered to summon the aforesaid Thomas Lovett to be here at the next court to make a fine with the lords for the things before granted, etc.

xii Transcription of Will of John Cole 1561. | indicates the end of each line in the original will.

In the name of God Amen the yere of owre Lorde | god 1561 the vijth daie of December I John Cole of ov_er_ Weedon | becke in the countie of Northampton being \sicke/ in bodye and | whole of mynde thanke be to almyghtie god make my testamente | and laste will in this forme and mann_or_ as here folowethe | First I bequethe my soule to almyghtie god trustinge to | be protecter? of his blessed passion my bodye to be buried in | the parishe churche yarde of wedon Item I gyve and bequethe | to Thomas Cole my sone A malte querne and a speyte Item | I gyve to William Cole iiij shepe. Item to John Cole xx^{ti} | marke to be paide within vj yeares after my decease by Thomas | Cole his brother Item to Helen my doughter xx^{ti} marke Item | to Agnes Chilleyes my wifes doughter five poundes and | other five poundes I owe of her fathers bequeste Item | to Henry Cole vj^{li} xiij^s and iiij^d and xx^{ti} of my beste ewes and | my best carte or els iiij markes of money A ploughe with | all thinges therto belonginge iij harrowes A garner to | put malte A newe stepe satt? A leade A salte troughe all | the tymbre bordes and every leyars in the stable and in cowe | house Item to Robert Cole my sone vj^{li} xiij^s iiij^d and a paire | of smythes bellowes A nansylde / nanfylde? and all the reste of my | fowles yt is to worke with a cowe and vj shepe Item to John Gibbis vj^{li} xiij^s iiij^d Item to Edmund Kinge vj^{li} | xiij^s iiij^d Item to John Gibbis vj^{li} xiij^s iiij^d Item to Margery | Kinge vj^{li} xiij^s iiij^d Item Agnes Cole vj^{li} xiij^s iiij^d Item | to Alice Cole vj^{li} xiij^s iiij^d Item to every one of my | childrens children A shippe [sheep] Item I will that Willyam Cole shall have all thinges that were gyven hyme by his grauntfathers will yt is a nanfylde A paire of | smythes bellowes An yron tourne? for a greenstone Twoo | great hammers A vice A beckehorne A heyfor and A carte | iiij^{oz} peces of pewter Item I gyve and bequethe all the Reste | of my goodes that be unbequethed to Margaret my wife | whome I make myne executrix Witnesses Robert Reynolds Thomas Cole John Byllyng with other men |

Probate: quinto die mensis Maij Anno Domini 1562 [5 May 1562]

xiii Eton, ECR27_232, 1561-2 (membrane 27), John Cole, Margaret and others.

Which same homage present that John Cole, out of court, viz on the 16th day of January last past before the date of this court, surrendered into the hands of the lord… one messuage, in which the aforesaid John Cole then inhabited… to the use and behoof of Henry Cole, son of the said John Cole, [and] the heirs and assigns of the same Henry. Who, being present in court, seeks to be admitted to the aforesaid premises with their appurtenances. To whom the lord by his steward granted seisin thereof by the rod.

To have and to hold the aforesaid messuages, lands, meadows and pastures with their appurtenances to the aforesaid Henry Cole and the heirs male of the body of the same Henry Cole lawfully begotten, and for lack of such issue, to the use and behoof of Robert Cole, another son of the aforesaid John Cole, and the heirs male of the body of the same Robert Cole lawfully begotten. And for lack of such issue, the remainder thereof to the right heirs of the aforesaid John Cole forever, of the lord by the rod at the will of the lord according to the custom of the aforesaid manor by the rent of 11s 2d a year, a heriot when it should befall, suit of court and all other charges, customs and services thereupon previously due and accustomed. And he gives to the lord as a fine £5. And he is admitted as tenant of the premises.

Provided, nevertheless, always that Margaret Cole, widow, mother of the said Henry, and also lately wife of the said late John Cole, deceased, will have and enjoy a moiety of all and singular the aforesaid premises for the part of her dower for the term of her life according to the custom of the aforesaid manor by the ancient rents, customs and services thereupon previously due and accustomed.

And at this court there came the aforesaid Margaret Cole, widow, late wife of the said John Cole, deceased, and seeks to be admitted both to a moiety of all and singular the aforesaid premises, viz one messuage… now in the seisin and possession of the said Henry Cole… and also to a moiety of another messuage… now in the seisin and possession of Thomas Cole senior, son of the said John Cole, of all and singular which premises the aforesaid John Cole, late husband of the aforesaid Margaret, was seised at the time that the marriage between the aforesaid John Cole and the same Margaret was celebrated and made.

To which same Margaret, the lord by his steward granted seisin thereof by the rod. To have and to hold the moiety of all and singular the aforesaid premises with their appurtenances to the aforesaid Margaret and her assigns for her dower for the term of her life according to the custom of the aforesaid manor, with remainder thereof after her decease to the aforesaid Thomas and Henry Cole, their heirs and assigns, of the lord by the rod at the will of the lord according to the custom of the aforesaid manor by the ancient rents, customs and services thereupon previously due and accustomed. And she gives to the lord as a fine [blank] and she made fealty and was admitted as tenant of the premises in the form, above said.

[Translation by Simon Neal]

xiv   Eton, ECR27_232 (membrane 5) 1585-6.
Homage: Thomas Cole and Henry Cole
Presentments: Thomas Byllynge and Thomas Cole

1st entry

At this court, it is found by the homage that Henry Marrette out of court after the last court surrendered into the hands of the lords by the hands of Richard Wawe, bailiff of the aforesaid manor, in the presence of Thomas Billinge and Thomas Cole, two customary tenants of this manor, bearing witness to this, according to the custom of the aforesaid manor, one cottage, one orchard and one close with appurtenances in Nether Weedon. And one acre and a half of arable land, lying in the fields of Weedon Beke, now in the occupation of the aforesaid Henry Marret. To the use of Edmund Gare, his heirs and assigns forever. Upon which the lord in this instant court by their steward granted the premises to the aforesaid Edmund Gare. To have to the same Edmund Gare, his heirs and assigns by the rod at the will of the lords according to the custom of the aforesaid manor, paying thereupon to the lords the rents, services and customs due for the premises and lawfully accustomed. And he gives to the lords as a fine for having such estate thereof 20s. And he did fealty to the lords and is admitted as tenant thereof.

2nd entry

At this court it is found by the aforesaid homage that John Clifford out of court after the last court surrendered into the hands of the lords in the presence of Thomas Billinge, Thomas Cole and Leonard Clifford, customary tenants of this manor, bearing witness to this, according to the custom of the aforesaid manor, the whole of his right, estate, title and interest of and in all the lands and tenements, which he holds in the right of Anne Clifford, his wife, the reversion of which pertains to Richard Wawe. To the use of the aforesaid Richard Wawe, his heirs and assigns. Upon which the lords by their steward in this instant court granted the premises to the aforesaid Richard Wawe. To have to the same Richard, his heirs and assigns by the rod at the will of the lords according to the custom of the aforesaid manor. Paying thereupon to the lords the rents, services and customs due for the premises and lawfully accustomed. And he gives to the lords as a fine for having such estate thereof 10s. And he did fealty to the lords and is admitted as tenant thereof.

[Translation by Simon Neal]

CHAPTER 7

[xv] It is also possible John Cole and Frances Gardyner were married in Culworth parish by vicar Edmund Rudierd who replaced Andrew King, but no records are known to exist for marriages before 1610.

[xvi] Since William Proudlove served as vicar of Fawsley earlier in his ministry career, he had known the Lord of the Manor, Sir Richard Knightley, for some thirty years. As happened for Thomas Cole in Pitsford, Thomas Billinge might also have been encouraged by a support system in Fawsley's parish—not far from Weedon Bec and much closer than Culworth.

[xvii] Former vicar Andrew King of Culworth was officially sanctioned as schoolmaster in Chessam/ Woburn Manor Buckinghamshire on 1 December 1595. In the Chessam parish records, he is also listed as minister and preacher of the word of God. He and his wife, Anne, celebrated the baptisms of at least three more sons there: Peregrine on 16 Nov 1597, Nathaniel on 13 Aug 1600, and Jacob on 1 Aug 1604. King faithfully served there until at least 1615.

[xviii] NRO Reference: X610/26. Photo 633, f. 81 - Dated 1596. WEC archive, Report 13a.
Northants: Wedunbeck vicarage granted by the said lord keeper of the great seal of England on the aforesaid day and year to William Proudlowe, clerk, Peterborough diocese, now void by the resignation of the last incumbent there and belonging by full right to our presentation. And it is worth clearly per annum £11.

[xix] NRO Reference: Visitation book no. 5 Dates: 1591-1597. Dated 1597. WEC archive, Report 13a.
Weedonbecke. Mr Proudlove, vicar. Robert Abby and Henry Cole, churchwardens. Thomas Gare and Robert Judkin also mentioned.

[xx] Eton, ECR27_266,1599, Thomas and Henry Cole. Translation by Simon Neal.
Item, they present that Thomas Cole out of court, viz on the 14th day of July in the 41st year of the reign of our Queen Elizabeth, surrendered into the hands of the lords...a moiety of a messuage... then in the occupation of the said Thomas. To the use of Henry Cole for the term of 21 years beginning on the said 14th day of July. Paying thereupon yearly to the aforesaid Thomas Cole, his heirs and assigns the yearly rent of 40s at the feasts of St Michael the Archangel and the Annunciation of the Blessed Virgin Mary by equal portions.

[xxi] William Russell, Grocer and Citizen of London, paid taxes in Southwark. TNA Lay Subsidy Rolls: E179/186/349, 362, 370. 377. 356, 370, 375A, 377.

1593 Aug: £3, Boroughside.	1594 Jun: £3, Boroughside.
1594 Aug: £3, Boroughside.	1598 Aug: £3, Boroughside.
1598 Aug: £4, Boroughside.	1599 Oct: £4, Boroughside.
1600 Aug: £4, Boroughside.	1600 Aug: £3, Boroughside.

xxii Puritan naming patterns continued in England into the reign of Charles II until nonconformity in the Church of England was outlawed in 1662. In 17th Century New England, 80% of children had Biblical names with a higher percentage (90%) in Boston.

xxiii NRO Reference: Institution book No. 3, Folio 7d - Vicarage of Wedunbecke: 24 Sep 1602:
Leonard Hutten, clerk, professor of sacred theology, instituted to the vicarage of Wedunbecke, void by lapse of time.
British Library, Lansdowne MS 445, Photo 642, page 16 WEC archive Report 13a Dated: 1602 Northants:
Wedunbecke vicarage granted by the said lord keeper of the great seal of England on the aforesaid day and year to Leonard Hutten, clerk, doctor of scared theology, Peterborough diocese, now lawfully vacant and belonging to our presentation by lapse of time on this occasion. And it is worth clearly per annum £11.
Note: The vicarage was located adjacent to the parish church. It is different from *Le Townhouse*.

xxiv Hopkins, 639-41. Elizabeth I selected James VI of Scotland as her successor.

xxv Stone of Scone, also called Stone of Destiny, in Scottish Gaelic Lia Fail.
This stone for centuries was associated with the crowning of Scottish kings. Then, in 1296, it was captured and taken to England and later placed under the Coronation Chair. The stone, weighing 336 pounds (152 kg), is a rectangular block of pale-yellow sandstone measuring 26 inches (66 cm) by 16 inches (41 cm) by 11 inches (28 cm). A Latin cross is its only decoration.
According to one Celtic legend, the stone was the pillow upon which the patriarch Jacob rested at Bethel when he beheld the visions of angels. From the Holy Land, it purportedly traveled to Egypt, Sicily, and Spain and reached Ireland about 700 BCE to be set upon the hill of Tara where the ancient kings of Ireland were crowned. It was taken by the Celtic Scots who invaded and occupied Scotland. About 840CE, it was taken by Kenneth MacAlpin to the village of Scone. At Scone, historically, the stone came to be encased in the seat of a royal coronation chair. John de Balliol was the last Scottish king crowned on it, in 1292, before Edward I of England invaded Scotland in 1296 and removed the stone to London. There, at Westminster Abbey in 1307, he had a special throne built, called the Coronation Chair, so that the stone fit under it. This symbolized that kings of England would also be crowned as kings of Scotland. Attached to the stone in ancient times was allegedly a piece of metal with a prophecy that Sir Walter Scott translated as

> Unless the fates be faulty grown | And prophet's voice be vain | Where'er is found this sacred stone | The Scottish race shall reign.

When Queen Elizabeth I died without issue in 1603, she was succeeded by King James VI of Scotland, who became James I of England. James was crowned on the Stone of Scone, and patriotic Scots said that the legend had been fulfilled, for a Scotsman then ruled where the Stone of Scone was.

xxvi A Puritan, later identified as Lewis Pickering, wrote an epitaph poem about the death of John Whitgift, Archbishop of Canterbury.

CHAPTER 8

xxvii TNA,STAC 8/302/4. Names of individuals involved, by alpha surname, forename, and location if known, in clearing William Gardyner's farm near Culworth on 12 Nov 1606.

Bradfilde, John	of Weedon Bec
Brynckoe, Robert – (olde Robert?)	
Caswell, John	of Weedon Bec

Cole, Frances – wife of John	of Weedon Bec
Cole, John	of Weedon Bec
Cosford, John	of Watford
Cowper, William	of Weedon Bec
Foxe, Anthony	of Culworth
Gardyner, Margaret – wife of Wm	of Culworth
Gardyner, William	of Culworth
Gardyner, wife of Thomas (no forename)	of Culworth
Kimbell, John	of Culworth
Kimbell, Margaret – wife of Nicholas	of Culworth
_____, Marye servant of Nicholas Kimbell	of Culworth
Kimbell, Nicolas – son-in-law of Wm Gardyner	of Culworth
Launden, Edward – son-in-law of Wm Gardyner	of Pitsford
Launden, Mary – wife of Edward	of Pitsford
Lowe, John (Lawe?)	
Shepard, Richard A (?)	
& others	

xxviii As a working theory, this letter from "Elizabeth of Weedon" may have been written by Thomas Gardyner's wife but never delivered. There is no verified source of identification for her, but the letter's content leads one to surmise that it came from someone close to its intended recipient, who appears to be the missing defendant. It also indicates, if the year is correct, that the intended recipient was absent almost a year prior to the deed of the farm's goods and chattels was executed which was in May 1606. If the date of the letter is actually in May 1606, the letter would better fit the timeline of actual events.

> p[er]swade thy self that so suerly as thou hast beene and art a most insolent, notable and infamous fellowe both of thy self and also by bauding others of like base, rascallike and slanderous carriadge ev[er]more against my selfe and others by many yeares toge--ither: only thereby to delight and disport thy most loathsome contentious and seditious disposition, whilest in the meane tyme most carelesly wretchedly and beastly thou utterly wastest thy best only and cheefest yeares and w[i]thall ?rivatest thy poore estate whereat the world so much do note and ?squibb

> So suerly, I thank God I have attayned so good meanes by such and so sufficient p[er]sons my kind and able aliance and frendes as I have longe wished yet nev[er] till of late attempted or tried to helpe call in question thy selfe and thy base tuppe--nye ?tewe yo[u]r severall, uncivill and rascally behaviours most impudently and cravenly ev[er]more uppon oddes put in ure against me and sundry others accountinge and re-countinge nev[er] once to come to reckening.

> Now therefore call thy prowde and hoggerly tewe togither closslye and wi- -ttilye I warne yee. How to resolve to answere when they are called viz w[i]th p[ro]found lying villanouse swearing and notorious facinges all in a ?tale ?see yea. else tell them thou dwellest in a strange countrey far from home and suspected of manye to goe god knowes, …whether, further unto Scottes borders by some sup--osed that therefore thou canst and easily give them the slippe if they feele once any the directions and so leave them hope lesse of all comfort for ev[er] and some of the harberlisse like ingrantes and beggars.

For tell them thou hast no reason to spend such side iourneis as wynter will make thee, so much tyme and many noted and mockt at of many and besides catche litle or nothinge for o[u]r livi- -nge here in Milton, w[hi]ch latelye were gott of hunger starved Linford at fast and loose unlesse they singe true descant, that is to say, keeping tyme and tyme as you have painfully oft taught them: And nowe I pray god once to make thee an honest man and if it be but to disprove the world.

Milton this 18 of May 1605 [1606?]
Elizab[eth] [f]Weedon

Hornecastle men report yo[u]r mault yo[u]r onely trad- -inge (except lawe w[i]th a bayley and some few others) is stincking ripe through a laske of continuall riding that you are hic and ubique; wandringly, God wot even after the old fashion thoughe not so far in compasse

NOTE: There is a village in Northampton called Milton Malsor which is just 11 miles from Weedon Bec to the South. Registers exist on Ancestry for Milton Malsor from 1558. There is a village called Great Linford in what is now the town of Milton Keynes, which is 26 miles from Weedon Bec; and a village called Lilford near Peterborough, which is 43 miles from Weedon Bec.

The term "Horncastles men" is unexplained. Google only offers Horncastle as a village in Lincolnshire or a more recent episode where some men in Horncastle did not like their washing machine.

NOTE: It is unclear what this page refers to. The document was double checked and nothing missing. The images look like there should be a page before the letter, but all the documents in the box are stitched together, so what is seen in the images is simply the previous document.

SECTION THREE

PROMISES

CHAPTER 9

PROMISES, PROSPERITY, A PLAGUE, AND COLONIES IN AMERICA

THE GLOBE OPENS IN SOUTHWARK

On the evening before Lent, 20 February 1599, the Lord Chamberlain's Men theatre troupe performed at Richmond Palace for Queen Elizabeth. The following morning, the Reverend Canon Doctor Lancelot Andrewes preached an Ash Wednesday sermon at the queen's court. Afterwards, six men who were stakeholders in the acting company—Burbage, Kemp, Heminges, Phillips, Pope, and Shakespeare—crossed River Thames for an afternoon meeting. Once there, they signed a land lease to build a new venue. Just two months prior, several of them had pulled down the old theatre, Shoreditch, with plans to erect a new "playehowse" on a plot of ground in Maid Lane. The harvested wood and timbers were repurposed to build a new theatre in Southwark.[1]

THE GLOBE THEATRE.

The Globe Theatre, 1612. Engraving.
Courtesy of the Yale Center for British Art. Public domain. (9.1)

---

[1] James Shapiro, *A Year in the Life of William Shakespeare: 1599* (HarperCollins: New York 2005): 77.

The success of the borough's two major theatres, the Rose and the Swan, had opened the eyes of playwrights and impresarios alike from the established Shoreditch district. An opportunity to reach new audiences in new ways in a new state-of-the-art venue offered promising prospects. As theatregoers observed the progress of construction, a buzz of excitement circulated throughout Southwark's Liberty of the Clink. With three open-air floors, it would hold 3,000 eager patrons. Its stage measured twenty-seven by forty-three feet and was raised off the ground to allow access by a trapdoor. Color-coded flags atop the playhouse indicated what type of play was featured. A black flag meant a tragedy, while a red flag indicated a historical play. A flag flying atop the theatre meant it was performance day.

When the Globe's grand opening performance finally arrived, a trumpet blast sounded to let people know the show was about to start.[2] The crowd streamed in and filled the Globe to its maximum capacity. The first performance was a hit and generated substantial crowds who clamored for more. Repeat performances of favorite plays offered variety and generated demand for new ones. Several playwrights wrote new plays, one of whom was William Shakespeare.

As Shakespeare's fame spread, demand for new plays heightened anticipation for opening night performances in a very short period. His early plays at the Globe included *Henry I, II, III, IV*, and *V, Julius Caesar, As You Like It, Hamlet, Measure for Measure, Othello, King Lear, Macbeth*, and *Antony and Cleopatra*. In 1600, Edmund, his younger brother and already a seasoned actor in his own right, followed him to London at age twenty.

The Globe soon offered up to ten different plays over a two-week period. Southwark's vibrant theatre district stimulated the economic growth of the borough. Brewhouses, pubs, and other enterprises flourished. The theatre's proximity next door to St. Saviour's Parish church helped energize the area around the property recently acquired by the church's parishioners. The economic development of the Liberty of the Clink in turn benefited all the parishes on the south bankside of River Thames and in the borough of Southwark.

THE ARNOLD AND CLARKE FAMILIES PROSPER

St Olave's parishioners, along with others nearby involved in England's cloth industry, flourished. In the early seventeenth century, about seventy percent of the occupations listed in its parish register involved weaving, dying, felt making, and hat making—both hatters and haberdashers. Twenty-five percent of occupations related to River Thames included fishmongers and watermen The remaining five percent were related to food provision, which included salters, grocers (which spun off apothecaries as a separate guild in 1617), brewhouses, pubs, and the like. Freemen who operated businesses in Southwark thrived. They included the grocer William Russell, and two dyers' businesses operated by John Arnold and Thomas Clarke.

Alice and John Arnold lived and worked just outside of St. Olave's Parish boundary. With their shop located on their property in St. Mary Magdalene Parish, their dyer's

---

2   Matthew Pearson, "'Did You Know? 10 Facts about Shakespeare's Globe Theatre," *London Pass*. Viewed on 23 July 2019. https://londonpass.com/en-us/blog/did-you-know-10-facts- about-shakespeares-globe-theatre.

enterprise was in a prime commercial location in the borough of Southwark, where shops lined the narrow street. John Arnold's wife blessed him as they partnered to grow their establishment and livelihood. As a woman with significant experience in the craft, having worked for more than a decade alongside her first husband, Henry Yates, together building up his dyer's business, Alice's ability to read and write and help with record keeping was a great advantage.[3] After Yates' death and her marriage to John in January 1594, she was already adept at administrative and support tasks while managing their household and her children.

The Clarkes' dyer business, located in nearby St. Olave's Parish, was likewise growing. Thomas' wife Jane had benefited from watching her mother, Alice, work alongside both her husbands. Since Jane's entire life had been spent in the family dyer businesses, she naturally took on administrative and support tasks, as had her mother before her, as she and Thomas built their business together. Their partnership was a model for young couples just starting out.

A little over a year after their marriage, Jane began feeling strange sensations. Unfamiliar with what she sensed within her body, she hurried to see her mother for counsel. As Jane rushed up Bermondsey Street to see her mum, she unlatched the door, and the two of them sat down.

As Jane described her symptoms, Alice knowingly nodded, paused a moment, and then smiled broadly at her daughter, confirming what Jane had suspected: "You're pregnant! God has blessed you and Thomas with your first child. I'm so happy for you, and I'm thrilled I will be a grandmother!" Jane cried tears of joy and exclaimed, "Thank you, mum. You and the Lord have blessed me greatly."

THE CLARKES' FIRST CHILD

As Jane's pregnancy progressed, Alice tutored her daughter on the finer points of caring for herself and the child she was carrying. She gave her insights only a mother can about the first-time experience of birthing a child. By September, Jane and Alice knew the time would soon be at hand. In late September, with the support of her mother and a midwife, Jane delivered her first child. Though her husband had hoped for a son, Thomas was thrilled with their healthy daughter, as was Jane. They named her Margaret, in honor of both her deceased sister and Thomas' mother. In their parish church just east of London Bridge, Margaret was baptized on 27 September 1605.[4] The baby's two grandmothers, Margaret Clarke and Alice Arnold, beamed proudly as they watched the christening ceremony. Thomas and Jane also smiled at a double blessing on the very same day: their first child's baptism and the second anniversary of their marriage. Jane was eighteen years and seven months old.

Child-rearing came naturally to Jane Clarke. With her mother's continued tutelage and encouragement, her own healthy and happy daughter thrived. In the spring when Jane felt

---

[3]   Martha C. Howell, *Women, Production, and Patriarchy in Late Medieval Cities* (Chicago and London: University of Chicago 1986): 9-48. Recommended reading.

[4]   St. Olave's Parish Registers (1583-1627)

familiar symptoms again, she swooped her daughter into her arms for a quick visit to the Arnold's home and shop. As she carried Margaret, Jane walked along Tooley Street toward the main intersection, then turned right to venture up Bermondsey Street. She largely ignored the shops on each side of the narrow street as she hurried her pace. She could hardly wait to share the good news with her mother. When Jane arrived at the Arnolds' dwelling, she shifted Margaret in her arms, unlatched the front door, and exclaimed, "Mum, I have great news. Another child is on the way. Praise the Lord!" Alice rushed in and embraced her daughter. She lifted her granddaughter, Margaret, into her arms and gave her a kiss. Knowing a second grandchild was on the way, Alice could not have felt happier or more blessed.

In mid-February 1607, seventeen months after the birth of her first child, Jane delivered a healthy baby boy. Her thrilled husband, Thomas, kissed her and then his son. They named the baby Thomas, after his father. He was baptized on the 17th of February.[5] Two weeks after Jane's twentieth birthday, she was the proud mother of two healthy children: a lass and a lad. With their business thriving, her husband added a servant to lend a hand and help support Jane in managing their household: "his man, Robert."[i]

HAPPENINGS IN ST. SAVIOUR'S AND SOUTHWARK

During this time period, St. Saviour's, the parish adjacent to St. Olave's just west of London Bridge, received a new vicar. In the aftermath of King James I's Hampton Court Conference in 1604, Puritans like Edmund Snape, who dreamed of promised reforms after Queen Elizabeth's reign ended, had retrenched and regrouped in expectation of later opportunities for reform. The bishop moved carefully and cautiously, and on 22 November 1605, replaced Edmund Snape with William Symonds as one of two vicars at St. Saviour's parish. Symonds, a Doctor of Divinity who matriculated at Oxford's Magdalen Hall in 1571, was a moderate choice and well-suited to follow the fiery Snape as far as the bishop was concerned.

As the second largest church in greater London, St. Saviour's and its parish had regained stature in the eyes of the diocese. In the late sixteenth century, when its vestry[6] and parishioners acquired the parish church and its land from the Crown, they revitalized its land by destroying pigsties and kilns previously used for the manufacturing of Delftware located on the church grounds. The bishop felt the vestry's renovation efforts and the clearing out of some unsavory aspects of its property had made vast improvements stimulated by the Globe's success.[7] In fact, James I granted favorable status to the theatre's acting troupe, the Lord Chamberlain's Men. By patent dated 19 May 1603, King James licensed

---

5 St. Olave's Parish Registers (1583-1627)
6 Vestry was a committee of local elected representatives and churchwardens to fundraise and administer church business affairs.
7 David Divers et al, *A New Millennium at Southwark Cathedral: Investigations into the First Two Thousand Years* (London: Pre-Construct Archaelogy Ltd. Monograph 8, 2008): 128.

Lawrence Fletcher, William Shakespeare, Richard Burbage, Augustyne Phillippes, John Heninges, Henrie Condell, William Sly, Robert Armyn, Richard Cowly, and the rest of theire Assosiates freely to use and exercise the Arte and faculty of playinge Comedies, Tragedies, histories, Enterludes, moralls, pastoralls, Stage plaies aswell for the recreation of our lovinge Subjectes, as for our Solace and pleasure . . . when the infection of the plague shall decrease . . . as well within theire nowe usual howse called the Globe within our County of Surrey, as alsoe within anie towne halls or Moute halls or other convenient places within the liberties and freedome of anie other Cittie, universitie, towne or Boroughe . . . within our said Realmes.[8]

Above all, the bishop wanted to retain the good grace of His Royal Majesty, King James.

As new businesses and tenements sprang up to replace the dingy and dirty outbuildings, the area, boosted by the economic opportunities stimulated by the nearby Globe, drew merchants, grocers, brewers, playwrights, and others, thereby broadening the base of parishioners. John Harvard was baptized in the church in November 1607, and a memorial chapel commemorates him.[9] One wealthy and prominent parishioner was Sir Robert Clarke, Knight and Baron of the Exchequer who lived in Liberty of the Clink. When he passed away in 1607, his wife, Dame Joyce Clarke, outlived him by nineteen years. Her son, William Austen, commissioned a stunning chapel in St. Saviour's dedicated to his mother and Sir Robert Clarke. Dame Joyce Clarke was a patron of Edward Alleyn, one of the most famous actors of the time and an impresario. The two would meet often for dinner and discussion of his plays and business ventures. Others came to live in the district as well.

Of the eight actors appointed with Shakespeare to be "King's Men" in the Letters Patent of 1603, three, Lawrence Fletcher (1604–10), Augustine Phillips (1593–1604), and William Sly (1593–97), are shown in the token books as living in the neighbourhood of Bankside at the dates indicated in brackets. Edward Juby, Martin Slater and Alexander Cook, who are all known to have been actors, also occur in the token books while Edmund Shakespeare is shown in Hunts Rents, Maid Lane, in 1607, the year of his death.[10]

When William Shakespeare's brother, Edmund, died at age twenty-seven, William sadly bade him farewell with a special tribute. It is said that Shakespeare paid twenty shillings for his brother's burial and arranged for "a forenoone knell of the great bell."[11] Edmund was buried inside St. Saviour's church in the chancel floor.[ii]

---

[8]   "The Bankside Playhouses and Bear Gardens," *British History Online*. Viewed on 19 December 2019. https://www.british-history.ac.uk/survey-london/vol22/pp66-77.

[9]   The memorial recognizes John Harvard's role with the university in Cambridge, Massachusetts that carries his name.

[10]   "The Bankside Playhouses and Bear Gardens," *British History Online*.

[11]   "Edmund Shakespeare," *Wikipedia*. Viewed on 7 November 2019. https://en.wikipedia.org/wiki/Edmund_Shakespeare.

Edmond Shakespeare Marker in St. Saviour's Church. Public domain.[12] (9.2)

Not long afterwards, the former vicar of St. Saviour's, Edmund Snape, in failing health wrote a detailed will on 4 March 1608. This devout and fiery Puritan, one of nine imprisoned Puritans who had faced the Star Chamber trials and tribulations and suffered a ten-year banishment from his livelihood, listed as his survivors his father, Thomas, his brothers Thomas and John, his wife, Anne, and eight underage children.[iii]

The parish register records that Edmund Snape, a clerk of the city of London, was buried in St. Saviour's Church on 21 March 1608.[13] His will proved on the 9th of July. Executors were Ralph Bovey of the Inner Temple; Andrew Ellim, merchant; Thomas Carpenter, haberdasher; William Crosley, apothecary; Arthur Lee, girdler; and Rice Webb, haberdasher.

MORE CHILDREN FOR THE CLARKE FAMILY

A few months later in 1608, Jane Clarke's third child, Joyce, was born and baptized on the 30th of August.[14] The Clarkes' successful and thriving enterprise provided well for their family of five. Jane's stepfather, John, and her mother, Alice, provided Thomas and Jane expert guidance that helped them expand their enterprise. The following month, the Clarke family gathered with John and Alice Arnold to celebrate Thomas and Jane's fifth wedding anniversary. With three healthy children, they recounted their blessings and anticipated a promising future ahead.

In 1609 on a summertime trip to visit her mum, Jane paused to admire the view of the south bankside of River Thames outside their parish church—one of the best views in all of greater London. As Jane strolled with her three children in tow, the bustling river activity

---

[12] "Edmund Shakespeare," *Wikipedia.*
[13] St. Saviour's Parish Registers (1609-1653)
[14] St. Olave's Parish Registers (1583-1627)

on her left and the merchant shops on her right fascinated her impressionable children. The sights, sounds, and smells constantly stimulated all their senses.

View of London Bridge from St. Olave's Stairs. Wikimedia Commons. Public domain. (9.3)

Her son, Thomas, now nearly three, was particularly entranced by watermen shuttling passengers and cargo to and fro and loading ships destined for foreign ports. His young eyes absorbed the scene, and he imagined adventures awaiting these seafaring mariners in his active mind.

When Jane Clarke reached Bermondsey Street east of the church, she turned right, carrying Joyce in her arms with her older daughter and son in tow. As they walked up the bustling street, Margaret peered in shop windows to see what treasures were inside. Tugging at her mother's sleeve, Margaret asked countless questions about the items she saw. With a saintly patience, Jane explained each of the things that caught her eye. Her son Thomas' natural restlessness was on full display as he trailed his sister and darted back and forth on the cobblestone street between the shops and his mother. Her active lad was at a most challenging age for any mother. Jane cradled her youngest daughter, Joyce, in her arms and spoke to her softly.

Arriving at their destination, Jane unlatched the door and called out, "Mum, we're here!" The children's grandmother, Alice, beamed and rushed to kiss them before the smell of cookies caught their attention. Cookies with grandma—always a special treat for the children!

As Jane sat with her mother and children to enjoy the refreshments, she and Alice discussed the future. The warm summer breeze blew into the open windows, providing some relief from the heat and humidity. Together, mother and daughter enjoyed a break from their normal routine. Just talking with her mum while holding Joyce, they kept a watchful eye over Margaret and Thomas as they explored every nook and cranny of their grandparents' home.

As Jane reflected on her life, she realized her painful memories of the Plague of 1593 that decimated her family, followed by the Plague of 1603 that took her sister, were fading into the past. She thought to herself, "The last six years of my life have been so blessed. I am truly thankful to the Lord for my husband, our three children, our business, our servant, and for the extra blessings of the nearness of my mother and her husband." As Jane closed her silent prayer, her thoughts of her prospering family encouraged her with promises and hopes for many good years to come—God willing.

Across the borough in St. Saviour's Parish, a young man crossed River Thames and strode toward the Guildhall. Once inside, he found the clerk's office and paid his fee of 3s 4d to be sworn in as a freeman.[15] William Collier had completed his grocer's apprenticeship with William Russell. On 16 August 1609, he was free from his master's control. With continuing guild membership, he had earned the right to establish a grocer's business as a Citizen and Grocer of London. He looked forward to applying his skills for his own benefit and advancement. Indeed, the future looked promising for William Collier at age twenty-six. He was beginning a new chapter in his life.

A month later, the Clarke family gathered once again with John and Alice Arnold to celebrate Thomas and Jane's sixth marriage anniversary. Near the end of the year, in December, Jane once again noticed early signs of life within her. She told her husband, Thomas, another child was on the way. He smiled broadly as he stroked her stomach. They embraced and kissed. Together they thanked God for their family's blessings. At age twenty-two, Jane already had three healthy children, two girls and a boy, and their dyer business was also healthy. As they looked forward to child number four sometime in summer next year, they counted their blessings. They believed in their hearts that their future together was filled with Promises.

When the time came, Jane's mother, Alice, was at her daughter's bedside alongside a midwife for the delivery. When Jane bore her second son, they named him Henry—in honor of her father, Henry Yates, who perished in the Plague of 1593. The Clarke family brought infant Henry to St. Olave's Parish church for his baptism on 22 July 1610. He is listed in the parish register as the son of Thomas Clarke, dyer.[16] But unfortunately, Henry died within days and was buried on the 27th of July. It may have been an omen of things to come as Thomas and Jane and their family wrenchingly accepted the loss of their infant son as God's will.

Within a few weeks, a plague struck Southwark. For a third time, Jane Clarke's family would experience its tragic consequences. Her husband, Thomas, was stricken in September and wrote his will.[17] He bequeathed £20 each to his three children and "the rest of [his] goods" to his wife, Jane. He named his father-in-law, Mr. Arnall [sic], executor, and his wife executrix.[18] Tragically, Thomas Clarke died soon afterwards and was buried on 16 September 1610.

---

15 Grocers' Guild, Wardens' Accounts, 1609-1610. MS11571/9 Folio 332. Guildhall Library, London.

16 Henry Clarke lived only a few days and was buried on 27 July 1610.

17 Will of Thomas Clarke, of St. Olave, 1610. London Metropolitan Archives Ref: DW/PA/S/1610/30.

18 Mr. Arnall was John Arnold, Jane's stepfather, husband of her mother Alice. This document is the will of the correct Thomas Clarke, first husband to Jane (Gates/Yates) (Clarke) Collier.

Within the space of two months, Jane lost her infant child, Henry, and her husband, Thomas. Now a twenty-three-year-old widow with three young children—Joyce, aged two, Thomas, three and a half, and Margaret not quite five—Jane found herself without a husband. Like her mother, Alice, had experienced previously in late 1593, Jane Clarke desperately needed to marry again. For now, the promises of a bright future Jane had believed and clung to in faith seemed dashed. She could not yet see what God had in store for her and her family.

Before Jamestown, King James I's Early Colonization Efforts

Early in the reign of King James I, not long after he presided over the Hampton Court Conference, global developments drew his attention to colonializing efforts in the New World. In the spring of 1604, French explorer Samuel de Champlain joined an expedition led by the nobleman and merchant Pierre Dugua de Mons. During the exploration, Champlain created detailed maps of Acadia[19] and claimed it as colonial territory for France, thereby expanding French colonial possessions to comprise what are now Canada's Maritime provinces: Newfoundland, Prince Edward Island, Nova Scotia, and New Brunswick. The following year, Champlain mapped along the eastern seaboard south to what is now the Maine coast and detailed its bays and islands. Acting under the auspices of French King Henri IV, in June 1604 Dugua established a settlement on Saint Croix Island.[20] When nearly half of its settlers perished due to the harsh winter and scurvy, the survivors moved north to Port-Royal, Nova Scotia, in the spring of 1605. With Spain having established settlements in Florida (St. Augustine 1565), the Caribbean, and Mexico, the rush to colonize the New World was a competition among these three kingdoms as well as the Dutch. And with two new French settlements established in America, King James set his sights on expanding his kingdom beyond England, Ireland, and Scotland.

In March 1605, James I authorized English Captain George Weymouth to explore the coasts of what are today's Penobscot, Maine, and Massachusetts, just south of the French settlements. Weymouth's instructions—to identify the resources of America—led to a most significant event in the history of both England and America.

King James granted a royal charter to the Virginia Company in 1606. It gave the company's investors permission to send ships and settlers to establish colonies in the New World. Two groups within the company, one from London and the other from Plymouth, started planning separate and competing journeys. The Plymouth group was granted rights to the coast between latitudes 38° and 45° North. Its rival London group was granted the coast between latitudes 34° and 41° North. The rival colonists were to plant first within their respective non-overlapping areas. King James' intent was to foster competition for the

---

[19] Present-day Nova Scotia, Canada.
[20] Right on the border of present-day Maine and Canada.

rights to expand their colonization efforts. A neutral area between 38° and 41° was set aside as the prize for whichever group proved itself strong enough to survive.[21]

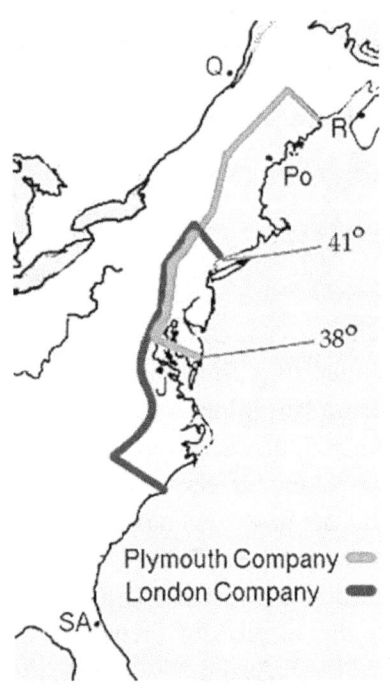

Virginia Co. Charter, 1606.
Public domain. (9.4)

The Virginia Company's first ship, the *Richard*, financed by the Plymouth group, sailed in August 1606. Off course near Florida, the Spanish intercepted and captured it in November. A second fleet of three ships, financed by the London group, left London with 104 men and boys on a voyage that took three months. In April 1607, the ships *Susan Constant*, *Godspeed*, and *Discovery* reached Virginia's Chesapeake Bay under the command of Captains Christopher Newport, Bartholomew Gosnold, and John Ratcliffe.[22] On the 13th of May, they named their settlement Jamestown and the main river James, in honor of their king. Within a month, they completed building a fort.[23]

A third group, also headed by the Plymouth investors, formed with the financial support of Sir John Popham, the Lord Chief Justice of England, and Sir Ferdinando Gorges, the military governor of Plymouth. Seeking to trade precious metals, spices, and furs, and to prove local forests could be used to build English ships, George Popham, a nephew of Sir John Popham, was appointed the colony's president. About 120 colonists (all men and boys) left Plymouth on 31 May 1607, in two ships which crossed the ocean in two and a half months. The first ship, the *Gift of God*, captained by John Elliott, arrived at the mouth of the Sagadahoc River on 13 August 1607.[24] The other, the *Mary and John* captained by Robert Davies, arrived three days later.[25]

Settlers included the Reverend Richard Seymour, grandson of Sir Edward Seymour, Duke of Somerset and brother to Jane Seymour, England's queen for nine days before Elizabeth's accession to the throne. Nine council members and six other gentlemen accompanied the expedition, while the rest were soldiers, artisans, farmers, and traders. They immediately set

---

21 Map image: "Wpdms king james grants," *Wikimedia Commons*. https://commons.wikimedia.org/w/index.php?curid=685738. Public domain.

22 "The Original Jamestown Settlers," *Encyclopedia Virginia*. Viewed on 5 April 2022. https://encyclopediavirginia.org/entries/the-original-jamestown-settlers-an-excerpt-from-the-generall-historie-of-virginia-new-england-and-the-summer-isles-by-john-smith-1624/.

23 "James VI and I (1566-1625)," *Encyclopedia Virginia*. Viewed on 5 April 2022. https://encyclopediavirginia.org/entries/james-vi-and-i-1566-1625/.

24 Today's Kennebec River in present day Maine.

25 Another source contradicts this account, arguing that Popham captained the *Gift of God* which accompanied the larger *Mary and John* captained by Raleigh Gilbert, the son of Sir Humphrey Gilbert and half nephew of Sir Walter Raleigh. Raleigh Gilbert was second in command of the colony.

to work to establish the colony, constructing buildings and shelters on the headlands which they named Sabino.

Seven weeks later, map maker John Hunt completed a draft plan for a star-shaped Fort St. George to protect the new colony. On 8 October 1607, Hunt returned to England on the *Mary and John* with the plan and a colony map to deliver to its investors. The ship re-stocked and departed again with provisions to re-supply the colony. But upon its second arrival, many settlers were discouraged by the harsh conditions. In December 1607, half the original settlers returned to England. In February 1608 when news of George Popham's death reached the colony, the remaining settlers were disheartened. By the following winter, the conditions defeated them. They completed a pinnace and christened her *Virginia*.[26] As they left Sabino headlands, the colonists glanced back one last time at their abandoned colony. With mixed emotions of sadness and relief, they turned their eyes forward. As they gazed at the vast ocean in front of them, the wind picked up and billowed *Virginia's* sails. The small ship's speed picked up and lurched ahead toward England.[27]

The failure of Popham Colony yielded two silver linings. No copy of the fort's plan and colony was ever found in England. But in 1888, historian Alexander Brown found the plan in the Simancas Archive in Spain, along with letters between Don Pedro Zuñiga (Spain's ambassador to England) and Spain's King Phillip III. John Hunt's plan precisely matched Sabino Head's topography and showed the colony, its star-shaped fort with ditches and ramparts, and eighteen buildings including the admiral's house, a chapel, a storehouse, a cooperage, and a guardhouse with nine guns. Since the plan was drafted when site work was just beginning, most likely the work on the fort and construction of the *Virginia* was just under way.

An archaeologist who conducted extensive site excavations between 1994 and 2013, Jeffrey Brain, confirmed the colony's location and the plan's accuracy. Brain called John Hunt's plan a visual time capsule of the site. There is no other similar plan for any early English settlement in the Americas: a treasure for present-day historians—truly a significant silver lining.[28]

---

[26] A pinnace is a small sailing ship often used as a tender to a larger ship.

[27] "John Hunt's plan of Fort St George (1607)," *Maine's First Ship*. Viewed on 20 Jan 2022. https://mfship. org/hunt-plan/.

[28] "Archaeology of Fort St George," *Maine's First Ship*. Viewed on 20 Jan 2022. https://mfship.org/home/ jostpru/archaeology/.

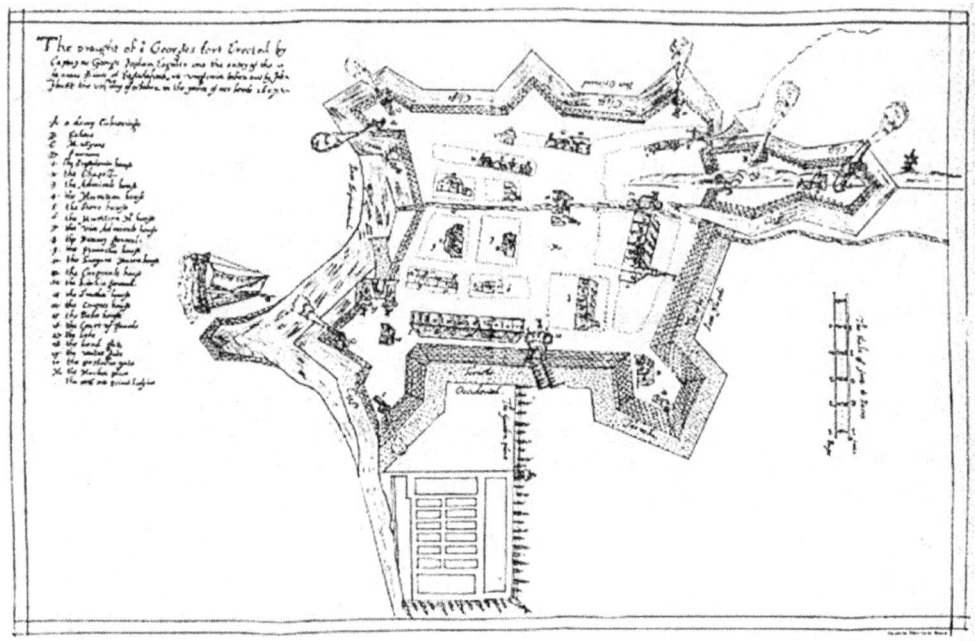

John Hunt. Map of Fort St. George, Popham Colony, 1607. Public domain. (9.5)

The second silver lining of Popham Colony's demise was the beginning of a major effort to support the fledgling Jamestown Colony—just eighteen months into its existence. But before that effort, King James clamped down on Puritan non-conformists in England. James hoped his oversight of the Hampton Court Conference had vanquished the Puritans, but he was mistaken—in particular, about one group that sought religious freedom.

FIVE PURITANS LEAD A SEPARATISTS' GROUP TO ESCAPE ENGLAND

In 1606, King James appointed a new church leader in the north of England. Tobias Matthew, James' choice as Archbishop of York, launched a campaign against Puritan Separatists in his region. From York south and throughout the East Midlands of England, non-conformist congregational groups were targeted. They included worshipers in Scrooby and Gainsborough. From within these congregations there emerged five individuals to lead their collective search for religious freedom outside of the auspices and control of the Church of England. Their sacrifices and exploits would echo throughout the ages with their bravery and courage in the face of adversity.

One was defrocked vicar Richard Clyfton, a Puritan minister who led a growing congregation in Babworth. A second was former vicar John Smyth, who led a congregation in Gainsborough. A third was John Robinson, another Lincolnshire Puritan dismissed by the Church of England who, along with his family, joined Smyth's illegal congregation. A fourth was William Bradford. An orphan at age seven, Bradford was shepherded by Clyfton as a youth. When Clyfton established a Separatist congregation at Scrooby, a fifth man, William Brewster, hosted gatherings at his Scrooby manor led by Clyfton and Robinson.

Brewster mentored Bradford and later resigned his lucrative Scrooby position as postmaster at age forty. Bradford recorded that they were "hunted and persecuted on all sides."[29] One Scrooby congregant, Gervase Nevyle, was arrested and put on trial 19 November 1607. He refused to take the required oath to testify, telling the court, "We ought to obey God rather than men." He also denounced the archbishop's authority as unbiblical, an "anti-Christian hierarchie."[30] These phrases bear a striking resemblance to those used by the Nine Puritans, including William Proudlove, in their trials before the Star Chamber in the early 1590s.

As the persecutions' intensity increased, "By joint consent they resolved to go into the Low countries, where they heard was freedom of religion for all men." Knowing that King James would not approve a petition for them to leave England, many Separatists from Scrooby and Gainsborough "sold their homes and belongings." From 1607 to 1608, "some were taken and clapped up in prisons, others had their houses beset and watched night and day, and hardly escaped with their hands."[31] When a large company of them were betrayed by the ship captain, the officers robbed them "of their money, the men being examined to their very shirts, and the women searched 'further than became modesty,' while their keepsakes, books, and other little effects were stolen or scattered." Many were imprisoned in Boston, England, and most were released after thirty days. But seven principal Puritan leaders, including William Brewster, William Bradford, probably the three ministers—Clyfton, Robinson, and Smith—and two others, "were kept in prison for the assizes."[32]

During one group's escape, which included William Bradford, an intense storm battered their ship at sea. In fear, the crew cried out, "We sink, we sink." The Separatists also cried out—but in faith. "Yet Lord, Thou canst save; yet, Lord, Thou canst save!" When the ship righted itself, and the storm began to abate, they praised God. Fourteen harrowing days after they embarked, they reached port "astonished at their deliverance, the storm having been so long and violent. In the end, notwithstanding the storms of opposition, they all got over, some from one place, some from another, and met together with no small rejoicing."[33] The Puritan pastors, having been detained—and some of them imprisoned—by the authorities, remained in England until 1608 when they were at last able to escape to Holland. Reunited with their fellow Separatists, "they were finally able to meet and worship as they felt led without fear."[34] A little more than a decade later, God's plan for the Leiden Puritans from Scrooby would require another enormous leap of faith.

---

29   Gragg, *The Pilgrim Chronicles*, 53-75. Gragg provides detailed eyewitness descriptions of these events. Recommended reading.

30   Gragg, 65-8.

31   Gragg, 69.

32   John A. Goodwin, *The Pilgrim Republic: An Historical Review of the Colony of New Plymouth* (Cambridge University Press 1920) Tercentenary Edition, 26-9. Viewed on 23 December 2022 on *The Internet Archive* (https://archive.org).

33   Gragg, 71-2.

34   Gragg, 75.

A Sermon Launches a Major Effort to Restock Jamestown Colony

On 25 April 1609, vicar William Symonds of St. Saviour's in Southwark readied himself before an illustrious and important audience. Summoned to preach a sermon at White-Chappel, across River Thames in London, he spoke "in the presence of many, honourable and worshipfull, the adventurers and planters for Virginia" of the great promises available "for the benefit and use of the colony, planted, and to bee planted there, and for the advancement of their Christian purpose."[35] Though Symonds probably never set foot in Virginia himself, he published a description promoting the colony settlement across the ocean in 1612.[iv]

A few weeks after this sermon was delivered, a fleet of nine ships was stocked with enough cargo to resupply the struggling Jamestown Colony for a year. Many of the fleet's passengers likely heard, or heard about, Symonds' sermon. One such passenger, with a particularly colorful story, was Stephen Hopkins. He had already cast his lot with those aiming to assist the struggling settlement of Jamestown. From his Hampshire home, Hopkins had signed on as a clerk for Richard Buck, who was to become Jamestown's minister. Stephen left his wife, Mary, and their three children, Elizabeth, Constance, and Giles, to care for their household without him.[36]

As the flotilla of ships assembled in Plymouth, its largest ship was the *Sea Venture*, a 300-ton merchant ship and the fleet's flagship. Her captain was the experienced Christopher Newport, who had transported the original settlers to Jamestown in 1607. An estimated five to six hundred colonists boarded the ships. Aboard *Sea Venture* were several who would be prominent in the colony: Sir Thomas Gates, lieutenant governor of Virginia; Sir George Somers, admiral of the fleet; and William Strachey, the future secretary of the Virginia Company in Jamestown. The fleet departed England in June of 1609.[37]

A week away from the fleet's destination, William Strachey recorded in his journal that "heavy clouds foretold a storm of unusual intensity . . . the morning brought a hurricane from the northeast . . . swelling and roaring as it were by fits, some hours with more violence

---

[35] William Symonds, preacher at Saint Saviors in Southwarke. *Virginia. A sermon preached at White-Chappel, in the presence of many, honourable and worshipfull, the aduenturers and planters for Virginia. 25. April. 1609. Published for the benefit and use of the colony, planted, and to bee planted there, and for the advancement of their Christian purpose.* (London: Printed by I. Windet, for Eleazar Edgar, and William Welby, and are to be sold in Paules Church-yard at the signe of the Windmill, 1609; Ann Arbor: Text Creation Partnership, 2011). Viewed on 2 November 2022. https://quod.lib.umich.edu/e/eebo2/A13290.0001.001. In today's world, we might consider this a motivational speech.

[36] Caleb Johnson, *Here Shall I Die Ashore* (Xlibris Corporation, 2007): 31. Recommended reading for descendants of Stephen Hopkins who include this author, and those interested in this incredible historic adventure.

[37] Stephanie Fitzwater, Jamestown-Yorktown Foundation Outreach Education Instructor, "The Story of the Sea Venture," *Jamestown-Yorktown Museums.* Viewed on 4 Feb 2022. https://jyfmuseums.org/learn/learning-center/the-story-of-the-sea-venture/.

than others, at length did beat all light from Heaven; which, lie an hell of darkness, turned black upon us."[38]

For three full days and four nights, the fierce storm of such intensity that many passengers and crew had never experienced wreaked havoc on the fleet. With dangerously high waves and winds, the fleet simply tried to ride it out and survive. Not surprisingly, the fleet's flagship lost sight of the other ships.

On Friday the 28th of July, when the terrifying storm abated briefly, a lookout spotted land. With the ship taking on water, and after three days and nights at the helm with little or no sleep, Admiral Somers made a fateful decision to beach the ship before it sank. About a half to three quarters of a mile offshore of the Isle of Devils,[39] he wedged the battered *Sea Venture* between two rocks to keep it from capsizing or sinking. The crew manned their boats and battled the elements to take all the passengers ashore as best they could. Amazingly, every one of about 150 men and women survived the shipwreck.

SHIPWRECKED ON DEVIL'S ISLAND

In the passing days, the crew retrieved their tools, salvaged the ship's goods, stored them ashore, and began disassembling its planks. Admiral Somers, as commander of the fleet, and Lieutenant Governor Gates, appointed to be governor of Jamestown, negotiated responsibilities, and assumed authority to establish order and discipline. The hallmarks of English society's hierarchical structures were swiftly implemented as necessary ingredients to organize the stranded colonists and crew and focus them on survival in unchartered territory. An immediate priority was to search for food sources. They discovered God's provision in abundance.

> A great store of fish . . . angelfish, salmon peal, bonitos, sting ray, bally, snappers, hoggish, sharks, dogfish, pilchards, mullets, and rockfish . . . We have taken also from under the broken rocks crevises [crayfish] oftentimes greater than any of our best English lobsters, and likewise abundance of crabs, oysters, and whelks.

> Fowl included a great store of small birds, sparrows, fat and plump like a bunting, bigger than ours, robins of divers colors, green and yellow . . . white and gray heronshaws, bitterns, teal, snipes, crows, and hawks . . . oxbirds, cormorants, bald coots, moor hens, owls, and bats.[40]

> There hath been taken in two or three hours, a thousand at the least; the bird being of the bigness of a good pigeon, and layeth eggs as big as hen eggs upon the sand, where they come and lay them daily . . . in one morning, one thousand of eggs.

---

[38] William Strachey, "A True Reportory of the Wreck and Redemption of Sir Thomas Gates, Knight," in Louis B. Wright (ed.), *A Voyage to Virginia in 1609: Two Narratives: Strachey's "True Reportory" and Jourdain's "Discovery of the Bermudas."* (Charlottesville and London: University of Virginia Press, 1964, 2013): xxi. Hereinafter referenced as Strachey.

[39] Today's Bermuda.

[40] Strachey, 27-30.

There are also great store of tortoises, (which some call turtles) and those so great, that I have seen a bushel of eggs in one of their bellies, which are sweeter than any hen egg; and the tortoise itself is all very good meat, and yieldeth great store of oil, which is as sweet as any butter, and one of them will suffice fifty men a meal, at the least, and, of these hath been taken great store, with two boats, at the least forty in one day.[41]

With seeds salvaged from the wreckage, Admiral Somers planted a garden and "sowed muskmelons, peas, onions, radish, lettuce, and many English seeds and kitchen herbs."[42] Unfortunately, wild hogs broke into the garden and rooted them up. But that indicated the presence of hogs and wild boars. They were hunted to provide an abundant source of meat.

"On October 1, the castaways celebrated their first Communion, with Rev. Richard Buck giving a godly sermon, and Stephen Hopkins reading the psalms. They would celebrate another Communion on Christmas Eve as well."[43] With these worship services, Hopkins gained visibility and status in the eyes of the colonists. After a few months, with no sign of a hoped-for rescue, Somers and Gates selected eight men to sail to Jamestown and return with help. After some false starts, they sailed away from the island in a pinnace and were never heard from again—a failed rescue attempt.

The admiral and governor decided two pinnaces would be built to carry everyone to Jamestown. Some crewmembers had discussed among themselves that they would be happy and content to stay on this idyllic island. The crew had heard stories of attacks by local natives at Jamestown, its starving settlers, and a lack of resources. By comparison, here was paradise, in their opinion, compared to the wilderness of the Virginia Colony.

When Governor Gates began a concerted effort to build a pinnace, six crewmen assigned to the task conspired to subvert its construction. When discovered, they were brought up on trial, convicted, and banished to an uninhabited island. After they pleaded for mercy, they were allowed to return and fill a need for their labor. But dissension and subversion of authority continued. In a heated dispute ending in a fatal shovel blow, sailor Robert Waters killed fellow crewman Edward Samuel. When Waters was tried for murder and sentenced to death the next morning, a few of his fellow sailors helped him escape. But as winter enveloped the island, work on the pinnaces progressed.

Stephen Hopkins questioned the wisdom of leaving their island for Jamestown as well. William Strachey observed that Hopkins "subtly began to shake the foundation of our quiet safety." He made

substantial arguments both civil and divine (the Scripture falsely quoted) that it was no breach of honesty, conscience, nor religion to decline from the obedience of the governor or refuse to go any further led by his authority (except it so pleased themselves), since his authority ceased when the wreck was committed, and, with it, they were all then freed from the government of any man, and for a matter of conscience it was not unknown to the meanest how much we were therin bound each one to provide for himself and his own family.

---

[41] Johnson, 226.
[42] Strachey, 23-4.
[43] Johnson, 42.

For which were two apparent reasons to stay them even in this place: first, abundance by God's providence of all manner of good food; next, some hope in reasonable time, when they might grow weary of the place, to build a small bark, with the skill and help of the aforesaid Nicholas Bennett, whom they insinuated to them, albeit he was now absent from his quarter and working in the main island with Sir George Somers upon his pinnace, to be of the conspiracy, that so might get clear from hence at their own pleasures.

When in Virginia, the first would be assuredly wanting and they might well fear to be detained in that country by the authority of the commander thereof and their whole life to serve the turns of the adventurers with their travails and labors.[44]

Enraged by Hopkins' mutiny which challenged his authority, the governor had him "arrested and brought before the whole company in manacles, where, at the tolling of the bell, the *corps de garde* assembled."[45] After he denied and pleaded the charges, the court found him guilty and sentenced him to death. Upon hearing his sentence, Hopkins dropped to his knees and pleaded for mercy.

But so penitent he was, and made so much moan, alleging the ruin of his wife and children in this his trespass, as it wrought in the hearts of all the better sort of the company, who therefore with humble entreaties and earnest supplications went unto our governor, whom they besought (as likewise Captain Newport and myself) and never left him until we had got his pardon.[46]

Hopkins promised to keep a low profile and resumed his duties. Within two months, another mutiny was discovered led by sailor Henry Paine, but Hopkins was not involved. Paine was sentenced to death and executed that evening. Word of his execution caused others to flee into the woods for fear of the same happening to them. They were ultimately left behind.

By the end of April 1610, two pinnaces were finished. Built by two different groups from the salvaged shipwreck's materials and the island's resources, one was completed under Admiral Somers' command and named *Patience*. The other, completed by Governor Gates' group, named *Deliverance*, was capable of an eighty-ton burden. Strachey captured this historic occasion in a letter.

Before we quitted our old quarter and dislodged to the fresh water with our pinnace, our governor set up in Sir George Somers' garden a fair mnemosynon [memorial] in figure of a cross, made of some of the timber of our ruined ship, which was screwed in with strong and great trunnels to a mighty cedar, which grew in the midst of the said garden and whose top and upper branches he caused to be lopped, that the violence of the wind and weather might the less power over her. In the midst of the cross, our governor fastened the picture of His

---

44 Strachey, 44.
45 Strachey, 45.
46 Strachey, 45.

Majesty in a piece of silver of twelvepence, and on each side of the cross he set an inscription graven in copper in the Latin and English to this purpose:

In memory of our great deliverance, both from a mighty storm and leak, we have set up this to the honor of God. It is the spoil of an English ship (of three hundred ton) called the *Sea Venture*, bound to Virginia, or Nova Britannia, in America. In it were two knights, Sir Thomas Gates, Knight, governor of the English forces and colony there, and Sir George Somers, Knight, admiral of the seas. Her captain was Christopher Newport; passengers and mariners she had beside (which came all safe to land) one hundred and fifty. We were forced to run her ashore (by reason of her leak) under a point that bore southeast from the northern point of the island, which we discovered first the eight-and-twentieth of July 1609.[47]

After ten months shipwrecked upon Devil's Island, the two pinnaces, *Deliverance* and *Patience*, departed for Jamestown with 142 survivors. In May, they were pleased to discover the fleet's other ships, including the pinnace *Virginia,* had made it through the hurricane and arrived safely in Jamestown. Among the new arrivals were two men who would later make significant contributions to England's colonization efforts in America: Stephen Hopkins and John Rolfe.

When William Strachey returned to London in 1610, he brought his journal of the voyage, letters describing the fierce storm and the shipwreck, and his descriptions of events on the Isle of Devils. In one of his letters, he described "a most dreadful tempest," referencing the storm. He also wrote a draft of a play and shared it with his friend, William Shakespeare. Taken with the story, Shakespeare reworked it into a new play, *The Tempest*. Its first recorded performance for King James and his Royal Court at the Banqueting House in Whitehall Palace occurred on Hallomas nyght [*sic*], 1 November 1611. The first scene opens on a ship during a fierce storm, with the remainder of the play set on an island and a theme of treason woven throughout. Many believe Shakespeare modeled his drunken butler, a comic relief character named Stefano, after Stephen Hopkins, albeit with much artistic license.

Events in Jamestown and England

Despite the difficulties faced by the Jamestown colonists, John Rolfe saw a tantalizing business opportunity. In 1612 he established a plantation, Varina Farms, thirty miles upstream from Jamestown. From his first harvest, he exported four barrels of tobacco leaf to England in March 1614. This cash crop was an immediate success. Soon, Rolfe and others exported large quantities of tobacco from plantations on the James River.

Meanwhile in England, Stephen Hopkin's "wife and children were struggling to maintain the family in his absence. They must have learned by now that he had survived the shipwreck in Bermuda and made it safely to Jamestown." However, Mary Hopkins "died and was buried at Hursley on 9 May 1613, only in her very early thirties." Her probate record, dated the following day, refers to "Mary Hopkins of Hursley in the Countie of

---

[47] Strachey, 58.

South[ampt]ton widowe deceased."[48] Her death left Stephen and Mary's three children, Elizabeth aged nine, Constance aged seven, and Giles aged five, under the guardianship of one Thomas Syms. Mary's estate was modest, and her daughter, Elizabeth, died soon after her mother, leaving two orphans, Constance and Giles.

About this time in Jamestown, the indigenous princess, Pocahontas, daughter of the chieftain, Powhatan, converted to Christianity. Baptized by Alexander Whitaker, she chose Rebecca as her Christian name. On 5 April 1614, Rebecca married John Rolfe. Minister Richard Buck officiated at their wedding, with Stephen Hopkins most certainly in attendance. John and Rebecca lived on Rolfe's plantation where their son, Thomas, was born in January 1615.

Just four months earlier, the colony's deputy governor, Sir Thomas Dale, dictated a letter on 10 September 1614 to his Virginia Company superiors requesting that Stephen Hopkins be released from his seven-year contract as a minister's clerk to return home. Stephen must have received news of his wife's death and asked for permission to go home to care for his children.[49]

The next ship available for his return to England likely departed Jamestown in the spring of 1616. John and Rebecca Rolfe had been invited to tour England as guests of the Virginia Company, with the goal of promoting the Virginia Colony and its opportunities. Accompanied by their baby, Thomas, twelve members of her tribe, and Governor Dale, they arrived in Plymouth, England, on 12 June 1616. It's likely Hopkins traveled with them, disembarked in Plymouth to reunite with his two surviving children in Hursley, and relocated to London. Early in 1618, on the 19th of February, Hopkins married Elizabeth Fisher at St. Mary Whitechapel. One year later, their first child, Damaris, was born.[50]

The celebrity couple, John and Rebecca formerly known as Pocahontas, and their entourage charmed Queen Anne and captured the hearts and minds of the English. Investments in the Virginia Company soared, owing in large part to Rolfe's tract, *A True Relation of the state of Virginia Lefte by Sir Thomas Dale Knight in May Last 1616.* Published in 1617, it touted the viability of the colony in Virginia. Unfortunately, as they prepared to return to

Pocahontas, 1616. Engraving by Simon van de Passe. Courtesy of Smithsonian, National Portrait Gallery. Public domain. (9.6)

---

[48] Johnson, 58.

[49] Recommended readings about the life of Stephen Hopkins include Caleb Johnson, *Here Shall I Die Ashore* (previously noted), and Jonathan Mack, *A Stranger Among Saints: Stephen Hopkins, the Man Who Survived Jamestown and Saved Plymouth* (Chicago: Chicago Review Press, 2020).

[50] Johnson, 60-61.

Jamestown, Rebecca fell seriously ill and died—probably of pneumonia. She was buried in St. George's cemetery in the town of Gravesend, Kent. This contemporary image is the only one of her known to exist.

JANE CLARKE MARRIES AGAIN

After the tragic losses of her infant son and her husband in the summer of 1610, Jane Clarke discussed her situation with her mother, Alice, and stepfather, John. As a twenty-three-year-old widow with three children under five years of age, how would they identify a suitable husband candidate for her? Through Jane's inheritance from her father and her deceased siblings' shares bequeathed to her, Jane had accumulated an attractive dowry of approximately £122, which was enhanced by her late husband's estate.[51]

John and Alice made inquiries of family and their business connections, many of them recommending the Freeman Grocer William Collier. In his late twenties and single, his successful grocer's business was now in its second year in St. Olave's Parish. After discussions among all the parties had concluded, Jane Clarke married William Collier in St. Olave's Parish on 16 May 1611.[52] She blended her three children into their marriage from its start.

Almost exactly nine months from their wedding day, their first child together, Mary, was born and was baptized on 18 February 1612.[53] The Collier household now had six mouths to feed: the parents, William and Jane, and their four children: Margaret, Thomas, Joyce, and infant Mary. The help and guidance of John and Alice Arnold was invaluable. Jane, with her years as a partner in her husband's dyer business, partnered with William in the same way and took on administrative and support tasks, just as her mother had done. That same year, John Arnold signed a surety on behalf of Collier to help him expand his business.

A FIERY PERFORMANCE AT THE GLOBE

In 1613, William Shakespeare retired as a playwright. With his move to Stratford-upon-Avon, he missed a most memorable performance of one of the last plays he penned. During a performance of *All is True*[54] on 29 June 1613, a fire broke out at the Globe in Southwark. Contemporary accounts recorded what happened. Sir Henry Wotton wrote this colorful description.

> I will entertain you at the present with what happened this week at the Banks side. The King's players had a new play, called *All is True*, representing some principal pieces of the reign of Henry VIII, which set forth with many extraordinary circumstances of pomp and majesty even to the matting of the stage; the knights of the order with their Georges and

---

[51] £16,500 in 2017 currency or approximately $21,870.
[52] Cole, "Jane Clarke," 46.
[53] Cole, "Jane Clarke," 46.
[54] Also known as *Henry VIII*.

Garter, the guards with their embroidered coats, and the like; sufficient in truth within awhile to make greatness very familiar, if not ridiculous.

Now King Henry making a masque at the Cardinal Wolsey's house, and certain cannons being shot off at his entry, some of the paper or other stuff, wherewith one of them was stopped, did light on the thatch, where, being thought at first but idle smoak, and their eyes more attentive to the show, it kindled inwardly, and ran round like a train, consuming within less than an hour the whole house to the very ground.

This was the fatal period of that virtuous fabrick, wherein yet nothing did perish but *wood* and *straw*, and a few forsaken cloaks; only one man had his breeches set on fire, that would perhaps have broyled him, if he had not, by the benefit of a provident wit, put it out with a bottle of ale.[55]

John Chamberlain mentioned to Sir Ralph Winwood, by a "fair Grace of God, that the People had so little Harm, having but two narrow Doors to get out."[56] Three thousand people rushing out two narrow doors to escape a fire—that must have been a harrowing sight!

A few days later, after having spied the smoke and fire from their parish, William Collier took his stepson, Thomas aged six, to view the Globe's destruction and its aftermath. As they stood there looking at the burnt timbers, ashes, and piles of debris, Thomas asked many questions about what happened, and William patiently answered them. His stepson had always been inquisitive, and William wanted to encourage and bring out that characteristic in him.

Since they were very close, William took the young lad into St. Saviour's church to view its massive interior. Again, Thomas asked many questions as he compared it in his mind to St. Olave's, the only other church he had been inside.

When Thomas' attention drifted as he seemed to lose interest, William took his stepson to introduce him to his former master, William Russell, who lived nearby. Russell introduced his current apprentice to his former one. As they sat together, the men reminisced about Collier's apprenticeship while Thomas observed and listened intently. His inquisitive mind absorbed their conversation as these two older men discussed the economic effects of the Globe's destruction on their respective grocer's businesses. After William and his master finished their discussion, they bade William and Anne Russell farewell, and thanked them for a lovely afternoon.

---

55 "On This Day in 1613," *The Tudor Chronicles*. Viewed on 10 August 2022. https://thetudorchronicles. wordpress.com/2015/06/29/on-this-day-in-1613-shakespeares-globe-theatre-was-burned-to-the-ground/.
56 "Globe Theatre Fire," *Bard Stage*. Viewed on 10 August 2022. https://www.bardstage.org/globe-theatre-fire.htm.

St. Saviour's Church Interior. Courtesy of Wikimedia Commons. Public domain (9.7)

On their way home, William and his stepson discussed the day. Thomas shared his impressions, and they chatted about what he had seen and heard. When they crossed through St. Olave's gate and walked along the bankside of River Thames, Thomas excitedly pointed at the ships, and asked, "Father, where are they going?" William described foreign ports where these ships would deliver their cargo. He explained that some were carrying wool and other materials, including some goods that were tied to Collier's grocer business. This conversation about trade, travel, and foreign ports elicited even more questions from the young lad. When they paused at bankside looking across the river at dozens of ships, Thomas said, "Father, one day I want to travel across the ocean on one of those ships." William responded, "One day, Thomas, if you apply yourself, work hard, and if it is God's will—I'm sure you will." Young Thomas smiled broadly at his father, and his eyes widened in excitement. He said, "I hope it will be soon!" William looked at his young son and replied, "All in God's timing, Thomas. All in God's timing."

Within a year, the Globe was rebuilt and reopened on the same site—but with a tile roof replacing a thatched one.[v] Fittingly, Taylor, the water poet, commemorated the event with "A doleful Ballad of the General Conflagration of the famous Theatre called the Globe."

> As gold is better that in fire's tried,
> So is the Bankside Globe, that late was burn'd;
> For where before it had a thatched hide,
> Now to a stately theatre 'tis turn'd;
> Which is an emblem that great things are won
> By those that dare through greatest dangers run.[57]

Three months later, William and Jane's second daughter, Hannah, was baptized on 14 September 1613, a little more than eighteen months after her older sister Mary's birth. William hired a servant, Gilbart Smyth, to take on support tasks for Jane, who managed their household and helped William with administrative tasks in their grocer's enterprise. Collier now felt their business was well-positioned for growth. Their third child, another daughter, Rebecca, was baptized sixteen months later, on 10 January 1615. Unfortunately, five days later, their servant died and was buried in St. Olave's Parish.[58] Collier moved quickly to hire a replacement servant, John Sayles, and his business flourished.

A few months later, the Guildhall provided another boost to the Colliers' business. A grocer's apprentice, William Langham, with about three years of experience working for another master, transferred his apprenticeship to William Collier on 26 April 1615.

William Langham, apprentice transfer in 1615. Reproduced with kind permission of the Grocers' Company of London. Sponsored by Alan and Linda O'Neill. (9.8)

The first Apprentice Entrance records "James Scruby apprenticed to William Dixon for 7 years on 6 May 1612. He paid 2s 6d." An unusual entry written in Latin in the left margin applies only to the second apprentice: "William Langham apprentice to Richard Wright for 7 years on the same day [6 May 1612] Paid 2s 6d." The Latin entry indicates that on 26

---

57 "Southwark Bankside in the Olden Times," *British History Online*. Viewed 10 August 2022. https://www.british-history.ac.uk/old-new-london/vol6/pp45-57.

58 Cole, "Jane Clarke," 53.

April 1615, Langham's apprenticeship was transferred to a new master, William Collier. ". . . *idem apprenticus ex assensu Magri' | eius commisus est Willelmo Collier pro residuo termini | eius adhuc venturi.*"[59]

A year later, the news of William Shakespeare's death in Stratford-upon-Avon might have reached London by the time the Colliers welcomed their fourth daughter, Sarah. She was baptized on 30 April 1616. While William certainly had hoped for a son of his own, he felt blessed in so many ways with his wife, Jane, their four daughters together, and two daughters and one son from Jane's previous marriage. Thomas, now aged nine, worked on simple tasks in their grocer's business, as did his older siblings, Margaret and Joyce. When Jane bore another son, they all rejoiced, and they named him John.[vi] He was baptized on 17 March 1617.

Now with a male heir to his name, William burst with pride. Jane was pleased that her children's grandparents, John and Alice Arnold, had their grandchildren so near to watch them grow up. But William, Jane, and Alice all noticed signs of John Arnold's advancing age. He was beginning to slow down. The following year, on 16 March 1618, Arnold recognized his mortality and prepared a will witnessed by his stepson-in-law, William, among others.[vii] Simply written, it bequeathed some money to three nephews and the residue to his wife, Alice. John was not ill but felt it wise to arrange his estate now. He prayed for a few more years to enjoy with his wife and his grandchildren, and for his family's successful enterprises.

Six months later, with Collier's business flourishing, they experienced a tragic personal loss. Their son, John, died at age seventeen months. He was buried in St. Olave's churchyard on 24 August 1618. As the family watched John's burial, they heard the familiar verse, "The Lord gave and the Lord hath taken away; blessed be the name of the Lord."[60] When the ceremony was finished, they comforted each other and asked for God's grace to fortify their close-knit family. The following spring, they celebrated the birth of a daughter, Elizabeth. Baptized on 9 March 1619 at St. Olave's, she was Jane's tenth child born with two husbands. While the losses of two boys who died young, infant Henry Clarke in 1610 and John Collier in 1618, were sad, the other eight children survived and were healthy and thriving—a higher percentage than normal for the era.

When her eldest child, Margaret, celebrated her thirteenth birthday that September, Jane thought, "It won't be much longer before we need to look for husband candidates for Margaret. She's only three years younger than I was when I first married! How fleeting has her childhood been!" Then she realized Thomas, 11, and Joyce, 10, were not far behind their older sister. When she thought of her children with William—Mary, 7; Hannah, 6; Rebecca, 4; Sarah, 3; and Elizabeth, eighteen months—Jane placed her hand on her husband's shoulder and looked directly into his eyes with a twinkling smile. "William, I love you. How much you have blessed me and our family. Thank you, dear. I praise the Lord for you and our children every day!" As the loving couple embraced, they sighed at how fast their children were growing up.

---

[59] Grocers' Guild, Wardens' Accounts, 1611–1622. MS11571/010 Folio 19v. Guildhall Library, London.
[60] Job 1:21 (Kings James Version)

The Colliers' business continued to flourish and grow. William paid £18 for his annual lease—the highest of his landlord's fourteen or more units.[61] His apprentice, William Langham, was making great strides in his final apprenticeship year. Collier had no doubt Langham would in turn one day make a fine master for his own grocer's apprentice.

When informed by some colleagues of an enticing business opportunity, William Collier was eager to find out more. A new group of Merchant Adventurers was forming to support another new colony in Virginia. When he first heard of it, the concept captured his imagination. A promising ground floor opportunity would give Collier the chance to expand his horizons beyond the shores of England. Intrigued and interested, William Collier underestimated just how life-changing this business opportunity would be. It offered great Promises, not only for him, but for his family, and others he had yet to meet.

---

[61] Cole, "Jane Clarke," 47. Article available at https:\\www.passionategenealogist.org.

CHAPTER 10

PROMISES; ADVENTURERS; *MAYFLOWER*; AN APPRENTICE

PURITANS CALLED TO WORSHIP GOD

By mid-1608, the three former ministers of English Separatist congregations, Richard Clyfton and John Robinson of Scrooby plus Gainsborough's John Smyth, were all in Amsterdam. Those who had escaped England before they did were thrilled to embrace their Puritan ministers again. They joined another existing congregation of English exiles, the Ancient Brethren, formed a decade earlier and led by Henry Ainsworth, and for a while all worshiped together, comprising a congregation of three hundred worshipers.

Some months later, John Smyth announced his adherence to doctrines outside the group's accepted theology. He proposed that Bible verses in worship services should be read only in Hebrew and Greek and translated on the spot by the preacher. In addition, he revealed a growing acceptance of Anabaptist doctrines, declaring his belief that "infant baptism had no solid Scriptural grounds, [that] any baptism performed in the Church of England was unbiblical, and therefore most of his congregation needed to be baptized again."[1] Because such teachings were unacceptable to the other Separatist ministers, their disunity led to a split. Robinson felt they should move again, but Clyfton wanted to remain in Amsterdam. The dilemma for the Puritans from Scrooby was resolved in February 1609 when, led by Robinson along with William Brewster and William Bradford, "they petitioned a Dutch court to allow 'one-hundred persons born in England' to move to Leiden by the first of May, promising that they would not be 'a burden in the least to anyone.'"[2]

Much foundational groundwork for the Puritan exiles in Holland had been established by Henry Jacob. A student at Cambridge with several early followers of Robert Browne in the mid-1580s, he relocated to Amsterdam with members of the London Underground Church after the executions of John Greenwood, Henry Barrowe, and John Penry in 1593. He remained and ministered to the exiles until his return to England in 1597.

Near the beginning of King James I's reign, Jacob published a call for Puritan reforms titled *Reasons taken out of God's Word and the best humane Testimonies proving a necessitie of reforming our Churches in England*. In the context of the Hampton Court Conference of 1604, King James saw Jacob's treatise, along with other Puritan calls for reform, as an affront to his own authority and the Church of England. As a result, Jacob was imprisoned for eight months. Upon his release, he returned to Holland and formed a congregation of other exiled English Puritans in Middelburg, Zeeland. In 1610, Jacob traveled to Leiden to

---

[1]   Gragg, 77.
[2]   Gragg, 75.

meet with John Robinson. These two Puritan reformers developed a mutual respect—even though each did not fully embrace the other on certain theological fine points.

In 1616, Jacob returned to London with the aim of founding a congregation similar to those in Holland. Once there, he discovered remnants of the Puritan church in Southwark secretly worshiping as Independents—the spiritual descendants of reform-minded believers who worshiped together before, during, and after the trials and tribulations of the nine Puritans in the early 1590s, which included Weedon Bec's William Proudlove. Jacob's group plus ten underground Puritan congregations operated throughout greater London. Ecclesiastical authorities were aware of them and kept track of their activities, but so long as they kept to themselves, the authorities did not disturb them. Collectively, they were known as the London Underground Church.

But Jacob's vision differed from that of the other underground Puritan leaders. He saw his congregation as coexisting alongside the Church of England with a separate but equal status. Well-known to ecclesiastical authorities from his publications and work in Holland, Jacob's semi-Separatist church became increasingly visible. His belief that independent congregations of equal status could operate outside the control of the State Church promoted an attitude among his followers of tolerant and diverse theological thinking, quite unusual for its time. He encouraged his members to circulate freely back and forth between his congregation and their own parish churches, effectively remaining free to continue their communicant status within the Church of England while retaining access to a more open community of like-minded believers. His church drew other theologians willing to engage in open dialogue, discussions, and debates. Church of England officials kept a watchful eye on them, but Jacob's approach eventually led to internal congregational controversies. By 1619, a division widened between semi-Separatist and pro-Separatist members of the congregation. Without unity, a church split occurred, and Henry Jacob resigned his position in Southwark's Puritan congregation.

LEIDEN SEPARATISTS' CONCERNS

During this same time in Holland, John Robinson and his flock grew concerned for their children's English identity. In addition to differences between Puritan and Lutheran theology, the Separatists experienced difficulties with occupational biases. And though the Dutch tolerated the English exiles, the Separatists kept to their own attitudes, beliefs, and culture. The Puritans weren't able to integrate into the local culture and were not sure they wanted to. With growing concerns for their children's future identity both culturally and spiritually, they prayerfully considered their options and began asking questions. Should they move again, and if so, where? With England unlikely to accept them, what if they were to establish an English colony overseas? They prayed and asked the Lord for guidance. Without the direct oversight of the Church of England in a Separatist colony, might they raise their children as loyal English subjects <u>and</u> pursue their Puritan beliefs and worship?

They discussed the merits of a settlement in the Caribbean and the Americas (north or south). Since King James had already established the Virginia Colony with Jamestown, John Robinson and William Brewster wrote to Edwin Sandys, a prominent politician and one of the founders of the Virginia Company, on 15 December 1617. With Brewster's close ties to this influential and sympathetic Puritan supporter, they hoped to gain his support in the Council of the Virginia Company.[3] Sandys brought forward their proposal to the council, and they responded enthusiastically. When the council petitioned King James, stressing that a Separatist colony in North America would fill his coffers from offshore fishing profits, the king reportedly exclaimed, "So God, have my soul, 'tis an honest trade, 'twas the apostles' own calling!" But officials inside the Church of England immediately expressed their displeasure with the concept. To maintain their support and avoid controversy, King James tempered his enthusiasm. Without endorsing the venture, he promised only to "not molest them, if they carried themselves peaceably."[4]

With the king's lukewarm response, the Virginia Company council marked time. Jamestown needed their help, attention, and resources in its struggle to survive. The Leiden Separatists heard frightening stories of dangerous and disastrous ocean voyages, which generated fear and threatened unity. Robinson still felt God's calling away from Leiden. He led his congregation in prayer, discussion, and discernment. Ultimately, they decided together that America was, in fact, the best destination. There, they could freely pursue the freedom of religion to worship God according to their beliefs and conscience. With consensus attained, the Separatists sent deacons John Carver and Robert Cushman to London as their agents. Carver and Cushman negotiated a conditional patent from the Virginia Company for "the most northern parts of Virginia" near the mouth of the Hudson River.[5] But the patent's key condition dictated the need for the Separatists to be self-supporting. At that time, they had no means or plan to accomplish that requirement. But a few Puritans, including William Bradford, sold their houses in faith, and trusted God to provide the answer.

MERCHANT ADVENTURERS FORMED IN LONDON

In the spring of 1620, Thomas Weston, a London iron merchant in his early forties, appeared unannounced in Leiden with a financial proposal for the Separatists. Weston had spearheaded a new investment group of the type known as Merchant Adventurers, with the goal of raising sufficient capital to obtain a patent from the Council of the Virginia Company.[6] This license granted the Merchant Adventurers the right to underwrite a new settlement on the pristine coast of America in the northern part of Virginia Colony. A nucleus of wealthy merchants and experienced traders, including John Beauchamp,[7] James Shirley, John Pocock, Richard Andrews, brothers John and William Peirce, and Edward

---

3   Gragg, 102-4.

4   Gragg, 104.

5   Today's New York City.

6   "Merchant Adventurers" had been in existence since the early fifteenth century, with the term originally applying to merchants engaged in any export trade. By the seventeenth century, the term more commonly referred to those involved in speculative investment projects.

7   The English pronounced this French surname as "Beacham."

Pickering, recruited dozens of small investors who invested £10 for each share.[8] A few Merchant Adventurers invested as much as £500.[9] In about a year, they raised enough capital to support a colonization effort. Estimates of the total capital necessary to support a colony ranged from a low of £1200 to a high of £7000.[10]

Thomas Weston may have developed the idea for a new venture of this type as early as 1615. In Holland that year, he collaborated with Edward Pickering to enable the export and distribution of nonconformist religious pamphlets. Pickering, of a notable Northamptonshire family, kept shops in London and Amsterdam. Together, they met with William Brewster and Thomas Brewer, who set up the Pilgrim Press in 1616 in Leiden to print pamphlets that Weston distributed in England. Brewer's contacts included Edwin Sandys, plus Puritan ministers Henry Jacob, Richard Lee, Henry Ainsworth, John Dod, and John Robinson. Through this venture, Thomas Weston became aware of the Separatists' growing concern of remaining in Leiden.[11]

Weston's offer to the Leiden Puritans was simple: he would raise capital and underwrite a colony in America. The Merchant Adventurers would pay for the voyage, the ship and crew, and the provisions necessary to support the undertaking. Once there, the colonists would work four days a week for the company, two days a week for themselves, and take one day off on the Sabbath. The venture would profit by fishing offshore, possibly fur trapping, and exporting lumber. After seven years, the colonists would gain their homes and property for themselves. To the Leiden Separatists, Weston appeared as an answer to prayer—a sign of God's blessings on their endeavor. Thrilled with this offer from a man they knew and trusted, they signed an agreement with Weston, the acting agent on behalf of the Merchant Adventurers. They praised God for his faithfulness, believing that the Lord had once again delivered on his promises and provided a way.

WILLIAM COLLIER, A MERCHANT ADVENTURER

When Jane Collier bore another son, she named him John in honor of their previously deceased son. William and Jane participated in his baptism and christening on 21 March 1620.[12] After the ceremony, the Collier family gathered in their residence to celebrate. William and Jane's household now consisted of nine children, a servant, and William's apprentice, William Langham. There were thirteen mouths to feed in their immediate household plus, on occasion, Jane's mother, Alice, and her stepfather, John.

---

[8] Fifty to seventy investors invested. The number fluctuated with the ups and downs of the Plymouth Colony.

[9] George F. Willison, *Saints and Strangers* (New York: Reynal & Hitchcock 1945): 119.

[10] The high estimate was from John Smith, which equates to nearly £1 million in today's money.

[11] Graham Taylor, *The Mayflower in Britain: How an Icon was Made in London* (Gloucestershire: Amberley Publishing, 2020): 75-6.

[12] St. Olave's Parish Registers (1583-1627)

A month prior, William Collier was listed as a tenant in his landlord's will dated 17 February 1620.[13] Collier's lease, £18 per year, was the highest of at least fourteen tenants, whose annual rents ranged from 16s. to £16 19s. Clearly, William was reasonably prosperous with a good income to comfortably support his growing family.

Blessed with their thriving grocer's business, William shared more good news with the family gathered for supper. "I have invested in a new venture—an exciting opportunity to glorify God and support trade beyond England and across the great ocean." Thomas, his stepson, now thirteen, asked if they could sail on the big ocean. William replied, "If it is God's will, it could be possible. Now that I am now a Merchant Adventurer, much work and effort will be required to support a new colony in America. Let us thank God for providing this opportunity. May the Lord guide our steps, and we will give God the glory." The enlivened supper conversation provoked many questions, along with excitement and enthusiasm from everyone for the Promises of what lay ahead.

As he completed the final five years of his apprenticeship with William Collier, William Langham expressed his gratitude for the experience that went well beyond learning a grocer's skills. He observed his master's actions and heard first-hand accounts about the dynamics of Merchant Adventurers and emigrants to develop a new colony across the ocean. What a great learning opportunity it was for him! And now, it was time to venture out on his own. On 26 May 1620, the Guildhall records, "William Langham late app to Richard Wright and afterwards served William Collier, Grocer entered as a freeman. Paid 3s 4d."[14]

Yes indeed, the first half of 1620 portended a year filled with promises. History would record William Collier "having been an Adventurer unto it at its first beginning."[15]

PROMISES BROKEN

When Thomas Weston returned to London with the Separatists' signed agreement, the Merchant Adventurers flinched and rejected it. Without exclusive fishing rights for the new settlement, it presented too much risk and not enough reward in their view. The investors instructed Weston to press them for more favorable investment terms. When the core leaders of the Separatists—John Robinson, Edward Winslow, Isaac Allerton, John Carver, and Robert Cushman—learned the Merchant Adventurers would not accept the signed contract, they were furious. The newly revised terms would require them to work six days a week for the company, not four as in the previous signed agreement. At the end of seven years, they would earn only half their homes and property, not all the property as previously agreed. Declaring the new requirements "fitter for thieves and bondservants than honest men," they instructed Robert Cushman, as their agent, to refuse the new terms. Cushman and John Carver were already in London acquiring provisions for their voyage and coordinating details with the Merchant Adventurers. Despite his instructions,

---

[13] Will of John Newton, elder of London, Prerogative Court of Canterbury, PROB 11: Will Registers, 1599–1623. Piece 135: Soame, Quire Numbers 1–64 (1619).

[14] St. Olave's Parish Registers (1583-1627)

[15] Nathaniel Morton, *New England's Memorial* (Cambridge: 1669): 9.

Cushman "pledged the congregation to accept it, fearing the proposed colonization would otherwise collapse."[16] But he did not communicate this to Leiden. Without that knowledge, the Leiden Separatists asked one of their own, Captain Blossom, to purchase a ship for the voyage. He bought the Speedwell, a 60-ton pinnace, and had it refitted in Delftshaven with two masts.[viii]

In early June, the Merchant Adventurers sent Thomas Weston and Robert Cushman to Rotherhithe, east of and adjacent to the borough of Southwark, to meet with an experienced sea captain, Christopher Jones. They examined a ship berthed in a nearby inlet, on the north side of Earl's Creek, and began discussions for a voyage to America.[17] Though a seasoned captain and one of the ship's owners, Jones had never been to America. However, his master's mate, John Clarke, had piloted several voyages there, and his other pilot, Robert Coppin, had also traveled to America.[18] A fifteen-year-old ship, the *Mayflower* had returned to London in May with its hold filled with Bordeaux wine from France. Rated at 180-tons, the *Mayflower* and her crew appeared to be an excellent match.[19] In addition, the Rector of Rotherhithe's St. Mary's Church, Thomas Gataker, had Puritan leanings and connections with London's Dutch Church. Two of the ship's owners, John Clarke and John Moore, lived in Rotherhithe, as did many crew members, and were strongly connected with its church. Thomas Weston, Robert Cushman, and another of the investors, William Peirce, finalized the agreement at a restaurant in Canterbury.

The Merchant Adventurers knew that not all the Separatists were committed to undertake the initial voyage to start the settlement. Among those was their minister, John Robinson. More colonists were needed to make the colony viable. Through their network of contacts, potential colonists were recruited to join the Separatists' colony. One man stood out with unique qualifications and experience. Living in London, he had worked as a minister's assistant. He was thought to be a Separatist by inclination. He had been to America before for an extended period. He had recently married a second time after the death of his first wife. If he agreed to become a colonist, he would likely bring his wife and three children with the promise of acquiring land through hard work. The candidate's name was Stephen Hopkins.[20]

The *Mayflower* Departs London

The crew of the *Mayflower*, with a few local passengers from Southwark, prepared the ship for departure in Rotherhithe. When that day came in mid-July, a few Merchant Adventurers from Southwark, likely including William Collier and Timothy Hatherley, bid farewell to *Mayflower's* crew. They wished them all God's speed on their voyage to

---

[16] Gragg, 107.

[17] Taylor, 122.

[18] Gragg, 129-31.

[19] A ship rated at 180 tons meant that its hold would carry 180 barrels of wine. Therefore, *Mayflower* had three times more cargo capacity than did *Speedwell*.

[20] Stephen Hopkins is the author's tenth great-grandfather through his daughter, Constance.

America.[21] As the ship left the inlet, it sailed to the north bankside of River Thames at either Blackwall or Wapping in London, "where each passenger and each item of cargo had to be documented." [22]

As passengers boarded the *Mayflower*, a few family members who remained behind and other Merchant Adventurers watched and waved at their friends and family. Stephen Hopkins led the largest passenger entourage, which included his wife Elizabeth, who was several months pregnant; their young daughter, Damaris, 2; Stephen's two surviving children with his first wife, Constance, 14, and Giles, 12; plus their two servants, Edward Doty and Edward Lester. A few other passengers included Thomas Williams, Richard Clarke, and Richard Warren whose wife, Elizabeth, and children remained behind.[23]

With approximately sixty-five passengers and at least thirty crew onboard, the *Mayflower* set sail on River Thames.[24] London's church towers disappeared as they sailed east toward the river's outlet to the sea. Sailing south for the English Channel and the port of Southampton, they looked forward to their rendezvous with the *Speedwell* coming from Leiden. The teenagers onboard, including Constance Hopkins and a few crewmembers, imagined what experiences lay ahead. While they and the younger children deeply breathed in the sea air, their eyes peered at never-before-seen sights of all types of vessels, many schools of fish, and large animals onshore. They heard squawks and cries of seagulls and other birds. As it all soaked into their young brains, the images implanted foretold and anticipated the promises of untold adventures in the days ahead. The *Mayflower* arrived in Southampton seven days before the *Speedwell*.

LEIDEN SEPARATISTS PREPARE TO LEAVE

As the Leiden Separatists prepared to depart, emotions ran high. About fifty of their community were leaving for America and many promised to come later. Before they left, minister John Robinson hosted a celebration at his house. "A feast . . . at which there was much singing, there being many of the congregation very expert in music."[25]

---

[21] On this topic, the author offers his research in presentations and an article (in preparation at the time of this writing): "A Grave Mistake: Oldcomer Thomas Clarke's English Origins."

[22] Taylor, 122-4. Taylor makes a comprehensive analysis of why he believes Rotherhithe was not the embarkation point for Mayflower's passengers.

[23] A complete listing of the passengers is provided on Caleb Johnson's website: *Mayflower History*. http:// mayflowerhistory.com/mayflower-passenger-list.

[24] Many scholars agree with author Charles Banks' estimation that the *Mayflower* had a crew of about fifty— thirty-six men 'before the mast' (crew) and 14 officers on the captain's staff. The officers included four mates, four quartermasters, surgeon, carpenter, cooper, cook, boatswain, and a gunner. "The Mayflower," *Wikipedia*. Viewed on 20 August 2020. https://en.wikipedia.org/wiki/Mayflower. For more details, see the author's forthcoming article with more details about the crew at https:\\passionategenealogist.org.

[25] Taylor, 125.

So they lefte that goodly and pleasante city which had been their resting place near twelve years; but they knew they were pilgrims, and looked not much on those things, but lift up their eyes to the heavens, their dearest countrie, and quieted their spirits.[26]

To support those members of his flock leaving for America, Robinson accompanied them to Delfthaven. He offered an emotional sermon onshore.

I am verily persuaded the Lord hath more truth yet to break forth out of His holy word . . . I beseech you remember it is an article of your church covenant that you be ready to receive whatever truth shall be made known to you from the written word of God . . . It is not possible that the Christian world should come so latterly out of such thick anti-Christian darkness and that perfection of knowledge should break forth at once.[27]

Robinson's message reinforced an important part of their church covenant: an openness to new ideas and seeking truth and knowledge from God's word. He handed them a letter in anticipation of any difficult people they might encounter—from profane Londoners to heathen natives in a distant land.

On 22 July 1620, the Separatists boarded the ship, and the *Speedwell* sailed from Delfthaven under the command of Captain Reynolds to rendezvous with the *Mayflower* in Southampton. But soon after departure, the *Speedwell* started leaking. Some Separatists must have wondered, "Is this a sign of God's displeasure?"

They arrived later than expected and anchored the ship for repairs. William Brewster, a leading Separatist and William Bradford's mentor, who had been in hiding after printing a booklet critical of King James, arrived and greeted them. The Leiden group embraced him warmly. They were comforted by his presence, and by the knowledge he and his wife, Mary, and sons Love and Wrestling, would accompany them to America. As they met the others from London, they joyfully welcomed each other and extended mutual congratulations. Families were assigned to each ship and food and drink supplies were loaded.

CONFLICT IN SOUTHAMPTON

With Leiden's leaders assembled, they met with Thomas Weston. He brought a revised agreement for them to sign, which included the "new and demanding terms his investors required." The Separatists were stunned. They had rejected these terms outright and instructed Robert Cushman, their London agent, to refuse them. Instead, Cushman apparently had pledged the Separatists to accept the new document, fearing the colonization attempt would collapse without agreeing to the new terms.[28]

In addition, Weston informed them that a new governor, Christopher Martin, was appointed to be in charge and would accompany them to America. To make matters worse, Martin had bought food in Kent and had loaded it in Southampton. He and John Carver

---

[26] Taylor, 91-2. Quoted from William Bradford, *Of Plymouth Plantation* (2006 ed. of 1856).
[27] Taylor, 45. Quoted from Woodhouse and Roots, *Puritanism and Liberty* (1992 ed. of 1938).
[28] Gragg, 130.

also hired a cooper, John Alden, to look after the barrels and casks. When the Separatists learned that Martin had spent £700 on food without a proper accounting, they were furious and refused to sign the revised agreement. Offended, Weston stormed off the dock, declaring that "they must, then, stand on their own legs."[29] Robert Cushman was distraught.

Without Weston's funds and confronted with continuing the voyage on their own, the Separatists sold "a large store of butter" from *Speedwell's* cargo hold. That raised £700—enough to satisfy their unanticipated costs and cover the port fees. With the *Speedwell's* repairs completed, the two disparate groups boarded the two ships. Robert Cushman boarded the *Speedwell* to make sure he was separated from Christopher Martin. Cushman described him as

> a monster. . . . He insulteth over our poor people, with such scorn and contempt as if they were not good enough to wipe his shoes . . . If I speak to him, he flies in my face as mutinous, and saith no complaints shall be heard or received but by himself.

Cushman further noted his concerns in a hastily written letter to a London friend.

> Friend, if ever we make a plantation God works a miracle, especially considering how scant we shall be of victals, and most of all un-united amongst ourselves and devoid of good tutors and regiment. Violence will break all. Where is the meek and humble spirit of Moses?[30]

With the leaks repaired and drama at port behind them, they had lost almost two weeks of prime sailing time. But the Separatists' leaders paused, prayed, and wrote a conciliatory letter to the Merchant Adventurers.

AN EPIC VOYAGE BEGINS

With approximately ninety passengers on the *Mayflower* and another thirty on the *Speedwell* plus two crews, the ships departed Southampton on the 5th of August. Not long after and barely underway, more leaks on the *Speedwell* forced them to harbor again, this time at Dartmouth on about 12 August. They made it only seventy-five miles west of Southampton. After repairs were accomplished, they were ready to leave again. But they had to wait for a good wind. Several *Mayflower* passengers wanted out of the voyage, willing to lose everything. But Governor Martin refused to let any passengers off the ship. After a long ten days of waiting, they departed on 23 August.

On 26 August, about 100 leagues into the voyage, disaster struck again.[31] The *Speedwell* sprang another leak. Captain Reynolds refused to go farther, and both ships returned to anchor in Plymouth Harbor on 28 August. As the crow flies, they were only fifty miles west of Dartmouth. In twenty-five days, the passengers and crew had traveled only 125 miles

---

[29]   Nathaniel Philbrick, *Mayflower: A Story of Courage, Community, and War* (New York: Penguin Books, 2006): 26.

[30]   Philbrick, 26-7.

[31]   345 miles.

west from the start of their journey. Already, some Leiden passengers had been on board for more than three and a half weeks. Under normal conditions, they could have crossed half the ocean in the same amount of time. On 29 August, they reached a decision to send the *Speedwell* back to London with about twenty discouraged passengers, including Robert Cushman. On 1 September, freight from the *Speedwell* was loaded onto the *Mayflower*. Eleven passengers from the *Speedwell* also boarded *Mayflower*, and a new governor, John Carver, was chosen for the remainder of the voyage. On 2 September, some passengers were entertained ashore by friends of their faith as the *Speedwell* sailed for London. The *Mayflower* departed Plymouth on 6 September 1620 with 102 passengers. Captain Jones noted in his log, "weighed anchor, wind E.N.E., a fine gale; laid course W.S.W. for northern coasts of Virginia."[32]

Once out in the open ocean, fair weather and a prosperous wind propelled the *Mayflower* forward. Since many Leiden passengers had never sailed before, they had no tolerance for the ship's motion and became quite seasick. William Bradford captured these details:

> And I may not omit here a special work of God's providence. There was a proud and very profane young man, one of the seamen, of a lusty, able body, which made him the more haughty; he would always be condemning the poor people in their sickness, and cursing them daily with grievous execrations, and did not let to tell them that he hoped to help cast half of them overboard before they came to their journey's end, and to make merry with what they had; and if he were gently reproved by any one, he would curse and swear most bitterly. But it pleased God, before they came half [the] seas over, to smite the young man with a grievous disease, of which he died in a desperate manner, and so was himself the first that was thrown overboard. Thus, his curses fell upon his own head, and it was an astonishment to all his fellows for they noted it to be the just hand of God upon him.[33]

Captain Jones noted this crewman's death on 23 September. "One of the seamen . . . sick with a grievous disease, died in a desperate manner. The first death and burial at sea of the voyage."[34] Unbeknownst to the passengers and crew, the hardest part of the voyage still lay ahead.

About a third of the way across the Atlantic Ocean, a fierce storm battered the ship with high winds and waves. As Stephen Hopkins steadied himself, he most certainly harkened back to the frightening storm he had experienced that lashed the *Sea Venture*. What was he thinking? Was God's wrath about to descend on them? Would another shipwreck resurrect his experiences on Devil's Island? Or would the Lord show his mighty power over the winds and waves to deliver them safely? The Leiden Landlubbers, as the crew called them, most certainly prayed fervently for God's deliverance. Captain Jones records:

---

[32] Azel Ames, *The May-flower and Her Log*. (Boston and New York: Houghton, Mifflin and Company, 1907). *Project Gutenberg*. Viewed on 20 August 2022. https://www.gutenberg.org/files/4107/4107-h/4107-h. htm. Hereinafter abbreviated Ames, *Mayflower Log*.

[33] Gragg, 168.

[34] Ames, *Mayflower Log*.

A sharp change. Equinoctial weather, followed by stormy westerly gales; encountered cross winds and continued fierce storms. Ship shrewdly shaken and her upper works made very leaky. One of the main beams in the midships was bowed and cracked. Some fear that the ship could not be able to perform the voyage. The chief of the company perceiving the mariners to fear the sufficiency of the ship (as appeared by their mutterings) they entered into serious consultation with the Master and other officers of the ship, to consider, in time, of the danger, and rather to return than to cast themselves into a desperate and inevitable peril.

In examining of all opinions, the Master and others affirmed they knew the ship to be strong and firm under water, and for the buckling bending or bowing of the main beam, there was a great iron screw the passengers brought out of Holland which would raise the beam into its place. The which being done, the carpenter and Master affirmed that a post put under it, set firm in the lower deck, and otherwise bound, would make it sufficient. As for the decks and upper works, they would caulk them as well as they could; and though with the working of the ship they would not long keep staunch, yet there would otherwise be no great danger if they did not over press her with sails. So they resolved to proceed.[35]

With the storm raging and no other choice, Captain Jones forced the ship to "lie ahull."[36] This maneuver, used as a last resort to steady the ship, furled the sails without a stitch of canvas set, secured the helm leeward away from the wind, and let the ship drift. When the *Mayflower II*, an exact replica built in England, encountered a similar storm 337 years later, Captain Alan Villers desperately performed the same maneuver. He reflected later that

as soon as the ship's bow swung into the wind, a remarkable change came over the *Mayflower II*. . . . Almost perfectly balanced [she] sat like a contented duck amid the roar of the storm. . . . I reflected that the Pilgrim Fathers, who tossed through many such a wild night in Atlantic storms, at least knew tranquility in great gales.[37]

But in 1620, with the ship ahull, the captain saw and described a lusty young man, John Howland, who came up on deck during the lull. Howland promptly stumbled and fell overboard. Somehow, John managed to grasp a line trailing the ship and held on for dear life. As the ship dragged him ten feet underwater, his strong hands held on tightly until he bobbed to the surface. The crew then used a boat hook to retrieve him from the ocean's grasp.

By late October, warmer and milder weather followed. In the timing of the weather's change, the Puritans saw God's providence, as Stephen Hopkins' wife, Elizabeth, went into labor. With her daughter, Constance, and probably the ship's doctor, Giles Heale, assisting, a baby boy was born and named Oceanus. As laws of the sea permit, Captain Christopher Jones baptized him. The colonists praised God and celebrated with Stephen Hopkins, the proud father, and his family. They had increased their number by one. But two days after a new life blessed the colonists, another was taken. William Butten, a servant of Samuel Fuller

---

[35] Ames, *Mayflower Log.*
[36] Philbrick, 31.
[37] Philbrick, 32.

and about the same age as Constance Hopkins, died on 6 November—the first passenger to die during the voyage.

Two days passed before the crew noticed the first signs of land. The word spread quickly with great excitement. Perhaps they would soon be on dry land! The following morning at daybreak on 9 November, land was sighted. Recognized as the bluffs of Cape Cod, the ship's master and the colonists' leaders conferenced. They were approximately ten leagues north of their intended destination: Hudson's River.[38] They decided to continue the voyage and headed SSW along the eastern bank of Cape Cod. When they reached the southern tip, the ship "fell amongst dangerous shoals and foaming breakers."[39] Captain Jones announced he was abandoning the effort. It was simply too dangerous to continue, and he turned the ship back. On Saturday, 11 November, the *Mayflower* lay at anchor in the sheltered bay inside the northern tip of Cape Cod.[40]

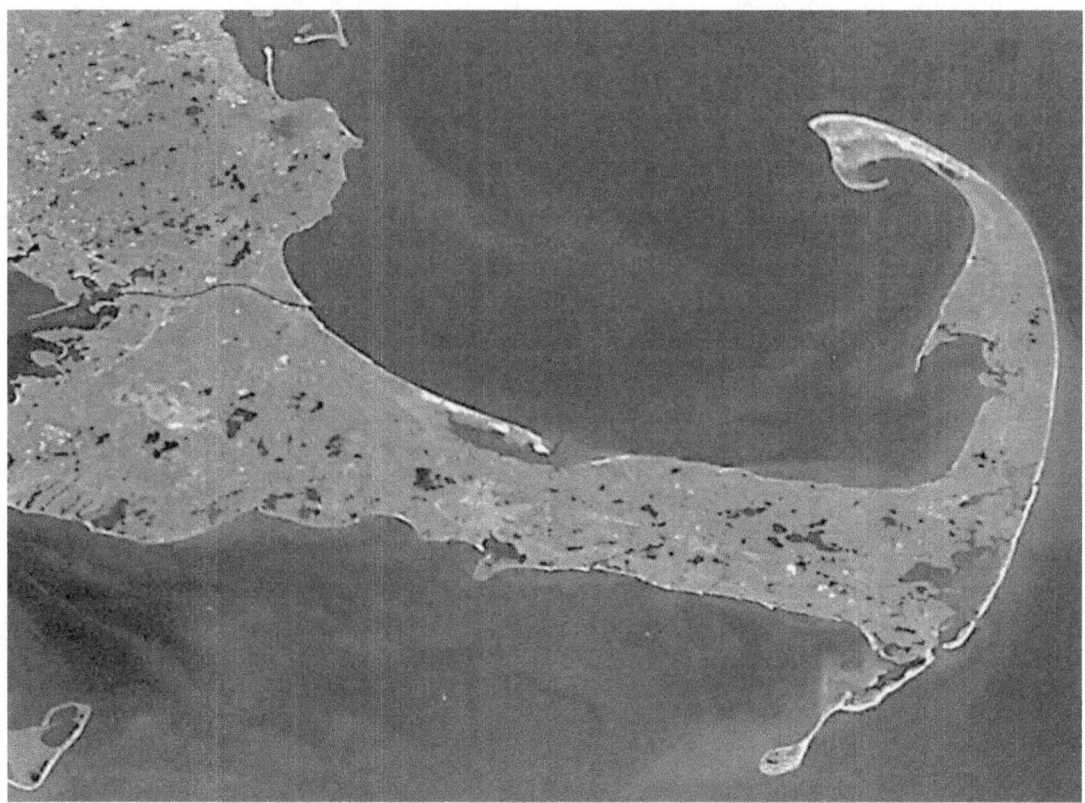

Cape Cod. Wikimedia Commons. Public domain. (10.1)

---

[38] Today's New York City.
[39] Ames, *Mayflower Log.*
[40] Near today's Provincetown.

THE *MAYFLOWER* IN AMERICA

At anchor, forty-one male colonists gathered in the ship's upper deck room. After sixty-six days of exhausting travel from Plymouth, they had faced extreme gales, high waves, a ruptured timber, two deaths, a birth, a man overboard and rescued, much sickness, and sundry unexpected events. Together, they had survived. Among those of age and well enough to participate, no male colonist was excluded. Whether they were servants or masters, from Leiden or London, all recognized the moment's significance and crammed into that upper room.

With no legal right to be where they were, they discussed and debated what to do. Stephen Hopkins' unique perspective and experience, eleven years earlier, was valuable and relevant. After being shipwrecked and stranded on Devil's Island, Hopkins had questioned the command structure and authority of both the ship captain and governor when a group of colonists found themselves ashore but not at their intended and approved destination. Hopkins clearly saw the parallels to what they now faced, and most certainly voiced his opinions and any concerns. In his previous situation, he was tried for mutiny, sentenced to death, but finally pardoned. The last thing he wanted was for history to repeat itself.

The colonists took a bold leap of faith. Forty-one adult men wrote and signed their own charter. They initiated a structure, "a civil Body Politick." In essence, they established a covenant to govern each other with "just and equal Laws, Ordinances, Acts, Constitutions, and Officers." Its opening, "undertaken for the Glory of God and Advancement of the Christian Faith, and the Honour of our King and Country," laid the foundation for the governing laws of the colony. Both Church and State are acknowledged from the beginning. This self-governing document, the first constitutional act of its kind in the New World, foreshadowed one that would create a nation in 1776.

The Mayflower Compact

IN THE NAME OF GOD, AMEN. We, whose names are underwritten, the Loyal Subjects of our dread Sovereign Lord King *James*, by the Grace of God, of *Great Britain*, *France*, and *Ireland*, King, *Defender of the Faith*, &c. Having undertaken for the Glory of God, and Advancement of the Christian Faith, and the Honour of our King and Country, a Voyage to plant the first Colony in the northern Parts of *Virginia*; Do by these Presents, solemnly and mutually, in the Presence of God and one another, covenant and combine ourselves together into a civil Body Politick, for our better Ordering and Preservation, and Furtherance of the Ends aforesaid: And by Virtue hereof do enact, constitute, and frame, such just and equal Laws, Ordinances, Acts, Constitutions, and Officers, from time to time, as shall be thought most meet and convenient for the general Good of the Colony; unto which we promise all due Submission and Obedience. IN WITNESS whereof we have hereunto subscribed our names at *Cape-Cod* the eleventh of November, in the Reign of our Sovereign Lord King *James*, of *England*, *France*, and *Ireland*, the eighteenth, and of *Scotland* the fifty-fourth, *Anno Domini*; 1620.

Mr. John Carver	John Craxton	Mr. Steven Hopkins	Francis Cooke
Mr. William Bradford	John Billington	Digery Priest	Thomas Rogers
Mr. Edward Winslow	Joses Fletcher	Thomas Williams	Thomas Tinker
Mr. William Brewster	John Goodman	Gilbert Winslow	John Ridgdale
Isaac Allerton	Mr. Samuel Fuller	Edmund Margesson	Edward Fuller
Myles Standish	Mr. Christopher Martin	Peter Brown	Richard Clark
John Alden	Mr. William Mullins	Richard Britteridge	Richard Gardiner
John Turner	Mr. William White	George Soule	Mr. John Allerton
Francis Eaton	Mr. Richard Warren	Edward Tilly	Thomas English
James Chilton	John Howland	John Tilly	Edward Doten
			Edward Liester[41]

Stephen Hopkins signed the Compact along with forty other colonists. Hopkins had come a long way since his death sentence on Devil's Island. In a little more than a decade, he progressed from being viewed as an unruly rogue to a founding father of an English colony in America. Stephen, the only colonist who had ever set foot in America and seen an indigenous native, would participate in many key events early in the life of this colony.

Two Concurrent Events in England

Within days of the colonists' creation and signing of the Mayflower Compact, two other events in England affected William and Jane Collier and William's former apprentice, William Langham. Langham had established himself as a freeman grocer in Southwark, the commercial center of the region's cloth trade as well as spices. As a wholesale grocer, Langham felt especially fortunate to have been apprenticed by Master Collier. Collier's well-established grocer's business, started in 1609, had flourished in St. Olave's Parish with his wife's support for over a decade. Collier also drew upon the expertise of his wife's mother, Alice, and husband, John Arnold, who operated a successful dyer's business on nearby Bermondsey Street for many years.

On 16 November 1620, six months after establishing his business, William Langham married Christian King.[42] Langham had invited his master and wife to attend their wedding ceremony. He respected and loved them as family. He intended to model his approach to family and business in the same way as William and Jane Collier did—working together as supportive partners. Certainly, the Colliers intended to witness and bless their ceremony. However, another sadder and more solemn event prevented their attendance: the death and burial of John Arnold. As Alice watched her second husband's burial in St. Olave's Parish churchyard, she was surely comforted by her daughter, Jane, and Jane's husband, William.

---

[41] "Mayflower Compact: 1620," *The Avalon Project*. Viewed on 29 August 2020. https://avalon.law. edu/17th_century/mayflower.asp. ("Mr" is a designation of class in English society. Those without it are viewed as commoners.)

[42] St. Mary Magdalene, Bermondsey, Parish Registers (1603-1642)

Both events occurred in mid-November 1620—almost exactly when the *Mayflower* anchored at the northern tip of Cape Cod sheltered in its inner bay.

PLYMOUTH COLONY'S FIRST WINTER AND ITS EARLY STRUGGLES

Captain Jones and the *Mayflower's* crew remained in Plymouth for the next five months. Jones had originally planned to return to England as soon as the colonists found a settlement site. But a strange sickness ravaged his ship's crew, as it did the *Mayflower's* passengers. About half the ship's crew died, including the gunner, boatswain, three of four quartermasters, the cook, and more than a dozen sailors. About half the Plymouth colonists died as well. That left only fifty ill-supplied colonists in terribly weakened conditions. They survived the first winter only with the indigenous natives' help and instruction.[ix]

When Captain Jones' remaining sailors recovered, the ship's empty hold received a ballast of stones from Plymouth Harbor's shoreline. On 5 April 1621, Jones weighed anchor and set sail for England. The *Mayflower* made excellent time on her return voyage as the westerly winds pushed her swiftly to England. She sailed into River Thames on 5 May 1621—less than half the time it took to sail to America.

Upon their arrival, Captain Jones, his officers, and crewmembers brought eyewitness accounts of the difficult voyage and the terrible losses in the first winter to the Merchant Adventurers. When Collier and the others heard their reports, they acted decisively on two critical items. First, the colonists lacked England's authority to operate where they settled. Second, the colonists needed help, support, and more colonists quickly.

PEIRCE PATENT OF 1621

The first task was assigned to Merchant Adventurer John Peirce, a Citizen and Clothworker of London. He was appointed to seek the right from the Council of New England for the settlers to live in America and establish their own government in Plymouth. Formally adopted on 1 June 1621, the council recognized that John Peirce and his associates, the Merchant Adventurers

> have already transported and undertaken to transporte at their cost and chardges themselves and dyvers persons into New England and there to erect and build a Towne and settle . . . diverse persons . . . for the advancement of the generall plantacon of that Country of New England.[43]

The patent assigned 100 acres to each male colonist and their heirs. If they "contynue three whole yeeres," they will have no other competition from other Englishmen. They were granted free liberty to fish in and upon the New England coast.

---

[43] "Peirce Patent," *Historical Archaeology and Public Engagement*. Viewed on 30 June 2020. http://www. histarch.illinois.edu/plymouth/piercepat.html.

For the second task, assigned to Thomas Weston, the Merchant Adventurers decided to re-supply the colony with another ship and more colonists. It took approximately two months to acquire supplies and recruit passengers. Some passengers, who left the *Mayflower* in Southampton and Plymouth a year earlier, were now willing to go, and others were recruited. A 55-ton merchant ship was commissioned for the voyage. Only one-third the size of the *Mayflower*, it didn't have enough capacity to restock the colony fully, but the Merchant Adventurers believed anything would be a blessing.

THE *FORTUNE*

Captained by William Peirce, John's brother and a fellow Merchant Adventurer, the *Fortune* arrived at the tip of Cape Cod on 9 November 1621—exactly one year after *Mayflower's* crew and passengers first sighted it. But it did not arrive in Plymouth until late November. Apparently, a number of passengers were shocked at the barren landscape and requested to return to England. For days, debates raged on about what to do. A delay of nearly three weeks caused much consternation for Peirce and other passengers. Peirce resolved the issue with a promise to take them elsewhere if they later were unwilling to stay in Plymouth. But by then they had consumed even more of the colony's food supply. Among the thirty-five passengers were William and Elizabeth Bassett, Jonathan Brewster, Robert Cushman and his son Thomas, Philip Delano, William Palmer, Thomas Prence, John Winslow, and William Wright.[44]

To further complicate the situation, the Plymouth colonists did not expect the ship. What they saw were new arrivals who strained the already limited food resources of the colony. As William Bradford recorded, "So they were landed; but there was not as much as biscuit-cake or any other victialls for them neither had they any beding, but some sorry things they had in their cabins, nor pot, nor pan, to dress meate in; nor over many cloathes."[45]

Robert Cushman brought the Merchant Adventurers' unsigned agreement with him. After Governor Carver died during the first winter's sickness, William Bradford was named governor by the colonists. Bradford knew his benefactors in London had received nothing in return for their investment so far. With Cushman's assurances that Thomas Weston could be trusted, Bradford and the other leaders signed the agreement. As a gesture of good faith, the colonists took two weeks to load hogsheads of beaver skins, otter skins, sassafras, and clapboards made from split oak that could be used to make barrel staves. The estimated cargo's value: £400-500, which would reduce their debt by half.

In preparation for his return trip, Robert Cushman put his fourteen-year-old son, Thomas, in William Bradford's care. On 13 December 1621, the *Fortune* left for England with Robert Cushman onboard. Unfortunately, the ship's master made a significant navigation error and was seized by a French warship. The ship's guns, cargo, and rigging

---

[44] Caleb Johnson, "Fortune," *Mayflower History*. Viewed on 10 July 2020. http://mayflowerhistory.com/fortune.

[45] William Bradford, *Of Plymouth Plantation 1620-1647 A New Edition by Samuel Eliot Morison* (New York: Alfred A. Knopf 1991): 172. Hereinafter abbreviated Bradford OPP.

were confiscated; the ship's master was locked up; and Cushman and the crew were kept on board under guard. They were freed thirteen days later, but their cargo was gone. On 17 February 1622, the *Fortune* arrived back in London with an empty hold.

The loss of *Fortune's* cargo dealt the Merchant Adventurers a severe financial blow. Thomas Weston abandoned the group. Some other investors followed Weston's lead and likewise left the group. None of the Merchant Adventurers, including William Collier, had made any return on their investment in almost two years.

THE COLLIER FAMILY MOVES

The month prior to *Fortune's* return from America, William and Jane Collier lost an infant child, Catheren. She was buried in St. Olave's churchyard in mid-January 1622.[46] But they praised God for blessing them with their remaining nine children: Margaret, 16; Thomas, 15; Joyce, 13; Mary, 10; Hannah, 8; Rebecca, 7; Sarah, 5; Elizabeth, almost three; and John, almost two. Only three of Jane's children were taken before their time. As Jane glanced at her eldest daughter, she realized she was looking at her younger self. Margaret was nearly the same age as Jane was when she married Thomas Clarke.

1622 was also a year when King James needed money and increased the tax burden on his more well-to-do subjects, including the Collier family. Jane's mother, the widow Alice Arnold, is recorded in tax rolls of the year as living "at the ninth listed dwelling on Bermondsey Street," with a tax imposition of £3 3s.[47] William Collier, whose residence was in St. Olave's Parish, also paid a tax of £3 3s. Two other of the Merchant Adventurers are recorded in the parish tax rolls as well: James Sherley, £3 3s, and John Peirce, £4 4s.[48]

In addition to their increased tax obligations, several other factors influenced the Colliers to consider consolidating their household with Alice. More than a year had elapsed since Alice was widowed. While everyone realized it might be somewhat crowded under one roof, Alice loved her grandchildren. She would be thrilled to have her family living with her. Even though Jane and William's grocer's business was doing well, William had not yet received any return from his investment in the Plymouth Colony in America. In fact, it needed even more financial support to survive. With Collier's tenement lease soon up for another year's renewal, it seemed a good and wise way to save on household expenses. Alice Arnold's home was located on Bermondsey Street, equidistant between St. Olave's Church, where renovations that began in 1617 were ongoing, and St. Mary Magdalene, Bermondsey. Though not common, a family's move from one parish to another did happen on occasion. With these elements all taken into account, the Collier family decided to move in with Alice Arnold.[49]

William Collier had remained in contact with his former apprentice, William Langham, who now operated his own freeman grocer's business in St. Olave's Parish and lived nearby.

---

46 St. Olave's Parish Registers (1583-1627).
47 The National Archives, E179/186/407, Poll tax of 1622. Bermondsey Parish.
48 The National Archives (Kew), E179/186/407, Poll tax of 1622, Rotuli 4 within St. Olave's Parish.
49 Cole, "Jane Clarke," 56.

Langham would occasionally ask his former master for advice, which Collier was happy to provide. When Collier had last seen him in the weeks after he married Christian, Langham asked him when he should consider taking on an apprentice. Collier encouraged him first to get more established. "Wait another year before taking that step," he advised. Collier now wondered how his former apprentice was doing. He also knew Langham was keenly interested in his Merchant Adventurer investments. Perhaps, he thought, it might be a good time to catch up with his former apprentice—before he moved to Bermondsey Street.

ZACHARY COLE LEAVES WEEDON BEC TO LEARN A TRADE

In Weedon Bec, in October 1621, the Cole family gathered around their second son, Zachary.[50] A teenager about fifteen, he was about to take a big step and leave his village and family to learn a trade in London. As his father, John, and his mother, Frances, embraced him tenderly, sharing words of love and encouragement, his brothers stood back. When it was their turn, Nathaniel, soon to be 27; Job, 13; John, 10; and young Daniel, 6; each tearfully said goodbye. The family prayed, placed hands on Zachary sitting in a chair, and asked for God's protection and blessing on his journey.

Zach's father, John, with his London experiences thirteen years earlier, gave him detailed instructions about the big city. He gifted Zach a horse for the journey. After father and son embraced, John instructed Zach to sell it when he arrived and use the money for expenses. As John watched his son mount his horse, he waved goodbye and bid him farewell. As Zach rode around a curve and disappeared, John wondered if he would ever see his second son again. He turned back to enter the messuage with a tear in his eye.

As Zach Cole left Weedon Bec to embark on this next stage of his life, he imagined what his future would be. For about two full days' travel, he soaked in the beautiful countryside of the East Midlands. But on the third day, as the sights, sounds, and smells of sprawling London emerged, it all seemed overwhelming for this young lad. Even though his father told him what London was like, he'd never experienced anything like it.

As Zach entered London Bridge, he saw the multitude of ships anchored to his left in River Thames. He thought, "I've never seen sights like this before! Where are all these vessels going? Commerce and trade. That's where my future lies." He slowed his horse to a walk, dodged pedestrians, and glanced at the multitude of shops with their goods inside. After leaving the bridge and entering Southwark, he rode south a few blocks and turned into a covered entrance on his left. On his right was George's Inn, which had been recommended to him. He dismounted and noticed the inn was "built of brick and timbers."[51] As he registered, an eager innkeeper helped young Zach sell his horse and set him up with a room.

---

[50] Records most often list him as Zacheus, but his immediate family called him Zachary or just Zach.

[51] "George Inn, Borough High Street, Southwark," *A London Inheritance*. Viewed on 15 September 2020. https://alondoninheritance.com/londonpubs/george-inn-borough-high-street-southwark/. This description occurred in 1622, right after Zachary Cole started his apprenticeship.

George's Inn, Southwark. Public domain. (10.2)

Within days, Zachary registered at the Guildhall and was formally appointed grocer's apprentice on 11 October 1621. The record states, "Zacheus Cole apprentice to William Langham for 8 years from this day the same day."[52]

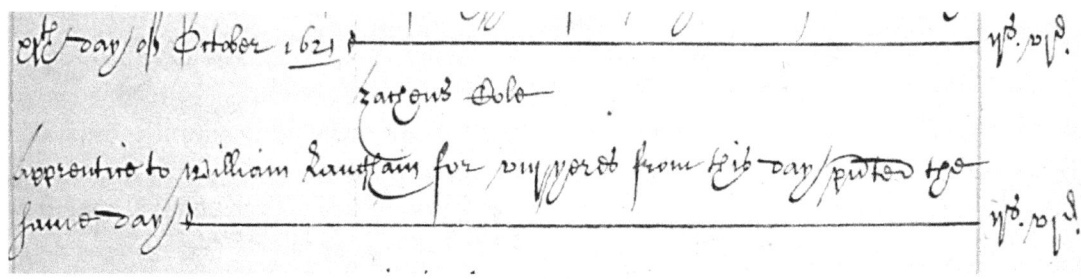

Apprenticeship Record of Zacheus Cole, 1621. Reproduced with kind permission of the Grocers' Company of London. Sponsored by Kitchen Mart, Inc. of Sacramento, California. (10.3)

As with any apprentice, Zachary Cole moved into a modest room in William and Christian Langham's tenement in St. Olave's Parish. Zach carefully observed everything his master did and threw himself into learning his craft. He was anxious to learn and knew that he, too, could become a Citizen Grocer in another eight years.

As William Collier entered William Langham's shop for a visit, the former apprentice welcomed his former master with an embrace. "I'm so glad you're here. Come in and meet my apprentice." Langham introduced Collier to Zachary Cole. Collier's initial impression of this young lad was that he was similar in size and bearing to his stepson, Thomas Clarke—they were about the same age.

---

52   Grocers' Guild, Wardens' Accounts 1611-1622. MS11571/10 Folio 470. Guildhall Library, London.

Apprentice Zach greeted him respectfully, "Pleased to meet you, Master Collier." The two chatted briefly about how he enjoyed the work and what he was learning. When asked about his home and background, Zach told him about the village, his parents, and his brothers. William Collier replied, "If any of your brothers wants to follow you here, let your master and me know. We're always looking for fine young men, just like you, Zachary, to join us." Zach smiled broadly and replied, "Thank you, sir. I will be sure to do that!" Zach took an instant liking to William Collier. Zach thought to himself, "Even though he's an old man, probably forty, he is wise and apparently in his prime."

Every week on his day off, Zach attended church with his master's family and occasionally explored his surroundings. River Thames with its watermen and ship traffic, London Bridge and its shops, the Globe Theatre, brewhouses, pubs, and even the bear and bull-baiting arenas were all within a short walking distance. For a young lad new to the borough, there was plenty to do on a day off. On workdays, he diligently applied himself to learning the grocer's trade. After his first year, Zach Cole knew this trade was for him.

As the Collier family settled into their new abode and life with Jane's mother, Alice Arnold's house on Bermondsey Street was now filled with her grandchildren's smiles, their lively antics, and loving embraces. And she was blessed with a steady income from tenements she managed for St. Mary Magdalene College in Oxford.[53] A servant helped Alice and Jane manage the household and other affairs. The extended family now attended worship services on Bermondsey Street at St. Mary Magdalene Parish church. Located just below the former Bermondsey Abbey, abandoned and dismantled after the Dissolution Act in 1538, this church, smaller than St. Olave's, was a pleasant walk up the cobblestone street. Each Sunday they made their way to worship services, the children peering in shop windows lining both sides of the street, as the bells of the church tower rang, giving notice the service would soon begin.

As the summer heat abated, Jane knew she was pregnant again. The following spring, she bore another son. Named James Collier, he was baptized on 16 March 1623.[54] Now, their family numbered ten children: Margaret, Thomas, Joyce, Mary, Hannah, Rebecca, Sarah, Elizabeth, John, and James.

Merchant Adventurers Prepare to Send More Ships

When William Collier came home from a Merchant Adventurers' meeting, his wife, Jane, greeted him with a kiss as usual. After they embraced, William looked at her and said, "We need to talk privately. Let's leave the children with Alice and go for a walk." Hand-in-hand, they strolled down Bermondsey Street, noticing the goods in shop windows, and then reached a spot with a view of River Thames. William asked Jane to sit with him on a bench.

---

[53] This detail is found in Alice Arnold's will: "To my son-in-law William Collier all the yearly rents of the premises in the occupation of Alexander Wylding [sic] situated in Bermondsey Street in the parish of St Olave's, which Alice holds by lease from St Mary Magdalene College in Oxford." The text of Alice Arnold's will is included in Chapter 11 endnotes.

[54] St. Mary Magdalene, Bermondsey, Parish Registers (1603-1642)

As they watched the ships and watermen travel the river with its bustling activity, William took a deep breath and sighed. Jane looked at him with concern in her eyes and asked, "Is something wrong? Are you ill?" "No dear. Nothing is wrong. We decided today to send two more ships to Plymouth Colony. They need help and strong young men of good character." He paused again as Jane's eyes widened. "How do you feel about us sending Thomas to America?" Jane gasped and looked at her husband. His eyes met hers. With tears in her eyes, she felt very strong emotions.

Thomas was her son, and his father's namesake. She thought of Thomas traveling alone across the vast ocean to the primitive coast of America. She had heard the horror stories: the fierce storms ships' passengers faced just getting there; colonists dying from strange sicknesses; the terrible cold and harsh winters; the lack of supplies and resources. And all for what? Jane was gripped by conflicting emotions and started to cry. "William, our boy is inquisitive, smart, strong-minded, independent, and strong for his age. But he's not yet fully grown—he's only sixteen!" Then William reminded her that Thomas was just a few months younger than she was when she first married, and that lads younger than that often traveled from the countryside to London to acquire a trade and prepare to make their way in the world.

As they conversed back and forth, issue by issue, William patiently listened to his wife's concerns and chose his words wisely. Her oldest boy leaving home, venturing across the vast ocean for a new life in a new place was the biggest step Thomas might ever take. It would have life-changing consequences. He understood what she was feeling. But William reminded her how often Thomas expressed interest in the Merchant Adventurers' business and the status of the Plymouth colonists. He viewed it as a great adventure. He wanted to experience and see first-hand the indigenous people with their unfamiliar customs. He imagined what his life could be in the New World. He could earn his own land. He could never achieve that if he stayed in England.

After their conversation exhausted them both, they prayed together for God's guidance. As they walked home arm-in-arm, Jane rested her head on William's shoulder. They stopped before they reached the front door, looked at each other, and prayer together, "May the Lord's hand be upon us and with Thomas." They unlatched the door, stepped inside, and asked for Thomas to sit with them. They had something important to discuss.

CHAPTER 11

TWO SHIPS, THREE MARRIAGES, CHALLENGES, AND A PLAGUE

TWO SHIPS DEPART FOR PLYMOUTH

In April 1623, the Merchant Adventurers completed preparations to resupply Plymouth Colony in America. A total of ninety-three passengers assembled to board two ships: the *Anne* and the *Little James*. Certainly, some passengers' family members were there to bid them farewell. They included William and Jane Collier with probably two of Jane's children: Margaret, 17, and Joyce, 14. The family was there to say goodbye to the children's brother and Jane's son, Thomas Clarke, at age sixteen. He was embarking on his life's greatest adventure. William was there to support his stepson, whom he had raised alongside Jane. When Thomas saw the two ships, his excitement grew by leaps and bounds. Even as a young lad, Thomas dreamt of crossing the vast ocean. Now, just two months after his sixteenth birthday, the moment had arrived. He was poised to begin a momentous step in his life's journey.

Collier was also there to say goodbye and bid farewell to his friend and fellow Merchant Adventurer, Timothy Hatherley. Other noteworthy passengers who boarded the *Anne* were well-known by the Plymouth Colonists. They included Edward Bangs, William Heard, Nicholas Snow, and widow Alice Carpenter Southworth. Also included were members of prominent families: two daughters of William Brewster, Patience, 23, and Fear, 17; and Mrs. Elizabeth Walker Warren, the wife of *Mayflower* passenger Richard Warren, with their five daughters: Mary, 15; Anna, 12; Sarah, 9; Elizabeth, 7; and Abigail, 5. The *Anne* was the primary 140-ton supply ship and carried about two-thirds of the passengers. Her master was Merchant Adventurer William Peirce, an experienced and seasoned mariner.

The second ship was the 44-ton pinnace, the *Little James*. Her master, John Bridges, also an experienced mariner, was paired with an inexperienced captain, Emmanuel Altham, a Merchant Adventurer. The crew signed on for the voyage with the agreement to spend six years in Plymouth Colony as shareholders instead of wage earners. The ship's investors would pay for the crew's food, drink, and clothing. After the voyage, the pinnace would remain in the colony for fishing, cargo, and military service. They expected to earn money from sharing in the fishing and trading profits. In addition, the pinnace was outfitted with six cannons to protect the colony.[1] Most passengers onboard the *Little James*, about thirty, were a group recruited by the Merchant Adventurer's Treasurer and unfamiliar to the other colonists.

---

[1]   "The ships Anne and Little James," *Wikipedia*. Viewed on 28 February 2021. https://en.wikipedia.org/wiki/The_ships_Anne_and_Little_James.

As the ships weighed anchors, Thomas Clarke waved to his family ashore and shouted goodbye. By then, he could not see the tears in his mother's eyes. He could hardly contain his excitement at what lay ahead. But not long after departure, the smaller ship became separated and encountered difficulties. With the vessel's cannons mounted, some crew members believed they could supplement their wages by capturing prized ships from enemy nations such as France or Spain. They were hugely disappointed to find out that was not true. When the crew spotted a French ship in the open sea, they pleaded with Captain Altham to capture it, but he refused. Under maritime law, prizes could only be taken if the ship carried letters issued by the Crown. The captain had none. Without authorization, he would not act, causing frustration and dissention. Two crewmen complained bitterly about the missed opportunity. William Stevens, a gunner, and Thomas Fell, a carpenter, hoped to augment their wages with plunder. Their disruptive behavior set the tone for the crew, and likely contributed to the voyage's length as much as the storms that churned up the water and waves. The voyage lasted about three months—nearly half again the length of *Mayflower's* sixty-six-day crossing.

The first ship, *Anne*, arrived in Plymouth on 10 July 1623, and *Little James* followed a week to ten days later. Governor Bradford's observations of the newly arrived colonists were distinctly mixed. He thought some were useful persons and would be "good members to the body." Some were wives and children of men there already. But Bradford saw some as unfit colonists and labeled them strangers. They were the independent emigrants recruited by the Merchant Adventurer treasurer. Led by John Oldham, aged twenty-one, this group was promised a settlement apart from the main community in Plymouth. Accompanying Oldham was his sister, Lucretia, destined to be the wife of Jonathan Brewster. In an apologetic letter to Bradford, Robert Cushman wrote:

> It greeveth me to see so weake a company sent you, and yet had I not been here they had been weaker. . . . such and such came without my constente: but the importunitie of their friends got promise of our Treasurer in my absence.[2]

A month after the *Anne's* arrival, the colony celebrated a special occasion. Alice Carpenter Southworth, one of its passengers, married Governor William Bradford on 14 August 1623. His first wife, Dorothy, had died tragically while the *Mayflower* anchored off the northern tip of Cape Cod before settling in Plymouth. Captain Emmanuel Altham of the *Little James* wrote about the marriage festivities in a letter dated that September.

> And now to say somewhat of the great cheer we had at the Governor's marriage. We had about twelve pasty venison, besides others, pieces of roasted venison and other such good cheer in such quantity that I could wish you some of our share. For here we have the best grapes that ever you [saw] and the biggest, and divers sorts of plums and nuts which our business will not suffer us to look for.[3]

---

[2]   Bradford OPP, 28.

[3]   Eugene Aubrey Stratton, *Plymouth Colony: Its History & People 1620-1691* (Salt Lake City: Ancestry Publishing, 2013): 25.

As Thomas Clarke participated in the festivities, he realized how much he had experienced in just four months. If he felt any twinges of homesickness, those emotions were likely fleeting. As a young man finding his way in a new environment, he had made many new friends. He thought, "My new family is right here. I need to make the most of the chance to prove myself." While the challenges were many, Thomas worked diligently as a carpenter, finishing planks for shipment back to England. He saw this pristine continent, filled with rich resources, as a land of true opportunities. He desperately wanted to succeed and leave his mark.

However, when the *Little James* first arrived at Plymouth Colony, its crewmembers were troubled by what they saw. The colonists were in worse condition than they anticipated. The crew's ringleaders believed they had been misled. Beyond their basic expenses, their agreement for wages was based on the colony's profits generated through fishing and trading. Consequently, crewmembers Stephens and Fell led a strike for an interim cash payment. When William Bradford offered to pay them personally, it placated them—temporarily.

TWO FAMILIES' FIRST MARRIAGES

In Weedon Bec, John and Frances Cole were excited about the first wedding in their family. Their eldest son Nathaniel, now twenty-eight, married Anne Clevely, nineteen, the daughter of Thomas and Anne Clevely, on 1 May 1623.[4] Zachary Cole, with his master's permission, arrived from Southwark to attend the ceremony and celebrate the family's special occasion. Zachary had not been home since his departure two years earlier. The entire family was anxious to hear about his experiences in the big city. As he detailed life in Southwark and his grocer's apprenticeship, Zachary spoke highly of his master, William Langham, as well as his master's master, William Collier. He excitedly described Master Collier's offer of a possible apprenticeship for Zachary's brothers. Job, 15, paid particularly close attention to his older brother. Job imagined what life would be like if he followed in Zachary's footsteps. John, 12, and Daniel, 9, were too young for such considerations, but perhaps a seed had been planted. After the celebration concluded, Zachary left promptly for London. He did not want to take advantage of his master's kindness in letting him attend.

A month before Nathaniel's wedding, another significant event in the village was finalized. Eton College, which held manorial rights over Weedon Bec, had authorized enclosures of the traditional village tenant properties.[x] John Cole was among the men who represented the village. The agreement, reached on 29 March 1623, was between the provost of Eton College, representing the Lords of the Manor of Weedon Bec; Thomas Thornton, Esquire, proprietor of the parsonage and patron of the vicarage there; Richard [sic] Smith, clerk, vicar, and incumbent of the church; John Thornton, gentlemen; John Billinge, John Cole, Robert Hunte, the residue of the copyholders of the said manor, and Mathew Bust, gentleman farmer. The agreement indicated the common fields enclosures

---

[4] Weedon Bec Parish Registers (1588-1665)

would be profitable for the manor, the local church, and the cottagers of the town, and at the same time beneficial to the copyholders. They would cause:

> no hurt to the com[m]on welth by any depopulac[i]on by reason that most of the said copyholders are copyholders of inheritance according to the custome of the said mannor and do dwell upon the same, It ys agreed betwene all the said lordes p[ro]prietors of the said p[ar]sonage vicar and copyholders that the said feildes of Weden Beck shalbe inclosed and layd in sev[er]alty every mans landes by them selves in sev[er]all plottes in forme following . . .

> First yt is agreed and willingly assent unto by the said lordes ten[a]ntes and copyholders and p[er]sons above menc[i]oned that the said vicarage and vicars lyveinge shalbe made better by xli by the yere at least, etc.[5]

A year later, in March 1624, John and Frances celebrated the birth of their first grandchild. Nathaniel and Anne Cole's daughter, Anne, was baptized by vicar Robert Smith on 17 March 1624 in the Weedon Bec Parish church.[6] Besides the grandparents, Nathaniel's brothers Job, John, and Daniel joined in the happy occasion.

As John Cole reflected while he held his granddaughter, he remembered his own parents, Thomas and Joan Cole. John's son, Nathaniel, knew his grandfather, but his grandmother had passed away before he was born. John heard stories of his grandfather John, for whom he was named, and some of his grandfather's memorable experiences with the manorial court nearly three-quarters of a century earlier. Of his grandfather's father, William, John knew very little. But for right now, John and Frances looked forward to what the Lord might have in store for their children and grandchildren. As Nathaniel and Anne began their family, John and Frances hoped for the same blessings for Zachary. Even though he was away learning a trade in London, they thought of him often and prayed for his well-being. They imagined their other sons might follow him, some day at some point. But at that moment, they could not have imagined the full scope of God's plan for their children.

In Southwark among Alice Arnold's tenants, one young man stood out. From a good family, Alexander Wilding seemed like a bright young man and had good prospects. In every interaction with him, Alice liked him and was impressed. One day, she thought, "He might be a good match for my granddaughter, Margaret. She is almost eighteen." Just as Alice was about to say something to her daughter, Jane came to her with Margaret. Margaret wanted their permission and blessing to marry. She was attracted to Alexander and believed he felt the same. Without delay, discussions opened between the families, and an agreement was reached.

A month after her eighteenth birthday, Margaret Clarke and Alexander Wilding sealed their marriage covenant in St. Olave's on 28 October 1623.[7] Her mother, Jane, her stepfather, William, and her grandmother, Alice, were pleased with the union. All the Clarke and Collier children were there, save one. Margaret's brother, Thomas Clarke, was in America.

---

5   NRO TH-660, "Articles of Agreement between Cranford and Cole in Weedon Bec, 1604 and Eton College."
6   Weedon Bec Parish Registers (1588-1665)
7   St. Olave's Parish Registers (1583-1627)

PLYMOUTH COLONY'S OPPORTUNITIES AND CHALLENGES

With an eye to protecting against the rigors and starvation of another coming winter, the colonists enacted the 1623 Division of Land. The land was allotted primarily to the Old Comer colonists on the first three ships sent by the investors: *Mayflower*, *Fortune*, and *Anne*. The colonists cast lots and were given one acre per family member. Two colonists granted land are of particular interest: "From the *Mayflower*, These lye on the South side of the brook to the woodward opposite to the former: Steven Hopkins 6." A mature man approaching age forty, Hopkins headed a large family. "From the *Anne*, South side - Tho. Clarke one acre 1."[8] The other was a single young man, not yet age seventeen, and a new arrival. Yet both achieved something in Plymouth Colony that neither could have attained in England: land ownership.

When a summer drought set in, Governor Bradford called for "a solemn day of humiliation." An important member of the colony, Edward Winslow, assisted Bradford and recorded the event.[9] All the colonists "assembled in the morning and prayed for eight or nine hours." After they adjourned, Winslow reported it "began raining that night and continued for two weeks." He wrote, it "distilled such soft, sweete, and moderate showers . . . it was hard to say whether our withered corne or drooping affections were most quickened and revived." Governor Bradford promptly called for another day of prayer to thank the Lord for his "mercies towards his Church and chosen ones." These new experiences for Thomas Clarke must have left an indelible impression on him. With God's providential help, the colonists "enjoyed a bountiful harvest. They had mastered at last the art of growing corn."[10] Of course, if it were not for their indigenous friends' teachings, they would never have learned how to plant corn correctly. The secret was to place a herring in each hole to fertilize each plant.[11]

Unfortunately, one of the new arrivals with Thomas Clarke on the *Anne*, Merchant Adventurer Timothy Hatherley, experienced a tragic loss in November 1623. He "lost his house in a conflagration that for a time threatened to consume the town."[12] With his belongings burned and lost, Hatherley returned on the *Anne* to England that winter "much impoverished and much discouraged."[13]

Once back in London, William Peirce and Timothy Hatherley informed their fellow investors about the ongoing challenges and lack of success with Plymouth's trading and fishing. The *Little James* and its crew had been nothing but trouble. Discouraged by the news, several investors dropped out of the group—but not William Collier.

---

8   Volume XII of the "Records of the Colony of New Plymouth," reprinted in *Mayflower Descendant*, 1:227-230, and posted online at *Historical Archaeology*, http://www.histarch.illinois.edu/plymouth/landdiv.html.

9   Mayflower passenger, Edward Winslow, was perhaps Bradford's most important assistant and supporter.

10 Willison, 239-40.

11 Stephen A. Mrozowski, "The Discovery of a Native Corn Field on Cape Cod," *Archaeology of Eastern North America* (1994 (22)): 47-62. Archaeological evidence unearthed has confirmed this technique.

12 Willison, 239.

13 Nathaniel Morton, *New England's Memorial*, 31. Viewed 29 September 2020. Caleb Johnson's website: www.mayflowerhistory.com.

As spring arrived, William and Jane celebrated the birth of another daughter, Martha. She was born twelve months after their son, James. On 28 March 1624, Martha was baptized in the parish church, St. Mary Magdalene, Bermondsey.[14] The Collier family now numbered an even dozen: the parents and ten children. Even with Thomas Clarke gone and living in Plymouth Colony, space in Alice Arnold's home was tight. With thirteen family members and a servant living under one roof, William and Jane discussed if it was time to move back to St. Olave's Parish.

At this time, the Merchant Adventurers met to regroup. The investors dwindled as enthusiasm for the project without profits waned. In April 1624, James Sherley, now treasurer of the Merchant Adventurers, wrote to Governor Bradford, Edward Winslow, and Isaac Allerton in the colony. In addition to Sherley, William Collier and six other Merchant Adventurers affixed their signatures to the letter.

> Two things (beloved friends) we have endeavoured to effect, touching Plymouth plantation, first, that the planters there might live comfortably and contentedly. 2d that some returns might be made hither for the satisfying and encouragement of the adventurers, but to neither of these two can we yet attain. Nay, if it be as some of them report which returned in the Catherine, it is almost impossible to hope for it, since, by their sayings, the slothfulness of one part of you, and the weakness of the other part, is such, that nothing can go well forward. And although we do not wholly credit these reports, yet surely, either the country is not good where you are, for habitation; or else there is something amiss amongst you; and we much fear the willing are too weak and the strong too idle.

A long list of questions and grievances followed. The main points were to explain why many investors had given up on the colony through the losses at sea and no profits. The letter concluded with these sentiments:

> At a word, though we be detected of folly, ignorance, want of judgment, yet let no man charge us with dishonesty, looseness or unconscionableness; but though we lose our labours or adventures, or charges, yea our lives; yet let us not lose on jot of our innocence, integrity, holiness, fear and comfort with God.

> And thus ceasing for this time to trouble you further; praying God to bless and prosper you, and sanctify all your crosses and losses, that they may turn to your great profit and comfort in the end, with hearty salutations to you all, we lovingly take leave of you, from London, April 7, 1624.

> Your assured lovers and friends,

> James Sherley, Thomas Fletcher, Thomas Brewer, John Ling,
> William Collier, William Thomas, Joseph Pocock, Robert Reayne[15]

---

14 Cole, "Jane Clarke," 59.
15 George Ernest Bowman (ed.), *Governor William Bradford's Letter Book*. (Boston: Massachusetts Society of Mayflower Descendants, 1906). Viewed on 10 July 2021. *Internet Archive*. https://archive.org/details/

The Merchant Adventurers' letter was sent to Plymouth with Captain William Peirce. Under his command, another ship, the *Charity*, carried more goods to stock the colony and additional passengers to consume the foodstuffs. Included were cattel [*sic*] for Plymouth—"3 heifers and a bull, the first beginning of any carte of that kind in ye land."[16] The term cattel often described other animals, including hogs and fowl. This trip probably helped Plymouth elder, William Brewster, provide instructions for the future transporting of such "beastes."

> For cattell the best and fittest tyme . . . is to carry them in the spring. . . . there are more easterly windes, Calmest seas, then they find plentifull foode . . . at their arrival. Thoess cattell that are fittest to be . . . are young heiffers of two yeers olde. The proportion of Water oates . . . that is usually laid aboord for the Cattell. . . .
>
> A shippe of 140 tunnes of two decks . . . will carrye about 60 young heiffers . . . the hold of the Lower decke myst be always open . . . The Cattell must be placed in the . . . holde of the shippe, Which is nearest to the hatches, With their Tylles to the inner syde of the shippe, and their heads outterwards bothe for aure and light. When it is faire wether yow must open all your hatches and ports for aure, and daily your cattell must be made cleene from their dung and it flung overboorde.
>
> And yow shall doe well daily to cause currey and rubbe them for this . . . will make them thrive . . . well at sea, and keepe them in health . . . They must have troughes and mangers . . . before them to eate their oates . . . if it be possible to be provided with asses . . . be verie useful.[17]

When the *Charity* arrived in Plymouth from London, returning colonist Edward Winslow brought "provisions including hooks and nets and other fishing gear, a ship's carpenter, a saltmaker, the Reverend John Lyford, and 3 heifers & a bull, the first beginning of any catle of that kind in ye land." A letter from Robert Cushman apologized for not sending "comfortable things as butter, sugar, &c." James Sherley described a particularly colorful Merchant Adventurers' meeting at his goldsmith's shop on London Bridge, during which the investors attempted to resolve their differences and frustrations about Plymouth. He wrote to Bradford, "ye loveingest and frendlyest meeting that ever I knew, and our greatest enemies offered to lend us 50. So I sent for apotle of wine (I would you could doe ye like), which we dranke friendly together. Thus God can turne ye harts of men when it pleaseth him."[18]

---

governorwilliam00bradgoog. Hereinafter abbreviated Bradford, *Letters*.

[16] Willison, 242.

[17] Caleb Johnson, *The Brewster Book Manuscript* (Massachusetts Society of Mayflower Descendants, 2019): 45-7.

[18] Willison, 242-3.

Challenges for Plymouth Colony and Its London Investors

During this time and without adequate trade goods from the Adventurers, the crew of the *Little James* was unable to obtain any prime furs to ship to England. This led to even more unrest. By winter of 1623/4, things went from bad to worse. When a winter gale damaged the pinnace while anchored in Plymouth harbor, the ship's crew bunked onboard in freezing weather. With only small rations and water to drink, no ale, their loyalty disintegrated during that winter of discontent.

In the spring of 1624, Captain Altham and Master Bridges took the *Little James* up the coast on a fishing and trading expedition, anchoring at Pemaquid.[19] There, the crew mutinied and threatened Altham and Master Bridges with the destruction of the ship. After a series of events culminating on the night of the 10th of April, wind and waves crashed the pinnace on the rocks, killing Master Bridges and two crewmen. Other in-port ships contacted Bradford and offered to salvage the ship in return for their beaver skins' quota. Bradford diverted the colony's beaver furs, stored for the Merchant Adventurers, in order to salvage the *Little James*. Within six weeks near the end of May, the *Little James* was again seaworthy. But at what cost?

About the time the salvage of *Little James* was completed, the *Charity* arrived in Plymouth. Captain William Peirce delivered the Merchant Adventurers' letter of 7 April 1624 to William Bradford. The governor clearly understood the investors' frustrations with the *Little James*. As its costs had increased, so had the colony's debts to the investors. But with the mutiny's aftermath, the deaths, the complete fiasco at Pemaquid and subsequent salvage effort and costs, Bradford ordered the *Little James* and her crew back to England. Other colonists, those who decided they were not cut out for living and working in such a primitive environment, shipped out to England with them. But Thomas Clarke was not one of them.

Unfortunately, one who remained, Reverend Lyford, created more turmoil in the colony. A graduate of Magdalen College in Oxford now in his forties, the cleric had spent years ministering to small parishes in England and Ireland. Since the Leiden Separatists had no ordained minister, because John Robinson remained in Leiden, they were unable to receive the sacraments and benefit from other ministerial support duties. The Merchant Adventurers selected Lyford to substitute for Robinson. Lyford was quickly admitted to the Separatists' church, and he shared teaching responsibilities with William Brewster every Sabbath. Unfortunately, he was not as the Separatists hoped or expected. Some colonists led by John Oldham, who had settled apart from the main Plymouth group, met secretly with Lyford. Dissatisfied with the Plymouth Separatists' practices, Lyford encouraged their dissension. Afterwards, Oldham and Lyford wrote slanderous and disparaging letters to their England contacts about the Separatists. Bradford observed a flurry of letters being posted and intercepted about twenty of them. He privately made copies of a few. In his words, the letters "grew very perverse, and showed a spirit of great malignancy, drawing as

---

[19]   On the coast of today's Maine.

many into faction as they could. Were they never so vile or profane, they did back them in all their doings . . . to speak against the church here."[20]

Growing in confidence with the support of Reverend Lyford, Oldham became quarrelsome, rude, and arrogant. He refused to stand his scheduled watch—a community duty required of all men. Unprovoked, he drew his knife on Myles Standish, the colony's military advisor, and denounced him as a "beggarly rascal." After detention, he was let go. But that was not the end of it. On one Sunday, without speaking to the governor or any church elders, and with Oldham's encouragement, minister Lyford set up his own public meeting. Bradford called the two men to account for their actions. He put them on trial for "plotting against them and disturbing their peace, both in respects of their civil and church state." When they denied the charges, Bradford read from their intercepted letters in front of the entire colony. Convicted, they both were banished from Plymouth Colony.[21]

MORE LONDON EVENTS

Southwark's summer heat of 1624 was unusually hot and dry. Whether or not the weather caused the next event cannot be determined. But regardless of the cause, the Collier family experienced a personal loss. Their youngest son, James, aged seventeen months, died. His burial was recorded in St. Olave's Parish Register on 24 August 1624.[22] The loss of their third child together caused William, Jane, their eight remaining children, and James' grandmother, Alice, to shed many tears as they bade him farewell. Deeply grieving the death of the precious child they lost well before his time, they prayed:

> "Almighty God, Father of mercies and giver of all comfort: Deal graciously with us as we mourn, that, casting all our cares on thee, we may know the consolation of thy love. Give unto thy servants the peace which the world cannot give. Through Jesus Christ our Lord, Amen."

When the *Little James* arrived in London in early November 1624, its two disgruntled crewmen, Fell and Stephens, left the ship in River Thames in a "very disordered and evil manner." They promptly sued the investor group and Plymouth Colony for £40, amounting to four to six years' wages—wages, they claimed, Bradford had promised them in Plymouth and not paid. In addition, the two Adventurers who invested the most to build and outfit the *Little James*, Thomas Fletcher and Thomas Goffe, demanded possession of the ship as payment for their debt.[23]

With jurisdiction over maritime matters, the High Court of Admiralty took custody of the *Little James* and all her goods pending resolution of the lawsuits filed in London. In November 1624, depositions were taken by the court. Five of these survive—from Edward

---

[20] Bradford OPP, 149.
[21] Bradford OPP, 148-57. See also, Philbrick, 161-162.
[22] St. Olave's Parish Registers (1583-1627)
[23] Caleb Johnson, "Troubles with Little James: Edward Winslow's depositions at High Court of Admiralty," *The Mayflower Quarterly* (Vol. 77, no. 1 (March 2011)): 51-54.

Winslow, William Peirce, Benedict Morgan, a passenger of the *Fortune*, Robert Cushman, and James Sherley, a Merchant Adventurer.[xi] The plaintiff crewmen lost the suit, and the court released the *Little James* back to its investors.

On 18 December 1624, the Merchant Adventurers sent another letter to Governor Bradford about the status of their group.

> To Our Loving Friends, Though the thing we feared be come upon us, and the evil we strove against has overtaken us, yet we cannot forget you, nor our friendship and fellowship which together we have had somme years . . . by a wonderful providence of God, we are so nearly united, we have thought good once more to write unto you, to let you know what is here befallen, and the reasons of it; as also our purposes and desires toward you for hereafter.
>
> The former course, for the generality here, is wholly dissolved from what it was, and whereas you and we were formerly sharers and partners in all voyages and dealings, this way is now no more.

They described what had transpired and the reasons for it:

> First and mainly, the many losses and crosses at sea, and abuses of seamen, which have caused us to run into so much charge, debts and engagements as our estates and means were not able to go on without impoverishing ourselves; except our estates had been greater and our associates cloven better unto us. Secondly, as here hath been a faction and siding amongst us now more than two years, so now there is an utter breach and sequestration amongst us; and in two parts of us a full desertion and forsaking of you, without any intent or purpose of meddling more with you.

They reaffirmed both God's sovereignty over all that happened and their collective response:

> For we know the hand of God to be in all these things, and no doubt he would admonish something thereby and to look at what is amiss. And although it be now too late for us or you to prevent and stay these things, yet is it not too late to exercise patience, wisdom, and conscience in bearing them, and in carrying ourselves in and under them for the time to come.

They pledged their continued support of the colonists:

> And as we ourselves stand ready to embrace all occasions that may tend to the furtherance of so hopeful a work, rather admiring of what is than grudging for what is not, so it must rest in you to make all good again.
>
> Let us endeavor to keep a fair and honest course, and see what time will bring forth, and how God in his providence will work for us. We still are persuaded you are the people that must make a plantation in those remote places when all others fail and return. . . . We have sent you here some cattle, cloth, hose, shoes, leather, etc.; but in another nature than formerly, as it stood us in hand to do. . . . Go on, good friends, comfortably; pluck up your spirits,

and quit yourselves like men in all your difficulties; that notwithstanding all displeasure and threats of men, yet the work may go on you are about, and not be neglected.[24]

Four Merchant Adventurers signed the letter: James Sherley, William Collier, Thomas Fletcher, and Robert Holland. The supportive closing words from these men came at a critical juncture for Plymouth. As one historian notes, these four original Adventurers had confidence in the colonists and shared their belief that God's hand was in the enterprise. They were "very keen to keep the business part of the enterprise going, as it was just beginning to pay dividends."[25]

In 1624, Captain John Smith, the famous explorer, described Plymouth Colony.

At New Plimouth there is about 180 persons, some cattell and goats, but many swine and poultry, 32 dwelling houses, whereof 7 were burnt the last winter, and the value of five hundred pounds in other goods; the Towne is impaled about half a mile compasse. In the towne upon a high Mount they have a Fort well built with wood, lome, and stone, where is planted their Ordnance: Also a fair Watch-tower, partly framed for the Sentinell, the place it seems is healthfull.

Most of them live together as one family or household, yet every man followeth his trad or profession both by sea and land, and all for a generall stocke, out of which they have all their maintenance, until there be a dividend betwixt the Planters and the Adventurers. Those Planters are not servants to the Adventurers here, but have only concells of directions from them . . . and all the master of families are partners in land or whatsoever, setting their labours against the stocke. . . . They have young men and boies for the Apprentises and servants, and some of them special families, as Ship-carpenters, Saltmakers, Fish-masterrs, yet as servants upon great wages.[26]

In support of the colony, two ships were again sent by the Adventurers, the *Little James* and the *Jacob*, the latter captained by William Peirce, to fish for cod during the 1625 trading season. In addition,

They consigned to Edward Winslow and Isaac Allerton a stock of cloth, hose, shoes, leather, etc., and four black heifers which were to be sold on the account of these Adventurers at seventy percent profit. The line of dry goods was poor in quality and did not sell well. The names of three of the black heifers, which sold very readily, were Raghorn, the Smooth-horned Heifer, and the Blind Heifer. . . . And three or four jades—the first horses to arrive in New England.[27]

---

[24] Bradford OPP, 172-4.

[25] Samuel Eliot Morison, editor of Bradford's journal, interprets the Merchant Adventurers' letter in this way (in Bradford OPP, 173 (footnote 4)).

[26] Stratton, 26.

[27] Anna C. Kingsbury, *A Historical Sketch of William Collier* (Privately Printed, 1925). Edward Winslow was in London in the winter for depositions at the High Court of Admiralty, accompanied by Isaac

In 1625, the Merchant Adventurers, William Collier among them, sent a letter informing Governor Bradford that the joint account had been closed. "After your necessities are served," the letter continued, "you gather together such commodities as ye country yields and send them over to pay debts and clear engagements here, which are not less than £1400."[28] Bradford knew it would take 3,000 beaver pelts to pay off the debt entirely—which they could not pay. But he authorized the colony to trade for 500 pelts as a good faith payment. He had them loaded on the *Little James* for shipment back to London.

Bradford wrote to Robert Cushman, hoping to add some positive news: "We have rid ourselves of the company of those, who have been so troublesome unto us."[29] This referred to Reverend John Lyford and John Oldham, who were expelled from the colony. As Bradford and the colonists wished the *Little James* God's speed, they were no doubt relieved at having shipped their good faith payment of beaver pelts. But once again, disaster struck on the return trip. In the English Channel, Barbary pirates captured the *Little James*. The cargo never reached England. It was another devasting loss for Plymouth Colony and the Merchant Adventurers.

LONDON'S UNUSUAL WEATHER, A MONARCH DIES, NEW LIFE BEGINS

At the beginning of 1625, January's weather was warm and mild. On 25 February, very high tides, perhaps once in a generation, flooded and wrecked Thames Street and Westminster Hall. It was described as a "full three feet in water all over."[30] The following month, King James, plagued by severe attacks of arthritis, gout, and fainting fits, suffered a stroke. On 27 March 1625, James I died, and Charles I succeeded his father at age twenty-four. James's funeral and burial in Westminster Abbey on the 7th of May was described as "a magnificent but disorderly affair."[31]

The following day, the Collier family celebrated a joyful event: the baptism of Jane Clarke Collier's first grandchild. Alexander and Margaret Clarke Wildinge's son, John, was baptized on 8 May 1625 in St. Olave's.[32] The extended family observed the ceremony. In attendance were Alice Arnold, the great-grandmother; William and Jane, the proud grandparents; Margaret's sister, Joyce; the Colliers' daughters, Mary, Hannah, Rebecca, Sarah, and Elizabeth; and their young son, John. What a grand celebration it was for the family! The only one missing was Thomas Clarke, now in Plymouth Colony.

Allerton on business for the colony. They probably returned on the *Little James* or the *Jacob* with William Peirce.

[28] Bradford OPP, 173-4.

[29] Stratton, 26.

[30] Charles Creighton, *A History of Epidemics in Britain from A.D. 664 to the Extinction of Plague* (Cambridge: Cambridge University Press, 1891): 508-9. *Project Gutenberg*. Viewed on 15 June 2021. https://www.gutenberg.org/ebooks/42686.

[31] David Harris Willson, *King James VI & I* (London: Jonathan Cape, 1956): 447.

[32] St. Olave's Parish Registers (1583-1627)

There for almost a year, Thomas had settled in nicely by now. On 5 June 1625, Bradford wrote to Cushman that the Plymouth colonists had "peace and health and contented minds." They had sufficient corn; they brought home 700 pounds of beaver, besides some other furs, and "never felt the sweetness of the country till this year; and not only we but all planters in the land begin to do it."[33] In sharp contrast, things were about to change dramatically in London.

The early summer of 1625 was unusually cold. On the 12th of June, Lord Chamberlain wrote: "We have had for a month together the extremist cold weather ever I knew in this season." The whole month of June was a time of "ceaseless rain in London." In England's countryside, the hay harvest was spoilt, and the corn harvest was only a half crop. Another account said that "the summer sun wore sallow hair and a languishing complexion; the air was full of black mists and damp, with no dewdrops at night, just a vaporous smoke." But the unusual weather paled in comparison to what was to happen next—the arrival of the Plague of 1625. "[I]t was not until July that a plague of the first degree declared itself."[34] It had been incubating and was about to strike metropolitan London. Southwark was destined to be the plague's epicenter. With tightly packed mazes of lanes, twisting passageways, and tenements of the poorer class, the borough was ripe as a breeding and spreading ground for this pestilence. The result was horrific.

St. Olave's Parish recorded the highest number of plague deaths of any London area parish. Other Southwark parishes suffered greatly, including St. Saviour's, St. George's, and St. Mary Magdalene in adjacent Bermondsey. The poor souls who contracted the plague experienced horrifying symptoms: high fever; delirium; vomiting; painful swellings of the armpits, legs, neck, and groin; and bleeding in the lungs. Once contracted, they most often died within two to four days. For perspective, the average number of *daily* recorded burials before the plague's outbreak in St. Olave's Parish was two or three. During the plague's peak months, the recorded *daily* burials frequently reached forty and fifty—a staggering increase.[35]

Plymouth Colony had sent Myles Standish to London with letters for the Merchant Adventurers and the Virginia Company Council. "But he came in a very bad time, for the State was full of trouble and the plague very hot in London, so as no business could be done."[36]

---

[33] Bradford, *Letters*, 13.
[34] Creighton, 508-9.
[35] Robert S. Wakefield, "The Children of William Collier," *The American Genealogist*, vol. 49, no. 4 (October 1973): 215.
[36] Bradford OPP, 177.

This is an illustration from a book printed in London in 1625, which was one of the worst plague years in London's history

Thomas Dekker, *A Rod for Run-aways*. (London: unknown publisher, 1625), title page.
Public domain. (11.1)

A Table of the Christenings and Mortality in London for the year 1625.[37]

Week ending		Christened	Buried	Of Plague	Parishes Infected
Mar.	3	185	207	0	0
	10	196	210	0	0
	17	175	262	4	3
	24	187	226	8	2
	31	133	243	11	4
Apr.	7	184	239	10	4
	14	154	256	24	10
	21	160	230	25	11
	28	134	305	26	9
May	5	158	292	30	10
	12	140	332	45	13
	19	182	379	71	17
	26	145	401	78	16
June	2	123	395	69	20
	9	125	434	91	25
	16	110	510	165	31
	23	110	640	239	32
	30	125	942	390	50
July	7	114	1222	593	57
	14	115	1741	1004	82
	21	137	2850	1819	96
	28	155	3583	2471	103
Aug.	4	128	4517	3659	114
	11	125	4855	4115	112
	18	134	5205	4463	114
	25	135	4841	4218	114
Sept.	1	117	3897	3344	117
	8	112	3157	2550	116
	15	100	2148	1674	107
	22	75	1994	1551	111
	29	78	1236	852	103
Oct.	6	77	838	538	99
	13	85	815	511	91
	20	91	651	331	76
	27	77	375	134	47
Nov.	3	82	357	89	41
	10	85	319	92	35
	17	88	274	48	22
	24	88	231	27	16
Dec.	1	93	190	15	12
	8	90	181	15	7
	15	94	168	6	5

Of London deaths recorded for 54,265 souls from city-wide statistics during the period December 1624 through December 1625, two-thirds [35,417] were attributed to the plague. Of the remaining third, half were attributed to the spotted fever and the flux which were the forerunners of the plague and continued alongside it.

	Total deaths	Plague deaths
St Giles's, Cripplegate	3988	2338
St Olave's, Southwark	**3689**	**2609**
St Sepulchre's, Newgate	3425	2420
St Mary's, Whitechapel	3305	2272
St Saviour's, Southwark	2746	1671
St Botolph's, Aldgate	2573	1653
St Botolph's, Bishopsgate	2334	714
St Andrew's, Holborn	2190	1636
St Leonard's, Shoreditch	1995	1407
St George's, Southwark	1608	912
St Bride's, Fleet St.	1481	1031
St Martin's in the Fields	1470	973
St Giles's in the Fields	1333	947
St Clement's Danes	1284	755
St James's, Clerkenwell	1191	903
St Magdalen's, Bermondsey	1127	889
St Katharine's, Tower	998	744
St Dunstan's in the West	860	642
97 parishes within the walls	14342	9197

---

37 Creighton, 508-509.

COLLIER FAMILY AND THE PLAGUE OF 1625

The Collier family was not spared in the Plague of 1625. The Colliers' grandson, John, died within a week of his birth and was buried about the 15th of May. William and Jane's young daughter Martha, aged one year and two months, died and was also buried about the same time, in mid-May. Two months later, Jane's eldest daughter, Margaret Clarke Wildinge, died before her twentieth birthday, and was buried on the 24th of July. Her husband, Alexander, lost his wife and only child within two months. Three weeks later, William and Jane lost another child, their son William; buried on the 12th of August. And finally, their daughter Hannah, two months shy of her twelfth birthday, died and was buried on 31 August.[38] It is hard to imagine the pain Jane and William Collier felt. Within fourteen weeks, five family members died: their first grandchild, John; a young daughter, Martha; Jane's eldest child, Margaret; another young child, William: and a budding lass, Hannah. Five deaths in such a short period must have been devastating for Jane, her mother Alice, her husband William, and their surviving children. Collier's former apprentice, William Langham, informed Collier that he lost his wife, Christian. While grieving, Langham felt fortunate that the plague did not take his apprentice. Zachary Cole survived one of the worst plagues the greater London area ever experienced.

Despite grieving their losses, William and Jane praised God for sparing their surviving children. But William also bowed the knee and thanked God fervently that both his wife and her mother, Alice, were spared. This plague was the fourth during which God protected Jane and Alice: 1593, 1603, 1610, and now 1625. William must have wondered why, in each successive wave of plague, his family members were spared. And now, once again, Jane felt the signs of life within her. Even though she had become a grandmother for a few short months, she was to have another child—probably the next spring.

What must have been the responses to their trials and tribulations faced by the Colliers at this time? From the magnitude of the tragic losses of so many loved ones, to the emotional pain Jane and William Collier suffered, their resiliency and perseverance are remarkable.

As a young child, Jane experienced the loss of nearly her entire family. She later lost her fourth child and first husband in short order. After her second marriage to William, they were greatly blessed with children and a prosperous business in their first decade together. After their investment in Plymouth Colony, they witnessed the tragic deaths of one grandchild and five children. How Jane and William Collier held themselves and their surviving family together is a testament to their character. With strong faith, they surely would have found solace and comfort in these Biblical texts: "The Lord hath given and the Lord hath taken it; blessed be the Name of the Lord;" and "Precious in the sight of the Lord is the death of his Saints."[39]

Six months after the family's devasting losses, the Collier family welcomed the birth of another daughter. Her baptism was recorded in St. Olave's Parish: Lidia, daughter of William Collier, Grocer baptized on 8 March 1626. Unfortunately, the infant died and

---

[38] St. Olave's Parish Registers (1583-1627)
[39] Job 1:21, Psalm 116:15 (Geneva Bible 1599)

was buried just three days later—on 11 March 1626.[40] What another sad occasion this was for the entire family! Within eight months, the family experienced yet another sad passing, their seventh death. And yet, the Grim Reaper was not yet finished with them.

ALICE ARNOLD SETS HER AFFAIRS IN ORDER

At about this time, Alice Yates Arnold knew instinctively her time was short until she would be called home to meet her Lord. She had worked on her will even before her granddaughter, Margaret, died last year. Since her second husband's death six years before, she thought, "So much has transpired! I do want to be buried next to John in St. Olave's burial ground." It was an easy decision for Alice to make. Her first husband, Henry Yates, was buried in an unmarked grave in the remote New Churchyard burial ground filled during the awful Plague of 1593.

Those painful memories resurfaced with sadness at how much of her family had been wiped out in a matter of weeks. Two months after her husband, Henry, had died, she was blessed with the birth of her daughter, Margaret. But Margaret only lived ten years until the Plague of 1603 took her. Fortunately, her daughter Jane survived both plagues and married Thomas Clarke. Jane's husband shared the same profession as did her first and second husbands. All three were successful and prosperous members of the Worshipful Company of Dyers.

As Alice finalized her will, she designated her daughter, Jane, as her sole executrix, with her husband, William, nominated if Jane was deceased. Alice anticipated her granddaughter Joyce, 17, might marry soon. Alice bequeathed £20 to Joyce and set aside some jewelry and household items "to be delivered to her when she reaches the age of 21 years or on the day of her marriage, whichever shall first happen, as long as she marries with her mother's consent." She also provided for her unmarried Collier granddaughters' future with proceeds from tenants' leases she controlled from St. Mary Magdalene College in Oxford. Alice placed her son-in-law, William, in charge of the tenants' receipts for fifteen years on behalf of her four Collier grandchildren. These tenants were situated in Bermondsey Street. Alice also declared a bequest to her grandson, Thomas Clarke: an inheritance of £10 "when he reaches the age of 21 years, if he can behave himself and take good courses whereby to live." Since Thomas was in Plymouth, her concerns are understandable considering what she had heard about the troubled state of the colony from her son-in-law. Alice also mentioned her widowed grandson-in-law, Alexander Wildinge [sic], as her tenant who owed £10—probably his annual lease—a full year after his wife, Margaret, died. To ensure that her extensive will of six pages was followed without question, she signed all six pages at the bottom of each one. For a woman born in the early 1560s, her ability to read and write must have come from either her parents or a tutor, not unheard of but somewhat rare.

---

40 St. Olave's Parish Registers (1583-1627)

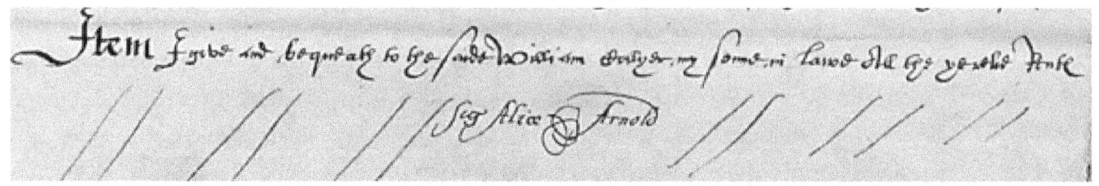

Signature of Alice Arnold. Reproduced with kind permission of the Diocese of Winchester.[41]
Sponsored by Scott L. Semans. (11.2)

After Jane's mother, Alice Arnold, passed, she was laid to rest in St. Olave's burial ground on 29 March 1626.[42] As the family observed Alice's body being lowered into the ground next to her husband, they celebrated her life. Unlike the many burials they attended in the past few months, Alice Arnold's life had been fully lived. She was probably in her mid-to-late sixties. On 8 April 1626, William and Jane gathered with two of her friends and overseers to review her will and bequests and to execute Alice's wishes.[xii]

One month later, William Collier's former apprentice William Langham, a freeman grocer and apprentice master of Zachary Cole, married Elizabeth Tence on 1 May 1626.[43] His first wife, Christian, died during the plague. Unfortunately, the plague lingered on, particularly in the English countryside outside of London. Weedon Bec was not spared.

PLAGUE STRIKES WEEDON BEC

The horrific Plague of 1625 that decimated so many Southwark families spread outward from London and lingered into 1626. It was not as ravaging for them as villagers heard it was in London, but nevertheless, it did strike down some well-respected residents. For one family, it was particularly sad. Their patriarch, John Cole, son of Thomas, grandson of John, great-grandson of William, was quickly taken by the plague—most likely in May. The town set aside a remote burial site for plague victims, which explains why his burial was not recorded. John Cole became the first known member of the Weedon Bec Cole family not buried in the parish churchyard. He was in his fifties.

John's wife, Frances Cole, would inherit the right to half their messuage and would live out her remaining years with her eldest son, Nathaniel, his wife Anne, and their children living in the other half of the messuage. A few months later, John's widow, Frances, after more than thirty years of marriage, arrived at *Le Townhouse* for a Weedon Bec Manor Court meeting on 18 November 1626. She petitioned the court to seek entry to her deceased husband's property. She testified, "I am the wife of John Cole. I seek to be admitted to a moiety of the aforesaid premises for the term of my life according to the custom of the

---

41 London Metropolitan Archives, Guildhall Library Manuscripts Section, Clerkenwell, London, England; Reference Number: DW/PA/5/1626; Will Number: 4. Testator Surname: *Arnold* – full name is Alice Arnold. In this image, the will Item references William Collier as her son-in-law.

42 Cole, "Jane Clarke," 57.

43 St. Mary Magdalene, Bermondsey, Parish Registers (1603-1642)

manor."[44] The lords' steward granted her "seisin by the rod." She gave them a "fine and did fealty and was thereupon admitted as tenant." The overseers of the court as Homage this day were John Cole, the son of Henry, John Billing, Martin Billing, Thomas Cleavely, John Cleavely, and Frances' son, Nathaniel Cole. Nathaniel, as John and Frances Cole's son and heir, presented a similar request after his mother, after which he was also admitted as tenant.[xiii] As had occurred in this family before, their tenant property formally passed from one generation to the next.

John Cole, his widow Frances seeks entry to his lands, 1626. Weedon Bec Manor Court.
Reproduced with kind permission of Eton College Archives, image 14.
Sponsored by Scott L. Semans. (11.3)

With his father gone, Job Cole, age eighteen, realized this was the time to pursue an apprenticeship. His brother Zachary's words relating his conversation with Master William Collier kept ringing in his ears. When Zachary received word of his father's passing and learned there would be no burial in the parish churchyard, he decided not to return home. But he did send word that he would speak to his master, William Langham, about a potential apprenticeship for Job with Collier.

---

[44] Weedon Bec Manor Court, 1626. Full citation and translation in endnotes.

Even though Frances Cole hated to see her son Job leave the village, she knew it was best for him. Happy that he would be near Zachary, she still had three sons close by: Nathaniel, John, and Daniel. After the family shared a final meal together before Job left, they grieved the loss of their patriarch, enjoyed the warmth and comfort of being together, and prayed for his travel and his future in London. Then Job left with the gift of a horse, waving goodbye, just as Zachary had done nearly five years earlier. It was the latter part of May.

William Collier Gains an Apprentice

After his mother-in-law's will was probated in April, William felt more confident in his financial situation and prospects. Even though the last few years had not yielded profits for him and the other Merchant Adventurers, his grocer's business had kept the family in a prosperous state. With the series of setbacks in Plymouth Colony, William could see his fellow investors' interest waning.

When William Langham, his former apprentice, mentioned that his apprentice's brother was anxious to learn a trade, Collier was receptive to be his master. With that referral, Job Cole started his training as William Collier's apprentice on 1 June 1626. The Guildhall recorded it: "Job Cole apprentice to William Collier for 8 years from 1st day of June last presented the same day."[45]

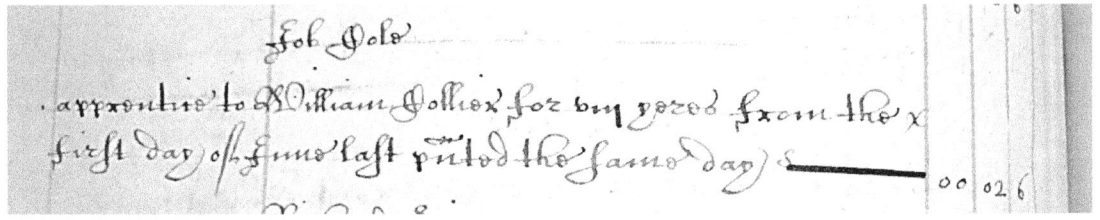

Job Cole, apprentice, 1626. Reproduced with kind permission of the Grocers' Company of London. Sponsored by Abacus Plumbing, Air Conditioning & Electrical of Houston, Texas. (11.4)

As he worked with his new apprentice, Master Collier first saw the family resemblance between Job and his brother, Zachary, whom he had met nearly five years earlier. Collier hoped that Job, at age eighteen; would be as beneficial for him as Zachary had been for William Langham. As Job settled into a room with the Collier family, he thought about how much he liked his master and his family. His master's wife Jane was intelligent and self-assured. Job thought, "She is very much like my mother, but younger." His master's daughters were slightly younger than he was: Mary, 14; Hannah, 12; Rebecca, 11; Sarah, 10; and Elizabeth, 7. Never having had younger sisters, Job thought, "This will be quite interesting, a new experience, and a real change." But he looked forward to learning the grocer's trade. And his master had many corresponding thoughts. "Job is an impressive young man. He could be quite successful. One day, he might be quite a catch for a young maiden."

---

[45] Grocers' Guild, Wardens' Accounts, 1622-1631. MS11571/11, Folio 181. Guildhall Library, London.

ANOTHER MARRIAGE IN THE FAMILY

Later in the year, the Collier family celebrated another daughter's marriage. Most likely because of the plague, as had happened with her parents in 1603, Joyce Clarke, Jane's daughter, and her betrothed, John Walker, applied for a license to marry outside their home parish of St. Olave's. The bishop granted their request.

Joyce Clarke marriage record, 1626-7. Reproduced with kind permission of the Society of Genealogists, London, England. Sponsored by Ronald E. Benson. (11.5)

"1626 John Walker of St. Olave's in Southwarke [sic] and Joyce Clarke of same parish were married the (blank) of (blank) 1626 by lyc [licence] from my Lord Grace of Canterbury."[46] The transcription indicates they were both from St Olave's and married in St. Peter Westcheap Parish. Licences issued by "my Lord Grace of Canterbury" refer to the Archbishop of Canterbury. Joyce Clarke was eighteen when she married—sometime between 8 November 1626 and 18 March 1627. Certainly, the Collier family would have attended the ceremony. It's also likely their new apprentice, Job Cole, attended, perhaps with his brother Zachary.

In England, the times were unsettled. The transition from King James I to his son, Charles I, was anything but smooth. A few months before Joyce Clarke's marriage, in June 1626—the same month Job Cole became William Collier's apprentice—Charles I dissolved Parliament.

"What does the future hold for England?" That question was on the minds of all subjects of the Crown. That was certainly true for the newlyweds. And it was true for merchants including William Collier, and two Cole brothers, Zachary and Job, both apprentices in the same profession as Collier, who would likely become Citizen Grocers in a few years.

---

[46] Transcript of the registers of St Matthew Friday Street and St Peter's Westcheap made by W Challen in Society of Genealogists *London Marriages vol 3* SoG ref MX/R325.

CHAPTER 12

PUSHES, PULLS, AND FINAL STRAWS LEAD TO AMERICA'S PROMISES

Almost immediately upon his accession to the throne, Charles I's policies provoked repeated clashes with members of Parliament. Very quickly his role in the Church of England became a prominent issue. Soon after he became king, in June 1625 Charles married the Catholic princess Henrietta Maria of France, apparently reneging on a promise he had made to Parliament. Adding to suspicions that he harbored pro-Catholic leanings, he continued his father's policy of toleration toward English Catholics. These concerns were heightened when it became clear he supported "High Church" policies and practices which emphasized the formality, rituals, and vestiges reminiscent of Catholic liturgy.

Charles I (Prince of Wales) 1623, Daniël Mijtens. Wikimedia Commons. Public domain. (12.1)

King Charles' efforts to establish conformity within the Church of England, with no tolerance of variations, took a tougher turn in 1626. Following the death of Lancelot Andrewes,[1] the Bishop of Winchester and Dean of the Chapel Royal, Charles cast about for promising church leaders who would carry out his policies. William Laud, then Bishop of Bath and Wells, was identified as one such like-minded clergyman. Appointed to succeed Andrewes as Chapel Dean in September of that year, he "rapidly ascended to a position of influence."[2]

As Charles I steadily applied more pressure to ecclesiastical authorities, Laud likewise gained in visibility and influence. He would soon be appointed Bishop of London, and ultimately rise to become Archbishop of Canterbury, the effective leader of the Church of England.

A second major issue in Charles' attempts to exert his own sovereignty concerned foreign diplomatic tensions that brought England ever closer to war with Spain and France. As conflicts intensified between the king and Parliament over his interference with long-standing agreements under his father's reign, Charles imposed taxes (impositions) without Parliament's approval, in large part to fund his looming potential war expeditions. But even worse were his policies toward merchants and trade. He took away lucrative

---

[1]   We have met Andrewes before. His palace as bishop was in Southwark. See above, chapter 9.

[2]   S. M. Towers, *Control of Religious Printing in Early Stuart England* (Suffolk: Boydell Press, 2003): 190.

commissions and charters and granted favors to his favorites. Many merchants' profitable trading and customs enterprises were eliminated or disrupted.

> Charles I definitively disrupted the great merchants' plans for the Americas when he refused to renew the commission for Virginia that his father had authorized. In May 1625, Charles put Virginia under royal control and set up a new Crown-appointed council for governing the colony instead of reviving the company.[3]

Relations between the Crown and Parliament were shattered. On 24 May 1626, the House of Commons declared all impositions not approved by Parliament unjustified and illegitimate. The king responded in the second half of 1626 with the imposition of what he called the "Forced Loan." This new levy on all taxpayers provoked intense hostility. Many merchants and shopkeepers simply refused to pay it, despite the

William Laud. Wikimedia Commons. Public domain. (12.2)

threat of imprisonment for their refusal. In typical English fashion, the Forced Loan yielded a new tongue-in-cheek phrase. Citizens began calling the Guildhall "the Yield All."[4]

This new tax certainly affected William Collier and his fellow Merchant Adventurers who had invested in Plymouth Colony. But its reach was much broader and affected almost any trader or merchant involved with the Americas as well. Those affected included:

> Thomas Stone, who was already a leading partner of Maurice Thomson's in Virginia and the West Indies; Stone's partner and cousin Andrew Stone; the cheese mongers Thomas Deacon and William Harris, later partners of Thomson's in the purchase of Berkeley Hundred in Virginia, as well as in many other ventures; Thomas Andrews, a Plymouth and Massachusetts Company backer, a New England trader, and later a partner of Thomson's in the West Indies and East Indies; and Joshua Foote, William Hitchcock, and John Pocock, all of whom were . . . major traders with New England.[5]

The looming prospects of war and disturbance to trade and shipping, combined with the political battles, created chaos for merchants and traders. However, "disruption of trade and destruction of goods and shipping . . . probably caused more damage to the merchants than did any other government policy."[6] These all directly impacted Collier's grocer's business.

---

[3]   Robert Brenner, *Merchants and Revolution: Commercial Change, Political Conflict, and London's Overseas Traders, 1550-1653* (London: Verso 2003): 223.

[4]   Brenner, 226.

[5]   Brenner, 226-7.

[6]   Brenner, 223.

MERCHANT ADVENTURERS RENEGOTIATE THEIR AGREEMENT WITH PLYMOUTH COLONY

In 1626, Plymouth's Governor William Bradford sent Old Comer Isaac Allerton as the colony's agent to renegotiate an agreement with the Merchant Adventurers in London. At a meeting held on 26 October and documented in a letter dated 15 November 1626, the Adventurers agreed to extend their commitment to the colony:

> To all Christian people, greetings, etc. At a meeting of the Merchant Adventurers on 26 October 1626, the Adventurers to New Plymouth in New England, were contented and agreed, in consideration of the sum of one thousand and eight hundred pounds sterling to be paid (in the manner and form following).[7]

By this agreement, the original investors' capital owed from before was written off by the investors. Since the Merchant Adventurers had already invested some £7000, this was offered at a considerable loss. They proposed the debt owed by the colonists would now be £1800. It was to be repaid in nine installments of £200 a year for nine years on the feast of St. Michael every September beginning in 1628. Five investors, John Pocock, John Beauchamp, Robert Keane, Edward Bass, and James Sherley would assume the debt liability. Isaac Allerton would continue acting as agent between the colonists and the Merchant Adventurers.

Given the tragic deaths experienced by the Collier family, King Charles' policies, and the trade disruptions, what happened next is either extraordinary, under a complex set of circumstances, or predictable when taking into account William Collier's character. He may have considered it a path to create a more promising future for his family. As one of the forty-two Adventurers who signed the letter detailing the new agreement, William had made a major commitment to Plymouth Colony. He subscribed, along with forty-one others in London and certain of the colonists themselves, to provide special aid as Purchasers, with the aim of helping to alleviate the increasing indebtedness of the colony.[8] Of William Collier it was said, "He had so generous a spirit, as not to be content with making profit by the enterprise of the pilgrims, unless he shared the hardships."[9]

With his increased commitment to Plymouth, Collier examined his business options and opportunities. His apprentice, Job Cole, was a diligent worker and learning his trade at a good pace. As Job's confidence grew daily, Collier felt the time was right for him to take on more responsibilities. That would free William to pursue other opportunities. After making inquiries, he was introduced to another Southwark freeman and merchant, a clothworker named James Monger who was seeking partners in an enterprise he wanted to expand.

To participate in this new venture, William Collier again moved his family. For the fourth time in fifteen years of marriage, William and Jane changed parishes. They moved

---

[7] Bradford OPP, 184.
[8] Stratton, 27-32.
[9] Lamont R. Healy, *Duxbury's Pilgrims and Their Land* (Duxbury MA: Duxbury Free Library, 2016): 38.

not far away from St. Olave's on the east side of London Bridge, to St. Saviour's Parish just west of London Bridge. William wanted to get settled into their new home. Jane was expecting another child.

In mid-summer 1627, Jane Collier at age forty bore her last child, a daughter. Ruth was baptized at St. Saviour's on 5 August 1627.[10] Jane and her husband, William, plus their remaining four daughters attended the christening, as did Job Cole.

The massive St. Saviour's Church, the second largest in all of London after St. Paul's, was a most impressive sight for the Collier children and Job Cole. William recalled the time he had visited the church with his stepson, Thomas Clarke, after they met with his former master, William Russell. "My goodness," William thought, "that was just after the original Globe Theatre burnt to the ground in 1613, fourteen years ago. So much has happened since then!" In the parish register's entry of Ruth's christening, William is identified as a brewer, not a grocer.

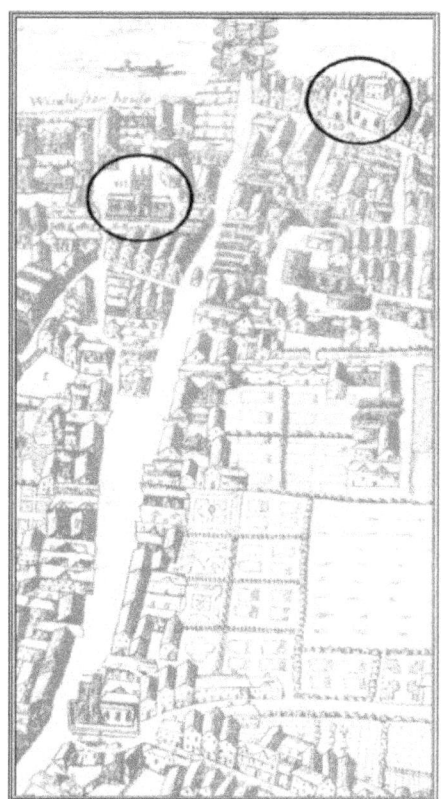

St. Saviour's and St. Olave's Churches.
Courtesy of Tony Sharp. (12.3)

WILLIAM COLLIER'S BREWHOUSE PARTNERSHIP

Within a few months of relocating to St. Saviour's Parish, the Minutes of the Brewers Company dated 3 March 1627/8 note that "William Collier of Southwark Grocer upon giving his bill to pay five pounds for a fine is this day admitted and sworn a free brother of this company." A second listing records him as "William Collier in Southwark partner with Mr. Monger," while another lists his partner as "James Monger in Southwark a clothworker."[11] There was no requirement that Collier obtain an additional guild membership in the Brewer's Company in order to partner in the brewhouse. That may account for the term "free brother" rather than "freeman." Though now a tavern proprietor, Collier continued paying his Grocer's Guildhall dues.

---

10 London Metropolitan Archives, St. Saviour's, Southwark. Composite Register 1609-1653, P92/SAV/3002. Ancestry.com. William E. Cole "English Origins of Job, John, Daniel, and Ruth Cole." *Mayflower Descendant*, Vol. 69, No. 1 Winter 2021, 38. Available at https://www.passionategenealogist.org.

11 Hunt, *TAG*, 42:120-21. [MS5445/15 and 5445/14] Author's note: in our research we were unable to verify this citation in the Minutes of the Court of the Brewers' Company at Guildhall, London. Also cited by Susan E. Roser. *Early Descendants of Daniel Cole of Eastham, Massachusetts* (Markham, Ontario: Stewart Publishing, 2010): 6.

A major attraction of this venture for Collier was its location. Leased to James Monger in 1620 by Sir John Bodley, the brewhouse was located on the property owned by Sir Matthew Bend. "The passage which led to the Globe Tavern, of which the playhouse formed a part, was . . . known by the name of Globe Alley."[12]

Yes, theatregoers attending the Globe Theatre passed right by the Globe Tavern. "It was called the Globe from its sign, which was a figure of Hercules, or Atlas, supporting a globe, under which was written, '*Totus mundus agit histrionem*' [All the world acts a play]."[13] As in real estate, the brewhouse's success was most likely based on three factors: location, location, location![xiv]

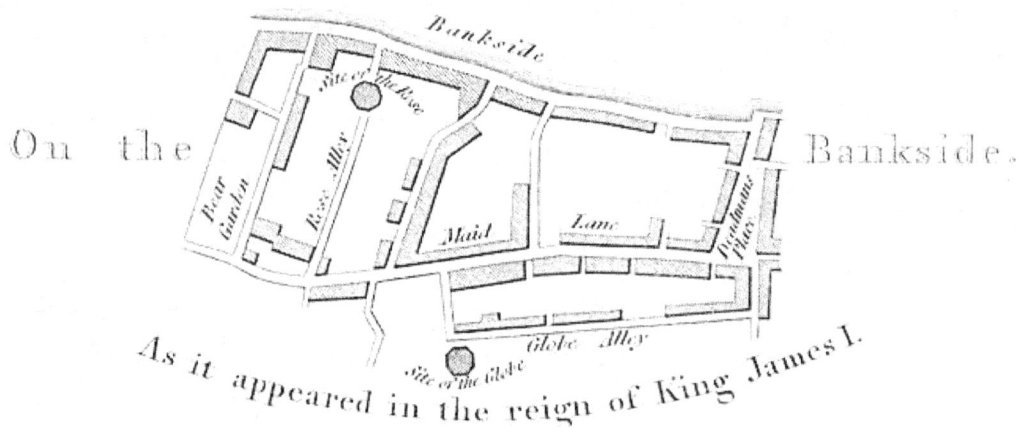

Site of the Globe Theatre and Tavern. Public domain. (12.4)

NEW AGREEMENT WITH PLYMOUTH COLONY

When Isaac Allerton returned to Plymouth with the new agreement signed by the Merchant Adventurers in hand, Governor Bradford was pleased.

> This agreement was well liked of and approved by all the Plantation, and consented unto, though they knew not well how to raise the payment and discharge their other engagements and supply the yearly wants of the Plantation, seeing they were forced for their necessities to take up money or goods at so high interests. Yet they undertook it, and seven or eight of

---

[12] Southwark: St. Saviour's Church. *British History Online*. Viewed on 17 September 2017. https://www.british-history.ac.uk/old-new-london/vol6/pp16-29.

[13] "Southwark: Bankside," *British History Online*. Viewed on 17 September 2017. https://www.british-history.ac.uk/old-new-london/vol6/pp45-47.

the chief of the place became jointly bound for the payment of this £1800 in the behalf of the rest.[14]

Though the colonists were grateful for the revision of their debt, questions remained as to how this could be paid. Their deliberations led to the Plymouth Division of Cattle, ratified on 22 May 1627. Governor Bradford recorded: "The heads of families, or single young men, that were of ability and free (and able to govern themselves with meet discretion, and their affairs, so as to be helpful in the commonwealth) into this partnership or purchase . . . This distribution gave generally good content and settled men's minds."[15] Four Merchant Adventurers retained their interest in the affairs of Plymouth Colony: James Sherley, Richard Andrews, Timothy Hatherley, and John Beauchamp. They were later known as the English Partners of the Purchasers. In return, the investors in London gave up all claims to all "the said stocks, shares, lands, marchandise and chatles" in Plymouth.

In July 1627, a small group of colonists, known as Undertakers, formed. The group included William Bradford, Captain Myles Standish, Isaac Allerton, Edward Winslow, William Brewster, John Howland, John Alden, and Thomas Prence. They agreed to undertake and pay the required sums in London. In the event of a default, they would become personally liable. In return, they would receive the profits from the beaver fur trade for six years for the whole colony, as well as profits from corn and tobacco. The agreement would be reassessed by the whole colony after 1633.[16]

Isaac Allerton, as agent of the colony, then returned to England with a signed copy of the agreement. He was authorized to deal with "some of their special friends to join with them in this trade."[17] James Sherley, goldsmith, and John Beauchamp, salter, were named as agents of the Plymouth Colony to receive all goods and merchandise sent to England, and to sell or barter their wares. These agents were also to purchase supplies for New England. If necessary, additional loans would come at high interest rates from Beauchamp, Sherley, Pocock, and others. In addition to his Plymouth Colony interests, Allerton arranged to invest £400 in William Collier's brewhouse partnership, at first under the James Sherley's name. This appears to be when the brewhouse obtained eight other tenant properties on Globe Alley for its brewery operations.[18]

Since Collier had not forfeited his Plymouth shares with the other investors, he may have retained the right for a land allocation if he later chose to emigrate to Plymouth.[19]

---

[14] Bradford OPP, 186.

[15] Bradford OPP, 186-8.

[16] Bradford OPP, 195-6.

[17] Bradford OPP, 196.

[18] "Chapter 9: The Anchor Brewery," *British History Online*. Viewed on 15 July 2019. https://www.british-history-ac.uk/survey-london/vol22/pp78-80. Originally published as Sir Howard Roberts and Walter H. Godfrey (ed.s), *Survey of London: Volume 22, Bankside (The Parishes of St. Saviour and Christchurch Southwark)* (London: London County Council, 1950).

[19] This scenario may explain why Collier chose later to emigrate to America. It's plausible but not proven.

On 17 November 1628, James Sherley wrote to Bradford of his willingness "to forebear my former £50 and two years' increase for the venture." He added that he had "persuaded Mr. Andrews and Mr. Beauchamp to do the like." This gesture greatly reduced the interest rate burden the colony experienced for loans at thirty to fifty to even seventy percent. Sherley attached a formal agreement with Plymouth dated the following day. It authorized him and John Beauchamp to act as "true and lawful agents" and to receive "goods, wares, and merchandise." The agreement was confirmed in Plymouth. Allerton retained authority to act on behalf of the colony. He also brought a patent for Kennebec to establish a trading house from the Council of New England paid for by James Sherley for £40.[20]

As King Charles continued to place increasing financial burdens and impose unfavorable treatment on London merchants, a new organization formed to support another colony in New England. New Plymouth would soon have a neighboring colony.

> The first major steps in constructing the alliance between colonizing lords, new-merchant leaders and Puritan ministers, most especially those associated with religious Independency, seem to have been take in the course of setting up the Massachusetts Bay Company in connection with the organization of the more general movement of religio-political opposition to the Crown at the end of the 1620s. Here, the Puritan lords showed their willingness to patronize a militantly Puritan project that they could influence but not effectively control. On 9 March 1628, the Earl of Warwick made a grant of land in Massachusetts that established the New England Company, the unincorporated predecessor of the Massachusetts Bay Company.[21]

WILLIAM LAUD APPOINTED BISHOP OF LONDON

In July 1628, the appointment of William Laud as Bishop of London increased the pressure on nonconformist clergymen, including any who were Puritan-leaning. One such individual was Puritan minister John Lathrop. Lathrop had denounced his ordination with the Church of England in 1623 and joined the Southwark Independent Church. Its church roots extended back at least to the early 1590s during Elizabeth I's reign, when Roger Rippon hosted gatherings at his house. In Puritan circles, the congregation was well-known. Anyone in London associated with the Leiden Separatists, Plymouth Colony, or the Merchant Adventurers, including William Collier, would have known of this church and may have attended at times.[22] Members were either Independents or non-separating Congregationalists. This church was one of six like it currently operating in London. Having been without a permanent pastor since Henry Jacob's resignation in 1619, the Southwark Independent Church called John Lathrop as its new minister in 1624. Four years later in July 1628, when Laud became London's bishop of London, he instructed his watchmen to keep close tabs on this group.

---

[20] Bradford OPP, 197-202.
[21] Brenner, 276.
[22] Taylor, *The Mayflower in Britain,* lists William Collier as "probably a Brownist church member:" 105.

Zacheus Cole Completes His Apprenticeship

On 22 October 1628, Zachary Cole completed his eight-year apprenticeship with Master William Langham one year early. This event is recorded in the Grocers' Company Guildhall records: "Zacheus Cole, Freeman, late apprentice to William Langham entered and sworn the same day [22 October 1628]. Paid 3s 4d."[23]

Zacheus Cole, Freeman, 1628. Reproduced with kind permission of Grocers' Company of London. Sponsored by the American Society of Genealogists. (12.5)

Maybe the disruptive economic climate created by the Crown's policies influenced Master Langham to accelerate his apprentice's completion. The Guildhall also changed its policy at one point to standardize apprenticeships at seven years, so that could have been the reason. Whatever the cause, Zachary's apprenticeship was completed early, and he became a freeman when he was in his mid-twenties. Effectively, he had achieved the same status as William Collier, Grocer, in October 1628 but without the same level of experience.

At that time, William Collier had apprenticed Zachary's brother Job for nearly two and a half years. Zachary's master, William Langham, had also been Collier's apprentice. Job Cole had more than five years remaining to fulfill his apprenticeship obligation. Given Collier's recent interest and investment in the brewhouse, he may have enlisted Zachary to work closely with him in his grocer's business. Or perhaps Collier had worked out an arrangement with William Langham to merge their enterprise interests and activities. With that move, Collier may well have become a business mentor for Zachary. Collier might have helped him to get started, employed him, or even partnered with him formally or informally as a mentor. Whatever the case, one thing is certain: Zachary Cole and William Collier had a close working relationship—so much so that Zachary would later call Collier "my loving friend."

It is possible, perhaps even likely, that these four men—Collier, with seventeen years of grocer's experience; Langham, with eight years on his own as a grocer and five years as Collier's apprentice; Zachary Cole, with seven years apprentice experience with Langham and just starting out as a freeman grocer; and Job Cole, Zachary's brother, with two and

---

[23] Grocers' Guild, Wardens' Accounts, 1622-1631. MS11571/11 Folio 270. Guildhall Library, London.

a half years as Collier's grocer apprentice—may have merged their efforts together into a single or aligned enterprise. Such an organization may well have been a superb way for Collier to focus on his brewhouse partnership with James Monger and still maintain his grocer's business interests.[24]

Collier's residence was located at the intersection of Globe Alley and Deadman's Place. Just west of Southwark's St. Saviour's, his residence was almost adjacent to the brewhouse. In the 1628 tax rolls, a Collier is found in Clink Liberty. His forename is missing, but it is most likely William, given its proximity to St. Saviour's and the brewery. He was assessed at £4 in goods and 10s 8d in value. Also living in St. Saviour's is William Langham, Citizen Grocer. His land is taxed at £1 with 4s in value. Timothy Hatherley, Collier's fellow Merchant Adventurer and friend, is found in St. Olave's. His goods are listed at £3 in goods and valued at 8s.[25] Joseph Collier, also a grocer in St. Saviour's, is taxed the same as (blank, probably William) Collier at £4 in goods and 10s 8d in value. This Collier's daughter, named Mary (but a different one from William and Jane Collier's eldest daughter), later married Malachi Browning and emigrated to Massachusetts.[26] Both William Langham and William Collier also appear in the St. Saviour's Token Books.

COLE FAMILY WEEDON BEC MANOR COURT PRESENTMENT BEQUESTS

In 1629, Zachary and Job Cole were summoned by their mother, Frances, and brother, Nathaniel, to appear in Weedon Bec. Although they were living in Southwark, settling the family estate after their father's death was a priority. Job must have received permission from William Collier to travel for the court appearance and be away from his apprenticeship work.

Held at *Le Townhouse* as was its custom, the Weedon Bec Manor Court met on its normal schedule. Nathaniel Cole, his mother Frances, and two of his brothers, Zachary and Job, appeared "in their own persons" and as "attorney for their brothers, John and Daniel." This hearing added further rights and privileges of inheritance for the younger brothers of Nathaniel. These guarantees were not included in the previous manor court held in 1626. One detail, that Zachary had not yet attained age twenty-four, is the only known documentation to calculate his birth year.

---

[24] While not proven, no facts disprove this analysis. It is a plausible explanation for how William Collier might have balanced his thriving grocer's enterprise and partnership in a brewhouse which quickly expanded into a brewery as well as his Merchant Adventurer interest in Plymouth Colony. Collier maintained his annual dues in the Grocer's Guild through at least 1631.

[25] E179/186/432 Southwark Lay Subsidy Tax Rolls, 1628.

[26] No connection between these two Collier families has been found at this point. However, it is a possible connection that should be proved or disproved.

Nathaniel Cole, his mother, Frances, and brothers' inheritance rights, 1629.
With kind permission of Eton College Archives, image 9. Sponsored by Scott L. Semans. (12.6)

And that Nathaniel Cole since the last court, namely on the 18th day of November in the second year of the reign of our lord Charles, by the grace of God of England, etc, surrendered into the hands of the lords by the hands of Robert Smith and John Billing, two customary tenants of the aforesaid manor, a moiety of one messuage, lying in Upper Weedon, and a moiety of three virgates of arable land, lying in the common fields of Weedon Beck, aforesaid, and all closes, meadows, pastures, commons and common of pasture pertaining to the same moiety of the messuage, and now in the occupation of the aforesaid Nathaniel Cole and Frances Cole, his mother.

To the use and behoof of Zachary Cole, Job Cole, John Cole and Daniel Cole, brothers of the aforesaid Nathaniel and their heirs forever to be equally divided. But with this condition, that the aforesaid Nathaniel Cole, his heirs, executors, administrators or assigns pay or cause to be paid to the aforesaid Zachary Cole the sum of £50 of good and lawful money of England, when he shall reach his age of 24 years; and to the aforesaid Job Cole the sum of £50 of lawful money of England, when he shall reach his age of 24 years; and to the aforesaid John Cole the sum of £50 of lawful money of England, when he shall reach his age of 24 years; and to the aforesaid Daniel Cole the sum of £60 of lawful money of England, when he reaches his age of 24 years.

And further that, if the above-said Zachary, Job and John or any one of them happen to die before they reach the aforesaid several ages of 24 years, the aforesaid Daniel then being alive and in full life, that then the first portion of them so dying is to remain to the aforesaid Daniel. But if the more than one of them happen to die before their several ages of 24 years, then their portion or portions of them so dying are to be equally divided, both to the above-said Nathaniel and also to the rest of them then surviving, then this surrender is to be void and no force.

Moreover, if the aforesaid Nathaniel, his heirs, executors or administrators make default in the payment of any of the aforesaid several sums of money on the several days and times and in the manner and form, above-mentioned, that then this surrender will remain in full power and virtue. And at this court there came the aforesaid Zachary Cole and Job Cole in their own proper persons, and the aforesaid John and Daniel by the aforesaid Zachary and Job as their attorneys, and they seek of the lords to be admitted to the premises as tenants according to the tenor and effect of the aforesaid surrender. To whom the lords by the aforesaid steward granted seisin by the rod.

To have and to hold to the aforesaid Zachary, Job, John and Daniel and their heirs at the will of the lords according to the custom of the aforesaid manor by the rents and other customs and services thereupon previously due and lawfully accustomed. They give to the lords as a fine £7 10s, of which 50s is paid in the present and the other pounds to be paid when it happens to be absolute. And they are admitted as tenants in the aforesaid manner and form.[27]

CLASHES INCREASE BETWEEN KING CHARLES AND PARLIAMENT

This same year, 1629, "the Personal Rule" of Charles I began—what later was labeled the Eleven Years' Tyranny. By the third year of his reign, Charles had already dissolved three Parliaments. Parliament members began to criticize the king more harshly than before. Charles realized that, if he could avoid war, he could rule without Parliament. Bishop Laud, an effective parliamentarian and a key royal adviser, became a policymaker for King Charles.[28] Distrustful of bargaining with Parliament, Laud resisted any encroachment on the king's ability to tax his subjects. Once again, Church and State were at the forefront of political, economic, and religious struggles. Laud recommended ambitious policy objectives to King Charles, disregarded special interests, and set up the ongoing conflict that would eventually lead to civil war in a little more than a decade.

These policies placed ongoing pressure and demands on London's merchants. James Sherley, in a letter this same year to Governor Bradford in Plymouth, apprised him of the status and continued support of several Merchant Adventurers, including William Collier.

Now Mr. Andrews, Mr. Beauchamp, and myself, are with your love and liking, joined partners with you ; the like is Mr. Collier, Mr. Thomas and Mr. Hatherly, but they no doubt will write unto you ; but Mr. Andrews, and Mr. Beauchamp rely wholly on me ; they are such as Mr. Hatherly could take up, for whose care and pains you and we, are much beholden unto him.[29]

Some London merchants occasionally were able to escape the city's pressures with residences in the countryside or other towns—including James Sherley. In addition to his

---

[27] Eton College Archives, Weedon Bec, Court Baron 1629. Cole Nathaniel Frances and brothers, ECR27_269.

[28] Mark Parry, "Bishop William Laud and the parliament of 1626," *Historical Research*, vol. 88, issue 240 (May 2015): 230-248. https://doi.org/10.1111.1468-2281.12097. Cited in "William Laud," *Wikipedia*. Viewed on 11 November 2022. https://en.wikipedia.org/wiki/William_Laud.

[29] Bradford, *Letters*, 45.

goldsmith shop on London Bridge and his Southwark domicile, he also had a residence in Bristol on England's west coast. Bristol's fishermen had fished the Grand Banks of Newfoundland since the sixteenth century.[30] The city's location and port gave its merchants a great trade advantage sailing to and from the New World. "Growth of the city and trade came with the rise of England's American colonies in the seventeenth century."[31] While in Bristol on 19 March 1630, James Sherley and Timothy Hatherley wrote a letter together to update Governor Bradford. In it, they sent news about William Collier.

> For Mr. Collier verily I could have wished it would have sorted his other affairs, to have been one of us but he could not spare money, and we thought it not reasonable to take in any partner, unless he were willing and able to spare money, and to lay down his portion of the stock; however, account of him as a sure friend, both ready and willing to do you all the offices of a firm friend.[32]

ANOTHER PLAGUE STRIKES LONDON

After only a few years' absence, another wave of plague struck. "The London plague of 1630 was a small affair (1317 deaths), the city being otherwise so healthy that the christenings exceeded the total burials (9315 to 9237)."[33] In a letter written on 2 August 1630 to Governor Bradford, Samuel Fuller mentions the plague in both city and country, but also brings news of a church covenant for prominent leaders in the new colony adjacent to Plymouth.

> Which brings this news out of England; that the plague is sore, both in the city and country, and that the University of Cambridge is shut up by reason thereof; also, that there is like to be a great dearth in the land by reason of a dry season. The Earl of Pembroke is dead, and Bishop Laud is Chancellor of Oxford; and that five sundry ministers are to appear before the High Commission, amongst whom, Mr. Cotton, of Boston, is one. The sad news here is, that many are sick, and many are dead, the Lord in mercy look upon them!

Some are here entered into a church covenant, the first four, namely, the Governour, Mr. John Winthrop, Mr. Johnson, Mr. Dudley, and Mr. Willson; since that, five more are joined unto them, and others it is like will add themselves to them daily.[34]

On 15 November 1630, Zachary Cole, Freeman Grocer and Citizen, gathered his closest friends and associates with him to write his will. Just two years after gaining this

---

[30] Brian Cathcart, "Rear Window: Newfoundland: Where fishes swim, men will fight," *The Independent* (London, 19 March 1995). "Bristol," *Wikipedia*. Viewed on 29 November 2022. https://en.wikipedia.org/wiki/Bristol.

[31] Kenneth Morgan, "Shipping Patterns and the Atlantic Trade of Bristol, 1749-1770," *The William and Mary Quarterly* Vol. 46, no. 3 (July 1989): 506–538. "Bristol," *Wikipedia*. Viewed on 29 November 2022. https://en.wikipedia.org/wiki/Bristol.

[32] Bradford, *Letters*, 73.

[33] Creighton, *A History of Epidemics*, 527.

[34] Bradford, *Letters*, 58.

status, in his mid-twenties and the prime of his life, Zachary already felt plague symptoms present throughout his body. He knew his mortal lifetime was short.[35]

WILL OF ZACHEUS COLE

In the name of God, Amen. The Sixteenth day of | November Anno Domini One thousand six hundred and thirty etc. I Zacheus Cole Citizen and Grocer | of London being sick in body but of sound and perfect mind and memory (thanks be to God | therefore) do make and declare my present last will and Testament in manner and form following |

That is to say First and principally I commend my soul unto God Almighty that gave it | me and my body I commit to the earth from whence it came, to be buried in such manner | and with such decent rites and solemnities as shall seem best to my Executors here under named |

And as touching my worldly estate wherewith it hath pleased the Lord to bless me withall (all | my debts which I shall truly owe at the time of my decease and my funeral charges being first | paid and discharged which I will and desire ~~define~~) I do demise, give, will and bequeath the same in manner | and form following, that is to say:

First I give and bequeath unto my dear and loving Mother | Francis Cole widow the sum of Five Pounds of lawfull money of England.

Item I give and | bequeath unto my loving cousin and friend <u>Amy</u> Billinge Five Pounds of like lawfull money | of England.

Item I give and bequeath unto my loving Brother Nathaniel Cole the like sum | of Five pounds of lawfull money English money.

I give and bequeath unto my loving brother Job | Cole the like sum of Five pounds of like lawfull money.

Item I give and bequeath unto my loving | Brother John Cole the like some of Five pounds of lawful English money of England.

And also I | give more unto my said brother Daniel Cole the sum of <u>Six</u> Pounds of lawfull money of England. And also I | give more unto my said Brother Daniel Cole the sum of <u>Ten</u> Pounds of like money the which I | had with him when he came to live with me.

Zachary's comment concerning his younger brother Daniel, "when he came to live with me," indicates that Daniel lived with Zachary prior to November 1630. Therefore, it is most

---

[35] Because of this will's importance, the conventions of Nicola Waddington's transcription are: 1) The spellings have been modernized; 2) the mark | denotes an end of line in the original, not to be confused with the personal pronoun "I;" and 3) each bequest has been put onto a separate line for ease of identification. In the original no such line breaks were used.

likely Daniel journeyed to London after Zachary became a freeman, as early as October 1628 or as late as 1629, after Zachary and Job both testified in person in the Weedon Bec Manor Court to settle their father's bequests. Zachary might have asked his youngest brother, Daniel at age thirteen or fourteen, to assist him in his grocer's business. It seems likely they traveled to Southwark together.

The residue and remainder of all and singular my | ready money, <u>wares</u>, debts, moveables and immoveables, implements, things, goods and chattels | whatsoever after my debts paid and my funeral charges discharged ~~and discharges~~ and the Legacies herein by me | given and bequeathed being first deducted and discharged the which I will and desire shall be done <u>xxx?</u> | accordingly. I do give, dispose, will and bequeath the same unto my said loving Mother Francis Cole and | my said Brothers Job Cole, John Cole and Daniel Cole to be equally divided amongst them share | and share alike.

And I do hereby ordain and make my said loving Mother Francis Cole and my | said brother Job Cole the sole Executors of this my present last will and Testament.

And I do | nominate and appoint my loving friend William Collier Grocer and my loving cousin Matheus <u>Mathew</u> | Billinge Scrivener whom I also entreat to be the Supervisors or Overseers of the <u>due execution</u> | of this my present last will and Testament that it be performed in all things as I have herein | willed and declared.

Zachary mentions my "loving friend," William Collier, and two "loving cousins," Amy and Mathew Billinge. Collier's designation signifies a close relationship but not a blood relative. It confirms a close working partnership or similar between Collier and Zachary in Collier's grocer enterprise or a mentorship. The "loving cousin" designation for Amy and Mathew Billinge signifies a blood relationship, but that has yet to be verified, even though both of them are in the Weedon Bec Parish registers.

And I do hereby revoke all other wills and Testaments by me heretofore made | hereby declaring and affirming the same to be void and of none effect.

In witness whereof I the | said Zacheus Cole to this my present last Will and Testament have hereunto set my hand | seal dated the day and year first above written.

Zacheus Cole. Signed sealed | published, declared and delivered by the said Zacheus Cole to be his last will and Testament | in the presence of us Peter Boddam, ~~The mark of~~ [inserted] Signam Thomas Williamson, William Collier, Jeanne | Collier and Mathew Billinge, Scr [Scrivener].[36]

Jeanne Collier is William's wife, Jane. Peter Boddam and Thomas Williamson were administrators. Zacheus Cole died not long after he wrote his will. Most plague victims passed within four days of the onset of symptoms. The will was proved on 29 November 1630.

---

[36] Will of Zacheus Cole, Prerogative Court of Canterbury, 106 Scrope, no. 1246.

Daniel, Job, and Zachary Cole were likely in Southwark together for a period of a year or longer. Since Job Cole was living with the Collier family, Daniel and Zachary probably lived nearby or possibly with them. Prior to his death, Zachary Cole lived in Southwark for nine years. When he passed away, his brother, Job, overlapped him in the same area for at least three and a half years. And his younger brother, Daniel, lived with him for at least a year.

FORMER VICAR OF WEEDON BEC, WILLIAM PROUDLOVE

The ravages of the 1630 plague were not limited to the Cole family. Another beloved friend, closely connected with them for decades, was also taken. William Proudlove, after leaving Weedon Bec in 1602, served as the vicar in the Chippenham Parish in Wiltshire beginning in the autumn of that year—before the end of Queen Elizabeth I's reign.[37] Although Proudlove might not have maintained contact with his former parishioners, any who were Nathaniel Cole's age or older would have remembered him kindly. Since he was at an advanced age when he left Weedon Bec, many thought he simply retired or died. But the opposite is true. After his wife, Isabella, died in 1611 in Chippenham, he kept ministering to his parishioners as a widower. Some twenty-two years after leaving Weedon Bec, he was still Chippenham's vicar. By then, he was likely in his nineties, remarkable for the times.

In the summer of 1626, William Proudlove wrote his will. William listed bequests to his living children, their children, and three brothers, a gift to his descendants beyond money. Proudlove mentions his sons in their birth order: John is his eldest; Thomas is his second. His eldest daughter is Elizabeth, the now wife of William Clarke, and he mentions his grandson, George Clarke. He lists his second daughter, Helen, who is the now wife of Christopher Evans, and his granddaughter, Jane Evans. He lists his youngest daughter, Grace, who was born in 1589 while he was imprisoned in London,[38] and "all and every [one of] her daughters." He also lists his youngest son, Elias, also in the Weedon Bec Parish registers. He names his natural brethren, meaning brothers: John Proudlove, Raphe Proudlove, and James Proudlove—a genealogical treasure trove for this family. Even more remarkable, Proudlove lived more than four years after writing his will and serving more than a quarter of a century in Chippenham. Four days after Zacheus Cole's will was written, Proudlove's will was proved on 19 November 1630.[39]

How can we be sure this is the same person who had served as Weedon Bec's vicar so long before? Besides matching his family members to the Weedon Bec Parish records, we have the evidence of his will's signature. It is printed as one might expect from someone in his nineties.

---

[37] See above, Chapter 7.
[38] See above, Chapter 2.
[39] Will of William Proudlove. Wiltshire and Swindon History Centre; Chippenham, Wiltshire, England; Wiltshire Wills and Probates; Reference Number: P3/P/176.

Signature of William Proudlove from his will written in 1626.
Sponsored by William E. Cole. (12.7)

His signature compares favorably with one on a petition to Queen Elizabeth I written in the early 1590s, when he was in his fifties, as one of the imprisoned Nine Puritans.[40] There are remarkable similarities, even though they were written thirty-five years apart.

Nine Puritans' Signatures from Petition sent to Queen Elizabeth in 1592. Courtesy of the British Library. Sponsored by the American Society of Genealogists. (12.8)

JOHN LATHROP AND WILLIAM LAUD: A TEST OF WILLS

In the spring of 1632, Puritan minister John Lathrop took a page off a printing press and read the text. "As faithful servants of Christ and as loyal subjects of Your Majesty, we seek to acquaint Your Majesty with our particular griefs." As he considered this pamphlet's opening, and his commitment to the cause he believed in with all his heart and soul, he and the printing assistant were interrupted. "The Stationers' men are coming!"[41]

Apparently, a reward had been posted for Lathrop's arrest. Fortunately for Lathrop, these henchmen did not know him by sight. They only had his description. They said, "We're searching the area and questioning everyone as to his whereabouts." Lathrop asked, "Why? What has he done?" They replied, "Bishop Laud's after him. He's an enemy to the King!"[42]

After they left, the supervisor of the Stationer's men informed them that Laud wanted Lathrop's entire congregation, not just him. They had information his group was meeting in a brewhouse. Undeterred, Lathrop continued preaching the truth as he always did. He did not fear men, and, in a sermon, he made clear his stance and his principles.

---

[40] See above, Chapter 3.
[41] Helene Holt, *Exiled: The Story of John Lathrop* (Moses Lake, WA: CrestHaven Publishing, 2005): 54.
[42] Holt, 55-56.

This I know. In a true Christian nation, all laws must respect the essential dignity of man, starting with man's right to personal conscience down to equality under the law. That's what Christ was all about! All laws must cohere with basic Christian origins and principles, or we disinherit ourselves, we cut ourselves off from the root and true vine, we turn our back and disown our very selves.

We have a measure of Christianity, but not a full measure. We are a concoction, an adulterated and polluted Christian nation. A quasi-Christian nation. A counterfeit. A sham. Perhaps a mockery . . . Where liberty is, there is Christ. Freedom survives only as long as Christian principles are upheld. It is no other way.[43]

In late April 1632, John Lathrop and his congregation met in the home of Humphrey Barnett, a brewer's clerk in Black Friars, London. The meeting was interrupted as his house was stormed by the bishop's henchmen. "Lathrop and forty-two members of his congregation were arrested, eleven of whom were women. Approximately eighteen escaped."[44] Those arrested were tried before the High Commission on 3 May 1632. John Lathrop and his congregational members all refused to take the oath *ex-officio*.

Unjustly imprisoned in Newgate, Lathrop petitioned Bishop Laud for release from captivity. A test of wills between this Puritan minister, John Lathrop, and the Bishop of London, William Laud, had begun—with striking similarities and parallels to the trials and tribulations the Nine Puritans faced with the Archbishop of Canterbury, John Whitgift, forty-two years earlier.

FINAL STRAWS

As December 1632 ended and January began, the winter cold enveloped London. John Lathrop was still imprisoned. William and Jane Collier assessed the impact of King Charles' policies. How was their family affected now, and what would be the future economic, religious, and political landscape of England? On all fronts, they found their homeland and all they had known for their entire lives, nearly five decades, was sorely lacking. They asked themselves, "Where is the promising future for our family?" They began to wonder if their family's future might be in America.

In the cold of London's winter, River Thames was almost frozen over. There, in February 1633, a catastrophe of epic proportions occurred. "There happened in the house of one Briggs [*sic*], a needle maker near St. Magnus Church, at the north end of the bridge (by the carelessness of a maidservant [*sic*], setting a tub of hot seacoal ashes under a pair of stairs), a sad and lamentable fire."[45] A prolific writer and Puritan, Nehemiah Wallington, captured the vivid details in his journal.

Holt, 67-8.
Holt, 246.
Nehemiah Wallington, *The Reign of Charles I* (London: Richard Bentley, 1869): 16-22.

On the 11th day of February, being Monday, 1633, began by God's just hand a fearful fire in the house of one Mr. John Brigges, near ten of the clock at night; it burnt down his house with all the goods that were in it; and as I hear, that Brigges, his wife, his child, and maid escaped with their lives very hardly, having on their bodies but their shirts and smocks; and the fire burnt so fiercely that it could not be quenched till it had burnt down all the houses on both sides of the way, from St. Magnus Church to the first open place.[46]

At one o'clock after midnight, loud shouts awakened Wallington, a wood turner who lived in the parish of St. Leonard Eastcheap, and his wife. They woke up their child, stepped outside, and looked down Fish Street Hill. The Wallington family

did behold such a fearful and dreadful fire, vaunting itself over the tops of houses like a captain flourishing and displaying his banner, and seeing so much means, and so little good it did, it made me think of that fire with the Lord threateneth against Jerusalem for the breach of His Sabbath.[47]

The house of John Brigges was located near the north end of London Bridge. The raging fire continued onto the bridge. For James Sherley, having been born on the bridge, it must have been terrifying to see it move toward Southwark. Not only was his shop in its path, but so was his family home of the last twenty-one years. What were his thoughts as the fire spewed embers in all directions, and spread totally out of control? Puritans would certainly have seen this fire as the wrath of God.

Even worse, River Thames was at low tide. The available equipment fighting the fire was ineffective, not being able to draw enough water. Emergency messages were sent out to the brewers of Southwark, calling on them to bring their water. Since the Globe Tavern was the closest establishment to London Bridge, William Collier, who lived right near Globe Alley and Deadman's Place, must have been awakened and involved in transporting water and helping to fight the fire. In all, forty-three shops on the bridge were destroyed overnight.[48] James Sherley's goldsmith's establishment "at the sign of the Golden Horseshoe" was burned to the ground.[49] Jane Langham, merchant, lost her mercer shop. Might she have been kin of William Langham, freeman grocer? Forty-one other shops were destroyed. It took a full week, until Tuesday the nineteenth, before the timber, wood, and coal embers were put out. The following day, London Bridge was cleared enough for passengers to go over it again. The whole Collier family, plus at least Job and Daniel Cole, must have been exhausted from the ordeal. Nehemiah Wallington cried out for his followers to be humbled before the Lord.

Let us all be humbled under the hand of the Lord. For the Lord is a Father that hangs betwixt anger and pity, resolved on neither, but inclined to this that the carriage of his children may call for, by striking further if they stoop not, and desisting from stripes if they

---

[46] Wallington, 17.
[47] Wallington, 18.
[48] Wallington, 19-20, lists the tenants' names and occupations of all forty-three shops destroyed.
[49] Willison, 294.

do. O how many dwelling places are become desolate! How are the labours of many a father, grandfather, great-grandfather, suddenly converted into smoke and rubbish in the space of a night and a day![50]

The Colliers and Coles were eyewitnesses of this historic event. As Puritans, they would have thought as Wallington did. Was the fire's destructive path a sign from God? Was God's wrath about to descend on London? Was it an omen of things to come? Wallington declared that he believed the fire to be a judgement on contemporary London's sins including "idolatry, superstition . . . adulteries, fornication, murders, oppressions which he saw around him."[51]

On 16 February 1633, with the fire's embers still hot, the gates of Newgate Prison opened for John Lathrop. He "was released from prison for a visit to his dying wife [Hannah] because she had been suffering with a lingering illness. Lathrop commended her to God; she died; he was returned to prison."[52] When William Collier received news of Hannah Lathrop's death and John's continued imprisonment, he must have wept. "Is there no more any justice for godly ministers, men, and women in England? Oh Lord, how much more must we endure?"

THE PROMISES OF AMERICA

For William Collier, his family, and close friends, the fire and the tragic news of the death of John Lathrop's wife and his continued unjust imprisonment were the final straws, or nails in London's coffin. God's message was clear to William. It was time to get serious about leaving London. William and Jane discussed the pros and cons. No family ties existed to keep them here. With their eldest daughter, Mary, at marrying age, and the next three girls approaching it, what would their lives be if they stayed in London? What would the future hold for young Ruth, at age five? Would all five daughters find suitable godly men here in London?

Being a London merchant and brewer for Collier was becoming more and more economically challenging. After Zachary Cole's death at the end of 1630, Collier's plan for his grocer's business expansion never came to fruition. He realized the London Bridge fire could have easily spread into Southwark and destroyed the brewhouse. That would have had disastrous consequences for Southwark and their livelihood. Even though his brewhouse partnership had great potential, perhaps this was the best time to exit from it. What other taxes would the king impose next? All these events and considerations converged to potentially push them away from London.

What if they all left together for Plymouth Colony? There were several factors to consider that might pull them to Plymouth. There would be freedom to live and worship in

---

[50] Wallington, 21.
[51] "Fire in the City," *City of London*, Viewed on 30 September 2018. https://www.cityoflondon.gov.uk/things-to-do/london-metropolitan-archives/the-collections/Pages/fire-in-the-city.aspx.
[52] Holt, 49.

a community with godly principles. The colony was committed to God's word. The colony was stronger now than it had ever been since the *Mayflower* arrived in 1620. Another larger colony in Charlestown, not far north from Plymouth, contained a substantial population of English men and women. In England, King Charles was strongly opposed to Puritanism. In 1632, the Bishop of London, William Laud, imprisoned John Lathrop, a godly Puritan minister, who led the underground Puritan church in Southwark. His wife and family had appealed for mercy, but he had been imprisoned for over a year already. Would Lathrop ever be released? The religious future for Puritans here was not promising. And it appeared that Bishop William Laud was next in line to become the Archbishop of Canterbury.[53]

Would his daughters have a better life in America than here in England? Their son, Thomas Clarke, had recently married in Plymouth. His wife, Susanna Ring, was from a good English family, and the Colliers received news the young couple was very happy. Thomas already owned land, and it seemed likely they would soon be grandparents. The Colliers knew that New Plymouth certainly contained enough godly men for their five daughters. William had retained his stock in the company. He knew he could become a landholder after he was formally brought into Plymouth Colony as a freeman. William felt God calling him to join Plymouth and contribute in a bigger way to the colony than he could ever do from London. William and Jane concluded: "The time is now. We will leave for America!"

With the decision made, William sprang into action. It typically took several weeks to prepare and stock a ship for the voyage across the ocean. Now his Merchant Adventurer experience and connections paid dividends. Captain John Rose of Southwark was hired. A ship, the *Mary and Jane*, was contracted for the voyage. Word spread among the Puritan network rapidly. William approached James Monger, his partner, to sell his shares in the brewhouse and brewery partnership. It had grown large enough to be a wholesale manufacturing enterprise, selling to retailers in London, and too large merely to be a brewhouse attached to an inn.[xv] With a fair agreement reached, William Collier recovered his investment and possibly a fair profit.

At age twenty-five, Job Cole saw the immediate benefits of emigration with his master to complete his commitment. He also felt a special attraction to one of Collier's daughters—Rebecca, age eighteen. Job thought, "Yes, Rebecca might be the one. But any of my master's other three eligible daughters, Mary, Sarah, or Elizabeth, would be a suitable wife!" He thought staying for a year with the Collier family to carve out a new life in America would be quite the adventure. Job's brother John, age twenty-two, was also a relatively new arrival in London. He easily grasped the significance of the moment, caught Job's excitement, and signed on as one of Collier's men.

However, Job's younger brother Daniel, at age eighteen, thought he should learn a trade first. He was ready to start an apprenticeship. "God willing, I will join you in America later,"

---

53   Archbishop of Canterbury George Abbot died on 4 August 1633 and Laud was nominated for the position two days later. As Archbishop of Canterbury, Laud immediately changed the Chapel services to privilege prayer over preaching, which pleased King Charles but increased the concerns of the Puritans.

he told his brothers and Mr. Collier. Then, Daniel Cole registered at the Merchant Taylors' Guild.

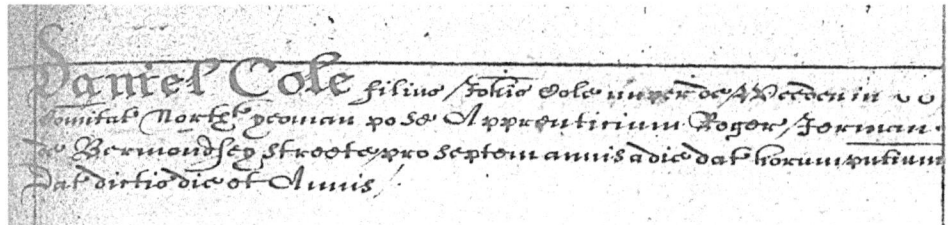

Daniel Cole, apprentice, 1633. With kind permission of the Merchant Taylors' Company.[54] Sponsored by William E. Cole, in honor of his eighth great-grandfather, Daniel Cole. (12.9)

Daniel Cole son of John Cole formerly of Weedon in the County of Northamptonshire, Yeoman, apprenticed himself to Roger Jerman of Bermondsey Street for seven years from the day given ---------- on the day and year given (9 Charles I) [1633-1634]

In the following list of presentments, Daniel Cole is listed in the fourth entry. His entry is on page 278. He was apprenticed *pro septem annis a die dat' horum presentium Dat' dictis die et annis,* "for seven years from the given date of these presents, Given on the said day and years."[55]

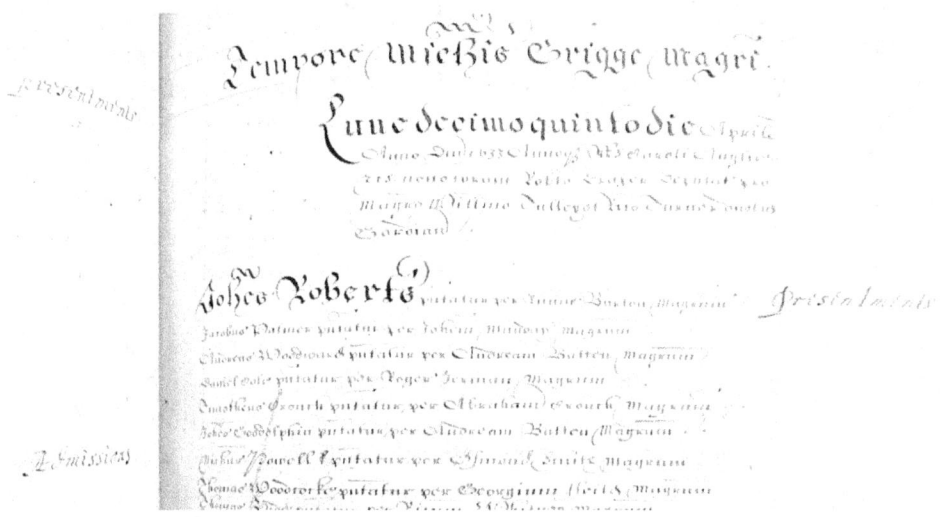

Daniel Cole, apprenticeship presentment, 15 April 1633. With kind permission of the Merchant Taylors' Company. Sponsored by William E. Cole, in honor of his eighth great-grandmother, Ruth Collier Cole. (12.10)

---

54   Merchant Taylors' Guild, Register of Apprenticeships, 1629-1635. MS 34038/10. Guildhall Library, London. A special thank you is due to Merchant Taylors' Company Archivist, Stephen Freeth, for his help and extra effort in finding these two never-before published images and answering additional follow-up questions about Daniel Cole's apprenticeship.

55   Merchant Taylors' Guild, Ordinary Court Minute Book. MS 34017/4 Folio 278. Guildhall Library, London.

As mid-April approached, the ship's officers, crew, passengers, and cargo were ready for the voyage to America.[xvi] Sometime right before Daniel started his apprenticeship, one can imagine the goodbyes and embraces between him and his two brothers. They agreed it would be up to Daniel to communicate all that had transpired to their brother, Nathaniel, and their mother, Frances. After they did say farewell, did Daniel envision when he might next see them? Was he sure he would join them in America? Would Job and John send letters to Daniel to inform him what Plymouth was like? Would Daniel keep them informed about his progress in learning his new trade? All these questions and thoughts must have raced through his mind.

When the *Mary and Jane* weighed anchor and headed downstream on River Thames, away from London, for the two Cole brothers and the Colliers—William and Jane, their children, Mary, Sarah, Rebecca, Elizabeth, and Ruth—it was the adventure of their lives. With 198 passengers onboard the *Mary and Jane*, the number was almost double the number of *Mayflower* passengers who departed England for Plymouth twelve and a half years earlier.

As the River Thames emptied into the North Sea, the ship headed south along the southeastern coastline of England. When it reached the English Channel, the passengers could see the coast of France and Calais off in the distance. When Captain Rose turned the ship westward into the channel with France on their left and England on their right, they gasped at the white cliffs of Dover. The beauty of the cliffs glistening in the late afternoon sun was stunning. Almost none of the passengers had ever seen sights like these before.

The ship continued past the Isle of Wight, outside of Southampton's major seaport, just as the *Mayflower* and countless other seafaring vessels had before. They passed the port of Plymouth, again on their right, and then past the far western tip of England known as Land's End. There, the vast ocean's panorama spread out before them. As the winds picked up, filling the ship's sails on all three masts, the passengers felt their speed quickening. For the most part, it was smooth sailing with very few idle moments waiting for wind. Within days, the teenagers and children had explored every available nook and cranny they were allowed to. Most adapted well to the ship's motion. Those who didn't were mostly out of sight in the lower deck stretched out trying to cope with their seasickness.

On the sixteenth of May, the ship's master and captain, John Rose, gathered the crew and his passengers on the main deck. Rose announced they had passed the two-thirds mark of their voyage. They were within two weeks of arriving in America, and everyone cheered. The captain then asked William and Jane Collier to step forward. Looking directly into their eyes, he projected his voice so everyone gathered could hear him. "For Mr. and Mrs. Collier, with respect and admiration, we want to celebrate today as a very special day in your life." Turning to the crowd, he continued, "It is their twenty-second wedding anniversary!" People clapped their hands, toasts were given, glasses raised, and cheers reverberated through the ship. William, age fifty, and Jane, forty-six, kissed and embraced. Their children hugged them. Many extended their congratulations including Job and John Cole, now known as Collier's men.

Young Ruth had never experienced anything like it. Indelibly etched in her mind, it was a memory she would carry with her throughout her entire life: A special celebration for her parents' special occasion in the middle of the Atlantic Ocean. As William and Jane gazed westward at the setting sun, they most certainly recalled their years together. What were their thoughts and conversation like on this day?

William had abandoned his promising partnership in the brewhouse and its brewery. He had built a successful grocer's enterprise and left it behind. Jane left behind her incredible experiences of family taken away in England during the plagues—lives lived that were much too short.[xvii] But William and Jane trusted God. They felt God's goodness in their lives. They knew God cared for them. His *Promises* were never broken. He would show them the way. With hearts filled with love, minds filled hope, and their spirits united, a prayer formed and came forth from William's voice.

"Blessed art thou, Lord God Almighty, King of kings and Lord of lords, whose goodness and mercy are everlasting, and whose faithfulness endureth through all generations. All honor, power, dominion, and glory are thine. Hallelujah! In thy divine providence, thou hast brought us to this new land. Through all our testing, trials, and tribulations—ours and those of our families before us—thou hast been our Rock and strength. We have been through fire and through water, and thou hast brought us into this goodly place of abundance. We are truly thankful. May thy Light shine brightly on our path ahead, that we may be found faithful, just, obedient, and righteous. Grant us grace to honor thee all the days of our lives and in every step we take, that we may show forth thy praise to all generations that follow. For these and all thy mercies, God's holy Name—Father, Son, and Holy Spirit—be blessed and praised. Through Jesus Christ our Lord, Amen."

The Colliers and Coles, and the other Puritans, were on a pilgrimage. Gazing out at the Atlantic Ocean, they affirmed their faith that had brought them this far. Two weeks after the Colliers celebrated their wedding anniversary, they would step off the *Mary and Jane* and step onto a new continent. There, they would find the *Promises* that awaited them in America.

Mayflower II.
Courtesy of 123rf.com. (12.11)

ENDNOTES

CHAPTER 9

i   Robert, his man, was given a bequest in Thomas Clarke's will in September 1610.

ii   Edmund Shakespeare's affair with an unknown woman resulted in a bastard child, Edward. One record noted him incorrectly with the surname Sharksbye. Edward died in about August 1607 and was followed in death by his father, Edmund, in December 1607. "Edmund Shakespeare," *Wikipedia*. Viewed on 7 November 2019. https://en.wikipedia.org/wiki/Edmund_Shakespeare.

iii   Will of Edmund Snape The National Archives, Prob.11/112/154, ff.117r-118v (register copy). Viewed on 5 September 2022. http://www-personal.umich.edu/~ingram/StSaviour/WILLS/wills-s.html#snapeedmund01.

> Snape listed eight underage children: Samuel, John, Nathaniel, Timothy, Hannah, Sarah, Elizabeth, and Ruth Snape. He also included Christopher Drayton his cousin. Henry Beridge of Steeple Gidding, Huntingdonshire, the father of his first wife. Judith Beridge his sister-in-law, and her unnamed husband. Nathaniel Williams his father-in-law. Mary Williams his cousin. The former children of his second wife, 'which she had by m^r morgan Sawden her former husband'. Elizabeth Sawden his wife's daughter, to have six silver spoons 'which were bestowed vppon her by m^r Abell Clerke when she was baptized'. He also gave a bequest to 'godlie ministers my poore brethren that are in necessitie and want'. He named a few others including George Throckmorton 'who lodged sometimes heretofore in my howse'. Richard Moore, carpenter, who owes him money. Sir Edward Phillips, knight, one of his majesty's serjeants at law. Elizabeth Stocke and her husband James Stocke, haberdasher. Ann Payne, widow. Stephen Egerton, preacher, to whom the testator owes money.
>
> In a memorandum four days later, "on ffriday March 18, in the morninge about twoe of the Clocke by Edmund Snape Preacher affirming his will and recording the names of the witnesses; and a schedule of debts to be annexed to the will. Witnesses: Edward Warren; Nathan Crosbye; Ephraim Hopkynson; Nathaniel Childe.
>
> Snape's will proved on the 9th of July. Executors approved were Ralph Bovey of the Inner Temple; Andrew Ellim, merchant; Thomas Carpenter, haberdasher; William Crosley, apothecary; Arthur Lee, girdler; and Rice Webb, haberdasher. No overseers were named.

iv   Virginia. A sermon preached at White-Chappel, in the presence of many, honourable and worshipfull, the adventurers and planters for Virginia. Published by William Symonds, preacher at Saint Saviors in Southwarke (1609). A map of Virginia with a description of the countrey, the commodities, people, government and religion. Written by Captaine Smith, sometimes governour of the countrey.

> Whereunto is annexed the proceedings of those colonies, since their first departure from England, with the discourses, orations, and relations of the salvages, and the accidents that befell them in all their iournies and discoveries.
>
> Taken faithfully as they were written out of the writings of Doctor Russell. Tho. Studley. Anas Todkill. Ieffra Abot. Richard Wiefin. Will. Phettiplace. Nathaniel Povvell. Richard Pots. And

the relations of divers other diligent observers there present then, and now many of them in England. By W.S., At Oxford: Printed by Joseph Barnes (1612).

v   Among the parish papers of St. Saviour's is a return of buildings made to the Earl Marshall in 1634/5. It refers to "The Globe Playhouse, nere Maidelane, built by the Company of Players, with timber, aboute 20 yeares past, vppon an old foundacion, worth 20 li per Annum, being the Inheritance of Sʳ Mathewe Brand kt. One house thereto adjoyninge, built aboute the same tyme with tymber in the possession of William Millet, gent', also of the Inheritance of Sʳ Mathew Brand kt., worth 4 per Annum." (fn. 11).

vi   John Collier, William's firstborn son, might possibly be a clue for the name of William's father. That naming pattern was quite common for English families in the early seventeenth century.

vii   The will of John Arnold. Prerogative Court of Canterbury Wills, PROB 11; Piece: 136. *Soame, Quire Numbers 65-120 (1620)*

Written 16 March 1617/18, Testator was John Arnold, Citizen and Dyer of London of the Parish of St Olave's. Arnold bequeathed: 1. To Richard Clark, Hugh Clarke and William Clark sons of my late sister Joyce Clarke 20s each. [Joyce would have died before March 1618] 2. To the children of his brother Thomas Arnold – 20s each. 3. Residue to wife Alice.

Witnesses: John Freebody Snr, Zachery Dixon [mark], William Collyar, Richard Hoy, Maria Macklyn [mark], John Arnold [mark]

Proved November 1620.

CHAPTER 10

viii   William Bradford wrote that the "overmasting" strained the ship's hull but attributed the cause of her leaking to actions on the part of the crew. Passenger Robert Cushman wrote from Dartmouth in August 1620 that the leaking was caused by a loose board approximately two feet long. Nathaniel Philbrick, author of *Mayflower: A Story of Courage, Community, and War* (New York: Penguin Books, 2006), theorized that the crew used a mast too big for the ship, and that the added stress caused holes to form in the hull.

ix   Many accounts detail the story of the early struggles of Plymouth Colony. William Bradford's extraordinary work, *Of Plymouth Plantation*, is the most relied upon eyewitness account. It is considered to be the first history book written in America. Recommended reading. Bradford's account of the first winter is also available online. "Surviving the First Winter of the Plymouth Colony, 1620-1621," *National Humanities Center.* Viewed on 24 January 2023. https://nationalhumanitiescenter.org/pds/amerbegin/settlement/text1/BradfordPlymouthPlantation.pdf.

CHAPTER 11

x   "Enclosure," *Britannica.* Viewed on 22 November 2022. https://www.britannica.com/topic/enclosure. Enclosures in England defined.

The division or consolidation of communal fields, meadows, pastures, and other arable lands . . . into the carefully delineated and individually owned and managed farm plots of modern times. Before enclosure, much farmland existed in the form of numerous, dispersed strips under the control of individual cultivators only during the growing season and until harvesting was completed for a given year. Thereafter, and until the next growing season, the land was at the disposal of the community for grazing by the village livestock and for other purposes. To enclose land was to put a hedge or fence around a portion of this open land and thus prevent the exercise of common grazing and other rights over it. In England the movement for enclosure began in the 12th century and proceeded rapidly in the period 1450–1640, when the purpose was mainly to increase the amount of full-time pasturage available to manorial lords.

xi   For researchers interested in more information about the *Little James* court case:

Caleb Johnson, "Troubles with Little James: Edward Winslow's depositions at High Court of Admiralty ," *The Mayflower Quarterly*, vol. 77, no. 1, March 2011, by,: p. 52-4; Eugene Aubrey Stratton, *Plymouth Colony: Its History and People, 1620-1691* (Salt Lake City: Ancestry Publishing 1986) p. 34-5.

High Court of Admiralty Examinations - Deposition: James Sherley, Goldsmith and Citizen of London, Treasurer of the New England Company who deposes, 20 November 1624, aged 33 years, "was borne upon London Bridge, within the parish of St. Magnus, and hath for fourteen years kept house and family in the parish of St. Michaels, Crooked Lane, and borne all offices there". He is now Renter-Warden of the goldsmith's Company. Author's note: Sherley also invested in the East India Company.

xii   London Metropolitan Archives and Guildhall Library Manuscripts Section, Clerkenwell, London, England; Reference Number: DW/PA/5/1626; Will Number: 4. Note that while Alice's husband's will proved in the PCC, Alice's will was proved in a lower court. Translation by Nicola Waddington.

Parish of St Olave's in Surrey.

The will was written 3 Feb 1625/6 and proved 8 April 1626.

Alice Arnold states she is the widow and Executrix of John Arnold

To be buried in the parish church of St Olave's alongside her husband.

To Joyce Clarke the daughter of my daughter Jane Collyer the now wife of William Collyer, £20, some jewellery and household items to be delivered to her when she reaches the age of 21 years or on the day of her marriage, whichever shall first happen, as long as she marries with her Mother's consent.

To her four grandchildren Mary Collyer, Sara Collyer, Rebecka Collyer and Elizabeth Collyer, daughters of my daughter Jane Collyer the debts of £10 owed by Alexander Wylding, Feltmaker of St Olave's. To be paid to them at the age of 21 years or upon marriage whichever is sooner.

If Joyce does not marry with her mother's consent then her portion is to go to the rest of 'her' [i.e Jane Collier's children].

To Thomas Clark, brother of Joyce Clark - £20 when he reaches the age of 21 years "if he can behave himself and take good courses whereby to live."

If Joyce or Thomas die before inheriting then their portions are to be divided between the rest of the children of the said Jane Collier.

To my son-in-law William Collier all the yearly rents of the premises in the occupation of Alexander Wylding situated in Bermondsey Street in the parish of St Olave's, which Alice holds by lease from St Mary Magdalene College in Oxford. William and Jane are to hold the tenements for 15 years the profits of which are to be given to their children, which they have now or in the future. At the end of 15 years the lease is to pass to Joyce Clark, unless she has died, when it passes to Jane.

To Mr Bramford, Preacher, 20s.

To my son-in-law William Collier £10.

[This clause was crossed through indicating she had likely died] To Kathryn Brooke, widow, my sister – 20s, and also her dwelling house rent free for life in St Olave's.

Small bequests made to various poor people.

To her son [name missing] Collyer £10 and some household items.

Sole Executrix – daughter Jane Collyer unless she is deceased and then William Collyer is nominated.

Overseers: Friends William Knight, Citizen and Fishmonger of London, and Robert Knight, Citizen and Dyer of London – 10s each for their efforts.

Residue to Jane Collyer.

xiii 1626 Weedon Bec Manor Court Presentments involving Frances and Nathaniel Cole.
Homage: John Cole, John Billing, Martin Billing, Thomas Cleavely. John Cleavely, Nathaniel Cole. Presentments:
John Cole has died and his widow Frances seeks entry to his lands – image taken and translated below. *Image name: Court Baron 1626 Cole John Frances and Nathaniel ECR27_269.*

> Item, that John Cole senior since the last court has died seised of one messuage in Overweedon Beck and one close of pasture pertaining to the same, and of three virgates of arable land and four virgates of meadow land within the fields of Weedonbeck, and all buildings, orchards, gardens, closes, commons, profits and commodities pertaining or belonging to the same messuage. And of three roods of cultivable land, lying in a close called Tween Townes. All and singular which premises were in the tenure or occupation of the aforesaid John Cole at the time of his death. And of one cottage with an area pertaining to the same, lying in Weedon Beck near to the tenement in the occupation of John Walker towards the east, and the cottage in the occupation of Alice Caswell towards the west, now in the tenure of Richard ?Watts. And that Nathaniel Cole is his son and next heir. And that Frances Cole is the wife of the aforesaid John, who came to this court and seeks to be admitted to a moiety of the aforesaid premises for the term of her life according to the custom of the aforesaid manor. To whom the lords by their aforesaid steward granted seisin by the rod. To have and to hold for the term of her life at the will of the lords according to the custom of the aforesaid manor by the yearly rent thereupon reserved and other customs and services thereupon previously due and lawfully accustomed. She gives to the lords a fine and did fealty and was thereupon admitted as tenant.

Nathaniel Cole seeks entry – image taken and translation below. *Image name: Court Baron 1626 Cole Nathaniel ECR27_26.*

Item, that the aforesaid Nathaniel Cole seeks to be admitted to the other moiety of the premises and to the reversion of the aforesaid moiety after the death of the aforesaid Frances his mother. To whom the lords by the aforesaid steward granted seisin by the rod. To have to him and his heirs at the will of the lords according to the custom of the aforesaid manor by the rents and other customs thereupon previously due and lawfully accustomed. He gives to the lords a fine and did fealty and was admitted as tenant thereof.

In addition to the preceding records, additional presentments were made in the hearing. The following transcriptions are provided.

Nathaniel Cole has lands adjacent to John Allen – image taken and translation below. *Image name: Court Baron 1626 Cole Nathaniel boundary ECR27_26.*

Item, that Edward Gare and John Smith in open court [came] before the homage and surrendered into the hands of the lords by the hands of the steward one tenement in Nether weedonbeck, situate and being near to the church way towards the east, and an area pertaining to the same tenement, now in the occupation of Alexander Waters, except for the house called 'le Kilne Howse', standing in the same area, with free egress and regress to the aforesaid Edward Gare for the repair of the stables adjacent to the same area, and common for one cow in the common fields of Weedonbeck, aforesaid. And also, all those three half acres of arable land, lying and being within the fields of Weedonbeck, aforesaid. One half acre of which lies in the field towards Dadford upon the furlong called 'le Middle Furlong' by the lands of the vicarage towards the west; and two roods lie in Cherry Pitt Hole in the fields of Stow by the lands of Nathaniel Cole towards the east; another half acre of them lies in the fields towards Everdon in the furlong upon Froxlade by the land of John Billing towards the north. Which same parcels of land are now in the tenure or occupation of the aforesaid Edward Gate. To the use and behoof of John Allen and his heirs forever. To which same John the lords by the aforesaid steward granted seisin by the rod. To have to him and his heirs at the will of the lords according to the custom of the aforesaid manor by the rents and other services thereupon previously due and lawfully accustomed. He gives to the lords as a fine three shillings, and he made fealty and was admitted as tenant thereof.

In the same court is a second paragraph showing Nathaniel as a boundary owner – image taken and translation below. *Image name:Court Baron 1626 Cole Nathaniel boundary 2nd para ECR27_269.*

Item, that William Goodman since the last court surrendered into the hands of the lords by the hands of Thomas Cleavley and John Cleavley, two of the customary tenants, one half acre and a rood of pasture with a hedge and ditch pertaining to the same, lying and being in the fields of Weedon, adjacent to the fields of Snascom, abutting upon the lane and the lands of Nathaniel Cole towards the south and east, one end thereof abutting by West Leaze, and the other end thereof by the royal way, now in the occupation of the aforesaid William Goodman. To the use and behoof of the aforesaid William Goodman and Joan his wife for the term of their lives, and after their decease, then to the use of John Goodman, son of the aforesaid William, and his heirs forever. To whom the lords by the aforesaid steward granted seisin by the rod. To have and to hold in the aforesaid manner and form at the will of the lords according to the custom of the aforesaid manor by the yearly rent of 2d and other customs and services thereupon previously due and lawfully accustomed. They give to the lord as a fine three shillings and made fealty and were admitted as tenants thereof.

In the same court came Thomas Cole – image taken and translation below. *Image name: Court Baron 1626 Cole Thomas boundary ECR27_269.*

Item, in open court there came Edward Gare and Arthur Reignolds and Rebecca his wife (the same Rebecca being examined by the steward of the lords previously alone and in secret), and they surrendered into the hands of the lords by the hands of the said steward the whole of that their messuage with all orchards, gardens, closes and three quarter-virgates of arable land with a meadow, pasture, pasturage and common pertaining to the same messuage, with appurtenances in Weedonbeck, aforesaid. And also, one piece of meadow, lying at Stowbrook, and one half acre of land at Hockley in the Hole, lying next to the land of Thomas Cole, and one rood of meadow, lying at Froile, and one rood of meadow, lying at Debden Hedge. To the use and behoof of John Allen and his heirs forever. To whom the lords by the aforesaid steward granted seisin by the rod. To have to him and his heirs at the will of the lords according to the custom of the aforesaid manor by the yearly rent of 6s 4d and the other customs and services thereupon previously due and lawfully accustomed. He gives to the lords as a fine £6 and he did fealty and was admitted as tenant thereof.

CHAPTER 12

xiv   As this author's English research partner, Nicola Waddington, strolled through Southwark's Borough Market section in the summer of 2019, she spied a memorial plaque. It was a magical moment all genealogists hope for.

Seeing the name Monger, Waddington accessed the Deeds of the Anchor Brewery. [Survey of London Vol. 22 fn. 123]. The deeds confirmed the brewhouse was established in the early seventeenth century by James Monger. The 1634 St. Saviour's Token Books yielded: "In the return of new buildings to St. Saviour's the Wardens made in 1634/5, there is an entry relating to a brewhouse and dwelling house in the tenure of James Monger built of timber on old foundations about 18 yeares since."

This time frame corresponds closely with the rebuilding of the Globe theatre after the fire in 1613. Given its location in the heart of the entertainment district, the brew-house thrived and expanded its operation into a brewery. In 1670, the brewery was sold to James (Josiah) Child, Citizen and Brewer, who owned it at his death in 1696. By the eighteenth century, the Anchor Brewery was the largest brewery in the world.

Will of a James Monger. Ref PROB11/265: Ruthen Quire number 208-259 (1657)

Proved on 6 June 1657, a James Monger, Citizen and Clothworker of London, listed his bequests:

£1000	to his granddaughter Brigett Monger.
£10	to the Worshipful Company of Clothworkers of which he was a member,
£10	to the poor children of the new Corporation of the Wardrobe London.
£5	to the poor of St Thomas Hospital in Southwark.
£5	to the Prisoners of Ludgate.
£5	to Woodstreet Compters,
£5	to the parishoners of St James Garlick London.

Monger gave smaller sums of money to poor widows and the poor of Guildford in Surrey. He left the rest of his estate, "all goods, lands and property to his son Henry Monger.

xv PETER MATHIAS, THE ANCHOR BREWERY: PARK STREET, SOUTHWARK originally published in 1953. Republished by The Brewery History Society, Brewery History Journal (2012) 145, 4-74.

In 1633 James Monger had the tenure of the brewery from a Hillarie Mempris, who in that year passed the lease to John Partridge for £400. The indenture survives and describes the property as being formed from eight tenements, doubtless very small, with their 'yards, backsides, gardens, garden plotts, chambers, rooms, casements, sheds ...' and so forth according to the legal formula. A small part of the property was leased by Sir John Bodley (probably a ground rent) to a Francis Carter for £6 p.a.; and the bulk of it to Monger for £21½ p.a.

The position here is probably that the ground rent as £21½ and the value of the buildings £400. Although not at all large in comparison with what it was later to become this document proves one important thing conclusively - which the fortunes of the owners of the brewery show indirectly. The brewery was large enough to be manufacturing for sale to retailers in London, and too large merely to be a brewhouse attached to an inn. The economic function of the business did not therefore change from this time onwards, although the scale of the operations grew with the scale of the market exploited.

xvi Typical preparations for a voyage to America took 6-8 weeks to acquire supplies. Author's Analysis:

The arrival of the ship that carried the Collier family and his men, the Cole brothers, was noted at the end of May. "The *Mary and Jane* arrived, Mr. Rose master. She came from London in seven weeks, and brought one hundred and ninety-six passengers, (only two children died)." Winthrop noted a smaller ship arrived in May before the *Mary and Jane* in a voyage of six weeks. By calculating the timing of the latest possible arrival date as 31 May 1633, the *Mary and*

Jane would have departed London on approximately the 17th of April, just after Daniel Cole's apprenticeship started.

Another interesting fact to note: Plymouth, most likely knew of William Collier's plans to emigrate. Collier was included on the tax list created at the new year: 25 March 1633, 33 days after London Bridge was reopened on the 20th of February. If a letter was sent immediately on a ship leaving for Plymouth, there's just enough time for it to have arrived for Governor Bradford to add him to the tax list. Or there may have been word sent before the fire. But William Collier was taxed before he arrived.

The taxes assessed for William Collier and Timothy Hatherley, both Merchant Adventurers, have identical rates—18 shillings. At this time, Hatherley had 2 assistants. By applying the same tax rate to Collier, his tax would also represent 2 men.

The tax assessment occurred two months before Collier arrived in late May 1633. This fact called into question previously published research that three brothers, Job, John, and Daniel Cole, were Collier's men. If only two Cole men were taxed, that lent credence to the published theory by Susan E. Roser that Daniel arrived later than did his two brothers, Job. This author arrived at this same conclusion and further substantiated by the previously unknown apprenticeship of Daniel Cole in the Merchant Taylor Guildhall Library Archive.

xvii   Jane Gates / Yates / Clarke / Collier bore four children with her first husband, Thomas Clarke. With her second husband, William Collier, Jane bore an additional thirteen children [nine proven, three are very likely, and one is probable]. That totals as many as seventeen children in a span of twenty-four years!

EPILOGUE

As my English origins research project expanded with more and more historic findings, it struck me that we had discovered more than would fit into one readable book. That's why I revised the book's subtitle from *Cole, Clarke, and Collier in England and America* to *Cole, Clarke, and Collier in England to America*. You have already journeyed far with the families Cole, Clarke, and Collier, and with others closely connected to them. And yet, *Puritans, Plagues, and Promises* has only scratched the surface of their epic saga. They haven't yet arrived in America!

Upon their arrival, William and Jane Collier became two important Puritan leaders in Plymouth Colony. Governor William Bradford relied upon William Collier as a key assistant. He held many important positions in the colony and lived a long life into his mid-eighties. But William and Jane's greatest legacy was probably their children.

Jane Clarke Collier's son, Thomas Clarke, married Susanna Ring before his mother and stepfather, William Collier, arrived. Clarke became a Freeman of the colony a few months before they arrived. Thomas and Susanna had many children, and Thomas led a long, productive life filled with excitement. He was well-known in Plymouth and lived in Boston for a time. He is interred at Plymouth's Burial Hill with the oldest visible gravestone in the cemetery. However, that is another story.[1]

On 15 May 1634, William and Jane Collier celebrated two weddings: their daughter, Rebecca, married Job Cole, and their daughter, Sarah, married Love Brewster. On 1 April 1635, daughter Mary wed widower Thomas Prence, who served many years as governor of Plymouth Colony. On 2 November 1637, daughter Elizabeth married Constant Southworth, who later became treasurer of Plymouth Colony. In about 1643, Ruth Collier married Daniel Cole. Thus, two Cole brothers married two Collier sisters, connecting the families and their legacy for generations to come. They were among the founders of Nauset/Eastham on Cape Cod in the 1640s. Both Daniel and Job Cole served in many leadership positions in their community. On 19 December 1645, Jane Clarke Collier's granddaughter, Sarah Walker, married Nathaniel Warren, son of Mayflower passenger Richard Warren. Born in 1624, Nathaniel was an early first-generation child born in America.

These interconnected families—Cole, Clarke, and Collier—raised many children with dozens of offspring who in turn produced hundreds of grandchildren. These immigrants, and their many descendants, lived most of their lives in Colonial America.

One can easily imagine the need for future publications of their stories. For example, a comprehensive Cole family history in America would be an equally compelling and epic story. A family's generational journey through the history of what ultimately became the United States of America is an enticing project. Its title could be: *The Cole Family: From*

---

[1]   William E. Cole, *"A Grave Mistake: Oldcomer Thomas Clarke's English Origins."* Available soon at https://www.passionategenealogist.org.

Cape Cod to California. It might cover the British Colonial period, the Revolutionary War, the War of 1812, the westward expansion, the California Gold Rush, the Civil War, and continue through the post-World War II era. Similar stories for the families of Clarke and Collier are likewise waiting to be written or enhanced.

The stories are out there. They should be told from the page or the stage. What is your story? As I like to remind readers and audiences, "Avoid dying with a story still inside you that needs to be told!"

ABOUT THE AUTHOR

William E. "Bill" Cole, M.A., is an internationally-known and respected family historian, genealogical researcher, and presenter. Bill's newest book, his third, *Puritans, Plagues, and Promises: Cole, Clarke, and Collier in England to America,* is the culmination of his eight-year English origins research project. It has revealed more than twenty historic genealogical breakthroughs.

Bill has inspired many and provided a roadmap for their own research. In his genealogical quests, he has discovered ancestors born at sea, a shipwrecked rogue who survived Jamestown, two Mayflower ancestors, multiple Revolutionary War patriots on both sides, and other fascinating characters—including one involved in a California stagecoach robbery.

Whether from the page or the stage, Cole's publications and presentations make him an in-demand presenter for conferences and societies. Acclaimed as a master storyteller and known as "The Passionate Genealogist," his virtual and in-person presentations are informational, impactful, and inspirational for all levels of genealogists and family historians.

William E. "Bill" Cole, M.A.

For more information:
https://www.passionategenealogist.org

PRIMARY SOURCES

British Library   London, England.
    Lord Burghley Papers.

Eton College Archives   Windsor, England.
    Manor Court Records, Weedon Bec, Everdon.

Grocers' Company of London Archives   London, England.
    Apprenticeships, Wardens' Account Books.

Lambeth Palace Library   London, England.
    Lord Burghley Papers.

London Metropolitan Archives   London, England.
    Guildhall Library Manuscripts, Wills.

Merchant Taylors' Company of London Archives   London, England.
    Apprenticeships, Presentments.

Northamptonshire Archives Services (NRO)   Northamptonshire, England.
    Previously known as Northampton Record Office. Wills,
    Diocese Records, Visitation Books, Correction Books.

Parish Registers   Ancestry.com.
    London, Southwark, Bermondsey, Northamptonshire.

Society of Genealogists   London, England.
The National Archives (TNA)   Kew, Surrey, England
    E179 Lay Subsidy Rolls, Chancery Court, Star Chamber Court.

SECONDARY SOURCES

Clergy of the Church of England Database (CCEd)   Theclergydatabase.org.uk/.

Find My Past   Findmypast.com.

Long Buckby Historical Society   Northamptonshire, England.

Weedon Bec Historical Society   Northamptonshire, England.

INDEX[1]

---

[1] "f" signifies footnote; "e" signifies endnote; and "c" signifies image caption.

www.ingramcontent.com/pod-product-compliance
Lightning Source LLC
Chambersburg PA
CBHW082140120626
46553CB00010B/2715